VINDICIAE GALLICAE
AND OTHER WRITINGS
ON THE FRENCH REVOLUTION

NATURAL LAW AND
ENLIGHTENMENT CLASSICS

Knud Haakonssen
General Editor

James Mackintosh

NATURAL LAW AND
ENLIGHTENMENT CLASSICS

Vindiciae Gallicae and Other Writings on the French Revolution

James Mackintosh

Edited and with an Introduction
by Donald Winch

LIBERTY FUND

Indianapolis

This book is published by Liberty Fund, Inc., a foundation established
to encourage study of the ideal of a society of free and responsible individuals.

𒈠𒄄

The cuneiform inscription that serves as our logo and as the design motif for
our endpapers is the earliest-known written appearance of the word
"freedom" (*amagi*), or "liberty." It is taken from a clay document written
about 2300 B.C. in the Sumerian city-state of Lagash.

Frontispiece: Portrait of Sir James Mackintosh by Sir Thomas Lawrence, oil
on canvas, exhibited 1804. Reproduced courtesy of the
National Portrait Gallery, London.

Library of Congress Cataloging-in-Publication Data
Mackintosh, James, Sir, 1765–1832.
Vindiciae Gallicae and other writings on the French Revolution/
James Mackintosh; edited with an introduction by Donald Winch.
p. cm.—(Natural law and enlightenment classics)
Includes bibliographical references and index.
ISBN-13: 978-0-86597-462-3 (alk. paper) ISBN-10: 0-86597-462-4 (alk. paper)
ISBN-13: 978-0-86597-463-0 (pbk.: alk. paper) ISBN-10: 0-86597-463-2 (pbk.: alk. paper)
1. Burke, Edmund, 1729–1797. Reflections on the Revolution in France.
2. France—Politics and government—1789–1799.
3. France—History—Revolution, 1789–1799—Causes.
I. Winch, Donald. II. Title. III. Series.
DC150.B9M2 2006
944.04—dc22   2005049402

LIBERTY FUND, INC.
8335 Allison Pointe Trail, Suite 300
Indianapolis, Indiana 46250-1684

CONTENTS

INTRODUCTION

The writings reprinted here trace James Mackintosh's involvement with the French Revolution from its hopeful beginnings in 1789 to the confused interlude between Napoleon's first and second abdications in favor of the restored Bourbon monarchy in 1815. They follow a path that was to become all too familiar to those who began as enthusiastic supporters of the Revolution, became disillusioned by its violence and autocratic outcome, and had to live with the consequences of renunciation for the rest of their lives. Those who wielded political ideas during this period ran the risks associated with handling high explosives—even those, like Mackintosh, who did so with eloquence, moderation, and learned illustration. Although Mackintosh shared this predicament with many others, his apostasy has some special features that lend historical interest to the way in which he attempted first to sustain and then to regain an intellectual stance on law and politics that would do credit to his upbringing as a Scottish "philosophic Whig."

Mackintosh was twenty-five when he published *Vindiciae Gallicae* in 1791. He had left Scotland four years earlier to make a career in England, and having failed as a medical practitioner he was taking the first steps toward becoming a lawyer. Once settled in London he supported himself by journalism and had formed close associations with circles that were seeking reforms in the system of parliamentary representation. His defense of the French Revolution and its English supporters against Edmund Burke's charges in *Reflections on the Revolution in France* proved successful in advancing his prospects within the Foxite wing of the Whig Party in Parliament. It led to an invitation from some of its younger members to act as honorary secretary to the Association of the Friends of the People, and it was on behalf of this body that Mackintosh wrote the second work reprinted here, an attack on the prime minister, Pitt the Younger, for reneging on his own record as parliamentary reformer.

As a result of the violent turn of events in France after the September massacres of 1792, and the execution of Louis XVI and the outbreak of war between France and England in the following year, Mackintosh was forced to stage a retreat on all fronts. Although he continued to regard the war conducted against France by a coalition of European powers as both unjust and inexpedient, a war that for Burke had taken on the character of a holy crusade against revolutionary principles, Mackintosh became increasingly anxious to distance himself from his earlier defense of the Revolution. By 1796 he had made an elaborate personal apology to Burke and had begun to think of ways of making a public declaration of his change of view. The third work reprinted here, the introductory discourse to a series of lectures he gave on the "law of nature and nations" in 1799 and 1800, was the means he chose for revealing his change of position. It also served to advance his legal career, and it was through ministerial patronage that, in 1804, he obtained the post of recorder of Bombay, a judicial appointment that carried with it a knighthood. This gave rise to charges that he had sacrificed "principles" to "connections," charges that dogged Mackintosh throughout his life and which his Whig friends were still anxious to rebut when they were repeated after his death in 1832.

Mackintosh hoped that his period of service in India would guarantee him financial independence and allow him to make progress with a number of scholarly projects: a history of England since the Revolution of 1688, a treatise on moral philosophy, and the life of Burke. Despite an ambitious program of reading, none of these projects was brought to fruition during the eight years he spent in India. Upon return to England in 1812, he resumed his political career and was returned as member of Parliament for Nairn in the following year. He also resumed his interest in French affairs and spent some weeks in Paris in 1814 before writing an article on the state of France for the *Edinburgh Review,* the last of the items reprinted here. It marks the end of a long period of engagement with French affairs and once more illustrates the hazards of attempting to combine punditry with sustaining a philosophical stance on politics. The article appeared during Napoleon's Hundred Days and ended with a firm prediction that a second Bourbon restoration was an impossibility, the event that actually occurred a few months later when Napoleon was defeated at Waterloo.

Although Mackintosh enjoyed a considerable reputation in Whig society, especially for his conversational powers, he never achieved the high executive office that his talents led him to expect. He found an outlet for his pedagogic skills as professor of law and general politics at the East India College at Haileybury, but he renounced a long-held dream of occupying the Edinburgh chair of moral philosophy when it became available in 1820 in favor of remaining at the disposal of his party in London. He managed to complete a three-volume *History of England* up to the Reformation but not the *History of the Revolution in England in 1688* (published in 1834 as a fragment). The nearest he came to writing a treatise on moral philosophy was his *General View of the Progress of Ethical Philosophy, Chiefly During the Seventeenth and Eighteenth Centuries,* a work for the *Encyclopedia Britannica* that completed a project begun by Dugald Stewart, who had held the chair of moral philosophy at Edinburgh when Mackintosh had been a student there.

Vindiciae Gallicae

Mackintosh's reply to Burke appeared late in a sequence of responses that began with Mary Wollstonecraft and continued with works by Catharine Macaulay, Joseph Priestley, and the first part of Thomas Paine's *Rights of Man.* As the Latin title indicates, and especially when compared with Paine's more popular and incendiary work (no mention of which appears in *Vindiciae*), Mackintosh's reply was written for an educated audience. While it vied with Burke in its use of rhetoric and historical learning, the distinguishing mark of Mackintosh's diagnosis of the state of French and English politics was his stress on "general causes." He claimed to be dealing with the "political and collective character" of institutions and events in France as opposed to Burke's emphasis on moral indictment and conspiracy between culpable individuals and groupings. On Mackintosh's reading of the evidence, prerevolutionary France suffered from a form of despotism attributable to the decline of its feudal aristocracy before other classes of citizen had risen to take its place. Unlike England, France had not enjoyed the "natural" (if also "accidental") benefits associated with the rise of the new commercial, professional, and moneyed classes, those who were better able to sustain representative institutions than the landed gentry. Since French society was incorrigibly diseased, the early measures taken to create new institutions around which the nation could be united were justified. These included the most revolutionary of the innovations, a unitary form of government centering on the National Assembly, the abolition of the corporate privileges attached to membership of the feudal ranks of nobility and clergy, and the nationalization of church property as backing for a new currency. Popular excesses and partial evils were not an essential part of the Revolution and could be attributed to the need to meet the threats posed by internal dissension and external invasion. In common with the Americans earlier, the French now had an opportunity to make conscious choices based on reason and the diffusion of more philosophical or scientific views on modern politics.

Mackintosh's diagnosis and defense of the Revolution was based on an exuberant mixture of authorities: David Hume on the role of opinion and the middle ranks in politics and the impermanence of "Gothic" forms of government; Adam Smith on the connections between commerce, productive labor, and liberty; and Montesquieu's account of the rise of absolutism in France at the expense of the *parlements*. To these was added invocation of a proud "Commonwealth" or republican tradition of resistance to absolute monarchy, with its Scottish heroes, George Buchanan and Andrew Fletcher, given due recognition. Finally, Mackintosh drew on the incipient historicism of "march-of-mind" assumptions contained in the work of the *philosophes* and Dugald Stewart: what could not be achieved at an earlier stage in the historical process was within the grasp of a new generation. Opinion was increasingly being formed by enlightened self-interest, giving philosophers a larger part to play in interpreting historical experience and in adapting institutions to meet the needs of a new "legislative age." To this heady brew Mackintosh added a dash of Machiavelli on the occasional need to return to first principles and an appeal to Jean-Jacques Rousseau's doctrines on equal "rights" and "general will."

Mackintosh convicted Burke of failure to grasp the true nature of French institutions and the strains placed upon them by the impending bankruptcy of the ancien régime. Instead of invoking English constitutional history as the standard against which French developments should be judged, Mackintosh appealed to a more cosmopolitan European perspective, one that linked the fortunes of nations and had been enlightened by international commerce in goods and ideas. In place of Burke's appeal to precedent and inheritance, he was shifting the criteria for legitimate government into a future tense. Transparency rather than "imposture" was now required; a regard for public utility rather than mere deference to established authority was the emerging basis for citizenly obligation.

The debate provoked by Burke was as much concerned with the nature of the English constitution and the meaning of 1688 as it was with events in France since 1789. For Mackintosh the legacy of 1688 was genuinely revolutionary in the principles it had adopted, but it was also incomplete and had become corrupted. Royal "influence" and parliamentary venality had undermined the vaunted system of ministerial responsibility. The powers of impeachment and control over the state's finances possessed by the House of Commons were now merely nominal. Inequalities in the system of representation had become a form of oppression. The English statute book was a testament to "superstitious barbarism"; dissenters were excluded from the political nation; and the House of Commons no longer reflected popular will. It had become a conspiracy designed to implement ministerial edicts rather than a check on executive power. Revolution was not "at present" required in England, but it could be averted only by adopting reform. Events in France had "called forth into energy, expanded, invigorated, and matured" principles that had "so long suffered to repose in impotent abstraction" in the land of their birth.

It was on this note that the first two editions of *Vindiciae Gallicae* ended. In the section Mackintosh added to the third edition he confidently predicted that the Revolution would be permanent and that the efforts of a "confederacy of despots" to suppress it would fail. Such efforts would merely unite the French around their new institutions, and failure would mark the end of Gothic governments throughout Europe. Similarly, the attempts by "church and king" mobs to harass dissenters and other English supporters of the Revolution were a desperate sign of the weakness of Toryism that could only contribute to its demise.

Letter to William Pitt

In *Vindiciae Gallicae* Mackintosh had charged Pitt with responsibility for reducing "popular control" over the House of Commons to a "shadow." In this anonymous pamphlet articulating the position of the Association of the Friends of the People, he spelled out the reforms needed to make good the defects in the English constitution. He had moved on in one respect: he had either become less confident about the outcome of French events or, for tactical reasons, was maintaining that reforms were necessary whatever might be the outcome. Dissociating domestic reform from French principles had now become an essential part of the case for moderate reform according to English principles. In maintaining that success or failure of the revolution in France made reform essential, however, Mackintosh was still attempting to occupy the middle ground between Tory reaction and an increase in monarchical power on one side and democratical Paineite republicanism on the other.

Mackintosh's proposals entailed—as previous reform efforts by Pitt himself had entailed—reduction in royal influence over the House of Commons via changes in the mode of election that would make it more "dependent upon the people, instead of being dependent on the Crown." This was to be achieved via redistribution of those seats that could clearly be shown to be, if not actively corrupt, then unrepresentative of the many. No new principles of representation were on display, and references to the "people" and greater equality of representation remained vague abstractions. The attempt to prove that safe middle ground existed was doomed to failure in the circumstances created by periodic social upheaval taking place against a background of pan-European war with revolutionary France. The pamphlet represents Mackintosh's most outspoken statement on the question of parliamentary reform. A quarter of a century was to elapse before he took up the cause again, and then it was to counter an equally dangerous foe, the philosophic radical case for a uniform system of representation based on number alone.

Discourse on the Law of Nature and of Nations

This introduction to natural jurisprudence, defined as "the science which teaches the rights and duties of men and of states," was initially published to allay the fears of Mackintosh's hosts, the benchers of Lincoln's Inn. He wanted to assure them that he was not about to repeat the errors of *Vindiciae Gallicae* by dealing with controversial constitutional issues, especially those connected with "first principles": the origin of governments and what made them fit for legitimate obligation. In this he followed the example of his friend Dugald Stewart in the almost contemporaneous course of lectures on politics he was giving in Edinburgh. In the course of his lectures Mackintosh also launched a thinly veiled attack on the views of former friends within the reformist camp, notably the perfectibilist speculations of William Godwin, an action for which he later felt it necessary to make partial amends. Thomas Babington Macaulay, who was to inherit the material Mackintosh collected for his history of England, later defended his friend by saying that he was neither a Jacobin nor an anti-Jacobin. While the former judgment may have been accurate, Mackintosh came close to the latter in his remarks on Godwin; he also distanced himself from such earlier authorities as Rousseau.

The foundations of justice and of the correlative science lay in the universal rules of individual morality, wherever these were to be observed in the historical record of mankind's moral sentiments based on "observation of common life." Mackintosh traces the history of attempts to codify systems of law, giving pride of place to Grotius, Pufendorf, and Montesquieu, while maintaining that circumstances were now ripe for a modern compend constructed on more scientific principles and encompassing the wider range of evidence of social life provided by modern communications and the travel literature. The lesson so far as innovations were concerned was one of prudence and caution, with time rather than human invention being credited with the most wisdom. The complicated machinery of the "mixed" English constitution was now held to embody liberties lost to less fortunate nations.

Mackintosh had taken a dim view of the lawyer's retrospective approach to liberty in *Vindiciae Gallicae*. Burke was indicted by being aligned with the "mysterious nonsense" of Coke and Blackstone, those who argued on the basis of mere prescriptive genealogy and precedent. In the discourse, gradualism, indeed denial of the wisdom of constructive innovation, was the message, with Burke now being cited positively for his understanding of the need for slow adaptation of institutions to local circumstances and habits. Mackintosh advised the lawyers in his audience that legal knowledge was essential to history but equally that legal skills without comparative-historical understanding were barren. History now supported caution; its laws, when not respected, will undo the unwary reformer. Constitutional guarantees of liberty could not be found in a single written document à la Paine and the declaration of rights.

Even when unnamed, Scottish authors remained influential. Thus Mackintosh followed the line taken by Hume and Smith in abandoning the idea of an original social contract in favor of a stadial form of history, in his stress on liberty as security under the rule of law, and in his desire to make the machinery of law and government proof against the knavery of rulers and fellow citizens. But he departs, in conclusion, from these secular mentors, as Stewart had done before him, in making the rules of justice part of "that eternal chain by which the Author of the universe has bound together the happiness and the duty of His creatures." A more mundane act of piety can be seen in Mackintosh's attempt to reconcile the positions of Fox and Burke, leaders of the two wings of the Whig Party sundered by the French Revolution.

On the State of France in 1815

Mackintosh's article was largely based on observations made during his visit in the previous year, though, ostensibly, it was prompted by two tracts by his friend Benjamin Constant and other recent works by English visitors to France. Between his own visit and the appearance of the article, Napoleon had escaped from Elba and formed an army that forced Louis XVIII to leave France. Mackintosh recalls the brief hope of the first restoration that legitimacy and the liberties established by the Revolution could be combined, while at the same time he draws attention to those changes in the "condition and character of the French people" generated by a quarter of a century's experience of revolution and war that made restoration of monarchy "as palpably hopeless as it is manifestly unjust." In scorning the deliberations of the allies at the Congress of Vienna, and when criticizing the conduct of the restored monarchs, he shows the same hostility to the "confederacy of despots" he had first revealed in *Vindiciae Gallicae*. Although Mackintosh proved to be no more prescient about French and European events in 1815 than he had been in 1791, this does not detract from his analysis of the permanent changes in the structure of French society produced by the Revolution.

NOTE ON THE
TEXTS USED IN THIS EDITION

The first edition of *Vindiciae Gallicae* appeared in April 1791, followed by a second in July correcting misprints that had arisen as a result of haste. A third edition appeared in August, containing an additional concluding section on the probable consequences of the French Revolution for European governments. The copy text employed here is that of the third edition, with the original pagination indicated by angle brackets. A fourth edition appeared in 1792; it varies only in its pagination. Since then the edition that has mostly been cited is that contained in Robert J. Mackintosh (ed.), *The Miscellaneous Works of Sir James Mackintosh* (3 vols., London, 1846, 3:2–166). This edition is marred by the numerous deletions and changes of wording and sense introduced by the editor, Mackintosh's son, presumably in an attempt to burnish his father's reputation.

All of Mackintosh's references to Burke's *Reflections* have been converted to refer to the Liberty Fund edition, Edmund Burke, *Reflections on the Revolution in France,* volume 2 of *Select Works of Edmund Burke* (Indianapolis: Liberty Fund, 1999).

The *Letter to Pitt* is based on the original pamphlet published in 1792.

The copy text of *A Discourse on the Law of Nature and Nations* is taken from the *Miscellaneous Works* (1:341–87). Additional material, chiefly footnotes, has been supplied from the third edition published in 1800. To this have been added extracts from the lectures printed in the son's edition of the *Memoirs of the Life of the Right Honourable Sir James Mackintosh* (2 vols., London, 1836, 1:111–22).

Finally, the copy text used here for Mackintosh's article for the *Edinburgh Review* on "The State of France in 1815," is taken from *Miscellaneous*

Works (1:185–202). The ending of the article omitted by the son has been added in an appendix and has been taken from the original article (no. 48, February 1815, pp. 505–37).

An asterisk, dagger, or double dagger indicates Mackintosh's original notes. Editorial notes identifying sources and giving translations are numbered. Editorial intrusions into the author's notes are made between square brackets.

ACKNOWLEDGMENTS

It would not have been possible to complete this edition without the expert assistance and persistence of Dr. Rachel Hammersley, Leverhulme Special Fellow at the University of Sussex and now lecturer in Historical Studies at the University of Newcastle-upon-Tyne, whose own work on the role of the Cordelier Club during the French Revolution will be published next year. The scholarly apparatus of notes, chronologies, and the dramatis personae are almost entirely her work. I am also grateful to Wendy Robins for help in the comparison of the various texts at an early stage in the project. For translation of most of the Latin and Greek quotations I am chiefly indebted to Leofranc Holford-Strevens, with my colleague Dr. James Shiel coming to the rescue on some quotations previously overlooked.

VINDICIAE GALLICAE.

DEFENCE

OF THE

FRENCH REVOLUTION

AND ITS

ENGLISH ADMIRERS,

AGAINST THE ACCUSATIONS OF

THE RIGHT HON. EDMUND BURKE;

INCLUDING

SOME STRICTURES ON THE LATE PRODUCTION

OF

MONS. DE CALONNE.

BY JAMES MACKINTOSH,

OF LINCOLN'S INN, ESQUIRE.

THE THIRD EDITION, WITH ADDITIONS.

LONDON:

PRINTED FOR G. G. J. AND J. ROBINSON,

PATERNOSTER-ROW.

1791

Advertisement

Had I foreseen the size to which the following volume was to grow, or the obstacles that were to retard its completion, I should probably have shrunk from the undertaking; and perhaps I may now be supposed to owe an apology for offering it to the Public, after the able and masterly Publications to which this controversy has given occasion.

Many parts of it bear internal marks of having been written some months ago, by allusions to circumstances which are now changed; but as they did not affect the reasoning, I was not solicitous to alter them.

For the lateness of its appearance, I find a consolation in the knowledge, that respectable Works on the same subject are still expected by the Public; and the number of my fellow-labourers only suggests the reflection—that too many minds cannot be employed on a controversy so immense as to present the most various aspects to different understandings, and so important, that the more correct statement of one fact, or the more successful illustration of one argument, will at least rescue a book from the imputation of having been written in vain.

Little Ealing, Middlesex,

April 26, 1791.

Advertisement to the Third Edition

I now present the following Work to the Public a third time, rendered, I hope, less unworthy of their favor.—Of *Literary Criticism* it does not become me to question the justice, but *Moral Animadversion* I feel it due to myself to notice.

The vulgar clamor which has been raised with such malignant art against the friends of Freedom, as the apostles of turbulence and sedition, has not even spared the obscurity of my name. To strangers I can only vindicate myself by *defying* the authors of such clamors to discover one passage in this *volume* not in the highest degree favorable to peace and stable government. Those to whom I am known would, I believe, be slow to impute any sentiments of violence to a temper which the partiality of my friends must confess to be indolent, and the hostility of enemies will not deny to be mild.

I have been accused, by *valuable friends,* of treating with ungenerous levity the misfortunes of the Royal Family of France. They will not however suppose me capable of *deliberately* violating the sacredness of misery in a palace or a cottage; and I sincerely lament that I should have been *betrayed* into expressions which admitted that constuction.

Little Ealing, August 28, 1791.

INTRODUCTION

The late opinions of Mr. Burke furnished more matter of astonishment to those who had distantly observed, than to those who had correctly examined the system of his former political life. An abhorrence for abstract politics, a predilection for aristocracy, and a dread of innovation, have ever been among the most sacred articles of his public creed. It was not likely that at his age he should abandon to the invasion of audacious novelties, opinions which he had received so early, and maintained so long, which had been fortified by the applause of the great, and the assent of the wise, which he had dictated to so many illustrious pupils, and supported against so many distinguished opponents. Men who early attain eminence, repose in their first <ii> creed. They neglect the progress of the human mind subsequent to its adoption, and when, as in the present case, it has burst forth into action, they regard it as a transient madness, worthy only of pity or derision. They mistake it for a mountain torrent that will pass away with the storm that gave it birth. They know not that it is the stream of human opinion *in omne volubilis aevum,*[1] which the accession of every day will swell, which is destined to sweep into the same oblivion the resistance of learned sophistry, and of powerful oppression.

But there still remained ample matter of astonishment in the Philippic of Mr. Burke. He might deplore the sanguinary excesses—he might deride the visionary policy that seemed to him to tarnish the lustre of the Revolution, but it was hard to have supposed that he should have exhausted against it every epithet of contumely and opprobium that language <iii>

---

1. "Rolling its flood forever." Horace, *Epistles,* in *Satires, Epistles, and Ars poetica,* trans. H. Rushton Fairclough (London and Cambridge, Mass.: Heinemann and Harvard University Press, 1978), 264–65 (I.ii.43).

can furnish to indignation; that the rage of his declamation should not for one moment have been suspended; that his heart should not betray one faint glow of triumph, at the splendid and glorious delivery of so great a people. All was invective—the authors, and admirers of the Revolution—every man who did not execrate it, even his own most enlightened and accomplished friends, were devoted to odium and ignominy.

This speech did not stoop to argument—the whole was dogmatical and authoritative; the cause seemed decided without discussion; the anathema fulminated before trial. But the ground of the opinions of this famous speech, which, if we may believe a foreign journalist, will form an epoch in the history of the eccentricities of the human mind, was impatiently expected in a work soon after announced.[2] The name of the author, the importance of the subject, and the singularity of his opinions, <iv> all contributed to inflame the public curiosity, which though it languished in a subsequent delay, has been revived by the appearance, and will be rewarded by the perusal of the work.

It is certainly in every respect a performance, of which to form a correct estimate, would prove one of the most arduous efforts of critical skill. "We scarcely can praise it, or blame it too much."[3] Argument every where dextrous and specious, sometimes grave and profound, cloathed in the most rich and various imagery, and aided by the most pathetic and picturesque description, speaks the opulence and the powers of that mind, of which age has neither dimmed the discernment nor enfeebled the fancy, neither repressed the ardor, nor narrowed the range. Virulent encomiums on urbanity, and inflammatory harangues against violence; homilies of moral and religious mysticism, better adapted <v> to the amusement than to the conviction of an incredulous age, though they may rouse the languor of attention, can never be dignified by the approbation of the understanding.

Of the Senate and people of France, his language is such as might have been expected to a country which his fancy has peopled only with plots,

2. Edmund Burke, *Substance of the Speech of the Right Honourable Edmund Burke, in the Debate on the Army Estimates, in the House of Commons, on Tuesday the 9th Day of February, 1790* (London: Debrett, 1790).

3. Oliver Goldsmith, "Retaliation: A Poem," in *Collected Works*, ed. A. Friedmann, 5 vols. (Oxford: Clarendon Press, 1966), 4:353.

assassinations, and massacres, and all the brood of dire chimeras which are the offspring of a prolific imagination, goaded by an ardent and deluded sensibility. The glimpses of benevolence, which irradiate this gloom of invective, arise only from generous illusion, from misguided and misplaced compassion—his eloquence is not at leisure to deplore the fate of beggared artizans, and famished peasants, the victims of suspended industry, and languishing commerce. The sensibility which seems scared by the homely miseries of the vulgar, is attracted only by the splendid sorrows of royalty, and agonizes at the slen-<vi>derest pang that assails the heart of sottishness or prostitution, if they are placed by fortune on a throne.

To the English friends of French freedom,[4] his language is contemptuous, illiberal, and scurrilous. In one of the ebbings of his fervor, he is disposed not to dispute "their good intentions."[5] But he abounds in intemperate sallies, in ungenerous insinuations, which wisdom ought to have checked, as ebullitions of passion, which genius ought to have disdained, as weapons of controversy.

The arrangement of his work is as singular as the matter. Availing himself of all the privileges of epistolary effusion, in their utmost latitude and laxity, he interrupts, dismisses, and resumes argument at pleasure. His subject is as extensive as political science—his allusions and excursions reach almost every region of human knowledge. It must <vii> be confessed that in this miscellaneous and desultory warfare, the superiority of a man of genius over common men is infinite. He can cover the most ignominious retreat by a brilliant allusion. He can parade his arguments with masterly generalship, where they are strong. He can escape from an untenable position into a splendid declamation. He can sap the most impregnable conviction by pathos, and put to flight a host of syllogisms with a sneer. Absolved from the laws of vulgar method, he can advance a groupe of

4. A general term for those in Britain who supported the French Revolution and called for reform at home. These included members of the London Corresponding Society, the Society for Constitutional Information, and other such societies. See A. Goodwin, *The Friends of Liberty: The English Democratic Movement in the Age of the French Revolution* (London: Hutchinson, 1979).

5. Edmund Burke, *Reflections on the Revolution in France,* vol. 2 of *Select Works of Edmund Burke,* 3 vols. (Indianapolis: Liberty Fund, 1999), 233.

magnificent horrors to make a breach in our hearts, through which the most undisciplined rabble of arguments may enter in triumph.

Analysis and method, like the discipline and armour of modern nations, correct in some measure the inequalities of controversial dexterity, and level on the intellectual field the giant and the dwarf. Let us then analyse the production of Mr. Burke, and dismissing what <viii> is extraneous and ornamental, we shall discover certain leading questions, of which the decision is indispensible to the point at issue.

The natural order of these topics will dictate the method of reply. Mr. Burke, availing himself of the indefinite and equivocal term, Revolution, has, altogether, reprobated that transaction. The first question, therefore, that arises, regards the general expediency and necessity of a Revolution in France.—This is followed by the discussion of the composition and conduct of the National Assembly, of the popular excesses which attended the Revolution, and the New Constitution that is to result from it. The conduct of its English admirers forms the last topic, though it is with rhetorical inversion first treated by Mr. Burke, as if the propriety of approbation should be determined before the discussion of the merit or demerit of what was approved. In pursuance <ix> of this analysis, the following sections will comprise the substance of our refutation.

Sect. I. *The General Expediency and Necessity of a Revolution in France.*

II. *The Composition and Character of the National Assembly considered.*

III. *The Popular Excesses which attended, or followed the Revolution.*

IV. *The new Constitution of France.*

V. *The Conduct of its English Admirers justified.*

With this reply to Mr. Burke will be mingled some strictures on the late publication of M. Calonne.[6] That minister, who has for some time exhib-

---

6. C. A. Calonne, *De l'état de la France, présent et à venir, par M. de Calonne ministre d'état* (Londres: T. Spilsbury & fils, 1790).

ited to the eyes of indignant Europe the spectacle of an exiled robber living
<x> in the most splendid impunity, has, with an effrontery that beggars
invective, assumed in his work the tone of afflicted patriotism, and delivers
his polluted Philippics as the oracles of persecuted virtue.

His work is more methodical than that of his coadjutor, Mr. Burke.* Of
his financial calculations it may be remarked, that in a work professedly
popular they afford the strongest presumption of fraud. Their extent and
intricacy seem contrived to extort assent from <xi> public indolence, for
men will rather believe than examine them. His inferences are so outrageously incredible, that most men of sense will think it more safe to trust
their own plain conclusions than to enter such a labyrinth of financial
sophistry.

The only part of his production that here demands reply, is that which
relates to general political questions. Remarks on what he has offered concerning them will naturally find a place under the corresponding sections
of the Reply to Mr. Burke. Its most important view is neither literary nor
argumentative. It appeals to judgments more decisive than those of criticism, and aims at wielding weapons more formidable than those of logic.

It is the manifesto of a Counter Revolution, and its obvious object is to
inflame every passion and interest, real or supposed, that has received any
shock in the establishment of <xii> freedom. He probes the bleeding
wounds of the princes, the nobility, the priesthood, and the great judicial
aristocracy. He adjures one body by its dignity degraded, another by its
inheritance plundered, and a third by its authority destroyed, to repair to
the holy banner of his philanthropic crusade. Confident in the protection
of all the monarchs of Europe, whom he alarms for the security of their

---

* It cannot be denied that the production of M. Calonne is, "eloquent, able," and
certainly very "instructive" in what regards his own character and designs. [Burke, *Reflections*, 295.] But it contains one instance of historical ignorance so egregious, that I
cannot resist quoting it.—In his long discussion of the pretensions of the Assembly to
the title of a National Convention, he deduces the origin of that word from Scotland,
where he informs us, p. 328, "On lui donna le nom de Convention Ecossoise, le résultat
de ses délibérations fut appellé *Covenant,* & ceux qui l'avoient souscrit ou qui y adhe-
roient *Covenanters!!*" ["It was given the name Scottish Convention, the result of its deliberations was called a *Covenant,* and those who subscribed or adhered to it Covenanters!!" Calonne, *De la France,* 328.]

thrones, and having insured the moderation of a fanatical rabble, by giving out among them the savage *war-whoop* of atheism, he already fancies himself in full march to Paris, not to re-instate the deposed despotism (for he disclaims the purpose, and who would not trust such virtuous disavowals!!) but at the head of this army of priests, mercenaries and fanatics, to dictate as the tutelar genius of France, the establishment of a just and temperate freedom, obtained without commotion and without carnage, and equally hostile to the interested ambition of demagogues and the lawless authority of kings. <xiii>

Crusades were an effervescence of chivalry, and the modern St. Francis has a knight for the conduct of these crusaders, who will convince Mr. Burke, that the age of chivalry is not past, nor the glory of Europe gone for ever. The Comte d'Artois,* that scyon worthy of Henry the Great, the rival of the Bayards and Sidneys, the new model of French Knighthood, is to issue from Turin with ten thousand cavaliers to deliver the peerless and immaculate Antonietta of Austria from the durance vile in which she has so long been immured in the Thuilleries, from the swords of the discourteous knights of Paris, and the spells of the sable wizards of democracy.

---

* *Ce digne rejeton du grand Henri*—Calonne, p. 413. *Un nouveau modèle de la Chevalerie Françoise.* Ibid. p. 114. ["This offspring worthy of Henry the Great"; "A new model of French chivalry." Calonne, *De la France,* 415 and 416. Mackintosh's page numbers are wrong.]

Vindiciae Gallicae
&c. &c.

<15>

ʂʘɿ SECTION I ʂʘɿ

The General Expediency and Necessity
of a Revolution in France.

It is asserted in many passages* of Mr. Burke's work, though no where with that precision which the importance of the assertion demanded, that the *French Revolution* was not only in its parts reprehensible, but in the whole was absurd, inexpedient, and unjust; yet he has no where exactly informed us what he understands by the term. The French Revolution, in its most popular sense, perhaps would be understood in England to <16> consist of those splendid events that formed the prominent portion of its exterior, the Parisian revolt, the capture of the Bastile, and the submission of the King. But these memorable events, though they strengthened and accelerated, could not constitute a Political Revolution. It must have been a change of Government, but even limited to that meaning, it is equivocal and wide.

It is capable of *three* senses. The King's recognition of the rights of the States General to a share in the legislation, was a change in the actual government of France, where the whole legislative and executive power had,

* Page 227, 236–37, 270, and many other passages.

without the shadow of interruption, for nearly two centuries been enjoyed by the Crown; in that sense the meeting of the States-General was the Revolution, and the 5th of May was its aera. The union of the three Orders in one assembly was a most important change in the forms and spirit of the legislature. This <17> too may be called the Revolution, and the 23d of June will be its aera. This body, thus united, are forming a new Constitution. This may be also called a Revolution, because it is of all the political changes the most important, and its epoch will be determined by the conclusion of the labours of the National Assembly.

Thus equivocal is the import of Mr. Burke's expressions. To extricate them from this ambiguity, a rapid survey of these events will be necessary. It will prove too the fairest and most forcible confutation of his arguments. It will best demonstrate the necessity and justice of all the successive changes in the State of France, which formed the mixed mass called the Revolution. It will discriminate legislative acts from popular excesses, and distinguish transient confusion from permanent establishment. It will evince the futility and fallacy of attributing to the <18> conspiracy of individuals, or bodies, a Revolution which, whether it be beneficial or injurious, was produced only by general causes, where the most conspicuous individual produced little real effect.

The Constitution of France resembled in the earlier stages of its progress the other Gothic governments of Europe. The history of its decline and the causes of its extinction are abundantly known. Its infancy and youth were like those of the English government. The *Champ de Mars,* and the *Wittenagemot,* the tumultuous assemblies of rude conquerors, were in both countries melted down into representative bodies. But the downfall of the feudal aristocracy happening in France before Commerce had elevated any other class of citizens into importance, its power devolved on the Crown. From the conclusion of the fifteenth century the powers of the States General had almost dwindled into formalities. <19> Their momentary reappearance under Henry III. and Louis XIII. served only to illustrate their insignificance. Their total disuse speedily succeeded.

The intrusion of any popular voice was not likely to be tolerated in the reign of Louis XIV. a reign which has been so often celebrated as the zenith of warlike and literary splendor, but which has always appeared to me to be the consummation of whatever is afflicting and degrading in the history of the human race. Talent seemed, in that reign, robbed of the conscious elevation, of the erect and manly part, which is its noblest associate and its surest indication. The mild purity of Fenelon,* the lofty spirit of Bossuet, the masculine mind of Boileau, the sublime fervor of Corneille, were confounded by the conta-<20>gion of ignominious and indiscriminate servility. It seemed as if the "representative majesty"[7] of the genius and intellect of man were prostrated before the shrine of a sanguinary and dissolute tyrant, who practised the corruption of Courts without their mildness, and incurred the guilt of wars without their glory. His highest praise is to have supported the stage trick of Royalty with effect; and it is surely difficult to conceive any character more odious and despicable, than that of a puny libertine, who, under the frown of a strumpet, or a monk, issues the mandate that is to murder virtuous citizens, to desolate happy and peaceful hamlets, to wring agonizing tears from widows and orphans. Heroism has a splendor that almost atones for its excesses; but what shall we think of him, who, from the luxurious and dastardly security in which he wallows at Versailles, issues with calm and cruel apathy his orders to butcher the Protestants of Languedoc, or <21> to lay in ashes the villages of the Palatinate?[8] On the recollection of such scenes, as a scholar, I blush for the prostitution of letters; as a man, I blush for the patience of humanity.

But the despotism of this reign was pregnant with the great events which have signalized our age. It fostered that literature which was one day destined to destroy it. Its profligate conquests have eventually proved the acquisitions of humanity; and the usurpations of Louis XIV. have served only

---

* And Cambray, worthy of a happier doom,
  The virtuous slave of *Louis* and of ROME.

[G. Lyttleton, first Baron Lyttleton, "To the Reverend Dr. Ayscough at Oxford. Writ from Paris in the Year 1728," in *Poems* (Glasgow, 1777), lines 45–46. Fénelon was archbishop of Cambray.]

  7. Burke, *Reflections*, 92.

  8. A reference to Louis XIV's revocation of the Edict of Nantes, October 22, 1685, which reversed the policy of toleration toward French Protestants introduced under Henry IV in 1598.

to add a larger portion to the great body of freemen. The spirit of its policy was inherited by the succeeding reign. The rage of conquest, repressed for a while by the torpid despotism of Fleury, burst forth with renovated violence in the latter part of the reign of Louis XV. France, exhausted alike by the misfortunes of one war and the victories of another, groaned under a weight of impost and debt, which it was equally difficult to remedy or to endure. <22> The profligate expedients were exhausted by which successive Ministers had attempted to avert the great crisis, in which the credit and power of the government must perish.

The wise and benevolent administration of M. Turgot, though long enough for his glory, was too short, and perhaps too *early,* for those salutary and grand reforms which his genius had conceived, and his virtue would have effected. The aspect of purity and talent spread a natural alarm among the minions of a Court, and they easily succeeded in the expulsion of such rare and obnoxious intruders.

The magnificent ambition of M. de Vergennes, the brilliant, profuse and rapacious career of M. de Calonne, the feeble and irresolute violence of M. Brienne, all contributed their share to swell this financial embarrassment. The *deficit,* or inferiority of the revenue to the expenditure, at length rose to <23> the enormous sum of 115 millions of livres, or about 4,750,000*l.* annually.* This was a disproportion between income and expence with which no government, and no individual, could long continue to exist.

In this exigency there was no expedient left, but to guarantee the ruined credit of bankrupt despotism by the sanction of the national voice. The States General were a dangerous mode of collecting it. Recourse was therefore had to the Assembly of the *Notables,* a mode well known in the history of France, in which the King summoned a number of individuals, selected, at *his* discre-<24>tion, from the mass, to advise him in great emergencies.

---

* For this we have the authority of M. de Calonne himself. See his late Publication, page 50. [Calonne, *De la France,* 56. Mackintosh's figures do not match those of Calonne.] This was the account presented to the Notables in April, 1787. He, indeed, makes some deductions on account of part of this *deficit* being expirable. But this is of no consequence to our purpose, which is to view the influence of the *present* urgency, the political, not the financial state of the question.

They were little better than a popular Privy Council. They were neither recognized nor protected by law. Their precarious and subordinate existence hung on the nod of despotism.

They were called together by M. Calonne, who has now the inconsistent arrogance to boast of the schemes which he laid before them, as the model of the Assembly whom he traduces. He proposed, it is true, the equalization of impost, and the abolition of the pecuniary exemptions of the Nobility and Clergy; and the difference between his system and that of the Assembly, is only in what makes the sole distinction in human actions—*its end*. He would have destroyed the privileged Orders, as obstacles to despotism. *They* have destroyed them, as derogations from freedom. The object of *his* plans was to facilitate *Fiscal* oppression. The motive of *theirs* <25> is to fortify general liberty. *They* have levelled all Frenchmen as men—*he* would have levelled them all as slaves.

The Assembly of the Notables, however, soon gave a memorable proof, how dangerous are all public meetings of men, even without legal powers of controul, to the permanence of despotism. They had been assembled by M. Calonne to admire the plausibility and splendor of his speculations, and to veil the extent and atrocity of his rapine. But the fallacy of the one, and the profligacy of the other, were detected with equal ease. Illustrious and accomplished orators, who have since found a nobler sphere for their talents, in a more free and powerful Assembly, exposed this plunderer to the Notables. Detested by the Nobles and Clergy, of whose privileges he had suggested the abolition; undermined in the favour of the Queen, by his attack on one of her favourites (*Breteuil*); <26> exposed to the fury of the people, and dreading the terrors of judicial prosecution, he speedily sought refuge in England, without the recollection of one virtue, or the applause of one party, to console his retreat.*

Thus did the Notables destroy their creator. Little appeared to be done to a superficial observer; but to a discerning eye, ALL was done; for the dethroned authority of Public opinion was restored. The succeeding Min-

---

* Histoire de la Revolution en 1789, &c. tom. i. p. 18 & 19. [F. M. de Kerverseau and G. Clavelin, *Histoire de la Révolution de 1789, et de l'établissement d'une constitution en France; précédée de l'exposé rapide des administrations successives qui ont déterminé cette Révolution mémorable,* 7 vols. (additional volumes appeared later) (Paris, 1790), 1:18–19.]

isters, uninstructed by the example of their predecessors, by the destruction of Public credit, and the fermentation of the popular mind, hazarded measures of a still more preposterous and perilous description. The usurpation of some share in the sovereignty by the Parliament of Paris had become popular and venerable, because its tendency was useful, <27> and its exercise virtuous.—That body had, as it is well known, claimed a right, which, in fact, amounted to a negative on all the acts of the King. They contended, that their registering his Edicts was necessary to give them force. They would, in that case, have possessed the same share of legislation with the King of England.

It is unnecessary to descant on the historical fallacy, and political inexpediency, of doctrines, which should vest in a narrow aristocracy of lawyers, who had bought their places, such extensive powers. It cannot be denied that their resistance had often proved salutary, and was some feeble check on the capricious wantonness of despotic exaction.—But the temerity of the Minister now assigned them a more important part. They refused to register two edicts for the creation of imposts. They averred, that the power of imposing taxes was vested only in the National <28> Representatives, and they claimed the immediate convocation of the States General of the kingdom. The minister banished them to Troyes. But he soon found how much the French were changed from that abject and frivolous people, which had so often endured the exile of its magistrates. Paris exhibited the tumult and clamour of a London mob.

The cabinet, which could neither advance nor recede with safety, had recourse to the expedient of a compulsory registration. The Duke of Orleans, and the magistrates who protested against this execrable mockery, were exiled or imprisoned. But all these hacknied expedients of despotism were in vain. These struggles, which merit notice only as they illustrate the progressive energy of Public opinion, were followed by events still less equivocal. *Lettres de Cachet* were issued against *M.M. d'Epresmenil & Goestard.* They took refuge in the sanctuary of justice, and the Par-<29>liament pronounced them under the safeguard of the law and the King. A deputation was sent to Versailles, to intreat his Majesty to listen to sage counsels. Paris expected, with impatient solicitude, the result of this deputation; when towards midnight, a body of 2000 troops marched to the palace where the Parliament were seated, and their Commander, entering into the Court of Peers, demanded his victims. A loud and unanimous acclamation replied, "We are all *d'Epresmenil & Goestard!*"⁹ These magistrates surrendered themselves, and the satellite of despotism led them off in triumph, amid the execrations of an aroused and indignant people.

These *spectacles* were not without their effect. The spirit of resistance spread daily over France. The intermediate commission of the States of Bretagne, the States of Dauphiné, and many other public bodies, began to assume a new and menacing tone. The Cabinet dis-<30>solved in its own feebleness, and M. Necker was recalled. That Minister, probably upright, and not illiberal, but narrow, pusillanimous, and entangled by the habits of detail* in which he had been reared, possessed not that erect and intrepid spirit, those enlarged and original views, which adapt themselves to new combinations of circumstances, and sway in the great convulsions of human affairs. Accustomed to the tranquil accuracy of commerce, or the elegant amusements of literature, he was "called on to ride in the whirlwind, and direct the storm."¹⁰ He seemed superior to his privacy while he was limited <31> to it, and would have been adjudged by history equal to his elevation had he never been elevated.† The reputation of few men, it is true, has been exposed to so severe a test; and a generous observer will be disposed to scrutinize less rigidly the claims of a Statesman, who has retired with the applause of no party, who is detested by the aristocracy as the

---

* The late celebrated Dr. Adam Smith, always held this opinion of Necker, whom he had known intimately when a Banker in Paris. He predicted the fall of his fame when his talents should be brought to the test, and always emphatically said, "He is but a man of detail." [Mackintosh himself appears to have been the source of this anecdote. See J. Rae, *Life of Adam Smith,* ed. J. Viner (New York: Augustus Kelley, 1965), 206.] At a time when the commercial abilities of Mr. Eden, the present Lord Auckland were the theme of profuse eulogy, Dr. Smith characterized him in the same words.

† *Major Privato visus dum privatus fuit et omnium consensú capax imperii nisi imperasset.*—TAC. ["He seemed too great to be a subject so long as he was subject, and all would have agreed that he was equal to the imperial office if he had never held it." Tacitus, *The Histories,* in *The Histories, The Annals,* trans. C. H. Moore, 3 vols. (London and Cambridge, Mass.: Heinemann and Harvard University Press, 1956), 1:82–83 (I.49).]

9. Kerverseau and Clavelin, *Histoire de la Révolution de 1789,* 1:46.

10. Joseph Addison, *The Campaign, A Poem, To His Grace the Duke of Marlborough,* 2d ed. (London: J. Jonson, 1705), 14.

instrument of their ruin, and despised by the democratic leaders for pusillanimous and fluctuating policy.

But had the character of M. Necker possessed more originality or decision, it could have had little influence on the fate of France. The minds of men had received an impulse. Individual aid and individual opposition were equally vain. His views, no doubt, extended only to palliation; but he was involved in a <32> stream of opinions and events, of which no force could resist the current, and no wisdom adequately predict the termination. He is represented by M. Calonne as the Lord Sunderland of Louis XVI. seducing the King to destroy his own power. But he had neither genius nor boldness for such designs.

To return to our rapid survey.—The Autumn of 1788 was peculiarly distinguished by the enlightened and disinterested patriotism of the States of Dauphiné. They furnished, in many respects, a model for the future Senate of France. Like them they deliberated amidst the terrors of ministerial vengeance and military execution. They annihilated the absurd and destructive distinction of Orders, the three estates were melted into a Provincial Assembly; and they declared, that the right of imposing taxes resided ultimately in the States General of France. They voted a deputation to the King to solicit the convocation of that <33> Assembly. They were emulously imitated by all the provinces that still retained the shadow of Provincial States. The States of Languedoc, of Velay, and Vivarois, the Tiers Etat of Provence, and all the Municipalities of Bretagne, adopted similar resolutions. In Provence and Bretagne, where the Nobles and Clergy, trembling for their privileges, and the Parliaments for their jurisdiction, attempted a feeble resistance, the fermentation was peculiarly strong. Some estimate of the fervor of public sentiment may be formed from the reception of the Count de Mirabeau in his native Provence, where the Burgesses of *Aix* assigned him a body-guard, where the citizens of Marseilles crowned him in the theatre, and where, under all the terrors of despotism, he received as numerous and tumultuous proofs of attachment as ever were bestowed on a favourite by the enthusiasm of the most free people. M. Caraman, the Governor of Provence, was even reduced to im-<34>plore his interposition with the populace, to appease and prevent their excesses. The contest in Bretagne was more violent and sanguinary. It had preserved its independence more than any of those Provinces which had been united to the Crown of France. The Nobles and Clergy possessed almost the whole power of the States, and their obstinacy was so great, that their Deputies did not take their seats in the National Assembly till an advanced period of its proceedings.

The return of M. Necker, and the recall of the exiled magistrates, re-stored a momentary calm. The personal reputation of the Minister for pro-bity, re-animated the credit of France. But the finances were too irreme-diably embarrassed for palliatives; and the fascinating idea of the States General, presented to the public imagination by the unwary zeal of the Parliament, awakened recollections of ancient freedom, and prospects <35> of future splendor, which the virtue or popularity of no Minister could banish. The convocation of that body was resolved—but many difficulties respecting the mode of electing and constituting it remained, which a sec-ond Assembly of Notables was summoned to decide.

The third Estate demanded representatives equal to those of the other two Orders jointly. They required that the number should be regulated by the population of the districts, and that the three Orders should vote in one Assembly. All the Committees into which the Notables were divided, except that of which MONSIEUR was President, decided against the Third Estate in every one of these particulars. They were strenuously supported by the Parliament of Paris, who, too late sensible of the suicide into which they had been betrayed, laboured to render the Assembly impotent, when they were unable to pre-<36>vent its meeting. But their efforts were in vain. M. Necker, whether actuated by respect for justice, or ambition of popu-larity, or yielding to the irresistible torrent of public sentiment, advised the King to adopt the propositions of the *Third Estate* in the two first partic-ulars, and to leave the last to be decided by the States General themselves.

Letters patent were accordingly issued on the 24th of January, 1789, for assembling the States General,* to which were annexed regulations for the detail of their elections. In the constituent assemblies of the several prov-inces, bailliages, and constabularies of the kingdom, the progress of the

* Lettre du Roi pour la convocation des Etats Generaux & regement pour l'execution des lettres de convocation, donné le 24 Janvier, 1789.

public mind became still more evident. The Clergy and Nobility ought not to be denied the praise of having emulously sacrificed their pe-<37>cuniary privileges. The instructions to the Representatives breathed every where a spirit of freedom as ardent, though not so liberal and enlightened, as that which has since presided in the deliberations of the National Assembly. Paris was eminently conspicuous. The union of talent, the rapid communication of thought, and the frequency of those numerous assemblies, where men learn their force, and compare their wrongs,* ever make a great capital the heart that circulates emotion and opinion to the extremities of an empire. No sooner had the convocation of the States General been announced, than the batteries of the press were opened. Pamphlet succeeded pamphlet, surpassing each other in boldness and elevation; and the advance of Paris to light and freedom was greater in three months than it had been in almost as many centuries. <38>

Doctrines† were universally received in May, which in January would have been deemed treasonable, and which in March were derided as the visions of a few deluded fanatics.

It was amid this rapid diffusion of light, and increasing fervor of public sentiment, that the States General of France assembled at Versailles on the 5th of May, 1789; a day which will probably be accounted by posterity one of the most memorable in the annals of the human race. Any detail of the parade <39> and ceremonial of their Assembly would be totally foreign to our purpose, which is not to narrate events, but to seize their spirit, and to mark their influence on the political progress from which the Revolution was to arise. The preliminary operation necessary to constitute the Assembly gave rise to the first great question—The mode of authenticating the

---

* *Conferre injurias & interpretando accendere.* —Tac. ["To compare their wrongs and inflame their significance." Tacitus, *Agricola,* in *Dialogus, Agricola, Germania,* trans. W. Peterson (London and New York: Heinemann and G. P. Putnam's Sons, 1920), 194–95 (§15).]

† The principles of freedom had long been understood, perhaps better than in any country of the world, by the philosophers of France. It was as natural that they should have been more diligently cultivated in that kingdom than in England, as that the science of medicine should be less understood and valued among simple and vigorous, than among luxurious and enfeebled nations. But the progress which we have noticed was among the less instructed part of society.

commissions of the Deputies. It was contended by the Clergy and Nobles, that according to ancient usage, each Order should separately scrutinize and authenticate the commissions of its own Deputies. It was argued by the Commons, that, on general principles, all Orders, having an equal interest in the purity of the national representative, had an equal right to take cognizance of the authenticity of the commissions of all the members who compose it, and therefore to scrutinize them in common. To the authority of precedent it was answered, that it would establish too much; for in the ancient States, their ex-<40>amination of powers was subordinate to the revision of Royal Commissaries, a subjection too degrading and injurious for the free and vigilant spirit of an enlightened age. This controversy involved another of more magnitude and importance. If the Orders united in this scrutiny, they were likely to continue in one Assembly; the separate voices of the two first Orders would be annihilated, and the importance of the Nobility and Clergy reduced to that of their individual suffrages.

This great Revolution was obviously meditated by the leaders of the Commons. They were seconded in the Chamber of the Noblesse by a minority eminently distinguished for rank, character, and talent. The obscure and useful portion of the Clergy were, from their situation, accessible to popular sentiment, and naturally coalesced with the Commons. Many who favoured the *division* of the Legislature in the ordinary arrangements of Go-<41>vernment, were convinced that the grand and radical reforms, which the situation of France demanded, could only be effected by its union as one Assembly.* So many prejudices were to be vanquished, so

---

* "Il n'est pas douteux que pour aujourd'hui, que pour cette premiere tenue une CHAMBRE UNIQUE n'ait été préferable & peut-être *necessaire.* Il y avoit tant de difficultés à surmonter, tant de prejugés à vaincre, tant de sacrifices à faire, de si vieilles habitudes à deraciner, une puissance si forte à contenir, en un mot, tant à detruire & *presque tout à creer.*"—"Ce nouvel ordre de choses que vous avez fait eclore, tout cela vous en êtes bien surs n'a jamais pu naître que de la reunion de toutes les personnes, de tous le sentiments, & de tous les coeurs."—*Discours de M. Lally Tolendahl à l'Assemblée Nationale.* 31 *Aout,* 1789, *dans ses Pieces Justificatifs, p.* 105–6. ["There is no doubt that today, that for this first meeting, a single chamber has been preferable and perhaps *necessary.* There have been too many difficulties to overcome, too many prejudices to conquer, too many sacrifices to make, and so many old habits to uproot, such a strong power to contain, in a word, so much to destroy and *almost everything to create.*" "This new order of

many difficulties to be surmounted, such obstinate habits to be extirpated, and so formidable a power to be re-<42>sisted, that there was an obvious necessity to concentrate the force of the reforming body. In a great Revolution, every expedient ought to facilitate change. In an established Government, every thing ought to render it difficult. Hence the division of a Legislature, which in an established Government may give a beneficial stability to the laws, must, in a moment of Revolution, be proportionably injurious, by fortifying abuse and unnerving reform. In a Revolution, the enemies of freedom are external, and all powers are therefore to be united. Under an establishment her enemies are internal, and power is therefore to be divided.

But besides this general consideration, the state of France furnished others of more local and temporary cogency. The States General, acting by separate Orders, were a body from which no substantial reform could be hoped. The two first Orders were interested <43> in the perpetuity of every abuse that was to be reformed. Their possession of two equal and independent voices must have rendered the exertions of the Commons impotent and nugatory, and a collusion between the Assembly and the Crown would probably have limited its illusive reforms to some sorry palliatives, the *price* of financial disembarrassment. The state of a nation lulled into complacent servitude by such petty concessions, is far more hopeless than the state of those who groan under the most galling yoke of despotism, and the condition of France would have been more irremediable than ever. Such reasonings produced an universal conviction, that the question, whether the States General were to vote individually, or in Orders, was a question, whether they were or were not to produce any important benefit. Guided by these views, and animated by public support, the Commons

---

things that you have brought into being, you are very sure could only emerge out of a meeting of all people, of all sentiments, and of all hearts." Trophime-Gérard, marquis de Lally-Tollendal, "Sur la Déclaration des Droits," in *Pièces justificatives contenant différentes motions et opinions de M. le comte de Lally-Tollendal* (Paris, 1789), 105–6.]—This passage is in more than one respect remarkable. It fully evinces the conviction of the Author, that changes were necessary great enough to deserve the name of a REVOLUTION; and, considering the respect of Mr. BURKE for his authority, ought to have weight with him.

adhered inflexibly to their principle of incorporating the three Orders. They <44> adopted a *provisory* organization, but studiously declined whatever might seem to suppose legal existence, or to arrogate constitutional powers. The Nobles, less politic or timid, declared themselves a legally constituted Order, and proceeded to discuss the great objects of their convocation. The Clergy affected to preserve a mediatorial character, and to conciliate the discordant claims of the two hostile Orders. The Commons, faithful to their system, remained in a wise and masterly inactivity, which tacitly reproached the arrogant assumption of the Nobles, while it left no pretext to calumniate their own conduct; gave time for the encrease of popular fervor, and distressed the Court by the delay of financial aid. Several conciliatory plans were proposed by the Minister, and rejected by the haughtiness of the Nobility and the policy of the Commons. <45>

Thus passed the period between the 5th of May and the 12th of June, when the popular leaders, animated by public support, and conscious of the maturity of their schemes, assumed a more resolute tone.

The Third Estate commenced the scrutiny of commissions, summoned the Nobles and Clergy to repair to the Hall of the States General, and resolved that the absence of the Deputies of some districts and classes of citizens could not preclude them, who formed the representatives of ninety-six hundred parts of the nation, from constituting themselves into a National Assembly.

These decisive measures betrayed the designs of the Court, and fully illustrated that bounty and liberality for which Lewis XVI. has been so idly celebrated. That feeble Prince, whose public character varied with every fluctuation in his Cabinet, the instru-<46>ment alike of the ambition of Vergennes, the prodigality of Calonne, and the ostentatious popularity of Necker, had hitherto yielded to the embarrassment of the finances, and the clamor of the people. The cabal that retained its ascendant over his mind, permitted concessions which they hoped to make vain, and flattered themselves with frustrating, by the contest of struggling Orders, all idea of substantial reform. No sooner did the Assembly betray any symptom of activity and vigor, than their alarms became conspicuous in the Royal conduct. The Comte d'Artois, and the other Princes of the Blood, published the boldest manifestoes against the Assembly; the credit of M. Necker at

Court declined every day; the Royalists in the Chamber of the Noblesse spoke of nothing less than an impeachment of the Commons for high treason, and an immediate dissolution of the States; a vast military force and a tremendous artillery were collected from all parts of the kingdom <47> towards Versailles and Paris, and under these menacing and inauspicious circumstances, the meeting of the States General was prohibited by the King's order till a Royal Session, which was destined for the 22d, but held on the 23d of June. The Commons, on repairing to their Hall on the 20th, found it invested with soldiers, and themselves excluded from it by the point of the bayonet. They were summoned by their President to a *Tennis-Court*, where they were reduced to hold their assembly, and which they rendered famous as the scene of their unanimous and memorable oath, never to separate till they had atchieved the regeneration of France.

The *Royal Session* thus announced, corresponded with the new tone of the Court. Its exterior was marked by the gloomy and ferocious haughtiness of despotism. The Royal puppet was now evidently moved by different persons from those who had prompted *its* <48> speech at the opening of the States. He probably spoke both with the same spirit and the same heart, and felt as little firmness under the cloak of arrogance, as he had been conscious of sensibility amidst his professions of affection. He was probably as feeble in the one as he had been cold in the other; but his language is some criterion of the system of his prompters.

This speech was distinguished by insulting condescension and ostentatious menace. He spoke not as the Chief of a free nation to its sovereign Legislature, but as a Sultan to his Divan. He *annulled* and *prescribed* deliberations at pleasure. He affected to represent his will as the rule of their conduct, and his bounty as the source of their freedom. Nor was the matter of his harangue less injurious than its manner was offensive. Instead of containing any concession important to public liberty, it indicated a relapse into a more lofty <49> despotism than had before marked his pretensions. Tithes, feudal, and seignorial rights, he consecrated as the most inviolable property; and of *Lettres de Cachet* themselves, by recommending the regulation, he obviously condemned the abolition. The distinction of Orders he considered as essential to the Constitution of the kingdom, and their present union as only legitimate by his permission. He concluded with commanding them to separate, and to assemble on the next day in the Halls of their respective Orders.

The Commons, however, inflexibly adhering to their principles, and conceiving themselves constituted as a National Assembly, treated these threats and injunctions with equal neglect. They remained assembled in the Hall, which the other Orders had quitted, in obedience to the Royal command; and when the Marquis de Breze, the King's Master of Ceremonies, reminded them of his <50> Majesty's orders, he was answered by *M. Bailli,* with Spartan energy, "The Nation assembled has no ORDERS to receive."[11] They proceeded to pass resolutions declaratory of adherence to their former decrees, and of the personal inviolability of the members.— The Royal Session, which the Aristocratic party had expected with such triumph and confidence, proved the severest blow to their cause. Forty-nine members of the Nobility, at the head of whom was M. de Clermont Tonnerre, repaired on the 26th of June to the Assembly.* The popular enthusiasm was enflamed to such a degree, that alarms were either felt, or affected, for the safety of the King, if the Union of Orders was delayed. The union was accordingly resolved on, and <51> the Duke of Luxemburg, President of the Nobility, was authorized by his Majesty to announce to his Order the request and even command of the King, to unite themselves with the other Orders. He remonstrated with the King on the fatal consequences of this step. The Nobility, he remarked, were not fighting their own battles, but those of the Crown. The support of the Monarchy was inseparably connected with the division of the States General. Divided, that body was subject to the Crown—united, its authority was sovereign, and its force irresistible.† The King was not, however, shaken by these con-

* It deserves remark, that in this number were Noblemen who have ever been considered as of the *moderate* party. Of these may be mentioned M.M. Lally, Virieu, and Clermont Tonnerre, none of whom certainly can be accused of democratic enthusiasm.

† These remarks of M. de Luxembourg are equivalent to a thousand defenses of the Revolutionists against Mr. Burke. They unanswerably prove that the division of Orders was supported *only* as necessary to palsy the efforts of the Legislature against the Despotism.

11. E. Madival and E. Laurent, *Archives Parlementaires 1787–1860,* 1e série, 99 vols., vols. 1–82 (Paris: Dupont, 1879–1914), vols. 83–99 (Paris, 1961–95), 8:137–38 (June 20, 1789).

siderations, and on the following day, in an official letter to the Presidents of the Nobility and Clergy, he notified his pleasure. A gloomy and re-<52>luctant obedience was yielded to this mandate, and the union of the National Representatives at length promised some hope to France.

But the general system of the Government formed a suspicious and tremendous contrast with this applauded concession. New *hordes* of foreign mercenaries were summoned to the blockade of Paris and Versailles, from the remotest provinces; an immense train of artillery was disposed in all the avenues of these cities; and seventy thousand men already invested the Legislature and Capital of France, when the last blow was hazarded against the public hopes, by the ignominious banishment of M. Necker. Events followed the most unexampled and memorable in the annals of mankind, which history will record and immortalize, but, on which, the object of the political reasoner is only to speculate. France was on the brink of civil war. The Pro-<53>vinces were ready to march immense bodies to the rescue of their Representatives. The Courtiers and their minions, Princes and Princesses, male and female favorites, crowded to the camps with which they had invested Versailles, and stimulated the ferocious cruelty of their mercenaries, by caresses, by largesses, and by promises. Mean time the people of Paris revolted, the French soldiery felt that they were citizens, and the fabric of Despotism fell to the ground.

These soldiers, whom posterity will celebrate for patriotic heroism, are stigmatized by Mr. Burke as "base hireling deserters,"[12] who sold their King for an increase of pay.* <54> This position he every where asserts or insinuates; but nothing seems more false. Had the defection been confined to Paris, there might have been some speciousness in the accusation. The Exchequer of a faction might have been equal to the corruption of the guards. The activity of intrigue might have seduced by promise, the troops can-

---

* Mr. Burke is sanctioned in this opinion by an authority not the most respectable, that of his late countryman *Count Dalton*, Commander of the Austrian troops in the Netherlands. In *September, 1789*, he addressed the *Regiment de Ligne*, at Brussels, in these terms, "J'espere que vous n'imiterez jamais ces laches François qui ont abandonné leur Souverain!" ["I hope that you will not imitate these cowardly French who have abandoned their sovereign." Unable to trace the source of this reference.]

12. Edmund Burke, *Substance of the Speech of the Right Honourable Edmund Burke, in the Debate on the Army Estimates, in the House of Commons, on Tuesday the 9th Day of February, 1790* (London: Debrett, 1790), p. 21.

toned in the neighbourhood of the capital. But what policy, or fortune, could pervade by their agents, or donatives, an army of 150,000 men, dispersed over so great a monarchy as France. The spirit of resistance to *uncivic* commands broke forth at once in every part of the empire. The garrisons of the cities of Rennes, Bourdeaux, Lyons, and Grenoble, refused, almost at the same moment, to resist the virtuous insurrection of their fellow citizens. No largesses could have seduced, no intrigues could have reached so vast and divided a body. Nothing but sympathy with the national spirit could have produced their <55> noble disobedience. The remark of Mr. Hume is here most applicable, that what depends on a few may be often attributed to chance (*secret circumstances*) but that the actions of great bodies must be ever ascribed to general causes.[13] It was the apprehension of *Montesquieu,* that the spirit of increasing armies would terminate in converting Europe into an immense camp, in changing our artizans and cultivators into military savages, and reviving the age of Attila and Genghis.[14] Events are our preceptors, and France has taught us that this evil contains in itself its own remedy and limit. A domestic army cannot be increased without increasing the number of its ties with the people, and of the channels by which popular sentiment may enter. Every man who is added to the army is a new link that unites it to the nation. If all citizens were compelled to become soldiers, all soldiers must of necessity adopt the feelings of citizens, and the despots cannot increase their <56> army without admitting into it a greater number of men interested to destroy them. A small army may have sentiments different from the great body of the people, and no interest in common with them, but a numerous soldiery cannot. This is the barrier which Nature has opposed to the increase of armies. They cannot be numerous enough to enslave the people, without becoming the people itself. The effects of this truth have been hitherto conspicuous only

13. David Hume, "Of the Rise and Progress of the Arts and Sciences," in *Essays Moral, Political, and Literary* (Indianapolis: Liberty Fund, 1985), 112.

14. Montesquieu, *Considérations sur les causes de la grandeur des Romains et de leur décadence* (Amsterdam: Mortier, 1734). For an English translation see Montesquieu, *Considerations on the Causes of the Greatness of the Romans and Their Decline,* trans. D. Lowenthal (Ithaca: Cornell University Press, 1965; repr. Indianapolis and Cambridge: Hackett, 1985, 1999).

in the military defection of France, because the enlightened sense of general interest has been so much more diffused in that nation than in any other despotic monarchy of Europe. But they must be felt by all. An elaborate discipline may for a while in Germany debase and brutalize soldiers too much to receive any impressions from their fellow men—artificial and local institutions are, however, too feeble to resist the energy of natural causes. The constitution of man survives the transient fashions of des-<57>potism, and the history of the next century will probably evince on how frail and tottering a basis the military tyrannies of Europe stand.

The pretended seduction of the French troops by the promise of the increased pay, is in every view contradicted by facts. This increase of pay did not originate in the Assembly. It was not therefore any part of their policy—It was prescribed to them by the instructions of their constituents, before the meeting of the States.* It could not therefore be the project of any cabal of demagogues to seduce the army; it was the decisive and unanimous voice of the nation, and if there was any conspiracy, it must have been that of the people. What had the demagogues <58> to offer. The soldiery knew that the States must, in obedience to their instructions, increase their pay. An increase of pay, therefore, was no temptation to sell their King, for of that they felt themselves already secure, as the national voice had prescribed it. It was in fact a necessary part of the system which was to raise the army to a body of respectable citizens, from a gang of mendicant ruffians.

It must infallibly operate to limit the increase of armies in the north. This influence has been already felt in the Netherlands, which fortune seems to have restored to Leopold, that they might furnish a school of revolt to German soldiers. The Austrian troops have there murmured at their comparative indigence, and supported their plea for increase of pay by the example of France. The same example must operate on the other armies of Europe. The solicitations of armed petitioners must be heard. The in-

* I appeal to M. Calonne, as an authority beyond suspicion on this subject—See his Summary of the *Cahiers,* or Instructions. Art. 73.— *"L'Augmentation de la Paie du Soldat."* Calonne, p. 390. ["The increase in soldiers' pay." C. A. Calonne, *De l'état de la France, présent et à venir, par M. de Calonne ministre d'état* (Londres: T. Spilsbury & fils, 1790), 390.]

digent de-<59>spots of Germany and the North will feel a limit to their military rage, in the scantiness of their Exchequer. They will be compelled to reduce the number, and increase the pay of their armies, and a new barrier will be opposed to the progress of that depopulation and barbarism, which philosophers had dreaded from the rapid increase of military force. These remarks on the spirit which actuated the French army in their unexampled, misconceived, and calumniated conduct, are peculiarly important, as they serve to illustrate a principle, which cannot too frequently be presented to view, that in the French Revolution all is to be attributed to general causes influencing the whole body of the people, and almost nothing to the schemes and the ascendant of individuals.

But to return to our rapid sketch. It was at the moment of the Parisian revolt, and of the defection of the army, that the whole <60> power of France devolved on the National Assembly. It is at that moment, therefore, that the discussion commences, whether that body ought to have re-established and re-formed the Government *which events had subverted,* or to have proceeded to the establishment of a new Constitution, on the general principles of reason and freedom. The arm of the ancient Government had been palsied, and its power reduced to formality, by events over which the Assembly possessed no controul. It was theirs to decide, not whether the monarchy was to be subverted, for that had been already effected, but whether, from its ruins, fragments were to be collected for the re-construction of the political edifice.

They had been assembled as an ordinary Legislature under existing laws. They were transformed by these events into a NATIONAL CONVENTION, and vested with powers to organize a Government. It is in vain that <61> their adversaries contest this assertion, by appealing to the deficiency of forms.* It is in vain to demand the legal instrument that changed their

---

* This circumstance is shortly stated by Mr. Burke. "I can never consider this Assembly as any thing else than a voluntary association of men, who have availed themselves of circumstances to seize upon the power of the State. They do not hold the authority they exercise under any Constitutional law of the State. They have departed from the instructions of the people that sent them, &c." Burke, p. 270. The same argument is treated by M. Calonne, in an expanded memorial of 44 pages, against the pretensions

Constitution, and extended their powers. Accurate forms in the conveyance of power are prescribed by the wisdom of law, in the regular administration of States. But great Revolutions are too immense for technical formality. All the sanction that can be hoped for in such events, is the voice of the people, however informally and irregularly expressed. This cannot be <62> pretended to have been wanting in France. Every other species of authority was annihilated by popular acts, but that of the States General. On them, therefore, devolved the duty of exercising their *unlimited** trust, ac- <63>cording to their best views of general interest. Their enemies have, even in their invectives, confessed the *subsequent adherence* of the people, for they have inveighed against it as the infatuation of a dire fanaticism. The authority of the Assembly was then first conferred on it by public confidence, and its acts have been since ratified by public approbation. Nothing can betray a disposition to puny and technical sophistry more strongly, than to observe with M. Calonne, that this ratification, to be valid, ought to have been made by France, not in her new organization of municipalities, but in her ancient division of bailliages and provinces. The same *individuals* act in both forms. The approbation of the *men* legitimates the Government. It is of no importance, whether they are assembled as bailliages, or as municipalities. If this latitude of informality, this subjection of laws to their principle, and of Government to its source, are not permitted in Revolutions, <64> how are we to justify the assumed authority

---

of the Assembly to be a convention, with much unavailing ingenuity and labour.—See his Work from p. 314 to 358.

* A distinction made by Mr. Burke between the *abstract* and *moral* competency of a Legislature (p. 107) has been much extolled by his admirers. To me it seems only a novel and objectionable mode of distinguishing between a *right* and the *expediency* of using it. But the mode of illustrating the distinction is far more pernicious than a mere novelty of phrase. This moral competence is subject, says our author, to "faith, justice, and fixed fundamental policy." Thus illustrated, the distinction appears liable to a double objection. It is false that the *abstract* competence of a Legislature extends to the violation of faith and justice. It is false that its *moral* competence does not extend to the most fundamental policy, and thus to confound fundamental policy with faith and justice, for the sake of stigmatizing innovators, is to stab the vitals of morality. There is only one maxim of policy truly fundamental—*the good of the governed*—and the stability of that maxim, rightly understood, demonstrates the mutability of all policy that is subordinate to it.

of the English Convention of 1688? "They did not hold the authority they exercised under any constitutional law of the State."[15] They were not even *legally* elected, as, it must be confessed, was the case with the French Assembly. An evident though irregular ratification by the people, alone legitimated their acts. Yet they possessed, by the confession of Mr. Burke, an authority only limited by prudence and virtue. Had the people of England given *instructions* to the Members of that Convention, its ultimate measures would probably have departed as much from them as the French Assembly have deviated from those of their constituents, and the public acquiescence in the deviation would, in all likelihood, have been the same.

It will be confessed by any man who has considered the public temper of England at the landing of William, that the majority of those instructions would not have proceeded < 65 > to the deposition of James. The first aspect of these great changes perplexes and intimidates men too much for just views and bold resolutions. It is by the progress of events that their hopes are emboldened, and their views enlarged.

This influence was felt in France. The people, in an advanced period of the Revolution, virtually recalled the instructions by which the feebleness of their political infancy had limited the power of their Representatives; for they sanctioned acts by which those instructions were contradicted. The formality of instructions was indeed wanting in England, but the change of public sentiment, from the opening of the Convention to its ultimate decision, was as remarkable as the contrast which has been so ostentatiously displayed by M. Calonne, between the decrees of the National Assembly and the first instructions of their constituents. < 66 >

Thus feeble are the objections against the authority of the Assembly.

We now resume the consideration of its exercise, and proceed to enquire, whether they ought to have reformed, or destroyed their Government? The general question of innovation is an exhausted common-place, to which the genius of Mr. Burke has been able to add nothing but splendor of eloquence and felicity of illustration. It has long been so notoriously of this nature, that it is placed by Lord Bacon among the sportive contests which

---

15. Burke, *Reflections*, 270.

are to exercise rhetorical skill. No man will support the extreme on either side. Perpetual change and immutable establishment are equally indefensible. To descend therefore from these barren generalities to a more near view of the question, let us state it more precisely. *Was the Civil Order in France* corrigible, *or was it necessary to* destroy *it?* Not to mention the extirpation of the feudal system, and <67> the abrogation of the civil and criminal code, we have first to consider the destruction of the three great corporations, of the Nobility, the Church, and the Parliaments. These three Aristocracies were the pillars which in fact formed the Government of France. The question then of *forming* or *destroying* these bodies is fundamental. There is one general principle applicable to them all adopted by the French Legislators—*that the existence of Orders is repugnant to the principles of the social union.* An Order is a *legal* rank, a body of men combined and endowed with privileges by law.—There are two kinds of inequality, the one personal—that of talent and virtue, the source of whatever is excellent and admirable in society—the other, that of fortune, which must exist, because *property* alone can stimulate to labour; and labour, if it were not necessary to the existence, would be indispensible to the happiness of man. But though it be necessary, yet, in its excess it is the great malady <68> of civil society. The accumulation of that power which is conferred by wealth in the hands of the few, is the perpetual source of oppression and neglect to the mass of mankind. The power of the wealthy is farther concentrated by their tendency to *combination,* from which, number, dispersion, indigence and ignorance equally preclude the poor. The wealthy are formed into bodies by their professions, their different degrees of opulence (called *ranks*), their knowledge, and their small number.—They necessarily in all countries administer government, for they alone have skill and leisure for its functions. Thus circumstanced, nothing can be more evident than their inevitable preponderance in the political scale. The preference of partial to general interests is however the greatest of all public evils. It should therefore have been the object of all laws to repress this malady, but it has been their perpetual tendency to aggravate it. Not content with the inevit-<69>able inequality of fortune, they have superadded to it honorary and political distinctions. Not content with the inevitable tendency of the wealthy to combine, they have embodied them in classes. They have fortified those conspiracies against the general interest, which they ought to have resisted, though they could not disarm. Laws, it is said, cannot equalize men. No. But ought they for that reason to aggravate the inequality which they cannot cure? Laws cannot inspire unmixed Patriotism—But ought they for that reason to foment that *corporation spirit* which is its most fatal enemy? All professional combinations, said Mr. Burke, in one of his late speeches in Parliament, are dangerous in a free State.[16] Arguing on the same principle, the National Assembly has proceeded further. They have conceived that the laws ought to *create* no inequality of combination, to recognize all only in their capacity of citizens, and <70> to offer no assistance to the natural preponderance of partial over general interest.

But besides the general source of hostility to Orders, the particular circumstances of France presented other objections, which it is necessary to consider more in detail.

It is in the first place to be remarked, that all the bodies and institutions of the kingdom participated the spirit of the ancient Government, and in that view were incapable of alliance with a free Constitution. They were tainted by the despotism of which they were members or instruments. Absolute monarchies, like every other consistent and permanent government, assimilate every thing with which they are connected to their own genius. The Nobility, the Priesthood, the Judicial Aristocracy, were unfit to be members of a free government, because their *corporate* character had been formed under arbitrary estab-<71>lishments. To have preserved these great corporations, would be to have retained the seeds of reviving despotism in the bosom of freedom. This remark may merit the attention of Mr. Burke, as illustrating an important difference between the French and English Revolutions. The Clergy, the Peerage, and Judicatures of England, had in some degree the sentiments inspired by a Government in which freedom had been eclipsed, but not extinguished—They were therefore qualified to partake of a more stable and improved liberty. But the case of France was different. These bodies had there imbibed every sentiment, and adopted every habit under arbitrary power. Their preservation in England, and their destruction in France, may in this view be justified on similar grounds. It

16. Possibly based on Burke, *Speech on the Army Estimates,* 24.

is absurd to regard the Orders as remnants of that free constitution which France, in common with the other Gothic nations of Europe, once enjoyed. Nothing remained of these ancient Orders <72> but the name. The Nobility were no longer those haughty and powerful Barons, who enslaved the people and dictated to the King. The Ecclesiastics were no longer that Priesthood, before whom, in a benighted and superstitious age, all civil power was impotent and mute. They have both dwindled into dependents on the crown. Still less do the opulent and enlightened Commons of France resemble its servile and beggared populace in the sixteenth century. Two hundred years of uninterrupted exercise had legitimated absolute authority as much as prescription can consecrate usurpation. The ancient French Constitution was therefore no farther a model than that of any *foreign* nation, which was to be judged of alone by its utility, and possessed in no respect the authority of establishment. It had been succeeded by *another* Government, and if France were to recur to a period antecedent to her servitude for legislative models, she might as well ascend to the aera of Clovis <73> or Charlemagne, as be regulated by the precedents of Henry III. or Mary of Medicis. All these forms of government existed only *historically.*

These observations include all the Orders. Let us consider each of them successively. The devotion of the Nobility of France to the Monarch was inspired equally by their sentiments, their interests, and their habits. "The feudal and chivalrous spirit of fealty,"[17] so long the prevailing passion of Europe, was still nourished in their bosoms by the military sentiments from which it first arose. The majority of them had still no profession but war, no hope but in Royal favor. The youthful and indigent filled the camps; the more opulent and mature partook the splendor and bounty of the Court: But they were equally dependents on the Crown. To the plentitude of the Royal power were attached those immense and magnificent privileges, which di-<74>vided France into distinct nations; which exhibited a Nobility monopolizing the rewards and offices of the State, and a people

17. Burke, *Reflections,* 172.

degraded to political *helotism.** Men do not cordially resign such privileges, nor quickly dismiss the sentiments which they have inspired. The ostentatious sacrifice of pecuniary exemptions in a moment of general fermentation is a wretched criterion of their genuine feelings. They affected to bestow as a gift, what they would have been speedily compelled to abandon as an usurpation, and they hoped by the sacrifice of a part to purchase security for the rest. They have been most justly stated to be a band of political *janissaries,*† far more valuable to a Sultan than mercenaries, because attached to him by unchangeable interest and indelible sentiment. Whether any reform could have extracted from this body a portion which <75> might have entered into the new constitution is a question which we shall consider when that political system comes under our review. Their existence, as a member of the Legislature, is a question distinct from their preservation as a separate Order, or great corporation, in the State. A senate of Nobles might have been established, though the Order of the Nobility had been destroyed, and England would then have been exactly copied.—But it is of the Order that we now speak, for we are now considering the destruction of the old not the formation of the new Government.—The suppression of Nobility has been in England most absurdly confounded with the prohibition of titles. The union of the Orders in one Assembly was the first step towards the destruction of a legislative Nobility. The abolition of their feudal rights, in the memorable session of the 4th of August, 1789, may be regarded as the second. They retained after these measures no distinction but what <76> was purely nominal, and it remained to be determined what place they were to occupy in the new Constitution. That question was decided by the decree of the 22d of December, in the same year, which enacted, that the Electoral Assemblies were to be composed without any regard to rank, and that citizens of all Orders were to vote in them indiscriminately. The distinction of Orders was destroyed by this decree, the Nobility were to form no part of the new Constitution, and they were

---

* I say *political* in contradistinction to *civil,* for in the latter sense the assertion would have been untrue.

† See Mr. ROUS's excellent "Thoughts on Government." [G. Rous, *Thoughts on Government, occasioned by Mr. Burke's Reflections, &c. in a letter to a friend* (London: Debrett, 1790).]

stripped of all that they had enjoyed under the old Government, but their titles.

Hitherto all had passed unnoticed, but no sooner did the Assembly, faithful to their principles, proceed to extirpate the external signs of ranks, which they no longer tolerated, then all Europe resounded with clamours against their Utopian and levelling madness. The *incredible** decree of the 19th of June, <77> 1790, for the suppression of titles, is the object of all these invectives, yet without that measure the Assembly would certainly have been guilty of the grossest inconsistency and absurdity. An *untitled* Nobility forming a member of the State, had been exemplified in some Commonwealths of antiquity. Such were the Patricians in Rome. But a titled Nobility, without legal privileges, or political existence, would have been a monster new in the annals of legislative absurdity. The power was possessed without the bauble by the Roman Aristocracy. The bauble would have been reverenced, while the power was trampled on, if titles had been spared in France. A titled Nobility, is the most undisputed progeny of feudal barbarism. Titles had in all nations *denoted offices,* it was reserved for Gothic Europe to attach them to *ranks,* yet this conduct of our remote ancestors admits explanation, for with them offices were hereditary, and hence the titles denoting them <78> became hereditary too. But we, who have rejected hereditary office, retain an usage to which it gave rise, and which it alone could justify.

So egregiously is this recent origin of titled Nobility misconceived, that it has been even pretended to be necessary to the order and existence of society: A narrow and arrogant bigotry, which would limit all political remark to the Gothic States of Europe, or establish general principles on events that occupy so short a period of history, and manners that have been adopted by so slender a portion of the human race. A titled Nobility, was equally unknown to the splendid Monarchies of Asia, and to the manly simplicity of the ancient Commonwealths.† It arose from <79> the pe-

---

* So called by M. Calonne. [Calonne, *De la France,* 232.]

† Aristocratic bodies did indeed exist in the ancient world, but *titles* were unknown. Though they possessed political privileges, yet as they did not affect the *manners,* they had not the same inevitable tendency to taint the public character as titular distinctions.

culiar circumstances of modern Europe, and yet its necessity is now erected on the basis of universal experience, as if these other renowned and polished States were effaced from the records of history, and banished from the society of nations. "Nobility is the Corinthian capital of polished states."[18] The august fabric of society is deformed and encumbered by such Gothic ornaments. The massy Doric that sustains it is Labour, and the splendid variety of arts and talents that solace and embellish life, form the decorations of its Corinthian and Ionic capitals.

Other motives besides the extirpation of feudality, disposed the French Legislature to the suppression of titles. To give stability <80> to a popular Government, a democratic character must be formed, and democratic sentiments inspired. The sentiment of equality which titular distinctions have, perhaps, more than any other cause, extinguished in Europe, and without which democratic forms are impotent and short-lived, was to be revived: a free Government was to be established, by carrying the spirit of equality and freedom into the feelings, the manners, the most familiar intercourse of men. The badges of inequality, which were perpetually inspiring sentiments adverse to the spirit of the Government, were therefore destroyed: Distinctions which only served to unfit the Nobility for obedience, and the people for freedom; to keep alive the discontent of the one, and to perpetuate the servility of the other; to deprive the one of the moderation that sinks them into citizens, and to rob the other of the spirit that exalts them into free men. A single example can alone dispel inveterate pre-<81>judices. Thus thought our ancestors at the Revolution, when they deviated from the succession, to destroy the prejudice of its sanctity. Thus also did the Legislators of France feel, when by the abolition of titles, they gave a mortal blow to the slavish prejudices which unfitted their country for freedom. It was a practical assertion of that equality which had been consecrated in the Declaration of Rights, but which no abstract assertion could have conveyed into the spirits and the hearts of men. It proceeded on the principle that

---

These bodies too being in general open to *property*, or *office*, they are in no respect to be compared to the Nobles of Europe. They might affect the *forms* of free Government as much, but they did not in the same proportion injure the *Spirit* of Freedom.

18. Burke, *Reflections*, 241.

the security of a revolution of *government* can only arise from a revolution of *character*.

To these reasonings it has been opposed, that hereditary distinctions are the *moral treasure* of a State, by which it excites and rewards public virtue and public service, which, without national injury or burden, operates with resistless force on generous minds. To this I answer, that of *personal* distinctions this de-<82>scription is most true, but that this moral treasury of honour is in fact impoverished by the improvident profusion that has made them hereditary. The possession of honours by the multitude, who have inherited but not acquired them, engrosses and depreciates these incentives and rewards of virtue. Were they purely personal, their value would be doubly enhanced, as the possessors would be fewer while the distinction was more honourable. Personal distinctions then every wise State will cherish as its surest and noblest resource, but of hereditary title, *at least in the circumstances of France,** the abolition seems to have been just and politic.

The fate of the Church, the second great corporation that sustained the French despo-<83>tism, has peculiarly provoked the indignation of Mr. Burke. The dissolution of the Church as a body, the resumption of its territorial revenues, and the new organization of the Priesthood, appear to him to be dictated by the union of robbery and irreligion to glut the rapacity of Stock-jobbers, and to gratify the hostility of Atheists. All the outrages and proscriptions of ancient or modern tyrants vanish, in his opinion, in the comparison with this confiscation of the *property* of the Gallican Church. Principles had, it is true, been on this subject explored, and reasons had been urged by men of genius, which vulgar men deemed irresistible. But with these reasons Mr. Burke will not deign to combat. "You do not imagine, Sir," says he to his correspondent "that I am going to compliment this *miserable description of persons* with any long discussion?"†[19] What im-

---

* I have been grossly misunderstood by those who have supposed this *qualification* an assumed or affected reserve. I believe the *principle* only as *qualified* by the *circumstances* of different nations.

† The Abbé Maury, who is not less remarkable for the fury of eloquent declamation, than for the *inept* parade of historical erudition, attempted in the debate on this subject to trace the opinion higher. Base lawyers, according to him, had insinuated it to the Roman Emperors, and against it was pointed the maxim of the Civil Law, *"Omnia tenes*

mediately follows <84> this contemptuous passage is so outrageously offensive to candor and urbanity, that an honourable adversary will disdain
to avail himself of it. The passage itself, however, demands a pause. It alludes to an opinion of which *I trust* Mr. Burke did not know the origin.
That the church-lands were national property was not first asserted among
the *Jacobins,* or in the *Palais Royal.*[20] The author of that opinion, the master
of that wretched <85> description of persons, whom Mr. Burke disdains
to encounter, was one whom he might have combated with glory, with
confidence of triumph in victory, and without fear or shame in defeat. The
author of that opinion was TURGOT! a name now too high to be exalted
by eulogy, or depressed by invective.—That benevolent and philosophic
Statesman delivered it in the article *Fondation* of the *Encyclopedie,*[21] as the
calm and disinterested opinion of a scholar, at a moment when he could
have no view to palliate rapacity, or prompt irreligion. It was no doctrine
contrived for the occasion by the agents of tyranny; it was a principle discovered in pure and harmless speculation, by one of the best and wisest of
men. I adduce the authority of Turgot, not to oppose the arguments (if

---

Caesar imperio sed non dominio." [Speech by the Abbé Maury in *Archives Parlementaires,*
9:610. "You hold all things, Caesar, by power of command, but not by ownership." The
ultimate source is Seneca: "Under the best sort of king everything belongs to the king
by his right of authority, and to his subjects by their individual rights of ownership."
Seneca, "De Beneficiis," in *Moral Essays,* trans. J. W. Basore, 3 vols. (London and Cambridge, Mass.: Heinemann and Harvard University Press, 1958) 3:468–69 (VII.v.10).]
Louis XIV. and Louis XV. had, if we may believe him, both been assailed by this Machiavelian doctrine, and both had repulsed it with magnanimous indignation. The
learned Abbé committed only one mistake. The despots of Rome and France had indeed
been poisoned with the idea that they were the immediate proprietors of their subjects'
estates. That opinion is execrable and flagitious, and it is not, as we shall see, the doctrine
of the French Legislators.

19. Burke, *Reflections,* 204.

20. The Jacobin Club was a popular political club. It was originally a meeting place
for deputies to the Estates General but later opened up its membership. The mother
society in Paris also became affiliated with a network of clubs across the country. The
Palais Royal was a focus for popular debate in the early years of the revolution.

21. One of the five articles that Turgot wrote for the *Encyclopédie.* It was included as
an appendix to Condorcet's *Vie de Turgot* in *Oeuvres,* vol. 5 (Paris: Firmin Didot Frères,
1847–49), 1–233. For a recent translation see R. L. Meek, ed., *Turgot on Progress, Economics, and Sociology* (London: Cambridge University Press, 1973).

there had been any) but to counteract the insinuations of Mr. Burke. The authority of his assertions forms a prejudice, which is thus to be removed before we can hope for a fair au-<86>dience at the bar of reason. If he insinuates the flagitiousness of these opinions by the supposed vileness of their origin, it cannot be unfit to pave the way for their reception, by assigning them a more illustrious pedigree.

But dismissing the genealogy of doctrines, let us examine their intrinsic value, and listen to no voice but that of truth. *"Are the lands occupied by the Church the* PROPERTY *of its Members?"* Various considerations present themselves, which may elucidate the subject.

I. It has not hitherto been supposed that any class of Public servants are proprietors. They are *salaried** by the State for the performance of certain duties. Judges are *paid* for the distribution of justice; *Kings* for execution of the laws; Soldiers, where there is a mercenary army, for public defence; and <87> Priests, where there is an established religion, for public instruction. The mode of their *payment* is indifferent to the question. It is generally in rude ages by land, and in cultivated periods by money. But a *territorial pension* is no more property than a *pecuniary one.* The right of the State to regulate the salaries of those servants whom it pays in money has not been disputed. But if it has *chosen to provide the revenue of a certain portion of land for the salary of another class of servants,* wherefore is its right more disputable, to resume that land, and to establish a new mode of payment? In the early history of Europe, before fiefs became hereditary, great landed estates were bestowed by the Sovereign, on condition of military service. By a similar tenure did the Church hold its lands. No man can prove, that because the State has intrusted its ecclesiastical servants with a portion of land, as the source and security of their *pensions,* they are in any respect more the *proprietors* of <88> it, than the other servants of the State are of that portion of the revenue from which they are paid.

II. The lands of the Church possess not the most simple and indispensible requisites of property. They are not even pretended to be held for the

---

* "Ils sont ou *salariés,* ou mendians, ou voleurs." *They are either salaried, or beggars, or robbers*—was the expression of M. Mirabeau respecting the Priesthood. [Unable to trace the source of this reference.]

benefit of those who enjoy them. This is the obvious criterion between private property and a pension for public service. The destination of the first is avowedly the comfort and happiness of the *individual* who enjoys it; as he is conceived to be the sole judge of this happiness, he possesses the most unlimited rights of enjoyment, alienation, and even abuse: But the lands of the Church, destined for the support of public servants, exhibited none of the characters of property—They were inalienable, because it would have been not less absurd for the Priesthood to have exercised such authority over these lands, than it would be for seamen to claim the property of a fleet <89> which they manned, or soldiers that of a fortress they garrisoned.

III. It is confessed that no individual Priest was a proprietor, and it is not denied that his utmost claim was limited to a possession for life of his stipend. If all the Priests, taken *individually,* were not proprietors, the Priesthood, as a *body,* cannot claim any such right. For what is a *body,* but an aggregate of individuals, and what new right can be conveyed by a mere change of name?—Nothing can so forcibly illustrate this argument as the case of other corporations. They are voluntary associations of men for their own benefit. Every member of them is an absolute sharer in their property, it is therefore alienated and inherited. Corporate property is here as sacred as individual, because in the ultimate analysis it is the same. But the Priesthood is a Corporation, endowed by the country, and destined for the benefit of other men. It is hence that the <90> members have no *separate,* nor the body any *collective,* right of property. They are only entrusted with the *administration* of the lands from which their *salaries* are paid.*

IV. It is from this last circumstance that their *legal semblance* of property arises. In charters, bonds, and all other proceedings of law, they are treated with the same formalities as real property.—"They are identified," says Mr. Burke, "with the mass of private property";[22] and it must be confessed, that if we are to limit our view to forms, this language is correct. But the repugnance of these formalities to legal truth proceeded from a very obvious

---

* This admits a familiar illustration. If a land-holder chuses to pay his steward for the collection of his rents, by permitting him to possess a farm *gratis,* is he conceived to have resigned his *property* in the farm? The case is precisely similar.

22. Burke, *Reflections,* 198.

cause. If estates are vested in the Clergy, to them most unquestionably ought to be entrusted the protection of these estates <91> in all contests at law, and actions for that purpose can only be maintained with facility, simplicity, and effect, by the *fiction* of their being proprietors.—Nor is this the only case in which the spirit and the forms of law are at variance respecting property. Scotland, where lands still are held by *feudal* tenures, will afford us a remarkable example. There, if we extend our views no further than legal forms, the *superior* is to be regarded as the proprietor, while the real proprietor appears to be only a tenant for life. Such is the language of the charter by which he obtains a legal right to his estate. In this case, the vassal is *formally* stript of the property which he in fact enjoys. In the other, the Church is *formally* invested with a property, to which in reality it had no claim. The argument of *prescription* will appear to be altogether untenable, *for prescription implies a certain period during which the rights of property had been exercised,* but in the case before us they *never* were exercised, because they never could be supposed to exist. <92> It must be proved that these possessions were of the nature of property, before it can follow that they are protected by prescription, and to plead it is to take for granted the question in dispute. If they never were property, no length of time can change their nature.* <93>

---

* There are persons who may not relish the mode of reasoning here adopted. They contend that property, being the creature of civil society, may be resumed by that Public will which created it, and on this principle they justify the National Assembly of France. But such a justification is adverse to the principles of that Assembly; for they have consecrated it as one of the first maxims of their Declaration of Rights, that the State cannot violate property, except in cases of urgent necessity, and on condition of previous indemnification. This defence too will not justify their selection of Church property, in preference of all others, for resumption. It certainly ought in this view to have fallen equally on all citizens. The principle is besides false in the extreme to which it is assumed. *Property* is, indeed, *in some senses* created by an act of the Public will; but it is by one of those *fundamental* acts which constitute society. Theory proves it to be essential to the social state. Experience proves that it has, in some degree, existed in every age and nation of the world. But those public acts which form and endow corporations, are subsequent and subordinate.—They are only *ordinary expedients* of legislation. The property of individuals is established on a *general principle,* which seems coeval with civil society itself. But *bodies* are instruments fabricated by the Legislator for a *specific* purpose, which ought to be preserved while they are beneficial, amended when they are impaired, and rejected when they become useless or injurious.

V. When the British Islands, the Dutch Republic, the German and Scandinavian States, reformed their ecclesiastical establishments, the howl of sacrilege was the only armour by which the Church attempted to protect its pretended property. The age was too tumultuous and unlettered for discussions of abstract jurisprudence. The clamour of sacrilege seems, however, to have fallen into early contempt. The Treaty of Westphalia[23] secularized many of the most opulent benefices of Germany, under the mediation and guarantee of the first Catholic Powers <94> of Europe. In our own island, on the abolition of episcopacy in Scotland at the Revolution, the revenues of the Church peaceably devolved on the Sovereign, and he devoted a portion of them to the support of the new establishment. When, at a still later period, the Jesuits were suppressed in most Catholic Monarchies, the wealth of that formidable and opulent body was every where seized by the Sovereign. In all these memorable examples, no traces are to be discovered of the pretended property of the Church.—The salaries of a class of Public servants are, in all these cases, resumed by the State, when it ceases to deem their service, or the mode of it, useful. It is in none of them recognized as property. That claim, now so forcibly urged by M. Calonne, was probably little respected by him, when he lent his agency to the destruction of the Jesuits with such peculiar activity and rancor. The sacredness of their property could not strongly impress him, <95> when he was instrumental in degrading the members of that accomplished Society, the glory of Catholic Europe, from their superb endowments to scanty and beggarly pensions. In all these contests, the inviolability of Church possessions was a principle that never made its appearance. A murmur of sacrilege might, indeed, be heard among the fanatical or interested few: But the religious horror in which the Priesthood had enveloped its robberies, had long been dispelled, and it was reserved for Mr. Burke to renew that cry of sacrilege, which, in the darkness of the sixteenth century, had resounded in vain. No man can be expected to oppose arguments to *epithets*. When a definition of sacrilege is given, consistent with good logic

---

23. The Treaty of Westphalia was signed at Munster on October 24, 1648, between the Holy Roman Emperor and his allies, and the king of France and his allies. It brought an end to the Thirty Years' War.

and plain English, it will be time enough to discuss it. Till that definition *(with the Greek Calends)* comes, I should as soon dispute about the meaning of sacrilege as about that of heresy or witchcraft. <96>

VI. The whole subject is indeed so evident, that little diversity of opinion could have arisen, if the question of church property had not been confounded with that of the present incumbents. The distinction, though neither stated by Mr. Burke nor M. Calonne, is extremely simple. The State is the proprietor of the Church revenues, but its faith, it may be said, is pledged to those who have entered into the Church, for the continuance of those incomes, for which they abandoned all other pursuits. The right of the State to arrange at its pleasure the revenues of any future Priests may be confessed, while a doubt may be entertained, whether it is competent to change the fortune of those to whom it has solemnly promised a certain income for life. But these distinct subjects have been confounded, that sympathy with suffering individuals might influence opinion on a general question, that feeling for the degradation of the hierarchy might supply the <97> place of argument to establish the property of the Church. To consider this subject distinctly it cannot be denied, that the mildest, the most equitable, and the most usual expedient of polished States in periods of emergency, *is the reduction of the salaries of their servants, and the suppression of superfluous places.* This and no more has been done regarding the Church of France. Civil, naval, and military servants of the State are subject to such retrenchments in a moment of difficulty. They often cannot be effected without a wound to individuals;* neither can the reform of a civil office, nor the reduction of a regiment: But all men who enter into the public service must do so with the implied condition of subjecting their emoluments, and even their official existence, to the exigencies of the State. The great grievance of such derangements is the shock they give to family settlements. This is precluded by the <98> compulsory celibacy of the Romish Church; and when the debts of the Clergy are incorporated with those of the State, and their subsistence insured by moderate incomes, though sensibility may, in the least retrenchment, find somewhat to lament, justice

---

* This is precisely the case of *"damnum absque injuria."* ["Loss without wrong"— Loss or damage for which there is no legal remedy.]

will, in the whole of these arrangements, discover little to condemn. To the individual members of the Church of France, whose hopes and enjoyments have been abridged by this resumption, no virtuous mind will refuse the tribute of its sympathy and its regrets. Every man of humanity must wish, that public exigencies had permitted the French Legislature to spare the income of present incumbents, and more especially of those whom they still continued in the discharge of active functions. But these sentiments imply no sorrow at the downfall of a great Corporation, the determined and implacable enemy of freedom; at the conversion of an immense public property to national use, nor at the reduc-<99>tion of a servile and imperious Priesthood to humble utility, as the moral and religious instructors of mankind. The attainment of these great objects console us for the portion of evil that was, perhaps, inseparable from them, and will be justly admired by a posterity too remote to be moved by these minute afflictions, or to be afflicted by any thing but their general splendor. The enlightened observer of an age thus distant will contemplate with peculiar astonishment, the rise, progress, decay, and downfall* of spiritual power in Christian Europe. It will attract his attention as an appearance which stands *alone* in history. Its connection in all stages of its progress with the civil power will peculiarly occupy his mind. He will remark the unpre-<100>suming humility by which it gradually gained the favor and divided the power of the Magistrate; the haughty and despotic tone in which it afterwards gave law to Sovereigns and subjects; the zeal with which, in the first desperate moments of decline, it armed the people against the Magistrate, and aimed at re-establishing spiritual despotism on the ruins of civil order; and the asylum which it at last found against the hostilities of reason in the prerogatives of temporal despotism, of which it had so long been the implacable foe.

The first and last of these periods will prove, that the Priesthood are servilely devoted when they are weak. The second and third, that they are dangerously ambitious when strong. In a state of feebleness, they are dan-

---

* Did we not dread the ridicule of political prediction, it would not seem difficult to assign its period.—Church power (unless some Revolution, auspicious to Priestcraft, should replunge Europe in ignorance) will certainly not survive the nineteenth century.

gerous to liberty; possessed of power, they are dangerous to civil government itself. But the last period of their progress will appear peculiarly connected with the <101> state of France. There was no protection for the
opulence and existence* of the European Priesthood in an enlightened period, but the Throne. It formed the only bulwark against the inroads of
reason; for the superstition which once formed their power was gone.
Around the Throne therefore they rallied. To the Monarch they transferred
the devotion which had formerly attached them to the Church, and the
fierceness of priestly† zeal was succeeded in their bosoms by the more peaceful sentiments of a courtly and polished servility. Such is, in a greater or
less degree, the present condition of the Church in every nation of Europe;
yet France has been reproached for the dissolution of such a body. It might
as well be maintained, that in her conquests over despotism, she ought to
have spared the strongest fortresses and most faithful troops of her adversary. Such <102> in truth, were the corporations of the Nobility and the
Church. The National Assembly ensured permanence to their establishments, by dismantling the fortresses, and disbanding the troops of their
vanquished foe.

In the few remarks that are here made on the Nobility and Clergy of
France, we confine ourselves strictly to their *political* and *collective* character. Mr. Burke, on the contrary, has grounded his eloquent apology purely
on their *individual* and *moral character.* This however is totally irrelevant
to the question, for we are not discussing what place they ought to occupy
in society as individuals, but as a body. We are not considering the demerit
of citizens whom it is fit to punish, but the spirit of a body which it is
politic to dissolve. We are not contending that the Nobility and Clergy were
in their private capacity bad citizens, but that they were mem-<103>bers
of corporations which could not be preserved with security to public
freedom.

The Judicial Aristocracy formed by the Parliaments, seems still less susceptible of union with a free Government. Their spirit and claims were
equally incompatible with liberty. They had imbibed a spirit congenial to

* I always understand their *corporate* existence.
† *Odium Theologicum.*

the authority under which they had acted, and suitable to the arbitrary genius of the laws which they had dispensed. They retained those ambiguous and indefinite claims to a share in the legislation, which the fluctuations of power in the kingdom had in some degree countenanced. The spirit of a *corporation* was from the smallness of their numbers more *concentrated* and vigorous in *them* than in the Nobles and Clergy; and whatever aristocratic zeal is laid to the charge of the Nobility, is imputable with tenfold force to the *ennobled Magistrates,* who regarded their recent honors with an enthusiasm of vanity, inspired <104> by that bigotted veneration for rank which is the perpetual character of upstarts. A free people could not form its tribunals of men who pretended to any controul on the Legislature. Courts of Justice, in which seats were legally purchased, had too long been endured: Judges who regarded the right of dispensing justice as a marketable commodity, could neither be fit organs of equitable laws, nor suitable magistrates for a free State. It is vain to urge with Mr. Burke the past services of these judicial bodies. It is not to be denied that Montesquieu is correct, when he states, that under bad Governments one abuse often limits another.[24] The usurped authority of the Parliaments formed, it is true, some bulwark against the caprice of the Court. But when the abuse is destroyed, why preserve the *remedial evil?* Superstition certainly alleviates the despotism of Turkey; but if a rational Government could be erected in that empire, it might with confidence disclaim the aid of <105> the Koran, and despise the remonstrances of the Mufti. To such establishments, let us pay the tribute of gratitude for past benefit; but when their utility no longer exists, let them be canonized by death, that their admirers may be indulged in all the plenitude of posthumous veneration.

The three Aristocracies, Military, Sacerdotal, and Judicial, may be considered as having formed the French Government. They have appeared, so far as we have considered them, incorrigible. All attempts to improve them would have been little better than (to use the words of Mr. Burke) "mean reparations on mighty ruins."[25] They were not perverted by the accidental

24. Montesquieu, *The Spirit of the Laws,* Cambridge Texts in the History of Political Thought, trans. and ed. Anne M. Cohler et al. (Cambridge: Cambridge University Press, 1989), 17–19, 25–27 (pt. 1, bk. 2, chap. 4; bk. 3, chap. 5).
25. Probably based on Burke, *Speech on the Army Estimates,* 30.

depravity of their members. They were not infected by any transient passion, which new circumstances would extirpate. The fault was in the essence
of the institutions themselves, which were irreconcileable with a free Government. But <106> it is objected, these institutions might have been *gradually* reformed.* The spirit of Freedom would have silently entered. The
progressive wisdom of an enlightened nation would have remedied, in process of time, their defects, without convulsion.

To this argument I confidently answer, *that these institutions would have
destroyed* LIBERTY, *before Liberty had corrected their* SPIRIT. Power vege-
tates with more vigor after these gentle prunings. A slender reform amuses
and lulls the people; the popular enthusiasm subsides, and the moment of
effectual reform is irretrievably lost. No important political improvement
was ever obtained in a period of tranquility. The corrupt interest of the
Governors is so strong, and the cry of the people so feeble, that it were vain
to expect it. If the effervescence of the po-<107>pular mind is suffered to
pass away without effect, it would be absurd to expect from languor what
enthusiasm has not obtained. If radical reform is not, at such a moment,
procured, all partial changes are evaded and defeated in the tranquility
which succeeds.† The gradual reform that arises from the presiding principle exhibited in the specious theory of Mr. Burke, is belied by the experience of all ages. Whatever excellence, whatever freedom is discoverable
in Governments, has been infused into them by the shock of a revolution,
and their subsequent progress has been only the accumulation of abuse. It
is hence that the most enlightened politicians have recognized the necessity

---

* See Mr. Burke's Reflexions, p. 273–76.

† "Ignore t'on que c'est en attaquant, en reversant tous les abus a la fois, qu'on peut
esperer de s'en voir delivré sans retour—que les reformes lentes et partielles ont toujours
fini par ne rien reformer: enfin que l'abus que l'on conserve devient l'appui et bientot le
restaurateur de tous ceux qu'on croioit avoir detruits."—*Adresse aux François par l'Eveque
d'Autun*—11 *Fevrier* 1790. ["You ignore [the fact] that it is in attacking, in reversing all
the abuse at once, that one can hope to be released without return . . . that slow and
partial reforms have always ended in reforming nothing; finally that the abuse that one
retains becomes the support and soon the restorer of all those which one thought had
been destroyed?" C. M. Talleyrand, bishop of Autun, "Adresse aux François," in E.
Madival and E. Laurent, *Archives Parlementaires 1787–1860*, 1e série, 99 vols., vols. 1–82
(Paris: Dupont, 1879–1914), vols. 83–99 (Paris: 1961–95), 11:549.]

of <108> *frequently recalling Governments to their first principles;* a truth equally suggested to the penetrating intellect of Machiavel, by his experience of the Florentine democracy, and by his research into the history of ancient Commonwealths.—Whatever is good ought to be pursued at the moment it is attainable. The public voice, irresistible in a period of convulsion, is contemned with impunity, when dictated by that lethargy into which nations are lulled by the tranquil course of their ordinary affairs. The ardor of reform languishes in unsupported tediousness. It perishes in an impotent struggle with adversaries, who receive new strength from the progress of the day. No hope of great political improvement (let us repeat it) is to be entertained from tranquility,* for its natural operation is to <109> strengthen all those who are interested in perpetuating abuse. The National Assembly seized the moment of eradicating the corruptions and abuses which afflicted their country. Their reform was total, that it might be commensurate with the evil, and *no part of it was delayed,* because to spare an abuse at such a period was to consecrate it; because the enthusiasm which carries nations to such enterprizes is short-lived, and the opportunity of reform, if once neglected, might be irrevocably fled.

But let us ascend to more general principles, and hazard bolder opinions. Let us grant that the state of France was not so desperately incorrigible. Let us suppose that changes far more gentle, innovations far less extensive, would have remedied the grosser evils of her Government, and placed it almost on a level with free and celebrated Constitutions. These concessions, though too large <110> for truth, will not convict the Assembly. By what principle of reason, or of justice, were they precluded from aspiring to give France a Government less imperfect, than *accident* had formed in other States?—Who will be hardy enough to assert, that a better Constitution is not attainable than any which has hitherto appeared? Is the limit of human wisdom to be estimated in the science of politics alone, by the extent of its present attainments? Is the most sublime and difficult of all arts, the improvement of the social order, the alleviation of the miseries of the civil

---

* The only apparent exception to this principle is the case where Sovereigns make important concessions to appease discontent, and avert convulsion. This, however, rightly understood, is no exception, for it arises evidently from the same causes, acting at a period less advanced in the progress of popular interposition.

condition of man, to be alone stationary, amid the rapid progress of every other art, liberal and vulgar, to perfection? Where would be the atrocious guilt of a grand experiment, to ascertain the portion of freedom and happiness, that can be created by political institutions?

That guilt (if it be guilt) is imputable to the National Assembly of France. They are <111> accused of having rejected the guidance of experience, of having abandoned themselves to the illusion of theory, and of having sacrificed great and attainable good to the magnificent chimeras of ideal excellence. If this accusation be just, if they have indeed abandoned *experience,* the basis of human knowledge, as well as the guide of human action, their conduct deserves no longer any serious argument; and if (as Mr. Burke more than once insinuates) their contempt of it is avowed and ostentatious, it was surely unworthy of him to have expended so much genius against so preposterous an insanity. But the explanation of *terms* will diminish our wonder—Experience may, both in the arts and in the conduct of human life, be regarded in a double view, either as furnishing *models,* or *principles.* An artist who frames his machine in exact imitation of his predecessor, is in the *first sense* said to be guided by experience. In this sense all improvements <112> of human life, have been *deviations* from experience. The first visionary innovator was the savage who built a cabin, or covered himself with a rug. If this be experience, man is degraded to the unimproveable level of the instinctive animals—But in the second acceptation, an artist is said to be guided by experience, when the inspection of a machine discovers to him principles, which teach him to improve it, or when the comparison of many both with respect to their excellencies and defects, enables him to frame another more perfect machine, different from any he had examined. In this latter sense, the National Assembly have perpetually availed themselves of experience. History is an immense collection of experiments on the nature and effect of the various parts of various Governments. Some institutions are *experimentally* ascertained to be beneficial; some to be most indubitably destructive. A third class, which produces partial good, obviously possess <113> the capacity of improvement. What, on such a survey, was the dictate of enlightened experience?—Not surely to follow the model of any of those Governments, in which these institutions lay indiscriminately mingled; but, like the mechanic, to compare and generalize; and, guided equally by experience, to imitate and reject. The process is in both cases the same. The rights and the nature of man are to the Legislator what the general properties of matter are to the Mechanic, the first guide, because they are founded on the widest experience. In the second class are to be ranked observations on the excellencies and defects of those Governments which have existed, that teach the construction of a more perfect machine. BUT EXPERIENCE IS THE BASIS OF ALL. Not the puny and trammelled experience of a *Statesman by trade,* who trembles at any change in the *tricks* which he has been taught, or the *routine* in which he has been accustomed to move, but an experience liberal <114> and enlightened, which hears the testimony of ages and nations, and collects from it the general principles which regulate the mechanism of society.

Legislators are under no obligation to retain a constitution, because it has been found *"tolerably* to answer the common purposes of Government."[26] It is absurd to *expect,* but it is not absurd to *pursue* perfection. It is absurd to acquiesce in evils, of which the remedy is obvious, because they are less grievous than those which are endured by others. To suppose the social order is not capable of improvement from the progress of the human understanding, is to betray the inconsistent absurdity of an arrogant confidence in our attainments, and an abject distrust of our powers. If indeed the sum of evil produced by political institutions, even in the least imperfect Governments, were small, there might be some pretence for this dread of innovation, this hor-<115>ror at remedy, which has raised such a clamour over Europe: But, on the contrary, in an estimate of the sources of human misery, after granting that one portion is to be attributed to disease, and another to private vices, it might perhaps be found that a *third equal* part arose from the oppressions and corruptions of Government, disguised under various forms. All the Governments that now exist in the world (except the United States of America) have been fortuitously formed. They are the produce of chance, not the work of art. They have been altered, impaired, improved and destroyed by accidental circumstances, beyond the foresight or controul of wisdom. Their parts thrown up against present emergencies

26. Burke, *Reflections,* 153.

formed no systematic whole. It was certainly not to have been presumed, that these *fortuitous Governments* should have surpassed the works of intellect, and precluded all nearer approaches to perfection. Their origin without doubt furnishes a strong presumption of an <116> opposite nature. It might teach us to expect in them many discordant principles, many jarring forms, much unmixed evil, and much imperfect good, many institutions which had long survived their motive, and many of which reason had never been the author, nor utility the object. Experience, *even in the best of these Governments,* accords with such expectations.

A Government of *art,* the work of legislative intellect, reared on the immutable basis of natural right and general happiness, which should combine the excellencies, and exclude the defects of the various constitutions which chance had scattered over the world, instead of being precluded by the perfection of any of those forms, was loudly demanded by the injustice and absurdity of them all. It was time that men should learn to tolerate nothing ancient that reason does not respect, and to shrink from no novelty to which reason may <117> conduct. It was time that the human powers, so long occupied by subordinate objects, and inferior arts, should mark the commencement of a new aera in history, by giving birth to the art of improving government, and increasing the civil happiness of man. It was time, as it has been wisely and eloquently said, that Legislators, instead of that narrow and dastardly *coasting* which never ventures to lose sight of usage and precedent, should, guided by the *polarity* of reason, hazard a bolder navigation, and discover, in unexplored regions, the treasure of public felicity.

The task of the French Legislators was, however, less hazardous. The philosophers of Europe had for a century discussed all objects of public oeconomy. The conviction of a great majority of enlightened men had, after many controversies, become on most questions of general politics, uniform. A degree of certainty, perhaps nearly equal to that which <118> such topics will admit, had been attained. The National Assembly were therefore not called on to make discoveries. It was sufficient if they were not uninfluenced by the opinions, nor exempt from the spirit of their age. They were fortunate enough to live in a period when it was only necessary to affix the stamp of laws to what had been prepared by the research of philosophy. They will here, however, be attacked by a futile common-place. The most specious *theory*, it will be said, is often impracticable, and any attempt to transfer speculative doctrines into the practice of States is chimerical and frantic. If by theory be understood vague conjecture, the objection is not worth discussion; but if by theory be meant inference from the moral nature and political state of man, then I assert, that whatever such theory pronounces to be true, must be practicable, and that whatever on the subject is impracticable, must be false. To resume the illustration from the <119> mechanical arts—Geometry, it may be justly said, bears nearly the same relation to mechanics that abstract reasoning does to politics.* The *moral forces* which are employed in politics are the passions and interests of men, of which it is the province of metaphysics to teach the nature and calculate the strength, as mathematics do those of the mechanical powers. Now suppose it had been mathematically proved, that by a certain alteration in the structure of a machine, its effect would be increased *four-fold,* would an instructed mechanic hesitate about the change? Would he be deterred, because he was the *first* to discover it? Would he thus sacrifice his own advantage to the blindness of his predecessors, and the obstinacy of his cotemporaries?—Let <120> us suppose a whole nation, of which the artizans thus rejected theoretical improvement. Mechanics might there, as a *science,* be most profoundly understood, while as an *art,* it exhibited nothing but rudeness and barbarism. The principles of Newton and Archimedes might be taught in the schools, while the architecture of the people might not have reached beyond the cabins of New Holland, or the ship-building of the Esquimaux. In a state of political science somewhat similar has Europe continued for a great part of the eighteenth century.† <121>

---

* I confess my obligation for this parallel to a learned friend, who though so justly admired in the republic of letters for his excellent writings, is still more so by his friends for the rich, original, and masculine turn of thought that animates his conversation. But the *Continuator* of "the History of Phillip III." little needs my praise. [William Thompson (1746–1817). Thomson wrote the final two chapters of R. Watson, *History of the Reign of Philip the Third, King of Spain* (London: J. Johnson, 1808).]

† Mechanics, because no passion or interest is concerned in the perpetuity of abuse, always yield to scientific improvement. Politics, for the contrary reason, always resist it. It was the remark of Hobbes, that if any interest or passion were concerned in disputing the theorems of geometry, different opinions would be maintained regarding them.

All the great questions of general politics had, as we have remarked, been nearly decided, and almost all the decisions had been hostile to established institutions—yet these institutions, still flourished in all their vigour. The same man who cultivated liberal science in his cabinet was compelled to administer a barbarous jurisprudence on the bench. The same MONTES-QUIEU, who at Paris reasoned as a philosopher of the eighteenth, was compelled to decide at Bourdeaux as a magistrate of the fourteenth century. The apostles of toleration and the ministers of the Inquisition were cotemporaries. The torture continued to be practised in the age of Beccaria. The Bastile devoured its victims in the country of Turgot. The criminal code, even of nations in which it was the mildest, was oppressive and savage. The laws respecting religious opinion, even where there was a *pretended* toleration, outraged the most evident deductions of reason. The true principles of commercial policy, <122> though they had been reduced to demonstration, influenced the councils of no State. Such was the fantastic spectacle presented by the European nations, who, philosophers in theory, and barbarous in practice, exhibited to the observing eye two opposite and inconsistent aspects of manners and opinions. But such a State carried in itself the seeds of its own destruction. Men will not long dwell in hovels, with the model of a palace before their eyes.

A State approaching to it in some measure existed indeed in the ancient world. But the art of Printing had not then provided a channel by which the opinions of the learned pass insensibly into the popular mind. A bulwark then existed between the body of mankind and the reflecting few. They were distinct nations, inhabiting the same country, and the opinions of the one (I speak *comparatively* with modern times) had little influence on the <123> other. But that bulwark is now levelled with the ground.— The convictions of philosophy insinuate themselves by a slow, but certain

---

[Thomas Hobbes, *Leviathan* (1651), pt. 1, chap. 11; p. 74 in the Richard Tuck edition for the Cambridge Texts in the History of Political Thought series (Cambridge and New York: Cambridge University Press, 1996).] It has actually happened (as if to justify the remark of that great man) that under the administration of TURGOT *a financial reform, grounded on a mathematical demonstration was derided as visionary nonsense!* So much for the sage preference of practice to theory.

progress, into popular sentiment. It is vain for the arrogance of learning to condemn the people to ignorance by reprobating superficial knowledge— The people cannot be profound, but the truths which regulate the moral and political relations of man, are at no great distance from the surface. The great works in which discoveries are contained cannot be read by the people; but their substance passes through a variety of minute and circuitous channels to the shop and the hamlet. The conversion of these works of unproductive splendor into latent use and unobserved activity, resembles the process of nature in the external world. The expanse of a noble lake, the course of a majestic river, imposes on the imagination by every impression of dignity and sublimity. But it is the moisture that insensibly arises from them, which, gradually ming-<124>ling with the soil, nourishes all the luxuriancy of vegetation, fructifies and adorns the surface of the earth.

It may then be remarked, that though liberal opinions so long existed with abusive establishments, it was not natural that this state of things should be permanent. The philosophers of antiquity did not, like ARCHIMEDES, want a spot on which to fix their engines, but they wanted an engine to move the moral world. The press is that engine, which has subjected the powerful to the wise, by governing the opinion of mankind. The discussion of great truths has prepared a body of laws for the National Assembly. The diffusion of political knowledge has *almost* prepared a people to receive them, and good men are at length permitted to indulge the *hope,* that the miseries of the human race are about to be alleviated; that hope may be illusive, for the grounds of its enemies are strong, the folly and villainy <125> of men. Yet they who entertain it will feel no shame in defeat, and no envy of the triumphant prediction of their adversaries. *Mehercule malim cum Platone errare.* [27] Whatever be the ultimate fate of the French Revolutionists, the friends of freedom must ever consider

---

27. "For goodness' sake, I had rather be wrong with Plato [than right with them]"; compare "I prefer, before heaven, to go astray with Plato [. . . rather than hold true views with his opponents]." Cicero, *Tusculan Disputations,* trans. J. E. King (London and Cambridge, Mass.: Heinemann and Harvard University Press, 1960), 46–47.

them as the authors of the greatest *attempt* that has hitherto been made in the cause of man. They never can cease to rejoice, that in the long catalogue of calamities and crimes which blacken human annals, the year 1789 presents one spot on which the eye of humanity may with complacence dwell. <126>

Of the Composition and Character of the National Assembly.

Events are rarely separated by the Historian from the character of those who are conspicuous in conducting them. From it alone they often receive the tinge which determines their moral colour.—What is admired as noble pride in SULLY, would be execrated as intolerable arrogance in RICHLIEU. But the degree of this influence varies with the importance of the events.— In the ordinary affairs of State it is great, because in fact they are only of importance to posterity, as they illustrate the characters of those who have acted distinguished parts on the <127> theatre of the world. But in events, which themselves are of immense magnitude, the character of those who conduct them becomes of far less relative importance. No ignominy is at the present day reflected on the Revolution of 1688 from the ingratitude of CHURCHILL, or the treachery of Sunderland. The purity of Somers, and the profligacy of Spencer are equally lost in the splendor of that great transaction, in the sense of its benefits, and the admiration of its justice. No moral impression remains on our mind, but that whatever voice speaks truth, whatever hand establishes freedom, delivers the oracles and dispenses the gifts of God.

If this be true of the deposition of James II. it is far more so of the French Revolution. Among many circumstances which distinguished that event, as unexampled in history, it was none of the least extraordinary, that it might truly be said to have been a <128> REVOLUTION *without Leaders*. It was the effect of general causes operating on the people. It was the revolt of a nation enlightened from a common source. Hence it has derived its peculiar character, and hence the merits of the most conspicuous individuals have had little influence on its progress.—The character of the National Assembly is of secondary importance indeed. But as Mr. Burke has expended so much invective against that body, a few strictures on his account of it will not be improper.

The representation of the third estate was, as he justly states, composed of Lawyers, Physicians, Merchants, Men of Letters, Tradesmen and Farmers. The choice was indeed limited by necessity, for except men of these ranks and professions, the *people* had no objects of election, the Army and the Church being engrossed by the Nobility.—"No vestige of the landed interest of the country appeared <129> in this representation."[28]—For an obvious reason—Because the *Nobility* of France, like the Gentry of England, formed almost exclusively the landed interest of the kingdom.— These professions then could only furnish Representatives for the *Tiers Etat.*—They form the majority of that middle rank among whom almost all the sense and virtue of society reside. Their pretended incapacity for political affairs is an arrogant fiction of Statesmen which the history of Revolutions has ever belied. These emergencies have never failed to create politicians. The subtle counsellors of Philip II. were baffled by the Burgomasters of Amsterdam and Leyden. The oppression of England summoned into existence a race of Statesmen in her Colonies. The lawyers of Boston, and the planters of Virginia, were transformed into ministers and negociators, who proved themselves inferior neither in wisdom as legislators, nor in dexterity as politicians. These facts evince that the powers <130> of mankind have been unjustly depreciated, the difficulty of Political affairs artfully magnified, and that there exists a quantity of talent *latent* among men, which ever rises to the level of the great occasions that call it forth.

But the predominance of the profession of the law, that profession which teaches men "to augur mis-government at a distance, and snuff the approach of tyranny in every tainted breeze,"* was the fatal source from which, if we may believe Mr. Burke, have arisen the calamities of France.

* Mr. Burke's Speech on American Affairs, 1775. ["Speech of Edmund Burke, Esq., On Moving His Resolutions for Conciliation with the Colonies, March 22, 1775," in *Select Works of Edmund Burke*, 3 vols. (Indianapolis, Liberty Fund, 1999), 1:242.]
  28. Burke, *Reflections*, 133.

The majority of the Third Estate was indeed composed of lawyers. Their talents of public speaking, and their professional habits of examining questions analogous to those of politics, rendered them the most probable objects of popular choice, especially in a *despotic* country, where political speculation was no natural amusement <131> for the leisure of opulence. But it does not appear that the majority of them consisted of the unlearned, mechanical members of the profession.* From the list of the States General, it should seem that the majority were *provincial advocates,* a name of very different import from *country attorneys,* and whose importance is not to be estimated by purely *English* ideas.

All *forensic* talent and eminence is *here* concentered in the capital. But in France, the institution of circuits did not exist. The provinces were imperfectly united, their laws various, their judicatures distinct, and almost independent. Twelve or thirteen Parliaments formed as many circles of advocates, who nearly emulated in learning and eloquence the Parisian Bar. This dispersion of talent was in <132> some respect also the necessary effect of the immensity of the kingdom. No liberal man will in England bestow on the Irish and Scottish bar the epithet *provincial* with a view of degradation. The Parliaments of many Provinces in France, presented as wide a field for talent as the Supreme Courts of Ireland and Scotland. The Parliament of Rennes, for example, dispensed justice to a Province which contained two million three hundred thousand inhabitants;† a population equal to that of some respectable kingdoms of Europe. The Cities of Bourdeaux, Lyons, and Marseilles, surpass in wealth and population Copenhagen, Stockholm, Petersburg, and Berlin. Such were the theatres on which the Provincial Advocates of France pursued professional fame. A general Convention of the British empire would yield perhaps as distinguished a place to <133> CURRAN and ERSKINE, and the other eminent and accom-

---

* See an accurate list of them in the Supplement to the *Journal de Paris,* 31st of May, 1789.

† See a Report on the Population of France to the National Assembly, by M. Brion de la Tour, Engineer and Geographer to the King, 1790. [L. Brion de la Tour, *Tableau de la population, avec les citations des auteurs . . . qui ont écrit sur cette partie de la statistique . . . suivi d'un tableau de l'étendue quarrée des généralités du royaume; avec une carte devisée par gouvernemens généraux et par généralités* (Paris, 1789).]

plished barristers of Dublin and Edinburgh, as to those of the capital. And on the same principles have the *Thourets* and *Chapeliers* of *Rouen,* and *Rennes,* acquired as great an ascendant in the National Assembly as the *Targets* and *Camus's* of the Parisian bar.

The proof that this *"faculty"* influence, as Mr. Burke chuses to phrase it, was not injuriously predominant, is to be found in the decrees of the Assembly respecting the judicial Order. It must on his system have been their object to have established what he calls "a litigious Constitution." The contrary has so notoriously been the case, all their decrees have so obviously tended to lessen the importance of lawyers, by facilitating arbitrations, by the adoption of juries, by diminishing the expence and tediousness of suits, by the destruction of an intricate and barbarous jurisprudence, and by the simplicity introduced <134> into all judicial proceedings, that their system has been accused of a direct tendency to extinguish the profession of the law. A system which may be condemned as leading to visionary excess, but which cannot be pretended to bear very strong marks of the supposed ascendant of *"chicane."*[29]

To the lawyers, besides the parochial clergy, whom Mr. Burke contemptuously stiles *"Country Curates,"** were added, those Noblemen whom he so severely stigmatizes as deserters from their Order. Yet the deputation of the Nobility who first joined the Commons, and to whom therefore that title best belongs, was not composed of men whom desperate fortunes and profligate ambition prepare for civil confusion. In that number were found the heads of the most ancient and opulent families in France, the Rochefoucaults, the Richlieus, <135> the Montmorencies, the Noailles. Among them was M. Lally, who has received such liberal praise from Mr. Burke, and it will be difficult to discover in one individual of that body any interest adverse to the preservation of order, the security of rank and wealth.

Having thus followed Mr. Burke in a very short sketch of the classes of men who compose the Assembly, let us proceed to consider his representation of the spirit and general rules which have guided it, and which ac-

---

* It is hardly necessary to remark that *Curé* means *Rector.*

29. The quotations from Burke in this and the previous paragraph are from *Reflections,* 132–35.

cording to him have presided in all the events of the Revolution. "A cabal of Philosophic Atheists had conspired the abolition of Christianity. A monied interest, who had grown into opulence from the calamities of France, contemned by the Nobility for their origin, and obnoxious to the people by their exactions, sought the alliance of these philosophers, by whose influence on public opinion they were to avenge themselves on the No-<136>bility, and conciliate the people. The Atheists were to be gratified with the extirpation of religion, and the Stock-jobbers with the spoils of the Nobles and the Church. The prominent features of the Revolution bear evidence of this league of impiety and rapine. The degraded establishment of the Church is preparatory to the abolition of Christianity, and all the financial operations are designed to fill the coffers of the monied *capitalists* of Paris."[30] Such is the theory of Mr. Burke respecting the spirit and character of the French Revolution. To separate the portion of truth that gives plausibility to his statement from the falsehood that invests it with all its horrors, will however neither be a tedious nor a difficult task.

The commercial, or monied interest, has in all nations of Europe (taken as a body) been less prejudiced, more liberal, and more intelligent, than the landed gentry. Their views are enlarged by a wider intercourse with <137> mankind, and hence the important influence of commerce in liberalizing the modern world. We cannot wonder then that this enlightened class of men ever prove the most ardent in the cause of freedom, the most zealous for political reform. It is not wonderful that philosophy should find in them more docile pupils; and liberty more active friends, than in a haughty and prejudiced aristocracy. The Revolution in 1688 produced the same division in England. The monied interest long formed the strength of *Whiggism,* while a majority of the landed gentlemen long continued zealous *Tories.* It is not unworthy of remark, that the pamphleteers of Toryism accused the Whigs of the same hostility to religion of which Mr. Burke now supposes the existence in France. They predicted the destruction of the Church, and even the downfall of Christianity itself from the influx of Heretics, Infidels, and Atheists, which the new Government of England protected. Their pamphlets <138> have perished with the topic which gave them birth, but

---

30. This is a composite quotation based on Burke, *Reflections,* 184.

the talents and fame of SWIFT have preserved his, which furnish abundant proof of this coincidence in clamour between the enemies of the English, and the detractors of the French Revolution.

That the philosophers, the other party in this unwonted alliance between affluence and literature, in this new union of authors and bankers, did prepare the Revolution by their writings, it is the glory of its admirers to avow.* <139>

What the speculative opinions of these philosophers were on remote and mysterious questions, is here of no importance. It is not as Atheists, or Theists, but as political reasoners, that they are to be considered in a political Revolution. All their writing, on the subjects of metaphysics and theology, are foreign to the question. If Rousseau has had any influence in promoting the Revolution, it is not by his *Letters from the Mountain,* but by his *Social Contract.* If Voltaire contributed to spread liberality in France, it was not by his *Philosophical Dictionary,* but by his Defences of Toleration. The obloquy of their Atheism (if it existed) is personal—it does not belong to the Revolution, for that event could <140> neither have been promoted nor retarded by abstract discussions of theology. The supposition of their conspiracy for the abolition of Christianity, is one of the most extravagant chimeras that ever entered the human imagination. Let us grant their infidelity in the fullest extent. Their philosophy must have taught them that the passions, whether rational or irrational, from which religion arises, could be eradicated by no human power from the heart of man.—Their incre-

---

* Mr. Burke's remark on the English Free-thinkers is unworthy of him. [Burke, *Reflections,* 184–85.] It more resembles the rant by which Priests inflame the languid bigotry of their fanatical adherents, than the calm, ingenuous and manly criticism of a philosopher and a scholar. Had he made extensive enquiries among his learned friends, he must have found many who read and admired COLLINS's incomparable tract on Liberty and Necessity. [Anthony Collins, *A Dissertation on Liberty and Necessity* (1729).] Had he looked abroad into the world, he would have found many who still read the philosophical works of Bolingbroke, not as philosophy, but as eloquent and splendid declamation. What he means by "their successors" I *will* not conjecture. I *will* not suppose that, with DR. HURD, he regards DAVID HUME as "a *puny* dialectician from the north!!" [Richard Hurd was an ally of William Warburton, an inveterate opponent of Hume's irreligion. The remark is that of Warburton as reported in an anonymous pamphlet with an introduction by Hurd, *Remarks on Mr. David Hume's Essay on the Natural History of Religion* (1757).]—yet it is hard to understand him in any other sense.

dulity must have made them indifferent what particular mode of religion might prevail. These philosophers were not the Apostles of any new Revelation that was to supplant the faith of Christ. They knew that the heart can on this subject bear no void, and they had no interest in substituting the Vedam, or the Koran for the Gospel. They could have no reasonable motives to promote any revolution in the popular faith. Their purpose was accomplished when the Priesthood was disarmed. What-<141>ever might be the freedom of their private speculations, it was not against religion, but against the Church, that their *political* hostility was directed.

But, says Mr. Burke, the degraded pensionary establishment, and the elective constitution of the new Clergy of France is sufficient evidence of the design. The Clergy are to be made contemptible, that the popular reverence for religion may be destroyed, and the way thus paved for its abolition. It is amusing to examine the different aspects which the same object presents to various minds.—Mr. Hume vindicates the policy of an opulent establishment, as a bribe which purchases the useful inactivity of the Priesthood.[31] They have no longer, he supposes, any temptation to court a dangerous dominion over the minds of the people, because they are independent of it. Had that philosopher been now alive, he must on the same principle have remarked, that <142> an elective Clergy and a scantily endowed Church, had a far greater tendency to produce fanaticism than irreligion. If the priests depend on the people, they can only maintain their influence by cultivating those passions in the popular mind, which gave them an ascendant over it. Their only influence is through the religious passions. To inflame these passions is their obvious ambition. Priests would be in a nation of sceptics contemptible, in a nation of fanatics omnipotent. It has not therefore been more uniformly the habit of a Clergy that depends on a court, to practise servility, than it would evidently be the interest of a Clergy that depends on the people to cultivate religious enthusiasm. Scanty endowments too would still more dispose them to seek a consolation for the absence of worldly enjoyments, in the exercise of a flattering authority over the minds of men.—Such would have been the view of a philosopher

31. David Hume, *The History of England,* 6 vols. (Indianapolis: Liberty Fund, 1983), 3:135–36.

who was *indifferent* to Christianity, on the <143> new Constitution of the
Gallican Church. He never would dream of rendering religion unpopular
by devoting her ministers to activity, contemptible by compelling them to
purity, or unamiable by divesting her of invidious splendor. He would have
seen in these changes the seeds of enthusiasm and not of laxity. But he
would be consoled by the reflection, that the dissolution of the Church as
a corporation had broken the strength of the priesthood, that religious liberty without limit would disarm the animosity of sects, and the diffusion
of knowledge restrain the extravagances of fanaticism.

I am here only considering the establishment of the Gallican Church as
an evidence of the supposed plan for abolishing Christianity. I am not discussing its intrinsic merits.—I therefore personate a Philosophic Infidel,
and it appears that he must have discerned the tendency of this plan to be
directly <144> the reverse of that conceived by Mr. Burke.* There is a fact,
which though little known, amounts almost to a proof of the solidity of
these speculations. It is in truth rather a *fanatical* than an irreligious spirit
which dictates the organization of the Church of France. A *Jansenistical*
party was formed in the Parlia-<145>ments of that kingdom by their long
hostilities with the Jesuits and the See of Rome.[32] Members of this party

---

* The theory of Mr. Burke on the subject of Religious Establishments, I am utterly
at a loss to comprehend. He will not adopt the impious reasoning of Mr. Hume, nor
does he suppose with Warburton any *"alliance* between Church and State,"* [Burke, *Reflections,* 149] for he seems to conceive them to be originally the same. When he or his
admirers translate his statements (*Reflections,* p. 187–91) into a series of propositions expressed in precise and unadorned English, they may become the proper objects of argument and discussion. In their present state they irresistibly remind one of the observations of Lord Bacon. "Pugnax enim philosophiae genus & sophisticum illaqueat
intellectum at illud alterum *Phantasticum* et *tumidum* et quasi *poeticum* magis *blanditur*
intellectui. Inest enim homini quaedam intellectus ambitio non minor quam voluntatis
praesertim in *ingeniis altis* et *elevatis."* Nov. Org. § LXV. ["For the contentious and sophistical kind of philosophy ensnares the understanding; but this kind, being fanciful
and timid and half poetical, misleads it more by flattery. For there is in man an ambition
of the understanding, no less than of the will, especially in high and lofty spirits." Francis
Bacon, "Novum Organum," in *The Works of Francis Bacon,* collected and ed. J. Spedding, R. L. Ellis, and D. Denon Heath, 14 vols. (London: Longman & Co., 1858–74),
1:175, LXV (English translation, 4:66).]

32. Jansenism was a movement within the Catholic Church inspired by the teachings
of the Dutch Roman Catholic theologian Cornelius Jansen (1585–1638), bishop of Ypres

have in the National Assembly, by the support of the inferior Clergy, acquired the ascendant in ecclesiastical affairs. Of this number is M. Camus. The new constitution of the Church accords exactly with their dogmas.* The Clergy are, according to their principles, to notify to the Bishop of Rome their union in doctrine, but to recognize no subordination in discipline. The spirit of a dormant sect thus revived in a new shape at so critical a period, the unintelligible subtleties of the Bishop of *Ypres* thus influencing the institutions of the eighteenth century, might present an ample field of reflexion to an enlightened observer of human affairs. But it is sufficient for our <146> purpose to observe the fact, and to remark the error of attributing to the hostile designs of atheism what in so great a degree has arisen from the ardour of religious zeal.

The establishment of the Church has not furnished any evidence of that to which Mr. Burke has attributed so much of the system of the National Assembly. Let us examine whether a short review of their financial operations will supply the defect.

† To the gloomy statement of French finance offered by M. Calonne,

---

from 1636. Jansenist beliefs, not least their adoption of the doctrine of predestination, brought them into conflict with both the Catholic Church and the Jesuits. In eighteenth-century France Jansenists in the parlements played an important role in the growing opposition to the monarchy. See D. Van Kley, *The Religious Origins of the French Revolution* (New Haven: Yale University Press, 1996).

* See the speech of *M. Syeyes* on Religious Liberty, where he reproaches the Ecclesiastical Committee with abusing the Revolution for the revival of *Port Royal,* the famous *Jansenistical* Seminary. See also M. CONDORCET *sur l'Instruction Publique.* [E. J. Sieyès, *Opinion de M. Emm. Sieyes, Député de Paris A l'Assemblée Nationale, Le 7 mai 1791; En réponse à la dénonciation de l'Arrêté du Département de Paris, du 11 Avril précédent, sur les Edifices religieux & la liberté générale des cultes* (Paris: Imprimerie Nationale, 1791), repr. in *Oeuvres de Sieyès,* ed. M. Dorigny, 3 vols. (Paris: EDHIS, 1989), vol. 2, no. 24. Condorcet, *Cinq mémoires sur l'instruction publique* (Paris, 1791). See the recent edition by C. Coutel and C. Kintzler (Paris: Flammarion, 1994).]

† It may be remarked, that on the subject of finance I have declined all details. They were not necessary to my purpose, which was to consider the Assembly's arrangements of revenue, more with a view to their SUPPOSED POLITICAL PROFLIGACY, than to their financial talents. I confine myself, therefore, to general remarks, and this I do with the greater pleasure, because I know the ability with which the subject will be treated by a gentleman, whom general sagacity and accurate knowledge of French finance, peculiarly qualify for exposing to the public the errors of Mr. Burke. [Thomas Christie. See footnote to page 91.]

let us oppose <147> the report of M. de la Rochefoucault, from the Committee of Finance on the 9th Dec. 1790,[33] which from premises that appear indisputable, infers a considerable *surplus* revenue in the present year. The purity of that distinguished person has hitherto been arraigned by no party. That understanding must be of a singular construction which could hesitate between the Duc de la Rochefoucault and M. Calonne. But without using this *argumentum ad verecundiam*,[34] we are to remark, that there are radical faults, which vitiate the whole calculations of that minister, and the consequent reasonings of Mr. Burke. They are taken from a year of confusion, of languishing and disturbed industry, and absurdly applied to the future revenue of peaceful and flourishing periods. They are taken from a year in which much of the old revenue of the State had been destroyed, and during which the Assembly had scarcely commenced its scheme of taxation. It is an error to assert <148> that the Assembly had destroyed the former oppressive taxes, which formed so important a source of revenue. These taxes perished in the expiring struggle of the ancient Government. No authority remaining in France could have maintained them. Calculations cannot fail of being most grossly illusive, which are formed from a period when so many taxes had failed before they could be replaced by new impost, and when productive industry itself, the source of all revenue, was struck with a momentary palsy.* Mr. Burke discusses the financial merit of the Assembly before it had begun its system of taxation. It is premature to examine their general scheme <149> of revenue, or to establish general maxims on the survey of a period which may be considered as an *interregnum* of finance.

The only financial operation which may be regarded as complete is their

---

* Mr. Burke exults in the deficiency confessed by M. Vernet of 8 millions sterling, in August, 1790. He follows it with an invective against the National Assembly, which one simple reflexion would have repressed. The suppression of the *gabelle* alone accounted for almost a half of that deficiency! Its produce was estimated at 60 millions of livres, or about two millions and a half sterling.

33. Possibly a reference to the speech by M. de la Rochefoucault which appears in the *Archives Parlementaires*, 21:261–63.

34. Argument from respect (modesty).

emission of *assignats*[35]—the establishment of a paper money, the representative of the national property, which, while it facilitated the sale of that property, should supply the absence of *specie* in ordinary circulation. On this, as well as most other topics, the predictions of their enemies have been completely falsified. They predicted, that no purchasers would be found hardy enough to trust their property on the tenure of a new and insecure establishment. But the national property has in all parts of France been bought with the greatest avidity. They predicted that the estimate of its value would prove exaggerated; but it has sold uniformly for double and treble that estimate. They have predicted that the depreciation of <150> the *assignats* would in effect heighten the price of the necessaries of life, and fall with the most cruel severity on the most indigent class of mankind: The event has however been, that the *assignats*, supported in their credit by the rapid sale of the property which they represented, have kept almost at *par*, that the price of the necessaries of life has lowered, and the sufferings of the indigent been considerably alleviated. Many millions of *assignats*, already committed to the flames, form the most unanswerable reply to the objections urged against them.*

Many purchasers, not availing themselves of that indulgence for gradual payment, which in so immense a sale was unavoidable, have paid the whole price in advance. This has been peculiarly the case in the Northern Provinces, where opulent farmers have been <151> the chief purchasers; a happy circumstance, if it only tended to multiply that most useful and respectable class of men, who are proprietors and cultivators of the ground.

The evils of this emission in the circumstances of France were transient; the beneficial effects permanent. Two great objects were to be obtained by it, one of policy, and another of finance. The first was to attach a great body of Proprietors to the Revolution, on the stability of which depended the security of their fortunes. This is what Mr. Burke terms, making them accomplices in confiscation, though it was precisely the policy adopted by the English Revolutionists, when they favoured the growth of a national debt,

---

* At this moment nearly *one-third*.

35. The revolutionary paper currency secured on the basis of the nationalized property of the church. Issued for the first time on December 19, 1789.

to interest a body of creditors in the permanence of their new establishment. To render the attainment of the other great object, the liquidation
of the public debt, improbable, M. Calonne has been reduced to so <152>
gross a misrepresentation, as to state the probable value of the national
property at only two *milliards,* (about 83 millions sterling) though the best
calculations have rated it at more than double that sum.[36] There is every
probability that this immense national estate will speedily disburden France
of the greatest part of her national debt, remove the load of impost under
which her industry has groaned, and open to her that career of prosperity
for which she was so evidently destined by the bounty of Nature. With
these great benefits, with the acquittal of the public debt, and the stability
of freedom, this operation has, it must be confessed, produced some evils.
It cannot be denied to have promoted, in some degree, a spirit of gambling,
and it may give an undue ascendant in the municipal bodies to the agents
of the paper circulation. But these evils are fugitive. The moment that witnesses the extinction of *assignats,* by the complete sale of the national lands,
must terminate <153> them; and that period, our past experience renders
probable, is not very remote. There was one general view, which to persons
conversant in political economy, would, from the commencement of the
operation have appeared decisive. Either the *assignats* were to retain their
value, or they were not. If they retained their value, none of the apprehended evils could arise from them. If they were discredited, every fall in
their value was a new motive to their holders to exchange them for national
lands. No man would retain depreciated paper who could acquire solid
property. If a great portion of them were thus employed the value of those
left in circulation must immediately rise, both because their number was
diminished, and their security become more obvious. The fall of their value
must have hastened the sale of the lands, and the sale of the lands must
have remedied the fall of their value. The failure, as a medium of <154>
circulation, must have improved them as an instrument of sale; and their
success as an instrument of sale must in return have restored their utility
as a medium of circulation. *This* action and re-action was inevitable,

---

36. C. A. Calonne, *De l'état de la France, présent et à venir, par M. de Calonne ministre
d'état* (Londres: T. Spilsbury & fils, 1790), 88 bis.

though the slight depreciation of the *assignats* had not made its effects very conspicuous in France.

So determined is the opposition of Mr. Burke to those measures of the Assembly which regard the finances of the Church, that even monastic institutions have in him found an advocate. Let us discuss the arguments which he urges for the preservation of these monuments of human madness. In support of an opinion so singular, he produces one *moral* and one *commercial* reason.* "In monastic institutions," in his opinion, "was found a great *power* for the mechanism of politic benevolence."—"To destroy any <155> *power* growing wild from the rank productive force of the human mind, is almost tantamount, in the moral world, to the destruction of the apparently active properties of bodies in the material." In one word, the spirit and the institutions of monachism were an instrument in the hand of the Legislator, which he ought to have converted to some public use. I confess myself so far to share the blindness of the National Assembly, that I cannot form the most remote conjecture concerning the various uses which "have suggested themselves to a contriving mind."[37] But without expatiating on them, let us attempt to construct an answer to his argument on a broader basis. The moral powers by which a Legislator moves the mind of man are his passions; and if the insane fanaticism which first peopled the deserts of Upper Egypt with anchorites, still existed in Europe, the Legislator must attempt the *direction* of a spirit which humanity forbad him <156> to persecute, and wisdom to neglect. But monastic institutions have for ages survived the spirit which gave them birth. It was not necessary for any Legislature to destroy "that power growing wild out of the rank productive force of the human mind,"[38] from which monachism had arisen. It was like all other furious and unnatural passions, in its nature transient. It languished in the discredit of miracles and the absence of persecution, and was gradually melted down in the sunshine of tranquility and opulence so long enjoyed by the Church. The soul which actuated

---

* Burke, p. 262–69.

37. Edmund Burke, *Reflections on the Revolution in France,* vol. 2 of *Select Works of Edmund Burke,* 3 vols. (Indianapolis: Liberty Fund, 1999), 263.

38. Ibid.

monachism had fled. The skeleton only remained to load and deface society.—The dens of fanaticism, where they did not become the recesses of
sensuality, were converted into the styes of indolence and apathy. The
moral power therefore no longer existed, for the spirit by which the Legislator could alone have moved these bodies was no more. The product of
fanaticism was therefore not <157> fit to be the instrument of wisdom. Nor
had any new spirit succeeded which might be an instrument in the hands
of legislative skill. These short-lived phrenzies leave behind them an *inert*
product, in the same manner as, when the fury and splendor of volcanic
eruption is past for ages, there still remains a mass of *lava* to encumber the
soil, and deform the aspect of the earth.* <158>

The sale of the monastic estates is also questioned by Mr. Burke on a
commercial principle. The sum of his reasoning may be thus expressed.
The surplus product of the earth forms the income of the landed proprietor. That surplus the expenditure of some one must disperse, and of what
import is it to society, whether it be circulated by the expence of one landholder, or of a society of monks. A very simple statement furnishes an unanswerable reply to this defence. The wealth of society is its stock of productive labour. There must, it is true, be unproductive consumers, but the
fewer their number the greater *(all things else being the same)* must be the
opu-<159>lence of a State. The possession of an estate by a society of

---

* It is urged by Mr. Burke, [Burke, *Reflections*, 263–66] as a species of incidental
defence of monachism, that there are many modes of industry, from which benevolence
would rather rescue men than from monastic quiet. This must be allowed, in one view,
to be true. But, though the laws *must permit* the natural progress which produces this
species of labour, does it follow, that they ought to create monastic seclusion? Is the
existence of one source of misery a reason for opening another! Because noxious drudgery *must* be tolerated, are we to *sanction* compulsory inutility?—Instances of similar bad
reasoning from what society *must* suffer to what she *ought* to enact, occur in other parts
of Mr. Burke's production. We in England, he says, do not think £.10,000 a year worse
in the hands of a Bishop than in those of a Baronet or a 'Squire. Excessive inequality is
in both cases an enormous evil. The laws *must* permit property to grow as the course of
things affect it. But ought they to add a new factitious evil to this natural and irremediable
one? They cannot avoid inequality in the income of *property,* because they must permit
property to distribute itself. But they can remedy excessive inequalities in the income of
office, because the income and the office are their creatures.

monks establishes, let us suppose forty, unproductive consumers. The possession of the same estate by a single landholder only necessarily produces one. It is therefore evident there is forty times the quantity of labour subtracted from the public stock, in the first case, than there is in the second. If it be objected that the domestics of a landholder are unproductive, let it be remarked that a monastry has its servants, and that those of a *lay* proprietor are not *professionally* and perpetually unproductive, as many of them become farmers and artizans, and it is to be observed above all, that many of them are married.—Nothing then can appear on a plain commercial view of the subject more evident than the distinction between lay and monkish landholders. It is surely unnecessary to appeal to the motives which has every where produced statutes of *Mortmain,* the neglected estate in which the land of ecclesiastical cor-<160>porations is suffered to remain, and the infinite utility which arises from changes of property in land. The face of those countries where the transfers have been most rapid, will sufficiently prove their benefit. Purchasers seldom adventure without fortune, and the novelty of their acquisition inspires them with the ardor of improvement.

No doubt can be entertained that the estates possessed by the Church will encrease immensely in their value. It is vain to say that they will be transferred to Stock-jobbers. Situations, not names, are to be considered in human affairs. He that has once tasted the indolence and authority of a landholder, will with difficulty return to the comparative servility and drudgery of a monied capitalist. But should the usurious habits of the immediate purchaser be inveterate, his son will imbibe the sentiments of a landed proprietor from his birth. The heir of the stock-jobbing <161> *Alpheus* may acquire as perfectly the habits of an active improver of his patrimonial estate, as the children of *Cincinnatus,* or *Cato.*

To aid the feebleness of these arguments, Mr. Burke has brought forward a panegyrical enumeration of the objects on which monastic revenue is expended. On this masterpiece of fascinating and magnificent eloquence it is impossible to be lavish of praise. It would have been quoted by QUINTILIAN as a splendid model of rhetorical common-place. But criticism is not our object, and, all that the display of such powers of oratory can on such a subject suggest, is what might perhaps have served as a characteristic motto to Mr. Burke's production.

Addidit *invalidae* robur FACUNDIA *causae.*[39] <162>

---

39. "His eloquence gave force to an unsound argument." Lucan, "The Civil War," in *Lucan,* trans. J. D. Duff (London and New York: Heinemann and G. P. Putnam's Sons, 1928), 372–73 (VII.67).

Popular Excesses which attended the Revolution.

That no great Revolutions can be accomplished without excesses and miseries at which humanity revolts, is a truth which cannot be denied. This unfortunately is true, in a peculiar manner, of those Revolutions, which, like that of France, are strictly *popular.* Where the people are led by a faction, its leaders find no difficulty in the re-establishment of that order, which must be the object of their wishes, because it is the sole security of their power. But when a general movement of the popular mind levels a despotism with the ground, it is far less easy to <163> restrain excess. There is more resentment to satiate and less authority to controul. The passion which produced an effect so tremendous, is too violent to subside in a moment into serenity and submission. The spirit of revolt breaks out with fatal violence after its object is destroyed, and turns against the order of freedom those arms by which it had subdued the strength of tyranny. The attempt to *punish* the spirit that actuates a *people,* if it were just, would be in vain, and if it were possible would be cruel. They are too *many* to be punished in a view of justice, and too *strong* to be punished in a view of policy. The ostentation of vigor would in such a case prove the display of impotence, and the rigor of justice conduct to the cruelty of extirpation. No remedy is therefore left but the progress of instruction, the force of persuasion, the mild authority of opinion. These remedies, though infallible, are of slow operation; and in the interval which elapses before a <164> calm succeeds the boisterous moments of a Revolution, it is vain to expect that a people, inured to barbarism by their oppressors, and which has ages of oppression to avenge, will be punctiliously generous in their triumph, nicely discriminative in their vengeance, or cautiously mild in their mode of retaliation. "They will break their chains on the heads of their oppressors."*

Such was the state of France, and such were the obvious causes that gave birth to scenes which the friends of freedom deplore as tarnishing her triumphs. They *feel* these evils as men of humanity. But they will not bestow the name on that womanish and complexional sensibility, towards which, even in the still intercourse of private life, *indulgence* is mingled with love. The only humanity <165> which, in the great affairs of men, claims their respect, is that manly and expanded humanity, which fixes its steady eye on the object of general happiness. The sensibility which shrinks at a present evil, without extending its views to future good, is not a virtue, for it is not a quality beneficial to mankind: It would arrest the arm of a Surgeon in amputating a gangrened limb, or the hand of a Judge in signing the sentence of a parricide. I do not say, (God forbid!) that a crime may be committed for the prospect of good. Such a doctrine would shake morals to their center. But the case of the French Revolutionists is totally different. Has any moralist ever pretended, *that we are to decline the pursuit of a good which our duty prescribed to us, because we foresaw that some partial and incidental evil would arise from it.* This is the true view of the question, and it is only by this principle that we are to estimate the re-<166>sponsibility of the leaders of the Revolution for the excesses which attended it.

If any of these leaders had crimes in contemplation for the attainment of their purpose, I abandon them to merited obloquy and execration. The man who would erect freedom on the ruins of morals, understands nor loves neither. But the number against whom *this* charge has ever been *insinuated,* is so small, that supposing (what I do not believe) its truth, it only proves that corrupt and ambitious men will mix with great bodies. The question with respect to the rest, is reducible to this—"Whether they were to abstain from establishing a free Government, because they foresaw that it could not be effected without confusion and temporary distress— Whether they were to be deterred from pursuing that Constitution which

---

* The eloquent expression of Mr. CURRAN in the Parliament of Ireland, respecting the Revolution. [John Philpot Curran. Unable to identify the source of this quotation.]

they deemed best for their country, by the <167> prospect of partial and transient evils, or to be consoled for these calamities by the view of that happiness to which their labours were to give ultimate permanence and diffusion?" A Minister is not conceived to be guilty of systematic immorality, because he balances the evils of the most just war with that national security that is produced by the reputation of spirit and power; nor ought the Patriot, who, balancing the evils of transient anarchy with the inestimable good of established liberty, finds the last preponderate in the scale.

Such, in fact, have ever been the reasonings of the leaders in those insurrections which have preserved the remnant of freedom that still exists among mankind. Holland, England, America, must have reasoned thus, and the different portions of liberty which they enjoy, have been purchased by the endurance of far greater calamities than have been suf-<168>fered by France. It is unnecessary to appeal to the wars which for almost a century afflicted the Low Countries. But it may be necessary to remind England of the price she paid for the establishment at the Revolution. The disputed succession which arose from that event, produced a destructive civil war in Ireland, two rebellions in Scotland, the consequent slaughter and banishment of thousands of citizens, with the widest confiscation of their properties; not to mention the continental connections into which it plunged England, the foreign wars in which it engaged us, and the necessity thus imposed upon us of maintaining a standing army, and accumulating an enormous public debt.* <169>

The freedom of America was purchased by calamities still more inevitable. The authors of the Revolution must have foreseen them, for they were not contingent or remote, but ready in a moment to burst on their heads. Their case is most similar to that of France, and best answers one

---

* Yet this was only the combat of reason and freedom against one prejudice, that of hereditary right, whereas the French Revolution is, as has been sublimely said by the BISHOP OF AUTUN, "Le premier combat qui se soit jamais livrée entre TOUS les PRINCIPES et TOUTES les ERREURS!"—*Addresse aux François,* 11 *Fev.* 1790. ["The first conflict which ever took place between ALL the PRINCIPLES and ALL the ERRORS!" Talleyrand, bishop of Autun, "Adresse aux François," in E. Madival and E. Laurent, *Archives Parlementaires 1787–1860,* 1e série, 99 vols., vols. 1–82 (Paris: Dupont, 1879–1914), vols. 83–99 (Paris: 1961–95), 11:549.]

of Mr. Burke's most triumphant arguments. They enjoyed *some* liberty, which their oppressors did not attack. The object of resistance was conceded in the progress of the war.—But like France, after the concessions of her King, they refused to acquiesce in an imperfect liberty, when a more perfect one was within their reach. They pursued what Mr. Burke, *whatever were his then sentiments,* on his *present* system, must reprobate as a speculative and ideal good. They sought their beloved independence through new calamities, through the prolonged horrors of civil war.—"Their resistance," *from that moment,* "was against concession. Their blows were <170> aimed at a hand holding forth immunity and favours."[40]—Events have indeed justified that noble resistance. America has emerged from her struggle into tranquility and freedom, into affluence and credit.—The authors of her Constitution have constructed a great permanent *experimental answer* to the sophisms and declamations of the detractors of liberty.

But what proportion did the price she paid for so great a blessing bear to the transient misfortunes which have afflicted France?—The extravagance of the comparison shocks every unprejudiced mind. No series of events in history have probably been more widely, malignantly, and systematically exaggerated than the French commotions. An enraged, numerous and opulent body of exiles, dispersed over Europe, have possessed themselves of every venal press, and filled the public ear with a perpetual buz of the <171> crimes and horrors that were acting in France.* Instead of entering on minute scrutiny, of which the importance would neither expiate the tediousness, nor reward the toil, let us content ourselves with opposing one general fact to this host of falsehoods. *No commercial house of importance has failed in France since the Revolution!*—How is this to be reconciled with the tales that have been circulated. As well might the trans-

---

* The *manoeuvres* of M. Calonne, in England, are too obvious from the complexion of some English prints. He informs us, that he had at once in contemplation to have inserted in a note at the end of his work extracts from the public papers in all the nations of Europe, demonstrating the general horror in which the French Revolution was held. This note would have been the more amusing, *as probably all these paragraphs were composed, and transmitted to these papers by M. Calonne himself.*—who would thus be the self-created organ of the voice of Europe.

40. Burke, *Reflections,* 127.

fers of the *Royal-Exchange*, be quietly executed in the ferocious anarchy of *Gondar*, <172> and the peaceful opulence of *Lombard-street*, flourish amidst *hordes* of *Galla* and *Agows*.—Commerce, which shrinks from the breath of civil confusion, has resisted this tempest, and a mighty Revolution has been accomplished with less commercial derangement than could arise from the bankruptcy of a second rate house in London, or Amsterdam. The manufacturers of Lyons, the merchants of Bourdeaux and Marseilles, are silent amidst the lamentations of the Abbé Maury, M. Calonne, and Mr. Burke. Happy is that people whose commerce flourishes in *Ledgers*, while it is bewailed in orations, and remains untouched in *calculation*, while it expires in the pictures of eloquence. This unquestionable fact, is on such a subject worth a thousand arguments, and to any mind qualified to judge, must expose in their true light those execrable fabrications, which have sounded such a "senseless yell" through Europe. <173>

But let us admit for a moment their truth, and take as a specimen of the evils of the Revolution, the number of lives which have been lost in its progress. That no possibility of cavil may remain, let us surpass in an exaggerated estimate the utmost audacity of falsehood. Let us make a statement, from which the most frontless hireling of *Calonne* would shrink. Let us for a moment suppose, that in the course of the Revolution 20,000 lives have been lost. On the comparison of even this loss with parallel events in history, is there any thing in it from which a manly and enlightened humanity will recoil? Can it be compared with the slaughter that established American freedom, or with the fruits of the English Revolution? But this comparison is an injustice to the argument. Compare it with the expenditure of blood by which in ordinary wars so many pernicious and ignoble objects are sought.—Compare it with the blood spilt by Eng-<174>land in the attempt to subjugate America, and if such be the guilt of the Revolutionists of France, for having, at the *hazard* of this evil, sought the establishment of freedom, what new name of obloquy shall be applied to the Minister of England, who with the *certainty* of a destruction so much greater, attempted the establishment of tyranny.

The illusion which prevents the effect of these comparisons, is not peculiar to Mr. Burke. The massacres of war, and the murders committed by the sword of justice, are disguised by the solemnities which invest them.

But the wild justice of the people has a naked and undisguised horror. Its slightest exertion awakens all our indignation, while murder and rapine, if arrayed in the gorgeous disguise of acts of State, may with impunity stalk abroad. Our sentiments are reconciled to them in this form, and we forget that the evils of anarchy must be short-<175>lived, while those of despotic government are fatally permanent.

Another illusion has particularly in England favored the exaggeration of the exiles. We judge of France by our own situation. This is to view it through a false medium. We ought to judge of it by a comparison with nations in *similar circumstances.* With us "the times may be moderate,* and therefore ought to be peaceable": But in France the times were not moderate, and could not be peaceable.

Let us correct that illusion of *moral optics* which makes near objects so disproportionately large. Let us place the scene of the French Revolution in a remote age, or in a distant nation, and then let us calmly ask our own minds, whether the most reasonable subject of wonder be not its unexampled mild-<176>ness, and the small number of individuals crushed in the fall of so vast a pile.

Such are the general reflexions suggested by the disorders of the French Revolution. Of these, the first in point of time as well as of importance, was the Parisian insurrection and the capture of the Bastile. The mode in which that memorable event is treated by Mr. Burke, is worthy of notice. It occupies no conspicuous place in his work. It is only obscurely and contemptuously hinted at as one of those examples of successful revolt, which have fostered a mutinous spirit in the soldiery. "They have not forgot the taking of the KING's CASTLES in Paris and at Marseilles. That they murdered with impunity in both places the Governors has not escaped their minds." (Burke, p. 324.) Such is the courtly circumlocution by which Mr. Burke designs the Bastile—*the King's Castle at Paris.* Such is the igno-<177>minious language in which he speaks of the summary justice executed on the titled ruffian who was its Governor; and such is the apparent art with which he has thrown into the back ground invective and asperity,

---

* Junius. [*The Letters of Junius,* ed. J. Cannon (Oxford: Clarendon Press, 1978), 288, letter 58, September 30, 1771.]

which if they had been prominent, would have provoked the indignation of mankind.

"Je sais," says Mounier, in the language of that frigid and scanty approbation that is extorted from an enemy, *"qu'il est des circonstances qui legitiment l'insurrection, & je mets dans ce nombre celles qui ont causé le siège de la Bastille." (Exposé de Mounier,* p. 24.)[41] But the admiration of Europe and of posterity, is not to be estimated by the penurious applause of M. Mounier, nor repressed by the insidious hostility of Mr. Burke. It will correspond to the splendor of an insurrection, as much ennobled by heroism as it was justified by necessity, in which the citizens of Paris, the unwarlike inhabitants of a vo-<178>luptuous capital, listening to no voice but that of the danger which menaced their representatives, their families, and their country, animated, instead of being awed, by the hosts of disciplined mercenaries that invested them on every side, formed themselves into an army, attacked with a gallantry and success equally incredible, a fortress formidable from its strength, and tremendous from its destination; dispelled every hostile project, and changed the destiny of France. To palliate or excuse such a revolt, would be abject treachery to its principles. It was a case in which revolt was the dictate of virtue, and the path of duty; and in which submission would have been the most dastardly baseness, and the foulest crime. It was an action not to be excused, but applauded; not to be pardoned, but admired. I shall not therefore descend to vindicate acts of heroism, which history will teach the remotest posterity to revere, and of which the recital is destined to <179> kindle in unborn millions the holy enthusiasm of Freedom.

Commotions of another description early followed the Revolution, partly arising from the general causes before stated, and partly from others of more limited and local operation. The peasantry of the provinces, buried for so many ages in the darkness of servitude, saw, indistinctly and confusedly, in the first dawn of liberty, the boundaries of their duties and their rights. It was no wonder that they should little understand that freedom

---

41. "I know that it is the circumstances which legitimate insurrection, and I place among this number those which caused the storming of the Bastille," J. J. Mounier, *Exposé de la conduite de M. Mounier, dans l'assemblée nationale: et des motifs de son retour en Dauphiné* (Paris: Buisson, 1789), 24n.

which so long had been remote from their views. The name conveyed to their ear a right to reject all restraint, to gratify every resentment, and to attack all property. Ruffians mingled with the deluded peasants, with hopes of booty, and inflamed their ignorance and prejudices, by forged acts of the King and the Assembly authorizing their licentiousness. From these circumstances arose many calamities in the <180> provinces. The country houses of many gentlemen were burnt, and some obnoxious persons were assassinated. But one may without excessive scepticism doubt, whether they had been the *mildest masters* whose *chateaux* had undergone that fate. Perhaps the peasants had oppressions to avenge, those silent grinding oppressions that form almost the only intercourse of the rich with the indigent; which though less flagrant than those of Government, are perhaps productive of more intolerable and diffusive misery.

But whatever was the demerit of these excesses, they can by no torture of reason be imputable to the National Assembly, or the leaders of the Revolution. In what manner were they to repress them? If they exerted against them their own authority with rigor, they must have provoked a civil war. If they invigorated the police and tribunals of the deposed Government, besides incurring the ha-<181>zard of the same calamity, they put arms into the hands of their enemies. Placed in this *dilemma,* they were compelled to expect a slow remedy from the returning serenity of the public mind, and from the progress of the new Government towards consistence and vigor.*

A degree of influence exerted by the people, far more than would be tolerated by a firm Government, or could exist in a state of tranquility, must be expected in the crisis of a <182> Revolution which the *people* have made.—They have too recent experience of their own strength to abstain at once from exerting it. Their political passions have been agitated by too

---

* If this statement be candid and exact, what shall we think of the language of Mr. BURKE, when he speaks of the ASSEMBLY as *"authorizing* treasons, robberies, rapes, assassinations, slaughters, and burnings, throughout all their harrassed land." P. 129. In another place he groupes together the legislative extinction of the *Order* of Nobles with the popular excesses committed against *individual* Noblemen, to load the Assembly with the accumulated obloquy. *See p.* 236–37. A mode of proceeding more remarkable for controversial dexterity than for candor.

fierce a storm to regain in a moment that serenity which would expect with patient acquiescence the decrees of their Representatives. From an inflamed multitude, who had felt themselves irresistible, and whose fancy annexed to the decision of every political question the fate of their freedom, an undue interposition in the proceedings of the Legislature was to have been expected. The passions which prompt it are vehement; the arguments which prove its impropriety are remote and refined. Too much, therefore, of this interposition was at such a conjuncture inevitable. It is without doubt a great evil, but it is irremediable. The submission of the people in a period of tranquility, degenerates into a listless and torpid negligence of public affairs, and the fervor which the moment of Revolu-<183>tion inspires, necessarily produces the opposite extreme. That, therefore, the conduct of the populace of Paris should not have been the most decorous and circumspect respecting the deliberations of the Assembly, that it should be frequently irregular and tumultuous, was, in the nature of things, inevitable. But the horrible picture which Mr. Burke has drawn of that "stern necessity" under which this "captive"[42] Assembly votes, is neither justified by this concession, nor by the state of facts. It is the overcharged colouring of a fervid imagination. Those whom he alludes to, as driven away by assassins, M.M. Lally and Mounier, might, surely, have remained with perfect safety in an Assembly in which such furious invectives are daily bellowed forth with impunity against the popular leaders. No man will deny, that that Member of the Minority enjoyed liberty of speech in its utmost plenitude, who called M. Mirabeau *"Le plus vil de tous les assassins."*[43] "The terrors <184> of the lamp-post and bayonet"[44] have hitherto been visionary. Popular fury has hitherto spared the most furious declaimers of Aristocracy, and the only *decree,* so far as I can discern, which has even been *pretended* to have been materially influenced by the populace, is that respecting the prerogatives of war and peace. That tumult has frequently derogated from the dignity and decorum which ought to distinguish the deliberations of a legislative Assembly, is not to be denied. But the only important question

42. Burke, *Reflections,* 160–61.
43. "The vilest of all the assassins." See Burke, *Reflections,* 167n in which Burke quotes from Lally-Tollendal's *Second Letter to a Friend.*
44. Burke, *Reflections,* 161.

regards the *effect* of these tumults on their decisions. That their debates have been tumultuous, is of little importance, if their decisions have been independent.—Even in the question of war and peace, "the highest bidder at the auction of popularity"* did not succeed. The scheme of M. Mirabeau, with few amendments, prevailed, while the more "splendidly popular" <185> propositions, which vested in the Legislature alone the prerogative of war and peace were rejected.

We are now conducted by the course of these strictures to the excesses committed at Versailles on the 5th and 6th of October, 1789. After the most careful perusal of the voluminous evidence before the *Chatelet,* of the controversial pamphlets of M.M. d'Orleans and Mounier, and of the official report of M. Chabroud to the Assembly,[45] the details of the affair seem to me so much involved in obscurity and contradiction, that they afford little on which a candid mind can with confidence pronounce.

They afford, indeed, to frivolous and puerile adversaries the means of convicting Mr. Burke of some minute errors. Mons. *Miomandre,* the centinel at the Queen's-gate, it is true, survives, but it is no less true, that <186> he was left for dead by his assassins. On the comparison of evidence, it seems probable, that the Queen's chamber was not broken into, *"that the asylum of beauty and Majesty was not profaned."*† But these slight corrections palliate little the atrocity, and alter not, in the least, the general complexion of these flagitious scenes.

The most important question which the subject presents is, whether the

---

* Burke, p. 362.

† The expression of M. Chabroud. Five witnesses assert that the ruffians did not break into the Queen's chamber. Two give the account followed by Mr. Burke, and to give this preponderance its due force, let it be recollected, that the whole proceedings before the *Chatelet* were *ex parte.* See *Procedure Criminelle fait au Chatelet de Paris, &c. deux Parties.* PARIS, 1790.

45. *Procedure criminelle fait au Chatelet de Paris* (Paris, 1790); *Justification de M. d'Orléans, du réflexions d'un bon citoyen sur la conduite du Chatelet au sujet de l'affaire du cinq octobre (1789)* ([Paris?], 1790); J. Mounier, *Appel au tribunal de l'opinion publique, du rapport de M. Chabraud, et du décret rendu par l'Assemblée Nationale le 2 octobre 1790. Examen du mémoire du Duc d'Orléans, et du plaidoyer du Comte de Mirabeau, et nouveaux ecclaircissemens sur les crimes du 5 et du 6 octobre 1789* (Génève, 1790); speech of M. Chabraud to National Assembly, *Archives Parlementaires,* 19:354.

Parisian populace were the instruments of conspirators, or whether their fatal march to Versailles was a spontaneous movement, produced by real or chimerical apprehensions of plots against their <187> freedom. I confess that I incline to the latter opinion.—*Natural causes* seem to me adequate to account for the movement. A scarcity of provision is not denied to have existed in Paris. The dinner of the body-guards might, surely have provoked a people more tranquil than those of a city scarce recovered from the shock of a great Revolution. The maledictions poured forth against the National Assembly, the insults offered to the patriotic cockade, the obnoxious ardor of *loyalty* displayed on that occasion, might have awakened even the jealousy of a people whose ardor had been sated by the long enjoyment, and whose alarms had been quieted by the secure possession of liberty. The escape of the King would be the infallible signal of civil war—the exposed situation of the Royal residence was therefore a source of perpetual alarm. These causes operating on that credulous jealousy, which is the malady of the Public mind in <188> times of civil confusion, which sees hostility and conspiracy on every side, seem sufficient to have actuated the Parisian populace.

The apprehensions of the people in such a period torture the most innocent and frivolous accidents into proofs of sanguinary plots.—Witness the *war* of *conspiracies* carried on by the contending factions in the reign of Charles the Second. The boldness with which such charges are then fabricated, and the facility with which they are credited, form indeed, in the mind of a wise man, the strongest presumptions against their truth. It is in perusing the history of such a period, that his scepticism respecting conspiracies is the most vigilant. The research of two centuries has not, in England, been able to decide disputes which these accusations have produced. The participation of Queen Mary in Babington's Plot against Elizabeth, is still the subject of controversy. We, at the present day, dispute <189> about the nature of the connection which subsisted between Charles the First and the Catholic insurgents of Ireland. It has occupied the labour of a century to separate truth from falsehood in the *Rye-house Plot,* to distinguish what both the friendship and enmity of cotemporaries confounded; the views of the leaders from the schemes of the inferior conspirators, and to discover that Russel and Sydney had, indeed, conspired a revolt, but that the underlings alone had plotted the assassination of the King.[46]

It may indeed be said, that ambitious leaders availed themselves of the inflamed state of Paris, that by false rumours, and exaggerated truths, they stimulated the revenge, and increased the fears of the populace; that their emissaries, mixing with the mob, and concealed by its confusion, were to execute their flagitious purposes; that conspiracy was thus joined to popular madness, and fanatics, as <190> usual, were the dupes of hypocritical leaders. Such is the accusation which has been made against M. d'Orleans and M. Mirabeau. Their defence is not imposed on the admirers of the French Revolution. That Revolution is not stigmatized, if its progress has not been altogether exempt from the interposition of profligate ambition, from which who can guard any of the affairs of men? Their cause is foreign from that of Revolution, and to become the advocate of *individuals,* were to forget the dignity of a discussion that regards the rights and interests of an emancipated nation. Of their guilt, however, I will be bold to say, evidence was not collected by the malignant activity of an avowedly hostile tribunal, which, for a moment, would have suspended their acquittal by an English Jury. It will be no mean testimony to the innocence of M. Mirabeau, that an opponent, not the mildest in his enmity, nor the most candid in his judgment, confessed, that he saw no seri-<191>ous ground of accusation against him.— *"J'avoue,"* says the Abbé Maury, *"que je ne vois aucune imputation grave contre M. de Mirabeau."**

One circumstance of repulsive improbability is on the face of the project attributed to them, that of intimidating the King into a flight, that there might be a pretext for elevating the Duke of Orleans to the office of Regent.

* Discours de M. l'Abbé Maury dans l'Assemblée Nationale, 1 Octobre, 1790. ["I avow that I see no serious charge against M. de Mirabeau." Probably a reference to Abbé Maury's speech to the National Assembly, in *Archives Parlementaires,* 19:399.]

46. The Rye House plot, which was foiled in June 1683, involved an attempt to seize the king and resulted in the execution of William Lord Russell and Algernon Sidney for their alleged involvement.

But the King could have had no rational hopes of escaping,* for he must have traversed 200 miles of a country guarded by a people in arms, before he could reach the nearest frontier of the kingdom. The object of the conspiracy then was too absurd to be pursued by conspirators, to whom talent and sagacity have not been denied by their enemies. That the popular leaders in France <192> did, indeed, desire to fix the Royal residence at Paris, it is impossible to doubt. The name, the person, and the authority of the King, would have been most formidable weapons in the hands of their adversaries. The peace of their country, the stability of their freedom, called on them to use every measure that could prevent their enemies from getting possession of that "Royal Figure."[47] The name of the King would have sanctioned foreign powers in supporting the aristocracy. Their interposition, which *now* would be hostility against the King and kingdom, would *then* have been only regarded as aid against rebellion. The name of the King would fascinate and inflame the people of the provinces. Against all these dreadful consequences, there seemed only one remedy, the residence of the King at Paris. Whether that residence is to be called a captivity, or by whatever other harsh name it is to be designed, I will not hesitate to affirm, that the Parliament of England would have merited <193> the gratitude of their country, and of posterity, by a similar prevention of the escape of Charles I. from London. The same act would have given stability to their limitations of kingly power, prevented the horrors of civil war, the despotism of Cromwell, the relapse into servitude under Charles II. and the calamities that followed the subsequent Revolution. Fortunate would it have been for England, if the person of James II. had been retained while his authority was limited. She would then have been circumstanced as France is now; where the odium of personal misconduct would have kept alive a salutary jealousy of power, the prejudices of *personal right* would not have been provoked to hostility against the Constitution, nor the people compelled to entrust their new Sovereign with exorbitant strength to defend *their* freedom and *his* contested throne. Such is the general view which a calm survey may

---

* The circumstances of his late attempt sanction this reasoning. [For flight to Varennes in 1791, see chronology of events.]

47. Burke, *Reflections,* 325.

suggest of the 6th October. The march to Versailles seems <194> to have been the spontaneous movement of an alarmed populace. Their views, and the suggestions of their leaders, were probably bounded by procuring the King to change his residence to Paris, but the collision of armed multitudes terminated in unforeseen excesses and execrable crimes.

In the eye of Mr. Burke, however, these crimes and excesses assume an aspect far more important than can be communicated to them by their own insulated guilt. They form, in his opinion, the crisis of a Revolution, far more important than any change of Government; a Revolution, in which the sentiments and opinions that have formed the manners of the European nations are to perish. "The age of chivalry is gone, and the glory of Europe extinguished for ever."[48] He follows this exclamation by an eloquent eulogium on chivalry, and by gloomy predictions of the future state of Europe, when the nation that has <195> been so long accustomed to give her the tone in arts and manners is thus debased and corrupted. A caviller might remark, that ages much more near the meridian fervor of chivalry than ours have witnessed a treatment of Queens as little gallant and generous as that of the Parisian mob. He might remind Mr. Burke, that in the age and country of Sir Philip Sidney, a Queen of France, whom no blindness to accomplishment, no malignity of detraction could reduce to the level of *Maria Antonietta*, was, by "a nation of men of honour and cavaliers,"[49] permitted to languish in captivity and expire on a scaffold; and he might add, that the manners of a country are more surely indicated by the systematic cruelty of a Sovereign, than by the licentious phrenzy of a mob. He might remark, that the mild system of modern manners which survived the massacres with which fanaticism had for a century desolated, and almost barbarized Europe, might, perhaps, <196> resist the shock of one day's excesses committed by a delirious populace. He might thus, perhaps, oppose specious and popular topics to the declamation of Mr. Burke.

But the subject itself is, to an enlarged thinker, fertile in reflexions of a different nature. That system of manners which arose among the Gothic nations of Europe, of which chivalry was more properly the effusion than

48. Ibid., 169–70.
49. Ibid., 169.

the source, is without doubt one of the most peculiar and interesting appearances in human affairs. The moral causes which formed its character have not, perhaps, been hitherto investigated with the happiest success. But to confine ourselves to the subject before us. Chivalry was certainly one of the most prominent features and remarkable effects of this system of manners. Candor must confess, that this singular institution is not *alone* admirable as a corrector of the ferocious ages in which it flourished. It contributed to polish <197> and soften Europe. It paved the way for that diffusion of knowledge and extension of commerce which afterwards, in some measure, supplanted it, and gave a new character to manners. Society is inevitably progressive.—In Government, commerce has overthrown that "feudal and chivalrous system"[50] under whose shade it first grew. In religion, learning has subverted that superstition whose opulent endowments had first fostered it. Peculiar circumstances softened the barbarism of the middle ages to a degree which favoured the admission of commerce and the growth of knowledge. These circumstances were connected with the manners of chivalry; but the sentiments peculiar to that institution could only be preserved by the situation which gave them birth. They were therefore enfeebled in the progress from ferocity and turbulence, and almost obliterated by tranquillity and refinement. But the auxiliaries which the manners of chivalry had in rude ages reared, ga-<198>thered strength from its weakness, and flourished in its decay. Commerce and diffused knowledge have, in fact, so compleatly assumed the ascendant in polished nations, that it will be difficult to discover any relics of *Gothic manners,* but in a fantastic exterior, which has survived the generous illusions that made these manners splendid and seductive. Their *direct* influence has long ceased in Europe,* but their *indirect* influence, through the medium of those causes, which would not perhaps have existed, but for the mildness which chivalry created in the midst of a barbarous age, still operates with encreasing vigor. The

---

* Those elfin charms that held in magic night
  Our elder fame, and dimm'd our genuine light,
  At length dissolve in TRUTH's meridian ray.

[Thomas Warton, "On the Birth of the Prince of Wales," in *Poems,* a new edition, with additions (London: T. Becket, 1777), 22.]

50. Burke, *Reflections,* 172.

manners of the middle age were, in the most singular sense, compulsory. Enterprizing benevolence was produced by general fierceness, gallant courtesy by ferocious rude-<199>ness, and artificial gentleness resisted the torrent of natural barbarism. But a less incongruous system has succeeded, in which commerce, which unites men's interests, and knowledge, which excludes those prejudices that tend to embroil them, present a broader basis for the stability of civilized and beneficent manners.

Mr. Burke, indeed, forebodes the most fatal consequences to literature from events, which he supposes to have given a mortal blow to the spirit of chivalry. I have ever been protected from such apprehensions by my belief in a very simple truth, *that diffused knowledge immortalizes itself.* A literature which is confined to a few, may be destroyed by the massacre of scholars and the conflagration of libraries; but the diffused knowledge of the present day could only be annihilated by the extirpation of the civilized part of mankind. <200>

Far from being hostile to letters, the French Revolution has contributed to serve their cause in a manner hitherto unexampled in history. The political and literary progress of nations has hitherto been the same; the period of their eminence in arts has also been the aera of their historical fame; and no example occurs in which great *political* splendor has been subsequent to the *Augustan age* of a people. Previous to the year 1789, this might have been considered as a maxim to which history furnished no exception. But France, which is destined to refute every abject and arrogant doctrine that would limit the human powers, presents a new scene. There the shock of a Revolution has infused the ardor of juvenile literature into a nation tending to decline. New arts are called forth when all seemed to have passed their zenith. France enjoyed one Augustan age, fostered by the favor of despotism. She seems about to witness another, created by the energy of freedom. <201>

In the opinion of Mr. Burke, however, she is advancing by rapid strides to ignorance and barbarism.* "Already," he informs us, "there appears a poverty of conception, a coarseness and vulgarity in all the proceedings of the Assembly, and of all their instructors. Their liberty is not liberal. Their

---

* Burke, p. 174.

science is presumptuous ignorance. Their humanity is savage and brutal."
To animadvert on this modest and courteous picture belongs not to the
present subject; and *impressions* cannot be disputed, more especially when
their grounds are not assigned. All that is left is, to declare opposite impressions with a confidence authorized by the example. The proceedings
of the National Assembly of France appear to me to contain models of
more splendid eloquence, and examples of more profound political research than have been exhibited by any public body <202> in modern
times. I cannot therefore augur, from these proceedings, the downfall of
philosophy, or the extinction of eloquence.

Thus various are the aspects which the French Revolution, not only in
its influence on literature, but in its general tenor and spirit, presents to
minds occupied by various opinions. To the eye of Mr. Burke it exhibits
nothing but a scene of horror. In his mind it inspires no emotion but abhorrence of its leaders, commiseration of their victims, and alarms at the
influence of an event which menaces the subversion of the policy, the arts,
and the manners of the civilized world. Minds who view it through another
medium are filled by it with every sentiment of admiration and triumph—
of admiration due to splendid exertions of virtue, and of triumph inspired
by widening prospects of happiness. <203>

Nor ought it to be denied by the candor of philosophy, that events so
great are never so *unmixed* as not to present a *double* aspect to the acuteness
and exaggeration of contending parties. The same ardor of passion which
produces patriotic and legislative heroism becomes the source of ferocious
retaliation, of visionary novelties, and precipitate change. The attempt were
hopeless to encrease the fertility, without favouring the rank luxuriance of
the soil. He that on such occasions expects unmixed good, ought to recollect, that the oeconomy of Nature has invariably determined the equal
influence of high passions in giving birth to virtues and to crimes. The soil
of *Attica* was remarked by antiquity as producing at once the most delicious
fruits and the most virulent poisons. It is thus with the human mind; and
to the frequency of convulsions in the ancient commonwealths, they owe
those examples of sanguinary tumult and virtuous heroism, <204> which
distinguish their history from the monotonous tranquillity of modern
States. The passions of a *nation* cannot be kindled to the degree which

renders it capable of great atchievements, without endangering the commission of violences and crimes. The reforming ardor of a *Senate* cannot
be inflamed sufficiently to combat and overcome abuses, without hazarding
the evils which arise from legislative temerity. Such are the immutable laws,
which are more properly to be regarded as libels on our nature than as
charges against the French Revolution. The impartial voice of History
ought, doubtless, to record the blemishes as well as the glories of that great
event, and to contrast the delineation of it which might have been given
by the specious and temperate *Toryism* of Mr. HUME, with that which we
have received from the repulsive and fanatical invectives of Mr. BURKE,
might still be amusing and instructive. Both these great men would be adverse to the Re-<205>volution; but it would not be difficult to distinguish
between the undisguised fury of an eloquent *advocate* and the well dissembled partiality of a philosophical JUDGE. Such would probably be the difference between Mr. Hume and Mr. Burke, were they to treat on the French
Revolution. The passions of the latter would only *feel* the excesses which
had dishonoured it; but the philosophy of the former would instruct him,
that the human feelings, raised by such events above the level of ordinary
situations, become the source of a guilt and a heroism unknown to the
ordinary affairs of nations; that such periods are only fertile in those sublime virtues and splendid crimes, which so powerfully agitate and interest
the heart of man. <206>

❦ SECTION IV ❦

New Constitution of France.*

A dissertation approaching to completeness on the new Constitution of France would, in fact, be a vast system of political science. It would include a development of the principles that regulate every portion of Government. So immense an attempt is little suited to our present limits. But some remarks on the prominent features of the French system are exacted by the nature of our vindication. They will consist chiefly of a defence of their grand THEORETIC PRINCIPLE, and their most *important* PRACTICAL INSTITUTION. <207>

The principle of theory which has actuated the Legislators of France has been, that the object of all legitimate Government is the assertion and protection of the NATURAL RIGHTS OF MAN. They cannot indeed be absolved of some deviations† from the path prescribed by this great principle; few indeed compared with those of any other body of whom history has preserved any record; but too many for their own glory, and for the happiness of the human race. This principle, however, is the basis of their edifice, and if it be false, the structure must fall to the ground. Against this principle, therefore, Mr. Burke has, with great judgment, directed his attack. Appeals to natural right are, according to him, inconsistent and preposterous. A complete abdication and surrender of all natural right is made

---

* I cannot help exhorting those who desire to have accurate notions on the subject of this section, to peruse and study the delineation of the French Constitution, which, with a correctness so admirable, has been given by Mr. CHRISTIE. [Thomas Christie, *Letters on the Revolution of France* (London: J. Johnson, 1791).]

† I particularly allude to their Colonial policy; but I think it candid to say, that I see in their full force the difficulties of that embarrassing business.

91

by man in entering into <208> Society, and the only rights which he retains are CREATED by the compact which holds together the society of which he is member. This doctrine he thus explicitly asserts.—"The moment," says he, "you abate any thing from the full rights of men each to govern himself, and suffer any artificial positive limitation on those rights, from that moment the whole organization of society becomes a consideration of convenience." Burke, p. 152. "How can any man claim under the conventions of civil society rights which do not so much as suppose its existence—Rights which are absolutely repugnant to it?" Ibid. p. 151. To the same purpose is his whole reasoning from p. 149 to p. 155. To examine this doctrine, therefore, is of fundamental importance. To this effect it is not necessary to enter on any elaborate research into the metaphysical principles of politics and ethics. A full discussion of the subject would <209> indeed demand such an investigation.* The origin of natural rights must have been illustrated, and even their existence proved against some theorists. But such an enquiry would have been inconsistent with the nature of a publication, of which the object was to enforce conviction on the people. We are besides absolved from the necessity of it in a controversy with Mr. Burke, who himself recognizes, in the most ample form, the existence of those natural rights.

Granting their existence, the discussion is short. The only criterion by which we can <210> estimate the portion of natural right surrendered by man on entering into society is the *object* of the surrender. If more is claimed than that object exacts, it becomes not an *object,* but a *pretext.* Now the *object* for which a man resigns any portion of his natural sovereignty over his own actions is, that he may be protected from the *abuse* of the same dominion in other men. No greater sacrifice is therefore necessary than is prescribed by this object, the resignation of *powers* that in their exercise might be injurious to ANOTHER. Nothing, therefore, can be more

---

* It might, perhaps, not be difficult to prove, that far from a *surrender,* there is not even a *diminution* of the natural rights of men by their entrance into Society. The existence of some union with greater or less permanence and perfection of public force for public protection (*the essence of Government*) might be demonstrated to be coeval, and co-extended with man. All theories therefore, which suppose the *actual existence* of any state antecedent to the social, might be convicted of futility and falsehood.

fallacious than to pretend, that we are precluded in the social state from *any* appeal to natural right.* It remains <211> in its full integrity and vigor, if we except that *portion* of it which men mutually sacrifice for protection against each other. They do not surrender all; that is not exacted by the object they have in view; and whatever <212> Government, under *pretence* of that surrender of natural right which is made for mutual security, assumes more than that object *rigorously* prescribes, is an usurpation supported by sophistry, a despotism varnished by illusion. It follows from this principle, that the surrender of right must be *equal* in all the members of society, as the object is to all precisely the same. In effect, society, instead of destroying, realizes and substantiates equality. In a state of *nature,* the equality of right is an impotent theory, which inequalities of strength and skill every moment violate. It is called into energy and effect only by society. As natural equality is not contested, and that the sum of right surrendered by every individual is equal, it cannot be denied that the remnant spared

---

* "Trouver une forme d'association qui defende & protege de toute la force commune la personne & les biens de chaque associé, & par laquelle chacun s'unissant a tous *n'obeisse pourtant qu'a lui-même & reste aussi libre qu'auparavant?*" Rousseau du Contrat Social, livre i. chap. vi. ["To find a form of association which defends and protects the person and goods of each associate with the force of all, and by which each uniting himself with all *obeys only himself and remains as free as before?*" Rousseau, *The Social Contract,* bk. 1, chap. 6, from *The Collected Writings of Rousseau,* vol. 4, ed. Roger D. Masters and Christopher Kelly (Hanover and London: Published for Dartmouth College by University Press of New England, 1990–2004).] I am not intimidated from quoting Rousseau by the derision of Mr. Burke. Mr. Hume's report of his literary secret seems most unfaithful. [The secret, according to Burke's version of Hume's report, was that Rousseau employed paradox to excite attention to his work; see Burke, *Reflections,* 277.] The sensibility, the pride, the fervor of his character, are pledges of his sincerity; and had he even commenced with the fabrication of paradoxes, for attracting attention, it would betray great ignorance of human nature to suppose, that in the ardor of contest, and the glory of success, he must not have become the dupe of his own illusions, a convert to his own imposture. It is indeed not improbable, that when rallied on the eccentricity of his paradoxes, he might, in a moment of gay effusion, have spoken of them as a sport of fancy, and an experiment on the credulity of mankind. The Scottish philosopher, inaccessible to enthusiasm, and little susceptible of those depressions and elevations, those agonies and raptures, so familiar to the warm and wayward heart of Rousseau, neither knew the sport into which he could be relaxed by gaiety, nor the ardor into which he could be exalted by passion. Mr. Burke, whose temperament is so different, might have experimentally known such variation, and learnt better to discriminate between effusion and deliberate opinion.

by the social compact must be equal also. *Civil* inequalities, or, more correctly, civil distinction, must exist in the social body, because it must possess
organs destined for different functions. But political inequality <213> is
equally inconsistent with the principles of natural right and the object of
civil institution.*

Men retain a right to a share in their own Government, because the
exercise of this right by one man is not inconsistent with its possession by
another, which is evidently the only case where the surrender of a natural
right can be exacted by society.

This doctrine is not more abstractly evident than it is practically important. The slightest deviation from it legitimates every tyranny. If the
only criterion of Governments be the supposed *convention* which forms
them, ALL are equally legitimate, for the <214> only interpreter of the convention is the usage of the Government, which is thus preposterously made
its own standard. Governors must, indeed, abide by the maxims of the
Constitution they administer; but what the Constitution is, must be on
this system immaterial. The King of France it does not, indeed, permit to
put out the eyes of the Princes of the Blood, nor the Sophi of Persia to
have recourse to *lettres de cachet.*[51] They must tyrannize by precedent, and
oppress in reverent imitation of the models consecrated by the usage of
despotic predecessors. But if they adhere to these, there is no remedy for
the oppressed, since an appeal to the rights of Nature were treason against
the principles of the social union. If, indeed, any offence against *precedent,*
in the kind or degree of oppression, be committed, this theory may (though
most inconsistently) permit resistance. But as long as the *forms* of any Government are preserved, it possesses, in a view of *justice,* (whatever be <215>
its nature) equal claims to obedience. This inference is irresistible, and it is
thus evident, that the doctrines of Mr. Burke are doubly refuted by the

---

* "But as to the share of power, authority and direction which each individual ought
to have in the management of a state, that I must deny to be among the direct original
rights of man in civil society." [Burke, *Reflections,* 150–51.] This is evidently denying the
existence of what has been called *political,* in contradistinction to *civil* liberty.

51. A warrant to hold a subject without trial that was signed by the king and minister.
For many revolutionaries warrants epitomized the arbitrary nature of justice under the
ancien régime.

fallacy of the logic which supports them, and the absurdity of the conclusions to which they lead.

They are also virtually contradicted by the laws of all nations. Were his opinions true, the language of laws should be *permissive,* not *restrictive.* Had men surrendered all their rights into the hands of the magistrate, the object of laws should have been to announce the portion he was pleased to return them, not the part of which he is compelled to deprive them. The criminal code of all nations consists of *prohibitions,* and whatever is not prohibited by the law, men every where conceive themselves entitled to do with impunity. They act on the principle which this language of law teaches them, that they retain rights which no power can impair or infringe, which <216> are not the boon of society, but the attribute of their nature. The rights of magistrates and public officers are truly the creatures of Society. They, therefore, are guided, not by what the law does not *prohibit,* but by what it authorizes or enjoins. Were the rights of citizens equally created by social institution, the language of the civil code would be similar, and the obedience of subjects would have the same limits.

This doctrine, thus false in its principles, absurd in its conclusions, and contradicted by the avowed sense of mankind, is even abandoned by Mr. Burke himself. He is betrayed into a confession directly repugnant to his general principle.—"Whatever each man can do without trespassing on others, he has a RIGHT to do for himself, and he has a RIGHT to a *fair portion* of ALL that society, with all its combinations of skill and force can do for him."[52] Either this right <217> is universal, or it is not. If it be universal, it cannot be the offspring of convention, for conventions must be as various as forms of government, and there are many of them which do not recognize this right, nor place man in this condition of just equality. All Governments, for example, which tolerate slavery neglect this right: for a slave is neither entitled to the fruits of his own industry, nor to any portion of what the combined force and skill of society produce. If it be not universal, it is no right at all, and it can only be called a *privilege* accorded by some Governments, and with-held by others. I can discern no mode of escaping from this dilemma, but the avowal that these civil claims are the remnant

52. Burke, *Reflections,* 150.

of those *metaphysic* rights which Mr. Burke holds in such abhorrence, but which it seems the more natural object of society to protect than destroy.

But it may urged, that though all appeals to the natural rights of men be not precluded <218> by the social compact, though their integrity and perfection in the civil state may *theoretically* be admitted, yet as men un-questionably may refrain from the exercise of their rights, if they think their exertion unwise: and as Government is not a scientific subtlety, but a *practical* expedient for general good, all recourse to these elaborate abstractions is frivolous and futile, and the grand question in Government is not its source, but its tendency; not a question of right, but a consideration of expediency. Political forms, it may be added, are only the *means* of ensuring a certain portion of public felicity. If the *end* be confessedly obtained, all discussion of the theoretical aptitude of the *means* to produce it is nugatory and redundant.

To this I answer, *first,* that such reasoning will prove too much, and that, taken in its proper extent, it impeaches the great system of morals, of which political principles form <219> only a part. All morality is, no doubt, founded on a broad and general expediency— *"Ipsa utilitas justi prope mater & equi,"*[53] may be safely adopted, without the reserve dictated by the timid and inconstant philosophy of the Poet. Justice is expediency, but it is ex-pediency, speaking by general maxims, into which reason has concentrated the experience of mankind. Every general principle of justice is demon-strably expedient, and it is this utility alone that confers on it a moral ob-ligation. But it would be fatal to the existence of morality, if the utility of every *particular act* were to be the subject of deliberation in the mind of every moral agent. A general moral maxim is to be obeyed, even if the inutility is evident, because the precedent of deviating more than balances any utility that may exist in the particular deviation. Political first principles are of this description. They are only moral principles adapted to the civil union of men. When I assert that a man has a right <220> to life, liberty, &c. I only mean to enunciate a MORAL MAXIM founded on *general interest,* which prohibits any attack on these possessions. In this primary and radical

---

53. "And so does Expedience herself, the mother, we may say, of justice and right." Horace, *Satires,* in *Satires, Epistles, and Ars poetica,* trans. H. Rushton Fairclough (Lon-don and Cambridge, Mass.: Heinemann and Harvard University Press, 1978), 40–41 (I.iii.98).

sense, all rights, natural as well as civil, arise from expediency. But the moment the moral edifice is reared, its basis is hid from the eye for ever. The moment these maxims, which are founded on an utility that is paramount and perpetual, are embodied and consecrated, they cease to yield to partial and subordinate expediency. It then becomes the perfection of virtue to consider, not whether an action be useful, but whether it be right.

The same necessity for the substitution of general maxims exists in politics as in morals. These precise and inflexible principles, which yield neither to the seductions of passion, nor the suggestion of interest, ought to be the guide of Public as well as private morals.—Acting according to the natural rights of men, <221> is only another expression for acting according to those GENERAL MAXIMS of *social morals* which prescribe what is *right and fit* in human intercourse. We have proved that the social compact does not alter these maxims, or destroy these rights, and it incontestibly follows, from the same principles which guide all morality, that no expediency can justify their infraction.

The inflexibility of general principles is, indeed, perhaps more necessary in political morals than in any other class of actions. If the consideration of expediency be admitted, the question recurs, who are to judge of it? They are never the *many* whose interest is at stake: They cannot judge, and no appeal to them is hazarded. They are the *few*, whose interest is linked to the perpetuity of oppression and abuse. Surely that Judge ought to be bound down by the strictest rules, who is undeniably interested in the decision; and he <222> would scarcely be esteemed a wise Legislator, who should vest in the next heir to a lunatic a discretionary power to judge of his sanity or derangement. Far more necessary then is the obedience to general principles, and the maintenance of natural rights, in politics than in the morality of common life. The moment that the slenderest infraction of these rights is permitted for motives of *convenience,* the bulwark of all upright politics is lost. If a small convenience will justify a little infraction, a greater pretended convenience will expiate a bolder violation. The Rubicon is past. Tyrants never seek in vain for sophists. Pretences are multiplied without difficulty and without end. Nothing, therefore, but an inflexible adherence to the principles of general right can preserve the purity, consistency, and stability of a free State.

We have thus vindicated the first theoretical principle of French legis-

lation. The doc-<223>trine of an absolute surrender of natural rights by
civil and social man, has appeared to be deduced from inadequate premises;
and to conduct to absurd conclusions, to sanctify the most atrocious despotism, to outrage the most avowed convictions of men, and, finally, to be
abandoned, as hopelessly untenable by its author. The existence and perfection of these rights being proved, the first duty of law-givers and magistrates is to assert and protect them. Most wisely and auspiciously then did
France commence her regenerating labours with a solemn declaration of
these sacred, inalienable, and imprescriptible rights—a declaration which
must be to the citizen the monitor of his duties, as well as the oracle of his
rights; by a perpetual recurrence to which the deviations of the magistrate
are to be checked, the tendency of power to abuse corrected, and every
political proposition (being compared with the *end* of society) correctly
and dispassionately estimated. These declara-<224>tions of the rights of
men originated from the juvenile vigor of reason and freedom in the new
world, where the human mind was unincumbered with that vast mass of
usage and prejudice, which so many ages of ignorance had accumulated,
to load and deform society in Europe. France learned this, among other
lessons, from America; and it is perhaps the only expedient that can be
devised by human wisdom to keep alive the public vigilance against the
usurpation of partial interests, by perpetually presenting the general right
and the general interest to the public eye. Thus far I trust will be found
correct the scientific principle which has been the Polar Star, by the light
of which the National Assembly of France has hitherto navigated the vessel
of the State, amid so many tempests howling destruction around them on
every side.

There remains a much more extensive and complicated enquiry, the consideration of their <225> political institutions. As it is impossible to examine all, we must limit our remarks to the most important. To speak then
generally of their Constitution, it is a preliminary remark, that the application of the word DEMOCRACY to it is fallacious and illusive.—If that
word, indeed, be taken in its *etymological sense,* as the power of the people,
it is a Democracy, and so is all legitimate Government. But if it be taken
in its historical sense, it is not so, for it does not resemble those Governments which have been called Democracies in ancient or modern times. In

the ancient Democracies there was neither representation nor division of powers. The rabble legislated, judged and exercised every political authority. I do not mean to deny that in Athens, the Democracy of which history has transmitted to us the most monuments, there did exist some feeble controls. But it has been well remarked, that a multitude, if it was composed of NEWTONS, must <226> be a mob. Their will must be equally unwise, unjust, and irresistible. The authority of a corrupt and tumultuous populace has indeed by the best writers of antiquity been regarded rather as an Ochlocracy than a Democracy, as the despotism of the rabble, not the dominion of the people. It is a degenerate Democracy. It is a febrile paroxysm of the social body, which must speedily terminate in convalescence or dissolution.

The New Constitution of France is almost directly the reverse of these forms. It vests the legislative authority in the Representatives of the people, the executive in an hereditary First Magistrate, and the judicial in Judges, periodically elected, unconnected either with the Legislature or with the executive Magistrate. To confound such a constitution with the Democracies of antiquity, for the purpose of quoting historical and experimental evidence against it, is to recur to the most paltry <227> and shallow arts of sophistry.—In discussing it, on the present occasion, the first question that arises regards the mode of constituting the Legislature, and the first division of this question, which considers the right of suffrage, is of primary importance in Commonwealths. Here I most cordially agree with Mr. Burke* in reprobating the impotent and preposterous qualification by which the Assembly have *disfranchised* every citizen who does not pay a direct contribution equivalent to the price of three days labour. Nothing can be more evident than its inefficacy for any purpose but the display of inconsistency, and the violation of justice. But these remarks were made at the moment of discussion in France, and the plan† was combated in the Assembly with

---

* P. 281–83.

† For the history of this decree, the 27th and 29th days of October, 1789, see the *Procès verbaux* of these days.—See also the *Journal de Paris,* No. 301, & *Les Revolutions de Paris,* No. 17, p. 73, *& seq.* These authorities amply corroborate the assertions of the text. [See E. Madival and E. Laurent, *Archives Parlementaires 1787–1860,* 1e série, 99 vols.,

all the force of reason and elo-<228>quence by the most conspicuous leaders of the popular party. M.M. Mirabeau, Target, and Petion more particularly distinguished themselves by their opposition. But the more timid
and prejudiced members of the democratic party shrunk from so bold an
innovation in political systems, as JUSTICE. They fluctuated between their
principles and their prejudices, and the struggle terminated in an illusive
compromise, the constant resource of feeble and temporizing characters.
They were content that *little* practical evil should in fact be produced.—
Their views were not sufficiently enlarged and exalted to perceive, that the
INVIOLABILITY of PRINCIPLES is the *Palladium* of virtue and of freedom.
The members of this description do not, indeed, form the majority of their
party; but Aristocratic minority, anxious for whatever might dishonor or
embarrass the Assembly, eagerly coalesced with them, and stained the infant
Constitution with this absurd usurpation. <229>

An enlightened and respectable antagonist of Mr. Burke has attempted
the defence of this measure. In a letter to *Earl Stanhope,* p. 78–79,[54] it is
contended, that the spirit of this regulation accords exactly with the principles of natural justice, because even in an unsocial state, the *pauper* has
a claim only on charity, and he who produces nothing has no right to share
in the regulation of what is produced by the industry of others. But whatever be the justice of disfranchising the unproductive poor, the argument
is, in point of fact, totally misapplied. Domestic servants are excluded by
the decree of the Assembly, though they subsist as evidently on the produce
of their own labour as any other class of men in society; and to them therefore the argument of our acute and ingenious writer is totally inapplicable.*
But it is the consola-<230>tion of the consistent friends of freedom, that

---

vols. 1–82 (Paris: Dupont, 1879–1914), vols. 83–99 (Paris: 1961–95), 9:589–601; *Journal
de Paris,* no. 301; *Les Révolutions de Paris,* no. 17, p. 73 ff.]

    * It has been very justly remarked, that even on the idea of *taxation,* all men have
equal rights of election. For the man who is too poor to pay a direct contribution to the
State, still pays a tax in the increased *price* of his food and cloaths. It is besides to be
observed, that life and liberty are more sacred than property, and that the right of suffrage
is the only shield that can guard them.

    54. Catharine Macaulay, *Observations on the Reflections of the Right Hon. Edmund
Burke, on the Revolution in France, in a letter to the Right Hon. the Earl of Stanhope* (London, 1790), 78–79.

this abuse must be short-lived. The spirit of reason and liberty, which has atchieved such mighty victories, cannot long be resisted by this puny foe. The number of primary electors is at present so great, and the importance of their single votes so proportionally little, that their interest in resisting the extension of the right of suffrage is insignificantly small. Thus much have I spoken of the usurpation of the rights of suffrage with the ardor of anxious affection, and the freedom of liberal admiration. The moment is too serious for compliment, and I leave untouched to the partizans of despotism, their monopoly of blind and servile applause.* <231>

I must avow, with the same frankness, equal disapprobation of the elements of territory and contribution which enter into the proportion of Representatives deputed by the various portions of the kingdom. Territorial or financial representation,† is a monstrous relic of ancient prejudice. Land or money cannot be represented. Men only *can* be represented, and population alone ought to regulate the number of Representatives which any district delegates. <232>

The next consideration that presents itself is, the nature of those bodies into which the citizens of France are to be organized for the performance of their political functions.—In this important part of the subject, Mr. Burke has committed some fundamental errors. It is more amply, more dexterously, and more correctly treated by M. de Calonne, of whose work this discussion forms the most interesting part.

The Assemblies into which the people of France are divided, are of *four* kinds.—Primary, Municipal, Electoral, and Administrative.

---

* "He who freely magnifies what has been nobly done and fears not to declare as freely what might have been done better, gives you the best covenant of his fidelity. His highest praise is not flattery and his plainest advice is praise." MILTON's *Areopagitica.* [John Milton, "Areopagitica," in *The Works of John Milton,* ed. F. A. Patterson, 18 vols. (New York: Columbia University Press, 1931–40), 4:294–95.]

† Montesquieu, I think, mentions a federative Republic in *Lycia,* where the proportion of Representatives deputed by each State was in a *ratio* compounded of its population and contribution. [Montesquieu, *Spirit of the Laws,* bk. 9, chap. 3.] There might be some plausibility in this institution among confederated independent States, but it is grossly absurd in a Commonwealth, which is *vitally* ONE. In such a state, the contribution of all being proportioned to their capacity, it is *relatively* to the contributors EQUAL, and if it can confer any political claims, they must derive from it equal rights.

To the *Municipalities* belong the care of preserving the police, and collecting the revenue within their jurisdiction. An accurate idea of their nature and object may be formed by supposing the *country* of England uniformly <233> divided, and governed, like its cities and towns, by magistracies of popular election.

The Primary Assemblies, the first elements of the Commonwealth, are formed by all the citizens, who pay a direct contribution, equal to the price of three days labour, which may be averaged at half a Crown English. Their functions are purely electoral. They send Representatives *directly* to the Assembly of the *Department,* in the proportion of one to every hundred active citizens. This they do not through the medium of the district, as was originally proposed by the Constitutional Committee, and has been erroneously stated by Mr. Burke.[55] They send, indeed, Representatives to the Assembly of the district, but it is the object of that Assembly not to depute electors to the department, but to elect the administrators of the district itself. <234>

The Electoral Assemblies of the *Departments,* formed by the immediate delegates of the people in their primary Assemblies, elect the Members of the Legislature, the Judges, the Administrators, and the* Bishop of the Department.

The *Administrators* are every where the organs and instruments of the Executive Power. As the provinces of France, under her ancient Government were ruled by Governors, Intendants, &c. appointed by the Crown, so they are now governed by these administrative bodies, who are chosen by the Electoral Assemblies of the Departments.

Such is the rude outline of that elaborate organization which the French Legislature have formed. Details are not necessary to my purpose; and I the more chearfully abstain <235> from them, because I know that they will be speedily laid before the Public by a person far more competent to deliver them with precision, and illustrated with a very correct and ingenious chart of the New Constitution of France.[56]

---

* Every Department is an Episcopal See.
55. Burke, *Reflections,* 282.
56. Christie, *Letters on the Revolution of France.*

Against the arrangement of these Assemblies, many subtle and specious objections are urged, both by Mr. Burke and the exiled Minister of France. The first and most formidable is, "the supposed tendency of it to dismember France into a body of confederated Republics."[57] To this objection there are several unanswerable replies. But before I state them, it is necessary to make one distinction. These several bodies are, in a certain sense independent, in what regards subordinate and interior regulation. But they are not independent in the sense which the objection supposes, that of possessing a separate will from that of the nation, or influencing, but by their Representatives, the general sys-<236>tem of the State. Nay, it may be demonstrated, that the Legislators of France have solicitously provided more elaborate precautions against this dismemberment than have been adopted by any recorded Government.

The first circumstance which is adverse to it is the *minuteness of the parts* into which the kingdom is divided. They are too small to possess a separate force. As elements of the social order, as particles of a great political body, they are something; but as insulated States, they would be impotent. Had France been moulded into great masses, each of them might have been strong enough to claim a separate will; but divided as she is, no body of citizens is conscious of sufficient strength to feel their sentiments of any importance, but as constituent parts of the general will. Survey the Administrative, the Primary, and the Electoral Assemblies, and nothing will be more evident than their impotence in indivi-<237>duality. The Municipalities, surely, are not likely to arrogate independence. A 48000th part of the kingdom has not energy sufficient for separate existence, nor can a hope arise in the Assembly of such a slender community of influencing, in a direct and dictatorial manner, the counsels of a great State. Even the Electoral Assemblies of the Departments do not, as we shall afterwards shew, possess force enough to become independent confederated Republics.

Another circumstance, powerfully hostile to this dismemberment, is the destruction of the ancient provincial division of the kingdom. In no part of Mr. Burke's work have his arguments been chosen with such infelicity of selection as in what regards this subject. He has not only erred, but his

57. Burke, *Reflections*, 143.

error is the precise reverse of truth. He represents as the harbinger of discord what is, in fact, the instrument of union. He mistakes the <238> cement of the edifice for a source of instability and a principle of repulsion.
France was, under the ancient Government, an union of Provinces acquired at various times, and on different conditions, differing in constitution, laws, language, manners, privileges, jurisdiction, and revenue. It
had the exterior of a simple Monarchy, but it was in reality an aggregate of
independent States. The Monarch was in one place King of Navarre, in
another Duke of Britanny, in a third Count of Provence, in a fourth Dau-
phin of Vienne. Under these various denominations, he possessed, at least
nominally, different degrees of power, and he certainly exercised it under
different forms.—The mass composed of these heterogeneous and discordant elements, was held together by the compressing force of despotism.
When that compression was withdrawn, the provinces must have resumed
their ancient independence, perhaps in a form more absolute than as members of a federative Repub-<239>lic. Every thing tended to inspire *provincial* and to extinguish *national* patriotism. The inhabitants of Bretagne, or
Guienne, felt themselves linked together by ancient habitudes, by congenial
prejudices, by similar manners, by the relics of their Constitution, and the
common name of their country; but their character as members of the
French Empire, could only remind them of long and ignominious subjection to a tyranny, of which they had only felt the strength in exaction, and
blessed the lenity in neglect. These causes must have formed the provinces
into independent Republics, and the destruction of their provincial existence was indispensible to the prevention of this dismemberment. It is impossible to deny, that men united by no previous habitude, (whatever may
be said of the policy of the union in other respects) are less qualified for
that union of will and force, which produces an independent Republic,
than provincials on whom every circumstance <240> tended to confer local
and partial attraction, and a repulsion to the common center of the national
system. Nothing could have been more inevitable than the independence
of those great provinces which had never been moulded and organized into
one Empire; and we may boldly pronounce, in direct opposition to Mr.
Burke, that the new division of the kingdom was the only expedient that
could have prevented its dismemberment into a confederacy of sovereign
Republics.

The solicitous and elaborate *division of powers,* is another expedient of infallible operation, to preserve the unity of the body politic. The *Municipalities* are limited to minute and local administration. The *Primary Assemblies* solely to elections. The *Assemblies of the District* to objects of administration and control of a superior class; and the *Assemblies of the Departments,* where this may be the most apprehended, possess functions pure-<241>ly electoral. They elect Judges, Legislators, Administrators, and Ministers of Religion, but they are to exert no authority legislative, administrative, or judicial. In any other capacity but that of executing their electoral functions, in voting an address, an instruction, or a censure, they are only simple citizens.*

But whatever danger might be apprehended from the assumption of powers by these for-<242>midable Assemblies, the depositaries of such extensive electoral powers are precluded by another circumstance, which totally disqualifies and unnerves them for any purpose but that for which they are created by the Constitution. They are *biennially* renewed, and their fugitive nature makes systematic usurpation hopeless. What power, indeed, could they possess of dictating to the National Assembly,† or what interest could the members of that Assembly have in obeying the mandates of those who held as fugitive and precarious a power as their own; not one of whom might, at the next election, have <243> a suffrage to bestow? The same

---

* Compare these remarks with the reasoning of M. Calonne under the head, *"Que faut-il penser de l'etablissement perpetuel de 83 Assemblées, composées chacune de plus 600 citoyens, chargées de choix des Legislateurs Supremes, du choix des Administrateurs Provinciaux, du choix des Juges, du choix des Principaux Ministres du Culte, & ayant en consequence le droit de se mettre en activité toutes fois & quantes?"* ["What must one think of the perpetual establishment of 83 Assemblies, each composed of at least 600 citizens, charged with choosing the Supreme Legislators, the Provincial Administrators, the Judges, the Principal Ministers of Religion, and having in consequence the right of putting it into action at any time or in any place." C. A. Calonne, *De l'état de la France, présent et à venir, par M. de Calonne ministre d'état* (Londres: T. Spilsbury & fils, 1790), 358–72.] The objection which we are combating is stated with great precision by M. de Calonne, from p. 358 to p. 372 of his work. The discussion must be maturely weighed by every reader who would fathom the legislation of France.

† I do not mean that their voice will not be there respected. That would be to suppose the Legislature as insolently corrupt as that of a neighbouring Government of pretended freedom. I only mean to assert, that they cannot possess such a power as will enable them to dictate instructions to their Representatives as authoritatively as Sovereigns do to their Embassadors; which is the idea of a confederated Republic.

probability gives the provincial Administrators that portion of independence which the Constitution demands. By a still stronger reason, the
Judges, who are elected for six years, must feel themselves independent of
constituents whom *three* elections may so radically and completely change.
These circumstances then, the minuteness of the divisions, the dissolution
of provincial ties, the elaborate distribution of powers, and the fugitive
constitution of the Electoral Assemblies, seem to form an insuperable barrier against the assumption of such powers by any of the bodies into which
France is organized, as would tend to produce the federal form. Thus the
first great argument of Mr. BURKE and M. DE CALONNE seems to be refuted in *principles,* if not in the expansion of detail.

The next objection that is to be considered is peculiar to Mr. Burke. The
subordination <244> *of elections* has been regarded by the admirers of the
French law-givers as a master-piece of legislative wisdom. It seemed as great
an improvement on representative Government, as representation itself
was on pure Democracy. No extent of territory is too great for a popular
Government thus organized; and as the Primary Assemblies may be divided
to any degree of minuteness, the most perfect order is reconcileable with
the widest diffusion of political right. Democracies were supposed by philosophers to be necessarily small, and therefore feeble; to demand numerous
Assemblies, and to be therefore venal and tumultuous. Yet this great discovery, which gives force and order in so high a degree to popular Governments, is condemned and derided by Mr. Burke. An *immediate* connection
between the representative and the *primary* constituent, he considers as
essential to the idea of representation. As the electors in the Primary Assemblies do not immediately <245> elect their law-givers, he regards their
rights of suffrage as nominal and illusory.* It will in the first instance be
remarked, from the statement which has already been given, that in stating
three interposed elections between the primary electors and the Legislature,
Mr. Burke has committed a most important error in point of fact. The
original plan of the Constitutional Committee was indeed agreeable to the

* P. 298. "For what are these Primary Electors complimented, or rather mocked with
a choice?—They can never know any thing of the qualities of him that is to serve them,
nor has he any obligation to serve them."

statement of Mr. Burke. The Primary Assemblies were to elect Deputies to the District, the District to the Department, and the Department to the National Assembly. But this plan was forcibly and successfully combated. It was represented as tending to introduce a vicious complexity into the Government, and, by making the channel <246> through which the national will passes into its public acts so circuitous, to enfeeble its energy under pretence of breaking its violence. It was accordingly radically changed. The series of three elections was still preserved for the choice of provincial Administrators, but the Electoral Assemblies in the *Departments,* who are the immediate constituents of the Legislature, are *directly* chosen by the *Primary Assemblies,* in the proportion of one elector to every hundred active citizens.* <247>

But to return to the general question, which is perhaps not much affected by these details, I profess I see no reason why the right of election is not as susceptible of delegation as any other civil function, why a citizen may not as well delegate the right of choosing law-givers, as that of making laws. Such a gradation of elections, says Mr. Burke, excludes responsibility and substantial election, since the primary electors neither can know, nor bring to account the members of the Assembly.

This argument has (considering the peculiar system of Mr. Burke) appeared to me to be the most singular and inconsistent that he has urged in his work. Representation itself must be confessed to be an infringement on <248> the most perfect liberty, for the best organized system cannot preclude the possibility of a variance between the *popular* and the *representative*

---

* For a charge of such fundamental inaccuracy against Mr. Burke, the Public will most justly and naturally expect the highest evidence. I do therefore boldly appeal to the *Decret sur la nouvelle Division du Royaume, Art.* 17.—to the *Procés Verbal* of the Assembly for the 22d Dec. 1789. [See *Archives Parlementaires,* 10:714–52.] If this evidence demanded any collateral aid, the authority of M. *Calonne* (which it is remarkable that Mr. Burke should have overlooked) corroborates it most amply. "On ordonne que chacune de ces Assemblées *(Primaires)* nommera un ELECTEUR a raison de 100 citoyens actifs."— Calonne, p. 360. "Ces cinquantes mille ELECTEURS *(des Departements)* choisis de deux ans en deux ans par les ASSEMBLEES PRIMAIRES." Id. ibid. ["It is decreed that each of these *(Primary)* Assemblies will name one elector for every 100 active citizens." "These 50,000 electors *(of the Departments)* chosen every two years by the PRIMARY ASSEMBLIES," Calonne, *De la France,* 360.] The Ex-Minister, indeed, is rarely to be detected in any departure from the solicitous accuracy of professional detail.

will. Responsibility, strictly and rigorously speaking, it can rarely admit, for the secrets of political fraud are so impenetrable, and the line which separates corrupt decision from erroneous judgment so indiscernibly minute, that the cases where the Deputies could be made properly responsible are too few to be named as exceptions. Their *dismission* is all the punishment that can be inflicted, and all that the best Constitution can attain is a *high probability* of unison between the constituent and his deputy. This seems attained in the arrangements of France. The electors of the *Departments* are so numerous, and so popularly elected, that there is the highest *probability* of their being actuated in their elections, and *re-elections,* by the sentiments of the Primary Assemblies. They have too many points of contact with the ge-<249>neral mass to have an insulated opinion, and too fugitive an existence to have a separate interest. It is besides to be remarked, that they come immediately from among the people, with all its opinions, and predilections, and enmities, to their elective functions; and it is surely improbable, that, too shortly united for the acquisition of a corporation spirit, they should have any will or voice but that of their constituents. This is true of those cases where the merits or demerits of candidates may be supposed to have reached the Primary Assemblies. In those far more numerous cases, where they are too obscure to obtain that notice, but by the polluted medium of a popular canvas, this delegation is still more evidently wise. The peasant, or artizan, who is a primary elector, knows intimately men among his equals, or *immediate* superiors, who have information and honesty enough to chuse a good representative. But among this class (the only one which he can know sufficiently <250> to judge) he rarely meets with any who have genius, leisure, and ambition for that situation themselves. Of the candidates to be electors in the *Department,* he may be a disinterested, deliberate, and competent judge. But were "he to be complimented, or rather mocked,"[58] with the direct right of electing to the legislative body, he must, in the tumult, venality, and intoxication of an election mob, give his suffrage without any *possible* just knowledge of the situation, character, and conduct of the candidates. So unfortunately false,

58. Burke, *Reflections,* 298.

indeed, seems the opinion of Mr. Burke, that this arrangement in the French Constitution is the only one that substantially, and in good faith, provides for the exercise of deliberate discrimination in the constituent.

The *hierarchy* of elections was obtruded on France by necessity. Had they rejected it, they had only the alternative of tumultuous electoral Assemblies, or a tumultuous Legis-<251>lature. If the primary electoral Assemblies were to be so divided as to avoid tumult, their deputies would be so numerous as to make the National Assembly a mob. If the number of electoral Assemblies were reduced according to the number of deputies that ought to constitute the Legislature, each of them would be numerous enough, on the other hand, to be also a mob. I cannot perceive that peculiar unfitness which is hinted at by Mr. Burke* in the right of *personal* choice to be delegated. It is in the practice of all States delegated to great officers, who are entrusted with the power of nominating their subordinate agents. It is in the most ordinary affairs of common life delegated, when our *ultimate* representatives are too remote from us to be within the sphere of our observation. <252>

It is remarkable that M. Calonne, addressing his work to a people enlightened by the masterly discussions to which these subjects have given rise, has not, in all the fervor of his zeal to criminate the new institutions, hazarded this objection. This is not the only instance in which the Ex-Minister has shewn more respect to the nation whom he addresses, than Mr. Burke has paid to the intellect and information of the English Public.†
<253>

---

* "Of all the powers to be delegated by those who have any real means of judging, that most peculiarly unfit is what relates to a personal choice." Burke, p. 298.

† Though it may, perhaps, be foreign to the purpose, I cannot help thinking one remark on this topic interesting. It will illustrate the difference of opinion between even the Aristocratic party in France and the rulers of England.—M. Calonne rightly states it to be the *unanimous instruction* of France to her Representatives, to enact the *equal* admissibility of ALL citizens to public employ!—England adheres to the Test Act! The arrangements of M. Necker for elections to the States General, and the scheme of M.M. Mounier and Lally Tolendahl for the new Constitution, included a representation of the people nearly exact. Yet the idea of it is regarded with horror in England!—The highest *Aristocrates* of France approach more nearly to the creed of general liberty than the most popular politicians of England, of which these two circumstances are signal proofs. Calonne [*De la France*], p. 383.

Thus much of the elements that are to generate the Legislative body. Concerning that body, thus constituted, various questions remain. Its *unity* or *division* will admit of much dispute, and it will be deemed of the greatest moment by the zealous admirers of the English Constitution, to determine, whether any semblance of its legislative organization could have been attained by France, if good, or ought to have been pursued by her, if attainable. Nothing has been asserted with more confidence by Mr. Burke than the facility with which the fragments of the long subverted liberty of France might have been formed into a British Constitution.* But of <254> this general position he has neither explained the mode, nor defined the limitations. Nothing is more favourable to the popularity of a work than these loftly generalities, which are light enough to pass into vulgar currency, and to become the maxims of a popular creed. Touched by definition, they become too simple and precise for eloquence, too cold and abstract for popularity. But exhibited as they are by Mr. Burke, they gratify the pride and <255> indolence of the people, who are thus taught to speak what gains applause, without any effort of intellect, and imposes silence, without any labour of confutation; what may be acquired without being studied, and uttered without being understood. Of this nature are these vague and confident assertions, which without furnishing any definite idea, afford a ready jargon for vulgar prejudice, flattering to national vanity, and sanctioned by

---

* To place this opinion in a stronger point of light, I have collected the principal passages in which it is announced or insinuated. "In your OLD STATES you possessed that variety of parts, corresponding with the various descriptions of which your community was happily composed." Burke, p. 123. "If diffident of yourselves, and not clearly the almost obliterated Constitution of your ancestors, seeing you had looked to your neighbours in this land, who had kept alive the principles and models of the old common law of Europe meliorated and adapted to the present state." Id. p. 125. "Have they never heard of a Monarchy directed by laws, controled and balanced by the great hereditary wealth and hereditary dignity of a nation, and both again controled by a judicious check from the reason and feeling of the people at large, acting by a suitable and permanent organ?" Id. p. 224. And in the same page he represents France as a nation which had it in its choice to obtain such a Government with ease, or *rather to confirm it when actually possessed.*"—"I must think such a Government well deserved to have its excellencies heightened, its faults corrected, and its *capacities* improved into a British Constitution." Id. p. 232. The precise question at issue is, whether the ancient Government of France possessed *capacities* which could have been improved into a British Constitution.

a distinguished name. It is necessary to enquire with more precision in what manner France could have assimilated the remains of her ancient Constitution to that of the English Legislature. Three modes only seem conceivable. The preservation of the *three* Orders distinct. The union of the Clergy and Nobility in one upper Chamber, or some mode of selecting from these two Orders a body like the House of Lords in England. Unless the insinuations of Mr. Burke point to one or other of these schemes, I cannot divine their meaning. The <256> first mode (the three Orders sitting in separate houses with equal privileges) would neither have been congenial in spirit nor similar in form to the Constitution of England. To convert the Convocation into an integrant and co-ordinate Member of our Legislature, would give it some semblance of the structure; but it would be a faint one. It would be necessary to arm our Clergy with an immense mass of property, rendered still more formidable by the concentration of great portions in the hands of a few, to constitute it in effect the same body with the Nobility, by granting them the monopoly of great benefices, and to bestow on this clerico-military aristocracy, in its two shapes of Priesthood and Nobility, *two* separate and independent voices in Legislation. This double body, from its necessary dependence on the King, must necessarily have in both forms become the organ of his voice. The Monarch would thus possess *three* negatives, *one* avowed and disus-<257>ed, two latent and in perpetual activity on the *single* voice which impotent and illusive formality had yielded to the Third Estate. Such and much more must the Parliament of England become before it could in any respect resemble the division of the French Legislature, according to those ancient Orders which formed the Gothic assemblies of Europe. So monstrous did the arrangement appear, that even under the reign of Despotism, the second plan was proposed by M. Calonne*—that the Clergy and Nobility should form an Upper House, to

---

* See his Lettre au Roi 9th February 1789. [C. A. Calonne, *Lettre adressée au Roi, Par M. de Calonne, Le 9 Février 1789* (London: T. Spilsbury, 1789); Calonne, *De la France,* 167.] See also Sur l'Etat de France, &c. p. 167. It was also, as we are informed by M. Calonne, suggested in the *Cahiers* of the Nobility of *Metz* and *Montargis.* It is worthy of incidental remark, that the proposition of such radical changes even by the Nobility is an incontestible evidence of the general conviction that a revolution or total change

exercise conjointly with the King and the Commons the Legislative Authority. It admits, however, of the clearest proof, that <258> such a Constitution would have been diametrically opposite in its spirit and principles to the English Government. This will at once be evident from the different description of the body of Nobles in France and England. In England they are a small body, united to the mass of the people by innumerable points of contact, receiving from it perpetual new infusions, and returning to it, undistinguished and unprivileged, the majority of their children. In France they formed an immense insulated *cast,* separated from society by every barrier that prejudice or policy could raise, receiving few plebeian accessions, and precluded, by the indelible character of nobility, the equal patrimony of all their children, from the possibility of their most remote descendants being restored to the general mass. The Nobles of England are a *Senate* of 200. The Noblesse of France were a *tribe* of 200,000. Nobility is in England only hereditary, so far as its professed object, the sup-<259>port of a hereditary Senate demands. It is therefore descendible only to one heir. Nobility in France was as widely inheritable as its real purpose, the maintenance of a privileged *cast,* prescribed. It was therefore necessarily descendible to all male children.

There are other points of contrast still more important. The Noblesse of France were at once *formidable* from their immense body of *property,* and *dependent* from the indigence of their Patrician rabble of *cadets,* whom honour inspired with servility, and servility excluded from the path to independence. They in fact possessed so large a portion of the landed property, as to be justly, and almost exclusively considered as the landed interest of the kingdom. To this formidable property were added the revenues of the Church, monopolized by the Children. The younger branches of these opulent families had in general no patrimony but their honours and their sword. They <260> were therefore reduced to seek fortune and distinction in military dependence on the Crown. If they were generous, the habits of military service devoted them, from loyalty; if they were prudent, the hope of military promotion devoted them, from interest, to the King.—How

---

in the Government was necessary. It is therefore an unanswerable reply to Mr. Burke and M. Calonne.

immense therefore and irresistible would the Royal influence have been in elections, where the majority of the voters were the servants and creatures of the Crown? What would be thought in England of a House of Lords, which, while it represented or contained the whole landed interest of the kingdom, should necessarily have a majority of its members septennially or triennially *nominated* by the King. Yet it would still yield to the French Upper House of M. *Calonne;* for the monied and commercial interests of England, which would continue to be represented by the Commons, are important and formidable, but in France they are comparatively insignificant. It would have been a <261> Government where the Aristocracy could have been strong only against the people, impotent against the Crown. This second arrangement then is equally repugnant to the *theory* of the British Constitution as the first. There remains only some mode of selection of a body from amidst the Nobility and Clergy to form an Upper House, and to this there are insuperable objections. Had the right of thus forming a branch of the Legislature by a *single* act of prerogative been given to the King, it must have strengthened his influence to a degree terrible at any period, but fatal in the moment of political reform. Had any mode of election by the Provinces, or the Legislature, been adopted, or if they had been vested with any control on the nomination of the Crown, the new dignity would have been sought with an activity of corruption and intrigue, of which, in such a national convulsion, it is impossible to estimate the danger. No general principle of selection, such as that <262> of *opulence* or *antiquity,* would have remedied the evil, for the excluded and *degraded* Nobles would feel the principle, that nobility is the equal and inalienable patrimony of all. By the abolition of nobility, no nobleman was *degraded,* for to degrade is to lower from a rank that continues to exist in society. No man can be *degraded* when the *rank* he possessed no longer exists. But had the rank of nobility remained in the mode of which we have been speaking, the great body of the Nobles would indeed, in a proper and *penal* sense, have been degraded, the new dignity of their former Peers would have kept alive the memory of what they once possessed, and provoked them to enterprizes far more fatal than resentment of an indignity, that is at least broken by division, and impartially inflicted on the greatest and most obscure.

So evident indeed was the impossibility of what Mr. Burke supposes attainable with such <263> ease, that no party in the Assembly suggested the imitation of the English model, the system of his oracles in French politics.* M.M. Lally and Mounier, approached more near to the Constitution of the American States. They proposed a Senate to be chosen for life by the King, from a certain number of candidates to be offered to his choice by the provinces.† This Senate was to enjoy an absolute negative on legislative acts, and to form the great national court for the trial of public delinquents. In effect, such a body would have formed a far more vigorous Aristocracy than <264> the English Peerage. The latter body only preserves its dignity by a wise disuse of its power. *Potentia ad impotentiam abusi*[59] would otherwise be descriptive of their fate. But the Senate of M. Mounier would be an Aristocracy moderated and legalized, which, because it *appeared* to have less independence, would in fact be emboldened to exert more. Deriving their rights equally with the Lower House from the people, and vested with a more dignified and extensive trust, they would neither shrink from the conflict with the Commons nor the King. The permanence of their authority must give them a superiority over the former; the spe-

---

* "De quelle manière sera compose le Senat? Sera-t-il formé de ce qu'on appelle aujourd'hui la Noblesse & le Clergé? NON SANS DOUTE. Ce seroit perpetuer cette separation d'Ordres, cette esprit de corporation qui est le plus grand ennemi de l'esprit Public." *Pièces Justificatifs* de M. Lally Tolendahl, p. 121. ["In what fashion will the senate be composed? Will it be formed of that which one calls today the Nobility and the Clergy? WITHOUT DOUBT NO. This would perpetuate this separation of Orders, this spirit of corporation which is the greatest enemy of the Public spirit." Trophime-Gérard, marquis de Lally-Tolendal, "Sur la Déclaration des Droits," in *Pièces justificatives contenant différentes motions et opinions de M. le comte de Lally-Tolendal* (Paris, 1789), 121.]

† "Après avoir examiné & balancé tous les inconveniens de chaque parti peut-être trouvera-t-on que faire nommer les Senateurs par le Roi, sur la presentation des provinces, & ne les faire nommer qu'à vie seroit encore le moyen le plus propre à concilier tous les interêts." Id. p. 124. ["After having examined & weighed all the inconveniences of each part, perhaps one will find that the means most suited to reconciling all interests is to have the King name Senators, on the recommendations of the provinces, and to have them named only for life." Lally-Tolendal, "Sur la Déclaration des Droits," in *Pièces justificatives*, 124.]

59. This is an adaptation of Velleius Paterculus on Pompey: "potentia sua numquam aut raro ad impotentiam usus" (never, or at least rarely, abusing his power). Velleius Paterculus, *Compendium of Roman History*, trans. F. W. Shipley (London and Cambridge, Mass.: Heinemann and Harvard University Press, 1961), 112–13 (II.xxix.3–4).

ciousness of their cause over the latter: and it seems probable, that they must have terminated in subjugating both. Those who suppose that a Senate for life might not be infected by the corporation spirit, may consider the ancient judicatures of France, who were as keenly <265> actuated by that spirit, as any body of hereditary Nobles that ever existed.

But to quit the details of these systems—a question arises for our consideration of a more general and more difficult nature—*Whether a simple representative Legislature, or a Constitution of mutual control, be the best form of Government?**—To examine this question at length is inconsistent with the object and limits of the present publication (which already grows insensibly beyond its intended size) but a few general principles may be hinted, on which the decision of the question perhaps chiefly depends.

1. It will not be controverted, that the object of a representative Legislature is to col-<266>lect the general will. To accord with this principle, there must be the same unity in the *representative* as in the *original* WILL.— That will is ONE. It cannot therefore, without solecism, be *doubly* represented. The social body supposes a perfect unity, and no man's will can have TWO discordant organs. Any *absolute*† negative opposed to the national will, decisively spoken by its Representatives, is radically null, as an usurpation of popular sovereignty. Thus far does the abstract principle of a representative Government condemn the division of the Legislature.

2. All bodies possessed of effectual control have a tendency to that great evil, which all laws have hitherto fostered, though it be the end of Legislation to repress, the preponde-<267>rance of partial interests. The spirit of corporation infallibly seizes every Public body, and the creation of every new Assembly creates a new, dexterous, and vigilant enemy to the general interest. This alone is a sufficient objection to a controling Senate. Such a body would be most peculiarly accessible to this contagious spirit. A representative body itself can only be preserved from it by those frequent elec-

---

* This question, translated into familiar language, may perhaps be thus expressed,— *"Whether the vigilance of the master, or the squabbles of the* servants, *be the best security for faithful service?"*

† The *suspensive veto* vested in the French King is only an appeal to the people on the conduct of their Representatives. The voice of the people clearly spoken, the negative ceases.

tions which break combinations, and infuse into it new portions of popular sentiments. Let us grant that a popular assembly may sometimes be precipitated into unwise decision by the seductions of eloquence, or the rage of faction. Let us grant that a controling Senate might remedy this evil, but let us recollect, that it is better the *Public interest should be occasionally mistaken than systematically opposed.*

3. It is perhaps susceptible of proof, that these Governments of balance and control <268> have never existed but in the vision of theorists. The fairest example will be the Constitution of England. If it can be proved that the two members of the Legislature, who are pretended to control each other, are ruled by the same *class* of men, the control must be granted to be imaginary. That opposition of interest, which is supposed to preclude all conspiracy against the people, can no longer exist. That this is the state of England, the most superficial observation must evince. The great proprietors, titled and untitled, possess the whole force of both Houses of Parliament that is not immediately dependent on the Crown. The Peers have a great influence in the House of Commons. All political parties are formed by a confederacy of the members of both Houses. The Court party, by the influence of the Crown, acting equally in both, supported by a part of the independent Aristocracy. The opposition by the remainder of the Aristocracy, whether Commoners <269> or Lords. Here is every symptom of collusion: No vestige of control. The only case indeed, where it could arise, is where the interest of the Peerage is distinct from that of the other great proprietors. But these separate interests are few and paltry, and have established so feeble a check, that the history of England will not afford one undisputed example of this vaunted control.

The rejection of the Peerage Bill of George the First is urged with great triumph by De Lolme.[60] There it seems the Commons rejected the bill, purely actuated by their fears, that the Aristocracy would acquire a strength from a limitation on the number of Peers, destructive of that balance of

---

60. The Peerage Bill of 1719 attempted to limit the creation of new peers in order to ensure a permanent Whig majority. It was, however, defeated in the Commons. See Jean Louis de Lolme, *The Rise and Progress of the English Constitution,* 2 vols. (New York: Garland, 1978; facsimile of 1838 edition), 2:939, chap. 17, "The English Constitution."

power which forms the Constitution. It is unfortunate that political theorists do not consult the *history* as well as the *letter* of legislative proceedings. It is a matter of perfect notoriety, that the rejection of that bill was occasioned by the secession of <270> Sir Robert (then Mr.) Walpole from the Cabinet, and the opposition of him and his party to it was *merely* as a ministerial measure. The debate was not guided by any general legislative principles. It was simply an experiment on the strength of two parties contending for power. The reader will no doubt feel a high reverence for the Constitutional principles of that Parliament, when he is informed that to it we owe the *Septennial Act!*[61]

In fact, if such a check existed in much greater force, it would be of little importance to the general question. "Through a diversity of members and interests," if we may believe Mr. Burke, "GENERAL LIBERTY had as many securities as there were separate views in the several Orders."[62] And if by GENERAL LIBERTY be understood the power of the collective body of these Orders, the position is undeniable. But if it means, what it ought to mean, the liberty of mankind, <271> nothing can be more false. The higher class in society, whatever be their names, of Nobles, Bishops, Judges, or possessors of landed and commercial wealth, have ever been united by a common view, far more powerful than those petty repugnancies of interest to which this variety of description may give rise. Whatever may be the little conflicts of ecclesiastical with secular, of commercial with landed opulence, they have one common interest to preserve, the elevated place to which the social order has raised them. There never was, or will be, in civilized society, but two grand interests, that of the RICH and that of the POOR. The differences of interest among the several classes of the rich will be ever too slender to preclude their conspiracy against mankind. In the mean time, the privileges of their several ORDERS will be guarded, and Mr. Burke will decide that GENERAL LIBERTY is secure!—It is thus that a Polish Palatine harangues in the Diet on the liberty of Poland, <272> without a blush at the recollection of his bondsmen.—It is thus that the Assembly of Jamaica,

---

61. The Septennial Act of 1716 extended the full lifetime of a parliament from three to seven years.

62. Burke, *Reflections,* 124.

amidst the slavery and sale of MEN, profanely appeal to the principles of freedom. It is thus that Antiquity, with her pretended political philosophy, cannot boast one philosopher who questioned the justice of servitude, nor with all her pretended public virtue, one philanthropist who deplored the misery of slaves.

One circumstance more remains concerning the Legislature—the exclusion of the King's Ministers from seats in it. This *self-denying Ordinance* I must unequivocally disapprove.—I regard all *disfranchisement* as equally unjust in its principle, destructive in its example, and impotent for its pretended purpose. The presence of Ministers in the Assembly would have been of great utility in a view of business, and perhaps, by giving publicity to their opinions, favorable on the whole to Public <273> Liberty. To exclude them from the Legislature, is to devote them to the purposes of the Crown, by giving them no *interest* in the Constitution. The fair and open influence of Ministers was never formidable. It is only that indirect and secret influence which this exclusion will perhaps enable them to practise with more impunity and success. It is also to be observed, that it is equivalent to an exclusion of all men of superior talent from the Cabinet. The object of liberal ambition will be a seat in the Supreme Assembly; and no man of genius will accept, much less pursue, branded and degraded offices, which banish him from the natural sphere of his powers.

Of the PLAN of JUDICATURE formed by the Assembly, I have not yet presumed to form a decided opinion. It certainly approaches to an experiment, whether a code of laws can be formed sufficiently simple and intelligible to supercede the necessity of lawyers <274> by profession.* Of all the attempts of the Assembly, the complicated relations of civilized society seem to render this the most problematical. They have not, however, concluded this part of their labours, and the feebleness attributed to the elective judicatures of the *Departments* may probably be remedied by the dignity and force with which they will invest the two high national tribunals

---

* The sexenial election of the Judges is strongly and ably opposed by M. Calonne, p. 294, chiefly on the principle, that the stability of judicial offices is the only inducement to men to devote their lives to legal study, which alone can form good magistrates.

(La Cour de Cassation & la Haute Cour Nationale) which they are about to organize.*

On the subject of the EXECUTIVE MAGISTRACY, there is a preliminary remark, which the advocates as well as the enemies <275> of the Revolution have too much neglected. The Assembly have been accused of violating their own principles by the assumption of executive powers, and their advocates have pleaded guilty to the charge. It has been forgotten that they had a double function to perform. They were not only to erect a new Constitution, but they were to guard it from destruction. Hence a necessary assumption of executive powers in the crisis of a Revolution. Had superstitious tenderness for the principle confined them to theoretical erections, which the breath of power was every day destroying, they would indeed have merited those epithets of visionaries and enthusiasts with which they have been loaded. To judge, therefore, of the future executive magistracy of France by its present state, is absurd. We must not, as has been justly observed, mistake for the new political edifice what is only the scaffolding necessary to its erection. The powers of the first magistrate <276> are not to be estimated by the debility to which the convulsions of the moment have reduced them, but by the provisions of the future Constitution.

The portion of power with which the King of France is invested, is certainly as much as pure theory demands for the executive magistrate. An organ to collect the Public will, and a hand to execute it, are the only necessary constituents of the social union. The popular representative forms the first; the executive officer the second. To the point where this principle would have conducted them, the French have not ventured to proceed. It has been asserted by Mr. Burke, that the French King has no negative on laws. This, however, is not true. The minority who opposed any species of negative in the Crown was only 100, when 800 members were present in the Assembly. The King possesses the power of with-holding his <277> assent to a proposed law for *two* successive Assemblies. If it is proposed by the *third,* his assent, indeed, becomes necessary. This species of suspensive

* I have on this subject read with much pleasure and instruction the profound and ingenious, though perhaps occasionally paradoxical, remarks of Mr. BENTHAM. [Jeremy Bentham, *Draught of a Code for the Organization of the Judicial Establishment [in France]* (London, 1791).]

veto is with great speciousness and ingenuity contended by M. Necker to be more efficient than the obsolete negative of the English Princes.* A mild and limited negative may, he remarked, be exercised without danger or odium, while a prerogative, like the absolute *veto,* must sink into impotence from its invidious magnitude. It is too *great* to be exercised, and must, as it has in England, be tacitly abandoned by disuse. Is not that negative really efficient, which is only to yield to the national voice, spoken after four years deliberation, and in two successive elections of Representatives? What Monarch of a free State, I will be bold to ask, could with decency or impunity oppose a negative the most unlimited in law to <278> the public sentiment, thus explicitly and constantly expressed? The most absolute *veto* must, if the people persist, prove eventually suspensive. A suspensive *veto* is therefore equivalent to an absolute one, and being of less invidious exercise, confers more real power. "The power of remonstrance,"† says Mr. Burke, "which was anciently vested in the Parliament of Paris, is now absurdly entrusted to the executive magistrate."[63] One might have supposed that this was a power of remonstrance like that of the Parliament of Paris to the *Legislature.* It is however, as we have seen, a power of a very different <279> description, a power of remonstrating to the people against their Representatives, the only share in legislation (whether it be nominally *absolute,* or nominally *limited*) that a free Government can entrust to its supreme magistrate.‡

---

* Rapport fait au Roi dans son Conseil, par le premier Ministre des Finances, à Versailles, le 11 Sept. 1789. [Jacques Necker, "Rapport fait au Roi dans son Conseil, par le premier Ministre des Finances, à Versailles, le 11 septembre 1789," in *Oeuvres Complètes,* 15 vols. (Paris, 1821; repr. Aalen: Scientia Verlag, 1971), 7:58–61.]

† The *negative* possessed by the King of France is precisely *double* of that which is entrusted to the Assembly. He may oppose his will to that of his whole people for *four years* or the term of two Legislatures, while the opposition of the Assembly to the general voice can only exist for *two years,* when a new election annihilates them. So inconsiderately has this prerogative been represented as nominal. The whole of this argument is in some measure *ad hominem,* for I myself am dubious about the utility of any species of Royal *veto,* absolute or suspensive.

‡ P. 315.

63. Burke, *Reflections,* 319.

On the Prerogative of WAR and PEACE, Mr. Burke* has shortly, and M. Calonne† at great length, arraigned the system of the Assembly.

In the Constitution of France, war is to be declared by a decree of the Legislature, on the proposition of the King. He possesses exclusively the *initiative*. It cannot originate with any member of the Legislature. The first remark suggested by this arrangement is, that the difference between it and the *theory* of the English Constitution is purely nominal. <280> That *theory* supposes an independent House of Commons, a rigorous responsibility, and an EFFECTIVE power of impeachment. Were these in any respect realized, it is perfectly obvious, that a decision for war must in every case depend on the deliberation of the Legislature. No Minister would hazard hostilities without the sanction of a body who held a sword suspended over his head; and, as this theory supposes the House of Commons perfectly uninfluenced by the Crown, the ultimate decision could in no respect depend on the executive magistrate, and no power remains to him but the *initiative*. The forms indeed, in the majority of cases, aim at a semblance of the theory. A Royal message announces imminent hostilities, and a Parliamentary address of promised support, re-echoes the message. It is this address alone which emboldens and authorizes the Cabinet to proceed in their measures. The Royal message corresponds to the French *initiative;* <281> and if the purity of our practice bore any proportion to the speciousness of our theory, the address would be a *decree* of the Legislature, adopting the proposition of the King. No man therefore, who is a sincere and enlightened admirer of the English Constitution, *as it ought, and is pretended to exist,* can consistently reprobate an arrangement which differs from it only in the most frivolous circumstances. To speak of our practical Government would be an outrage on common sense. There no trace of those discordant powers which are supposed in our theoretical Constitution remains. The most beautiful simplicity prevails. The same influence determines the executive and legislative power. The same Cabinet makes war in the name of the King, and sanctions it in the name of the Parliament. But France, destitute of the cement which united these jarring powers, was

---

* Burke, p. 313.
† Calonne, p. 170–200.

reduced to imitate our theory instead of our practice. Her Exchequer was
<282> ruined. She could not, therefore, adopt this admirable system.

Supposing however, but not granting, that this formidable prerogative
was more abridged in France than it is by the *theory* of our Government,
the expediency of the limitation remains to be considered. The chief objections are its tendency to favour the growth of foreign factions, and to
derogate from the promptitude so necessary to military success. To both
these objections there is one general answer. They proceed on the supposition of the frequency of wars. They both suppose, that France will retain
part of that political system which she has disclaimed. But if she adheres
with good faith to her declarations, war must become to her so rare an
occurrence, that the objections become insignificant. Foreign Powers have
no temptation to purchase factions in a State which does not interpose in
foreign politics; and a wise nation, which re-<283>gards victorious war as
not less fatally intoxicating to the victors, than widely destructive to the
vanquished, will not surrender their probability of peace from the dread
of defeat, nor purchase the hope of victory by provisions for facilitating
war. France, after having renounced for ever the idea of conquest, can, indeed, have no source of probable hostility but her colonies. Colonial possessions have been so unanswerably demonstrated to be commercially useless, and politically ruinous, that the conviction of philosophers cannot
fail of having, in due time, its effect on the minds of enlightened Europe,
and delivering the French Empire from this cumbrous and destructive
appendage.

But even were the exploded villainy that has obtained the name of politics to be readopted in France, the objections would still be feeble. The first,
which must be confessed to have a specious and formidable air, <284>
seems evidently to be founded on the history of Sweden and Poland, and
on some facts in that of the Dutch Republic. It is a remarkable example of
those loose and remote analogies by which sophists corrupt and abuse history. Peculiar circumstances in the situation of these States disposed them
to be the seat of foreign factions. It did not arise from war being decided
by public bodies, for if it had, it must have existed in ancient Rome and
Carthage—in modern Venice, and Switzerland—in the republican Parliament of England, and in the Congress of the United States of America.—

Holland too, in her better and more vigorous days, was perfectly exempt from this evil.—No traces of it appear in her history till the age of Charles II. and Louis XIV. when, divided between jealousy of the commerce of England and dread of the conquests of France, she threw herself into the arms of the House of Orange, and forced the partizans of freedom into a <285> reliance on French support. In more recent periods, domestic convulsions have more fatally displayed her debility, and too clearly evinced, that of that splendor which she gained from the ignorant indolence of the world, she now only retains the shadow, by the indulgence and courtesy of Europe. The case of Sweden is with the utmost facility explicable. An indigent and martial people, whether it be governed by one or many despots, will ever be sold by its tyrants to the enterprizes of opulent ambition; and recent facts have proved, that a change in the Government of Sweden has not changed the *stipendiary* spirit of its military system. Poland is an example still less relevant. There an independent anarchy of despots naturally *league* themselves variously with foreign Powers. Yet Russian force has done more than Russian gold; and Poland has suffered still more from feebleness than venality. No analogy can be supposed to exist between these <286> cases and that of France. I hazard the issue of the discussion on one plain point. All the Powers of Europe could not expend money enough to form and *maintain* a faction in their interest in France. Let us suppose it possible that the Legislature of this vast and opulent kingdom could *once* be corrupted; but let us recollect, that a series of Legislatures, collected by the most extensively popular election, are to be in succession purchased, to obtain any permanent ascendant, and it will be evident, that *Potosi* would be unequal to the attempt. If we consider that their deliberations are conducted under the detecting eye of a vigilant and enlightened people, the growth of foreign factions will appear still more chimerical. All the States which have been quoted were poor, therefore cheaply corrupted; their Government was an Aristocracy, and was therefore only to be *once* bought; the people were ignorant, and could therefore be sold by their Governors with impunity. The reverse of <287> these circumstances will save France, as they have saved England, from this "worst of evils."[64] Their wealth makes

64. Burke, *Reflections*, 192.

the attempt difficult; their discernment makes it hazardous; their short trust of power renders the object worthless, and its permanence impossible. That subjecting the decision of war to the deliberations of a popular assembly will, in a great measure, derogate from its energy, and unnerve it for all destructive purposes, I am not disposed to deny. France must, however, when her constitution is cemented, be, in a *defensive* view, invincible; and if her Government is unfitted for aggression, it is little wonder that the Assembly should have made no provision for a case which their principles do not suppose.

This is the last important arrangement respecting the executive power which Mr. Burke has considered, and it conducts us to a subject of infinite delicacy and difficulty, which <288> has afforded no small triumph to the enemies of the Revolution—The ORGANIZATION OF THE ARMY. It must be confessed, that to conciliate an army of a hundred and fifty thousand men, a navy of a hundred ships of the line, and a frontier guarded by a hundred fortresses, with the existence of a free Government, is a tremendous problem. It cannot be denied, that history affords no example in which such a Public force has not recoiled on the State, and become the ready instrument of military usurpation. And if the State of France were not perfectly unexampled, and to which these historical arguments are not therefore applicable or pertinent, the inference would be inevitable. An army, with the sentiments and habits which it is the system of modern Europe to inspire, is not only hostile to freedom, but incompatible with it. A body of men possessed of the whole force of a State, and systematically divested of every civic sentiment, is a monster that no <289> rational polity can tolerate, and every circumstance clearly shews it to be the object of French legislation to destroy it, not *as a body of armed citizens*—but as an ARMY. This is wisely and gradually to be effected. Two grand operations conduct to it—arming the people, and *unsoldiering* the army.* The first of these measures, the formation of the municipal army, certainly makes the nation independent of its military servants. An army of four millions can

---

* To use the language of M. Calonne, *"armant le peuple & popularisant l'armée."* ["Arming the people and popularizing the army." Quotation not found in C. A. Calonne, *De l'état de la France, présent et à venir, par M. de Calonne ministre d'état* (Londres: T. Spilsbury & fils, 1790).]

never be coerced by one of a hundred and fifty thousand; neither can they have a separate sentiment from the body of the nation, for they are the same. Whence the horror of Mr. Burke at thus arming the *nation,* under the title of a *municipal army,* has arisen, it is even difficult to conjecture. Has it ceased to be true, that the defence of a free State is only to be committed to its citizens? Are the long opposition to a standing <290> army in England, its tardy and jealous admission, and the perpetual clamor (at length illusively gratified) for a militia, to be exploded, as the gross and uncourtly sentiments of our unenlightened ancestors? The Assembly have put arms into the hands of the citizens, and by that means have for ever precluded both their own despotism and the usurpation of the army. "They must rule," says Mr. Burke, "by an army."[65] If that be their system, their policy is still more wretched than he has represented it. For they systematically strengthen those who are to be governed, while they systematically enfeeble their engine of Government. They fortify the people, and weaken the army. They reduce themselves and their army to dependence on the nation, whom alone they strengthen and arm. A *Military Democracy,* if it means a deliberative body of soldiers, is the most execrable of tyrannies; but if it be understood to denote a popular Government, where every citizen <291> is disciplined and armed, it must then be pronounced to be the only free Government which retains within itself the means of preservation.

The professed soldiers, rendered impotent to any dangerous purpose by the strength of the municipal army, are by many other circumstances invited to throw off those abject and murderous habits which form the perfection of a modern soldier. In other States the soldiery were in general disfranchised. They were too poor to be citizens. But in France a great part may enjoy the full rights of citizens. They are not then likely to sacrifice their superior to their inferior capacity, nor to elevate their military importance by committing political suicide. They feel themselves servile as soldiers, they are conscious of being sovereign as citizens. That diffusion of political knowledge among them, which is ridiculed and reprobated by Mr. <292> Burke, is the only remedy that could have fortified them against

65. Burke, *Reflections,* 334.

the seduction of an aspiring Commander. That alone will teach them, that in lending themselves to his views, they submit themselves to his yoke; that to destroy the liberty of others, they must sacrifice their own. They have, indeed, gigantic strength, and they may crush their fellow citizens, by dragging down the social edifice, but they must themselves be overwhelmed by its fall. THE DESPOTISM OF ARMIES IS THE SLAVERY OF SOLDIERS. An army cannot be strong enough to tyrannize, that is not itself cemented by the most absolute *interior* tyranny. The diffusion of these great truths will perpetuate, as they have produced, a revolution in the character of the French soldiery. They will therefore, in the sense of despotic disciplinarians, cease to be an army; and while the soldiers assume the sentiments of citizens, and the citizens acquire the discipline of soldiers, the military character will be diffused, and the military profession an-<293>nihilated. Military services will be the *duty* of all citizens, and the *trade* of none.* To this object their system evidently and inevitably tends. If a separate body of citizens, as an army, is deemed necessary, it will probably be formed by rotation. A certain period of military service will be exacted from every citizen, and may, as in ancient Republics, be made a necessary qualification for the pursuit of civil honors. In the present state of France, the national guard is a sufficient bulwark against the enemy, should it relapse into its ancient habits; and in its future state, no body susceptible of such dangerous habits <294> seems likely to exist. *"Gallos quoque in bellis floruisse audivimus,"*[66] may indeed be the sentiment of our children. The glory of

---

* Again I must encounter the derision of Mr. Burke, by quoting the ill-fated citizen of Geneva, whose life was embittered by the cold friendship of a Philosopher, and whose memory is proscribed by the alarmed enthusiasm of an orator. I shall presume to recommend to the perusal of every reader his tract entitled, *"Considerations sur le Gouvernement de Pologne, &c."* more especially what regards the military system. *Oeuvres de Rousseau, Geneve,* 1782, tome ii. p. 381–397. [Rousseau, "Considerations sur le Gouvernement de Poland," in *Oeuvres de Rousseau* (Genève, 1782), 2:381–97. For a recent English translation see Rousseau, *The Social Contract and Other Later Political Writings,* ed. V. Gourevitch (Cambridge: Cambridge University Press, 1997), 177–260.] It may be proper to remark, that my other citations from Rousseau are from the same edition.

66. "The Gauls also, according to history, once shone in war." The immediate source is Edmund Burke, *Substance of the Speech of the Right Honourable Edmund Burke, in the Debate on the Army Estimates, in the House of Commons, on Tuesday the 9th Day of February, 1790* (London: Debrett, 1790), 5. The text comes from Tacitus, *Agricola,* in *Dia-*

heroism, and the splendor of conquest, have long enough been the patrimony of that great nation. It is time that it should seek a new glory, and a new splendor, under the shade of freedom, in cultivating the arts of peace, and extending the happiness of mankind.—Happy if the example of that "Manifesto of Humanity"[67] which has been adopted by the Legislators of France into their constitutional code, made an adequate impression on surrounding nations.

> Tume genus humanum positis sibi consulat armis
> Inque vicem gens omnis amet.—[68] <295>

---

logus, Agricola, Germania, trans. W. Peterson (London and New York: Heinemann and G. P. Putnam's Sons, 1920), 188–89 (§11).

67. This is a reference to the Declaration of the Rights of Man and of the Citizen proclaimed by the National Assembly on August 26, 1789.

68. "In that day let mankind lay down their arms and seek their own welfare, and let all nations love one another." Lucan, "The Civil War," in *Lucan,* trans. J. D. Duff (London and New York: Heinemann and G. P. Putnam's Sons, 1928), 6–7 (bk. 1, lines 60–61). This quotation was also used as the epigraph to J. J. Rousseau, *Jugement sur le projet de paix perpétuelle de L'Abbé de Saint Pierre.*

English Admirers vindicated.

It is thus that Mr. Burke has spoken of the men and measures of a foreign nation, where patriotism could neither excuse his prepossession nor asperity; where no duty nor feeling ought to preclude him from adopting the feelings of disinterested posterity, and assuming the dispassionate tone of a philosopher and a historian. What wonder then that he should wanton still less temperately in all the eloquence and virulence of an advocate against fellow-citizens, to whom he attributes the flagitious purpose of stimulating England to the imitation of such enormities. The Revolution and Constitutional Societies, and Dr. Price, whom he regards as their oracle and guide, are the grand objects of his hostility. <296> For them no contumely is too debasing, no invective is too intemperate, no imputation too foul. Joy at the downfall of despotism is the indelible crime, for which no virtue can compensate, and no punishment can atone. An inconsistency however betrays itself not unfrequently in literary quarrels. He affects to despise those whom he appears to dread. His anger exalts those whom his ridicule would vilify; and on those whom at one moment he derides as too contemptible for resentment, he at another confers a criminal eminence, as too audacious for contempt. Their voice is now the importunate chink of the meagre shrivelled insects of the hour, now the hollow murmur, ominous of convulsions and earthquakes, that are to lay the fabric of society in ruins. To provoke against the doctrines and persons of these unfortunate Societies this storm of execration and derision, it was not sufficient that the French Revolution should be traduced, every record of English policy and law is to be distorted. <297>

The Revolution of 1688 is confessed to have established principles by those who lament that it has not reformed institutions. It has sanctified the theory, if it has not insured the practice of a free Government. It declared, by a memorable precedent, the right of the people of England to revoke abused power, to frame the Government, and bestow the Crown. There was a time, indeed, when some wretched followers of Filmer and Blackwood lifted their heads in opposition. But more than half a century had withdrawn them from public contempt to the amnesty and oblivion which their innoxious stupidity had purchased.

It was reserved for the latter end of the eighteenth century to construe these innocent and obvious inferences into libels on the Constitution and the laws. Dr. Price had asserted (I presume without fear of contradiction) that the House of Hanover owes the Crown <298> of England to the choice of their people, that the Revolution has established our right "to choose our own Governors, to cashier them for misconduct, and to Frame a Government for ourselves."[69] The first proposition, says Mr. Burke, is either false or nugatory. If it imports that England is an elective Monarchy, "it is an unfounded, dangerous, illegal, and unconstitutional position."* If it alludes to the election of his Majesty's ancestors to the Throne, it no more legalizes the Government of England than that of other nations, where the founders of dynasties have generally founded their claims on some sort of election. The first member of this dilemma merits no reply. The people may certainly, as they have done, *chuse* hereditary rather than elective Monarchy. They may *elect* a race instead of an individual. Their *right* is in all these cases equally unimpaired. <299> It will be in vain to compare the pretended elections in which a council of Barons, or an army of mercenaries, have imposed usurpers on enslaved and benighted kingdoms, with the solemn, deliberate, national *choice* of 1688. It is, indeed, often expedient to sanction these deficient titles by subsequent acquiescence. It is not among the projected innovations of France to revive the claims of any of the posterity of Paramond and Clovis, nor to arraign the usurpations of Pepin or Hugh Capet. Public tranquility thus demands a

* Page 100, p. 101.
69. Richard Price, "A Discourse on the Love of our Country," in *Political Writings*, ed. D. O. Thomas (Cambridge: Cambridge University Press, 1991), 190.

veil to be drawn over the successful crimes through which Kings have so often waded to the Throne. But wherefore should we not exult, that the Supreme Magistracy of England is free from this blot; that as a *direct* emanation from the sovereignty of the people, it is as legitimate in its origin as in its administration. Thus understood, the position of Dr. Price is neither false nor nugatory. It is not nugatory, for it honourably distinguishes the English Monarchy among the <300> Governments of the world; and if it be false, the whole history of our Revolution must be a legend. The fact was shortly, that the Prince of Orange was elected King of England, in contempt of the claims, not only of the exiled Monarch and his son, but of the Princesses Mary and Anne, the undisputed progeny of James II. The title of William III. was then clearly not *succession;* and the House of Commons ordered Dr. Burnet's tract to be burnt by the hands of the hangman for maintaining that it was *conquest.* [70] There remains only *election,* for these three claims to Royalty are all that are known among men. It is futile to urge, that the Convention deviated only *slenderly* from the order of succession. The deviation was indeed slight, but it destroyed the principle, and established the right to deviate, the point at issue. The principle that justified the elevation of William III. and the preference of the posterity of Sophia of Hanover to those of Henrietta of Orleans, would <301> equally, *in point of right,* have vindicated the election of Chancellor Jefferies or Colonel Kirk. The *choice* was, like every other choice, to be guided by views of policy and prudence, but it was a choice still.

From these views arose that repugnance between the conduct and the language of the Revolutionists, of which Mr. Burke has availed himself. Their conduct was manly and systematic. Their language was conciliating and equivocal. They kept measures with prejudice which they deemed necessary to the order of society. They imposed on the grossness of the popular understanding, by a sort of compromise between the Constitution and the abdicated family. "They drew a politic, well-wrought veil,"[71] to use the expressions of Mr. Burke, over the glorious scene which they had acted. They affected to preserve a semblance of succession, to recur for the objects of

70. Bishop Gilbert Burnet's pastoral letters urging the taking of the oath of allegiance to William and Mary in 1689 were burned by the public hangman in 1692.

71. Edmund Burke, *Reflections on the Revolution in France,* vol. 2 of *Select Works of Edmund Burke,* 3 vols. (Indianapolis: Liberty Fund, 1999), 105.

their election to the posterity <302> of Charles and James, that respect and loyalty might with less violence to public sentiment attach to the new Sovereign. Had a Jacobite been permitted freedom of speech in the Parliaments of William III. he might thus have arraigned the Act of Settlement—"Is the language of your statutes to be at eternal war with truth?—Not long ago you profaned the forms of devotion by a thanksgiving, which either means nothing, or insinuates a lie. You thanked Heaven for the preservation of a King and Queen on the *Throne of their ancestors;* an expression which either was singly meant of their descent, which was frivolous, or insinuated their hereditary right, which was false.—With the same contempt for consistency and truth, we are this day called on to settle the Crown of England on a Princess of Germany, 'because' she is the granddaughter of James the First. If that be, as the phraseology insinuates, the *true* and <303> *sole* reason of the choice, consistency demands that the words after 'excellent' should be omitted, and in their place be inserted 'Victor Amadeus, Duke of Savoy, married to the daughter of the most excellent Princess Henrietta, late Duchess of Orleans, daughter of our late Sovereign Lord Charles I. of glorious memory.'—Do homage to loyalty in your actions, or abjure it in your words—avow the grounds of your conduct, and your manliness will be respected by those who detest your rebellion." What reply Lord Somers, or Mr. Burke, could have devised to this Philippic, I know not, unless they confessed that the authors of the Revolution had one language for novices and another for adepts. Whether this conduct was the fruit of caution and consummate wisdom, or of a narrow, arrogant, and dastardly policy, which regarded the human race as only to be governed by being duped, it is useless to en-<304>quire, and might be presumptuous to determine. But it certainly was not to be expected, that any controversy should have arisen by confounding their *principles* with their *pretexts.* With the latter the position of Dr. Price has no connexion; from the former, it is an infallible inference.

The next doctrine of this obnoxious sermon that provokes the indignation of Mr. Burke is, that the Revolution has established "our right to cashier our Governors for misconduct."[72] Here a plain man could have foreseen scarcely any diversity of opinion. To contend that the deposition of

---

72. Ibid., 102. Compare Price, "A Discourse on the Love of Our Country," 190.

a King for the abuse of his powers did not establish a principle in favour
of the like deposition, when the like abuse should again occur, is certainly
one of the most arduous enterprizes that ever the heroism of paradox en-
countered. He has, however, not neglected the means of retreat. "No Government," he tells us, <305> "could stand a moment, if it could be blown
down with any thing so loose and indefinite as opinion of *misconduct*."[73]
One might suppose, from the dexterous levity with which the word misconduct is introduced, that the partizans of Democracy had maintained
the expediency of deposing Kings for every frivolous and venial fault, of
revolting against a Monarch for the choice of his titled or untitled valets,
for removing his footmen, or his Lords of the Bedchamber. It would have
been candid in Mr. Burke not to have dissembled what he must know, that
by *misconduct* was meant that precise species of misconduct for which
James II. was dethroned—A CONSPIRACY AGAINST THE LIBERTY OF HIS
COUNTRY.

Nothing can be more weak than to urge the *Constitutional irresponsibility*
of Kings or Parliaments. The law can never suppose them responsible, because their responsibility supposes the dissolution of society, which is
<306> the annihilation of law. In the Governments which have hitherto
existed, the power of the magistrate is the only article in the social compact.
Destroy it, and society is dissolved. A legal provision for the responsibility
of Kings would infer, that the authority of laws could co-exist with their
destruction. It is because they cannot be legally and constitutionally, that
they must be morally and rationally responsible. It is because there are no
remedies to be found within the pale of society, that we are to seek them
in nature, and throw our parchment chains in the face of our oppressors.
No man can deduce a precedent of *law* from the Revolution, for law cannot
exist in the dissolution of Government. A precedent of reason and justice
only can be established on it; and perhaps the friends of freedom merit the
misrepresentation with which they have been opposed, for trusting their
cause to such frail and frivolous auxiliaries, and for seeking in the profligate
<307> practices of men what is to be found in the sacred rights of Nature.
The system of lawyers is indeed widely different. They can only appeal to

73. Burke, *Reflections*, 115.

usage, precedents, authorities, and statutes. They display their elaborate frivolity, their perfidious friendship, in disgracing freedom with the fantastic honor of a pedigree. A pleader at the Old Bailey, who would attempt to aggravate the guilt of a robber, or a murderer, by proving that King John, or King Alfred, punished robbery and murder, would only provoke derision. A man who should pretend that the reason why we had right to property is, because our ancestors enjoyed that right 400 years ago, would be justly contemned. Yet so little is plain sense heard in the mysterious nonsense which is the cloak of political fraud, that the Cokes, the Blackstones, and Burkes, speak as if our right to freedom depended on its possession by our ancestors. In the common cases of morality we would blush at such an absurdity. No <308> man would justify murder by its antiquity, or stigmatize benevolence for being new. The genealogist who should emblazon the one as coeval with Cain, or stigmatize the other as upstart with Howard, would be disclaimed even by the most frantic partizan of Aristocracy. This Gothic transfer of *genealogy* to truth and justice is peculiar to politics. The existence of robbery in one age makes its vindication in the next; and the champions of freedom have abandoned the strong hold of right for precedent, which, when the most favorable, is, as might be expected from the ages which furnish it, feeble, fluctuating, partial, and equivocal. It is not because we *have* been free, but because we have a right to be free, that we ought to demand freedom. Justice and liberty have neither birth nor race, youth nor age. It would be the same absurdity to assert, that we have a right to freedom, because the Englishmen of Alfred's reign were free, as that three and three are six, <309> *because* they were so in the camp of Genghis Khan. Let us hear no more of this ignoble and ignominious pedigree of freedom. Let us hear no more of her Saxon, Danish, or Norman ancestors. Let the immortal daughter of Reason, of Justice, and of God, be no longer confounded with the spurious abortions that have usurped her name.

But, says Mr. Burke, we do not contend that right as created by antiquarian research. We are far from contending that possession legitimates tyranny, or that fact ought to be confounded with right. But, (to strip Mr. Burke's eulogies on English wisdom of their declamatory appendage) the impression of antiquity endears and ennobles freedom, and fortifies it by rendering it august and venerable in the popular mind. The illusion is useful. The expediency of *political imposture* is the whole force of the argument. A principle odious and suspected to the friends of <310> freedom, as the grand bulwark of secular and spiritual despotism in the world. To pronounce that men are only to be governed by delusion is to libel the human understanding, and to consecrate the frauds that have elevated Despots and Muftis, Pontiffs and Sultans, on the ruin of degraded and oppressed humanity. But the doctrine is as false as it is odious. Primary political truths are few and simple. It is easy to make them understood, and to transfer to Government the same enlightened self-interest that presides in the other concerns of life. It may be made to be respected, not because it is ancient, or because it is sacred, not because it has been established by Barons, or applauded by Priests, but because it is useful. Men may easily be instructed to maintain rights which it is their *interest* to maintain, and duties which it is their *interest* to perform. This is the only principle of authority that does not violate justice and insult humanity. It is also the only <311> one which can possess stability. The various fashions of prejudice and factitious sentiment which have been the basis of Governments, are short-lived things. The illusions of chivalry, and the illusions of superstition, which give splendor or sanctity to Government, are in their turn succeeded by new modes of opinion and new systems of manners. Reason alone, and natural sentiment, are the denizens of every nation, and the cotemporaries of every age. A conviction of the utility of Government affords the only stable and honorable security for obedience.

Our ancestors at the Revolution, it is true, were far from feeling the full force of these sublime truths; nor was the public mind of Europe, in the seventeenth century, sufficiently enlightened and matured for the grand enterprizes of legislation. The science which teaches the rights of man, the eloquence that kindles the spirit of freedom, had for ages <312> been buried with the other monuments of the wisdom and relics of the genius of antiquity. But the revival of letters first unlocked only to a few the sacred fountain. The necessary labors of criticism and lexicography occupied the earlier scholars, and some time elapsed before the spirit of antiquity was transfused into its admirers. The first man of that period who united elegant learning to original and masculine thought was Buchanan,* and he

* It is not a little remarkable, that Buchanan puts into the mouth of his antagonist,

too seems to have been the first scholar who caught from the ancients the noble flame of republican enthusiasm. This praise is merited by his neglected, though incomparable <313> tract, *De Jure Regni,* in which the principles of popular politics, and the maxims of a free Government, are delivered with a precision, and enforced with an energy, which no former age had equalled, and no succeeding has surpassed.[74] But the subsequent progress of the human mind was slow. The profound views of Harrington were derided as the ravings of a visionary; and who can wonder, that the frantic loyalty which depressed Paradise Lost, should involve in ignominy the eloquent apology of Milton* for the people of England <314> against a feeble and venal pedant. Sidney "by ancient learning, to the enlightened love of ancient freedom warmed,"[75] taught the principles which he had sealed with

---

MAITLAND, the same alarms for the downfall of literature that have been excited in the mind of Mr. Burke by the French Revolution. We can smile at such alarms on a retrospect of the literary history of Europe for the 17th of 18 centuries; and should our controversies reach the enlightened scholars of a future age, they will probably, with the same reason, smile at the alarms of Mr. Burke.

* "Pessime enim vel naturâ vel legibus comparatum foret si arguta servitus, libertas muta esset; & haberent tyranni qui pro se dicerent, non haberent qui tyrannos debellare possunt: Miserum esset si haec ipsa ratio quo utimur Dei munere non multo plura ad homines conservandos, liberandos, et *quantum natura fert* INTER SE AEQUANDOS quam ad opprimendos et sub UNIUS Imperio malè perdendos argumenta suppe ditaret. CAUSAM itaque PULCHERRIMAM hâc certè fiduciâ laeti aggrediamur; illinc fraudem, fallaciam, ignorantiam atque barbaeriem; hinc lucem, veritatem rationem et seculorum omnium studia atque doctrinam nobis cum stare."

Joannis Miltoni Defensio Populi Anglicani apud Opera,
tom. 2. p. 238. Ed. Lond. 1738.

["Nature and laws would be in ill case if slavery were eloquent and liberty mute; if tyrants should find defenders, and they that are potent to master and vanquish tyrants should find none. And it were deplorable indeed, if the reason mankind is endued withal, which is God's gift, should not furnish more arguments for men's preservation, for their deliverance, and, as much as the nature of the thing will bear, for their equality, than for their oppression and utter ruin under one man's dominion. Let me therefore enter upon this noble cause with cheerfulness grounded upon the assurance that on the other side are cheating, and trickery, and ignorance and outlandishness, and on my side the light of truth and reasons, and the practice and theory of the best historic ages." Milton, "The First Defence," in *The Works of John Milton,* ed. F. A. Patterson, 18 vols. (New York: Columbia University Press, 1931–40), 7:10–13.]

74. George Buchanan, *De jure regni apud Scotos. Or A dialogue, concerning the due priviledge of government in the kingdom of Scotland* (1579).

75. James Thompson, *The Seasons: Summer* (London: H. Jennings, 1779), 73 (lines 1520–21).

his blood; and Locke, whose praise is less that of being bold and original, than of being temperate, sound, lucid, and methodical, deserves the immortal honour of having systematized and rendered popular the doctrines of civil and religious liberty. In Ireland, Molyneux, the friend of Locke, produced the *"Case of Ireland,"* a production of which it is sufficient praise to say, that it was ordered to be burnt by a despotic Parliament;[76] and in Scotland, Andrew Fletcher, the scholar of Algernon Sidney, maintained the cause of his deserted country with the force of ancient eloquence, and the dignity of ancient virtue.

Such is a rapid enumeration of those who had before, or near the Revolution, contributed to the diffusion of political light. But <315> their number was small, their writings were unpopular, their dogmas were proscribed. The habits of reading had only then begun to reach the great body of mankind, whom the arrogance of rank and letters has ignominiously confounded under the denomination of the vulgar. Many causes too contributed to form a powerful Tory interest in England. The remnant of that Gothic sentiment, the extinction of which Mr. Burke so pathetically deplores, which engrafted loyalty on a point of honor in military attachment, formed one part, which may be called the *Toryism of Chivalry.* Doctrines of a divine right in Kings, which are now too much forgotten even for successful ridicule, were then supported and revered.—This may be called the *Toryism of Superstition.* And a third species arose from the great transfer of property into an upstart commercial interest, which drove the ancient gentry of England, for protection against its inroads, behind the Throne. This <316> may be called the *Toryism of Landed Aristocracy.** Religious prejudices, outrages on natural sentiments, which any artificial system is too

---

* Principle is respectable, even in its mistakes, and these Tories of the last century were a party of principle. There were accordingly among them men of the most elevated and untainted honor. Who will refuse that praise to Clarendon and Southampton, Ormond and Montrose?—But Toryism, as a party of principle, cannot now exist in England; for the principles on which we have seen it to be founded, exist no more. The Gothic sentiment is effaced, the superstition is exploded, and the landed and commercial interests are completely intermixed. The Toryism of the present day can only arise from an abject spirit or a corrupt heart.

76. William Molyneux, *The Case of Ireland's being bound by the Acts of Parliament of England* (1698).

feeble to withstand, and the stream of events which bore them along to extremities which no man could have foreseen, involved the Tories in the Revolution, and made it a truly national act.

But their repugnance to every shadow of innovation was invincible. Something the Whigs may be supposed to have conceded for the sake of conciliation, but few even of their <317> leaders, it is probable, had grand and liberal views. What indeed could have been expected from the delegates of a nation, in which, a few years before, the University of Oxford, representing the national learning and wisdom, had, in a solemn decree offered their congratulations to Sir George Mackenzie (infamous for the abuse of brilliancy and accomplishment to the most servile and profligate purposes) as having confuted the abominable doctrines of Buchanan and Milton, and demonstrated the divine rights of Kings to tyrannize and oppress mankind! It must be evident, that a people which could thus, by the organ of its most learned body, prostrate its reason before such execrable absurdities, was too *young* for legislation. Hence the absurd debates in the Convention about the palliative phrases of abdicate, desert, &c. which were better cut short by the Parliament of Scotland, when they used the correct and manly expression, that James II. had FOR-<318>FEITED THE THRONE. Hence we find the Revolutionists perpetually belying their political conduct by their legal phraseology.—Hence their impotent and illusive reforms.—Hence their neglect of foresight* in not providing bulwarks against the natural tendency of a disputed succession to accelerate most rapidly the progress of Royal influence, by rendering it necessary to strengthen so much the possessor of the Crown against the pretender to it, and thus partially sacrificing freedom to the very means of preserving it. <319>

But to elucidate the question more fully, "let us listen to the genuine

---

* This progress of Royal influence from a disputed succession has, in fact, most fatally taken place. The Protestant succession was the supposed means of preserving our liberties, and to that *means* the end has been most deplorably sacrificed. The Whigs, the sincere, though timid and partial friends of freedom, were forced to cling to the Throne as the anchor of liberty. To preserve it from utter shipwreck, they were forced to yield something to its protectors. Hence a national debt, a septennial Parliament, and a standing army. The avowed reason of the two last was Jacobitism. Hence the unnatural Coalition between Whiggism and Kings during the reigns of the two first Princes of the House of Hanover, which the pupillage of Leicester-house so totally broke.

oracles of Revolution policy";[77] not to the equivocal and palliative language of their statutes, but to the unrestrained effusion of sentiment in that memorable conference between the Lords and Commons, on Tuesday the 5th of February, 1688, which terminated in establishing the present Government of England. The Tories yielding to the torrent, in the *personal* exclusion of James II. resolved to embarrass the Whigs, by urging that the declaration of the abdication and vacancy of the Throne, was a change of the Government, *pro hac vice,*[78] into an elective Monarchy. The inference is irresistible, and it must be confessed, that though the Whigs were the better citizens, the Tories were the more correct logicians. It is in this conference that we see the Whig leaders compelled to disclose so much of those principles, which tenderness for prejudice, and reverence for usage, had influenced <320> them to dissemble. It is here that we shall discover sparks kindled in the collision of debate sufficient to enlighten the "politic gloom" in which they had enveloped their measures.

If there be any names venerable among the constitutional lawyers of England, they are those of Lord Somers and Mr. Serjeant Maynard. They were both conspicuous managers for the Commons in this conference, and the language of both will more than sanctify the inferences of Dr. Price, and the creed of the Revolution Society. My Lord Nottingham, who conducted the conference on the part of the Tories, in a manner most honorable to his dexterity and acuteness, demanded of the Managers for the Commons, "Whether they mean the Throne to be so *vacant* as to null the succession in the hereditary line, and so all the heirs to be cut off? which we (the Lords) say, will make the Crown *elective.*"[79] Maynard, whose argument al-<321>ways breathed much of the old republican spirit, replied with force and plainness, "It is not that the Commons do say the Crown of England is ALWAYS AND PERPETUALLY ELECTIVE, but it is necessary there be a supply where there is a defect." It is impossible to mistake the import of these words. Nothing can be more evident, than that by the mode

77. Burke, *Reflections,* 104.

78. "For this occasion"—An appointment for a particular occasion only.

79. *Parliamentary History of England from the Norman Conquest, in 1066, to the Year 1803,* 36 vols. (London: Hansard, 1806–20), vol. 5, *Comprising the Period from the Revolution, in 1688, to the Accession of Queen Anne, in 1702,* 72.

of *denying* that the Crown was ALWAYS AND PERPETUALLY ELECTIVE, he confesses that it was for the then exigency *elective*. In pursuance of his argument, he uses a comparison strongly illustrative of his belief in dogmas anathematized by Mr. Burke. "If two of us make a mutual agreement to help and defend each other from any one that should assault us in a journey, and he that is with me turns upon me, and breaks my head, he hath undoubtedly *abdicated* my assistance, and revoked."[80] Sentiments of the Kingly office, more irreverent and correct, are not to be <322> found in the most profane evangelist that disgraces the Democratic canon. It is not unworthy of incidental remark, that there were then persons who felt as great horror at novelties, which have since been universally received, as Mr. Burke now feels at the "rights of men."[81] The Earl of Clarendon, in his strictures on the speech of Mr. Somers, said, "I may say thus much in general, that this breaking the original contract is a language that has not long been used in this place; nor known in any of our law-books, or Public records. It is sprung up but as taken from some late authors, and those none of the best received!"[82]—This language one might have supposed to be that of Mr. Burke. It is not however his; it is that of a Jacobite Lord of the 17th century!

The Tories continued to perplex and intimidate the Whigs with idea of *election.*—Maynard again replies, "The word *elective* is none of the Commons word. The provi-<323>sion must be made, and if it be, that will not render the kingdom *perpetually* ELECTIVE."[83] If it were necessary to multiply citations to prove, that the Revolution was to all intents and purposes an *election,* we might hear Lord Nottingham, whose distinction is peculiarly applicable to the case before us. "If," says he, "you do once make it *elective,* I do not say you are always *bound* to go to *election,* but it is enough to make it so, if by that precedent there be a breach in the hereditary succession."[84] The reasoning of Sir Robert Howard, another of the Managers for the Commons, is bold and explicit. "My Lords, you will do well to consider; have you not yourselves limited the succession, and cut off some that might

80. Ibid., 5:72–73. *Revolted,* not *revoked,* in original.
81. Burke, *Reflections,* 150.
82. *Parliamentary History,* 5:76.
83. Ibid., 5:89.
84. Ibid., 5:92.

have a line of right? Have you not concurred with us in our vote, that it is inconsistent with our religion and our laws to have a Papist to reign over us? *Must* we not then come to an ELECTION, if the next heir be a Papist?"[85] The precise fact which followed.—But what <324> tends the most strongly to illustrate that contradiction between the *exoteric* and *esoteric* doctrine, the legal language, and the real principles, which forms the basis of this whole argument, is the avowal of Sir Richard Temple, another of the Managers for the Commons—"We are in as natural a capacity as any of our predecessors were to provide for a remedy in such exigencies as this."[86] Hence it followed infallibly, that their posterity to all generations *would be in the same "natural capacity,"* to provide remedy for exigencies. But let us hear their Statutes. There "the Lords Spiritual and Temporal, and Commons, do, in the name of all the people of England, most humbly *and faithfully submit themselves, their heirs and posterity, for ever,"* &c.[87] Here is the triumph of Mr. Burke—a solemn abdication and renunciation of right to change the Monarch or the Constitution! His triumph is increased by this statutory abolition of the rights of men <325> being copied from a similar profession of eternal allegiance made by the Parliament of Elizabeth!—It is difficult to conceive any thing more preposterous. In the very act of exercising a right which their ancestors had abdicated in their name, they abdicate the same right in the name of their posterity. To increase the ridicule of this legislative farce, they impose an *irrevocable* law on their posterity in the precise words of that law irrevocably imposed on them by their ancestors, at the moment when they are violating it. The Parliament of Elizabeth submit themselves and their posterity for ever. The Convention of 1688 spurn the submission for themselves, but re-enact it for their posterity. And after such a glaring inconsistency, this language of statutory adulation is seriously and triumphantly brought forward as "the *unerring oracles* of Revolution policy."[88] <326>

Thus evidently has it appeared, from the conduct and language of the

85. Ibid., 5:98.
86. Ibid., 5:99.
87. *The Statutes of the Realm. Printed by Command of His Majesty King George the Third,* 10 vols. (London, 1810–24; repr. 1963), 6:144, 1 William and Mary, session 2 C.2.
88. Burke, *Reflections,* 104.

leaders of the Revolution, that it was a *deposition* and an *election;* and that all language of a contrary tendency, which is to be found in their acts, arose from the remnant of their own prejudice, or from concession to the prejudice of others, or from the superficial and presumptuous policy of imposing august illusions on mankind. The same spirit regulated, the same prejudices impeded their progress in every department. "They acted," says Mr. Burke, "by their ancient States."[89] They did not—Were the Peers, and the members of a dissolved House of Commons, with the Lord-Mayor of London, &c. convoked by a summons from the Prince of Orange, the Parliament of England?—No. They were neither lawfully elected nor lawfully assembled. But they affected a semblance of a Parliament in their convention, and a semblance of hereditary right in their election. The subsequent <327> act of Parliament is nugatory; for as that Legislature derived its whole existence and authority from the Convention, it could not return more than it had received, and could not therefore *legalize* the acts of the body which created it. If they were not previously legal, the Parliament itself was without *legal* authority, and could, therefore, give no legal sanction. It is therefore without any view to a prior, or allusion to a subsequent Revolution, that Dr. Price, and the Revolution Society of London, think themselves entitled to conclude, that abused power is revocable, and corrupt Governments ought to be reformed. Of the first of these Revolutions, that in 1648, they may, perhaps, entertain different sentiments from Mr. Burke. They will confess that it was debased by the mixture of fanaticism; they may lament that history has so often prostituted her ungenerous suffrage to success, and that the Commonwealth was obscured and overwhelmed by the splendid pro-<328>fligacy of military usurpation. But they cannot arrogate the praise of having been the first to maintain, nor can Mr. Burke support his claim to have been the first who reprobated, *since that period,* the audacious heresy of popular politics. The prototype of Mr. Burke is not a less notorious personage than the predecessor he has assigned to Dr. Price. History has preserved fewer memorials of Hugh Peters than of Judge Jeffries. It was the fortune of that luminary and model of lawyers to sit in judgment on one of the fanatical apostles of Democracy. In the

89. Ibid., 109.

present ignominious obscurity of the sect in England, it may be necessary to mention that the name of this criminal was Algernon Sidney. He had, it is true, in his time acquired some renown: He was celebrated as the hero, and deplored as the martyr of freedom. But the learned magistrate was above this "epidemical fanaticism."[90] He inveighed against his pestilential dogmas in a spirit that deprives Mr. Burke's <329> invective against Dr. Price of all pretensions to originality. An unvarnished statement will so well evince the harmony both of the culprits and the accusers, that remark is superfluous—

ALGERNON SIDNEY (*Indictment against him.*)	DOCTOR PRICE *His Sermon.*
"And that the aforesaid Algernon Sidney did make, compose and write, or cause to be made, composed and written, a certain false, scandalous and seditious libel, in which is contained the following English words— *The Power originally in the people is delegated to the Parliament*—He (meaning the King) is subject to the laws of God, as he is a man, and to the people that made him a King, inasmuch as he is a King." And in another place of the said libel he says, "We may therefore take away Kings without breaking any yoke, or that is made a yoke, which ought not to be one, and the injury therefore is making or imposing, and there can be none in breaking it," &c.[91]	"We have a right to chuse our own Governors, to cashier them for misconduct, and to frame a Government for ourselves."[92] <330>

90. Ibid., 257.

91. Algernon Sidney, *Discourses Concerning Government* (Indianapolis: Liberty Fund, 1996), 313, 314; and see "Trial of Algernon Sidney for High Treason," in *A Complete Collection of State Trials, and Proceedings upon High Treason, and Other Crimes and Misdemeanours, from the Reign of King Richard II to the End of the Reign of King George I,* 8 vols. (London, 1730), 3:710–40.

92. Price, "A Discourse on the Love of Our Country," 190.

Thus we see the harmony of the culprits. The one is only a perspicuous and precise abridgment of the other. The harmony of the Judges will not be found less remarkable. Mr. Burke, "when he talks as if he had made a discovery, only follows a precedent."[93]

JUDGE JEFFRIES' *Charge to the Jury.*	MR. BURKE
"The King, it says, is responsible to them, and he is only their trustee. He has misgoverned, and he is to give it up, that they may be all Kings themselves. Gentlemen, I must tell you, I think I ought, more than ordinarily to press this on you, because I know the misfortunes of the late unhappy rebellion; and the bringing of the late blessed King to the scaffold was first begun by such kind of principles."*	"The Revolution Society chuses to assert, that a King is no more than the first servant of the Public, created by it, and responsible to it."[94]—"The second claim of the Revolution Society is cashiering the Monarch for misconduct," p. 114. "The Revolution Society, the heroic band of fabricators of Governments, electors of Sovereigns," p. 159. "This sermon is in a strain which has never been heard in this kingdom in any of the pulpits which are tolerated or encouraged in it since 1648." p. 97. <331>

Thus does Mr. Burke chaunt his political song in exact unison with the strains of the venerable Magistrate; they indict the same crimes; they impute the same motives; they dread the same consequences.

The Revolution Society felt, from the great event which they professedly commemorated, new motives to exult in the emancipation of France. The Revolution of 1688 deserves more the attention of a philosopher from its indirect influence on the progress of human opinion, than from its immediate effects on the Government of England. In the first view, it is perhaps difficult to estimate the magnitude of its effects. It sanctified, as we have seen, the general principles of freedom. It gave the first example in civilized modern Europe of a Government which reconciled a semblance

---

* Trial of Algernon Sidney for High Treason. State Trials, vol. iii. page 710, & seq.
93. Burke, *Reflections,* 158.
94. Ibid., 117.

of *political,* and a large portion of *civil* liberty with stability and peace. But above all, Europe owes to it the <332> inestimable blessing of an asylum for freedom of thought. Hence England became the preceptress of the world in philosophy and freedom. Hence arose the school of sages, who unshackled and emancipated the human mind; from among whom issued the Lockes, the Rousseaus, the Turgots, and the Franklins, the immortal band of preceptors and benefactors of mankind. They silently operated a grand *moral* Revolution, which was in due time to meliorate the social order. They had tyrants to dethrone more formidable than Kings, and from whom Kings held their power. They wrested the sceptre from superstition, and dragged prejudice in triumph. They destroyed the arsenal whence despotism had borrowed her thunders and her chains. These grand enterprizes of philosophic heroism must have preceded the reforms of civil Government. The Colossus of tyranny was undermined, and a pebble overthrew it.—From this progress of opinion arose the Ame-<333>rican revolution, and from this, most unquestionably the delivery of France. Nothing, therefore, could be more natural, than that those who, without blind bigotry for the forms, had a rational reverence for the principles of our ancestors, should rejoice in a Revolution, where these principles, which England had so long suffered to repose in impotent abstraction, were called forth into energy, expanded, invigorated, and matured. If, as we have presumed to suppose, the Revolution of 1688 may have had no small share in accelerating that progress of light which has dissolved the prejudices that supported despotism, they may be permitted, besides their exultation as friends of humanity, to indulge some pride as Englishmen.

It must be confessed that our ancestors in 1688, confined, in their practical regulations, their views solely to the urgent abuse. They punished the usurper without meliorating the <334> Government, and they proscribed usurpations without correcting their source. They were content to clear the turbid stream, instead of purifying the polluted fountain. They merit, however, veneration for their atchievements, and the most ample amnesty for their defects, for the first were their own, and the last are imputable to the age in which they lived.—The true admirers of the Revolution will pardon it for having spared abusive establishments, only because they revere it for having established grand principles. But the case of Mr. Burke is different;

he deifies its defects, and derides its principles; and were Lord Somers to
listen to such misplaced eulogy, and tortured inference, he might justly say,
"You deny us the only praise we can claim, and the only merit you allow
us is in the sacrifices we were compelled to make to prejudice and ignorance.
Your glory is our shame." Reverence for the principles, and pardon to the
defects of civil changes, which <335> arise in ages partially enlightened, are
the plain dictates of common-sense. Admiration of Magna Charta does
not infer any respect for villainage. Reverence for Roman patriotism is not
incompatible with detestation of slavery; nor does veneration for the Revolutionists of 1688 impose any blindness to the gross, radical, and multiplied absurdities and corruptions in their political system. The true admirers of Revolution principles cannot venerate institutions as sage and
effectual protection of freedom, which experience has proved to be nerve-
less and illusive. "The practical claim of impeachment," the vaunted responsibility of Ministers is the most sorry juggle of a political empiricism
by which a people were ever attempted to be lulled into servitude. State
prosecutions in free states have ever either languished in impotent and despised tediousness, or burst forth in a storm of popular indignation, that
at once overwhelms its object, without discrimination <336> of innocence or guilt. Nothing but this irresistible fervor can destroy the barriers
within which powerful and opulent delinquents are fortified. If this fervor
is not with eminent hazard of equity and humanity gratified in the moment, it subsides. The natural influence of the culprit, and of the accomplices interested in his impunity, resumes its place. As these trials are necessarily long, the facts which produce conviction, and the eloquence
which rouzes indignation, being effaced from the Public mind by time,
by ribaldry and sophistry, the shame of a corrupt decision is extenuated.
Every source of obloquy or odium that can be attached to the obnoxious
and invidious character of an accuser, is exhausted by the profuse corruption of the delinquent. The tribunal of Public opinion, which alone
preserves the purity of others, is itself polluted, and a people wearied,
disgusted, irritated, and corrupted, suffer the culprit to re-<337>tire in
impunity* and splendor. *Damnatus inani judicio quid enim salvis infamia*

---

* Part of this description is purely *historical.* Heaven forbid that the sequel should *nummis.*[95] Such has ever been the state of things, when the force of the Government has been sufficient to protect the accused from the first ebullition of popular impetuosity. The Democracies of antiquity presented a spectacle directly the reverse. But no history affords any example of a just medium. State trials will always either be impotent or oppressive, a persecution or a farce. Thus vain is the security of impeachment, and equally absurd, surely, is our confidence in "the control of Parliaments,"[96] in their present constitution, and with their remaining powers. To begin with the last. They possess the *nominal* power of impeachment. Not to mention its disuse in <338> the case of any Minister for more than seventy years, it is always too late to remedy the evil, and probably always too weak to punish the criminal. They possess a pretended power of with-holding supplies. But the situation of society has in truth wrested it from them. The supplies they must vote, for the army must have its pay, and the Public creditors their interest. A power that cannot be exercised without provoking mutiny, and proclaiming bankruptcy, the blindest bigot cannot deny to be purely *nominal.* A practical substitute for these theoretical powers existed till our days in the *negative* exercised by the House of Commons on the choice of the Minister of the Crown. But the elevation of Mr. Pitt established a precedent which extirpated the last *shadow* of popular control from the Government of England—

---

prove *prophetic.* When this subject presents Mr. Burke to my mind, I must say, TALIS *cum sis utinam noster esses.* [As Agesilaus said to his enemy Pharnabazus, "They are so good that I wish they were on our side." Quoted in Bacon, "Of the Dignity and Advancement of Learning," in *The Works of Francis Bacon,* collected and ed. J. Spedding, R. L. Ellis, and D. Denon Heath, 14 vols. (London: Longman & Co., 1858–74), 3:277, (I.3.1). Compare Xenophon, *Hellenica,* in *Hellenica, Anabasis,* trans. C. L. Brownson, 3 vols. (London and Cambridge, Mass.: Heinemann and Harvard University Press, 1961), 1:278–79 (IV.1.38).]

95. "Condemned by a futile verdict—for what matters infamy if the cash be kept?" Juvenal, "Satires," in *Juvenal and Persius,* trans. G. G. Ramsay, rev. ed. (London and Cambridge, Mass.: Heinemann and Harvard University Press, 1965), 6–7 (satire 1, 47–48).

96. Burke, *Reflections,* 116.

Olim vera fides
Sulla Mario que receptis libertatis obit
Pompeio rebus adempto nunc & ficta perit.[97] <339>

But in truth, the force and the privileges of Parliament are almost indifferent to the people, for it is not the guardian of their rights, nor the organ of their voice. We are said to be *unequally* represented. This is one of those contradictory phrases that form the political jargon of half-enlightened periods. Unequal freedom is a contradiction in terms. It ought not to be called freedom, but the power of some, and the slavery of others—the oppression of one portion of mankind by another. The law is the deliberate reason of ALL, guiding *their* occasional will. Representation is an expedient for peacefully, systematically, and unequivocally collecting this universal voice. So thought and so spoke the Edmund Burke of better times. "To follow, not to force the Public inclination, to give a direction, a form, a technical dress, and a specific sanction to the general sense of the community is the true end of Legislature." *Burke's two Letters to Gentlemen in Bristol,* <340> *page* 52.[98] There spoke the correspondent of Franklin,* the Champion of America, the enlightened advocate of humanity and freedom!—If these principles be true, and they are so true that it seems almost puerile to repeat them, who can without indignation hear the House of Commons of England called a popular representative. A more insolent and preposterous abuse of language is not to be found in the vocabulary of tyrants. The criterion that distinguishes *laws* from *dictates,* freedom from servitude, rightful Government from usurpation, *the law being an expression of the general will,* is wanting. This is the grievance which the admirers of the Revolution in 1688 desire to remedy according to its *principles.* This is that

---

* Mr. Burke has had the honor of being traduced for corresponding, during the American war, with this great man, because he was a *Rebel!*

97. "Sincere belief in Rome's freedom died long ago, when Sulla and Marius were admitted within the walls; but now, when Pompey has been removed from the world, even the sham belief is dead." Lucan, "The Civil War," in *Lucan,* trans. J. D. Duff (London and New York: Heinemann and G. P. Putnam's Sons, 1928), 518–21 (IX. 204–6).

98. Burke, "Letter to the Sheriffs of Bristol, 3 April 1777," in *The Writings and Speeches of Edmund Burke,* general ed. P. Langford, vol. 3, *Party, Parliament, and the American War 1774–1780,* ed. W. M. Elofson and John Woods (Oxford: Clarendon Press, 1996), 315.

perennial source of corruption which has increased, is increasing, and ought to be diminished. If the general <341> interest is not the object of our Government, it is, it must be, because the general will does not govern. We are boldly challenged to produce our proofs; our complaints are asserted to be chimerical, and the excellence of our Government is inferred from its beneficial effects. Most unfortunately for us, most unfortunately for our country, these proofs are too ready, and too numerous. We find them in that "monumental debt," the *bequest* of wasteful and profligate wars, which already wrings from the peasant something of his hard-earned pittance, which already has punished the industry of the useful and upright manufacturer, by robbing him of the asylum of his house, and the judgment of his peers, to which the madness of political Quixotism adds a million for every farthing that the pomp of Ministerial empiricism pays, and which menaces our children with convulsions and calamities, of which no age has seen the parallel. We find them in the black and bloody <342> Roll of persecuting statutes that are still suffered to stain our code; a list so execrable, that were no monument to be preserved of what England was in the eighteenth century but her statute book, she might be deemed still plunged in the deepest gloom of superstitious barbarism. We find them in the ignominious exclusion of great bodies of our fellow citizens from political trusts, by tests which reward falshood and punish probity, which profane the rites of the religion they pretend to guard, and usurp the dominion of the God they profess to revere. We find them in the growing corruption of those who administer the Government, in the venality of a House of Commons which has become only a cumbrous and expensive chamber for registering Ministerial edicts—in the increase of a Nobility arrived to a degradation, by the profusion and prostitution of honors which the most zealous partizans of Democracy would have spared them. We find them, ABOVE <343> ALL, in the rapid progress which has been made to silence the great organ of Public opinion, the Press, which is the true control on Ministers and Parliaments, who might else, with impunity, trample on the impotent formalities that form the pretended bulwark of our freedom. The mutual control, the well-poised balance of the several members of our Legislature, are the visions of theoretical, or the pretext of practical politicians.

It is a Government, not of check, but of conspiracy—a conspiracy which can only be repressed by the energy of popular opinion.

These are no visionary ills, no chimerical apprehensions. They are the sad and sober reflections of as honest and enlightened men as any in the kingdom; nor are they alleviated by the torpid and listless security into which the people seem to be lulled—*Summum otium forense non quiescentis sed senescentis civitatis.*[99] It is in this fatal temper that men <344> become sufficiently debased and embruted to sink into placid and polluted servitude. It is then that it may most truly be said, that the *mind* of a country is slain. The admirers of Revolution principles naturally call on every aggrieved and enlightened citizen to consider the source of his oppression. If penal statutes hang over our Catholic brethren,* <345> if test acts outrage our Protestant fellow-citizens, if the remains of feudal tyranny are still suffered to exist in Scotland, if the press is fettered, if our right to trial by jury is abridged, if our manufacturers are proscribed and hunted down by EXCISE, the reason of all these oppressions is the same. No branch of the Legislature represents the people. Men are oppressed, because they have no share in their own government. Let all these classes of oppressed citizens melt their local and partial grievances into one great mass. Let them cease

---

* No body of men in any State that pretends to freedom have ever been so insolently oppressed as the *Catholic* MAJORITY of Ireland. Their cause has been lately pleaded by an eloquent Advocate, whose virtues might have been supposed to have influenced my praise as the partial dictate of friendship, had not his genius extorted it as a strict tribute to justice. I perceive that HE retains much of that *admiration* which WE cherished in common by his classical quotation respecting Mr. Burke—

> Soli quippe vacat, studiisque adiisque carenti
> Humanum lugere genus ———

See "The CONSTITUTIONAL INTERESTS of IRELAND with respect to the POPERY LAWS." P. IV. Dublin, 1791. ["Who, actually left alone without studies or shrines, has the task of weeping for the human race" (*aditisque* for *adiisque*). As quoted in *The Constitutional Interests of Ireland with Respect to the Popery Laws Impartially Investigated* (Dublin: J. Moore, 1791), iv.]

99. "The forum is profoundly tranquil, but that indicates senile decay, rather than acquiescence, on the part of the State." Cicero, *The Letters to His Brother Quintus,* trans. W. Glynn Williams (London and Cambridge, Mass.: Heinemann and Harvard University Press, 1972), 534–35 (bk. 2, letter 15a, line 5).

to be suppliants for their rights, or to sue for them like mendicants, as a precarious boon from the arrogant pity of usurpers. Until the Legislature speaks their voice, it will oppress them. Let them unite to procure such a reform in the representation of the people, as will make the House of Commons their representatives. If dismissing all petty views of obtaining their own particular ends, they unite for this great object, they must succeed. <346> The co-operating efforts of so many bodies of citizens must awaken the nation, and its voice will be spoken in a tone that virtuous Governors will obey, and tyrannical Governors must dread. It is impossible to suppose the existence of such insolent profligacy as would affect to despise the national voice, if it were unequivocally spoken.

This tranquil and legal reform is the ultimate object of those whom Mr. Burke has so foully branded. In effect this would be amply sufficient. The powers of the King and the Lords have never been formidable in England, but from discords between the House of Commons and its pretended constituents. Were that House really to become the vehicle of the popular voice, the privileges of other bodies, in opposition to the sense of the people and their representatives, would be but as dust in the balance. From this radical improvement all subaltern reform <347> would naturally and peaceably arise. We dream of no more, and in claiming this, instead of meriting the imputation of being apostles of sedition, we conceive ourselves entitled to be considered as the most sincere friends of tranquil and stable Government.—We desire to avert revolution* by reform; subversion by correction. We admonish our Governors to reform, while they retain the force to reform with dignity and security; and we conjure them not to wait the moment, which *will infallibly* arrive, when they shall be obliged to supplicate that people, whom they oppress and despise, for the slenderest pittance of their present powers. <348>

The grievances of England do not now, we confess, justify a change by violence. But they are in a rapid progress to that fatal state, in which they

---

* Let the Governors of all States compare the convulsion which the obstinacy of the Government provoked in France, with the peaceful and dignified reform which its wisdom effected in POLAND. The moment is important, the dilemma inevitable, the alternative awful, the lesson most instructive!—

will both justify and produce it. It is because we sincerely love tranquil*
freedom, that we earnestly deprecate the moment when virtue and honor
shall compel us to seek her with our swords. Are not *they* the true friends
to authority who desire, that whatever is granted by it "should issue as a
gift of her bounty and beneficence, rather than as claims recovered against
a struggling litigant? Or, at least, that if her beneficence obtained no credit
in her concessions, they should appear the salutary provisions of wisdom
and foresight, not as things wrung with blood by the cruel gripe of a rigid
necessity."† We desire that the political light which is to break in on England
<349> should be "through well-contrived and well-disposed windows, not
through flaws and breaches, through the yawning chasms of our ruin."‡

Such was the language of Mr. Burke in cases nearly parallel to the present. But of those who now presume to give similar counsels, his alarm and
abhorrence are extreme. They deem the "present times," favorable "to all
exertions in the cause of liberty."¹⁰⁰ They naturally must. Their hopes in
that great cause are from the determined and according voices of enlightened men. The shock that destroyed the despotism of France has widely
dispersed the clouds that intercepted reason from the political and moral
world; and we cannot suppose, that England is the only spot that has not
been reached by this "flood of light" that has burst upon the human race.—
We might suppose <350> too, that Englishmen would be shamed out of
their torpor by the great exertions of nations whom we had long deemed
buried in hopeless servitude. Thus far we might be pardoned for thinking

---

* Manus haec inimica Tyrannis
  Ense petit placidam sub libertate quietem.—
["This hand hostile to tyrants / seeks with a sword quiet peace with liberty." The first
half of the sentence was written by Algernon Sidney in the visitors' book of the University of Copenhagen. It has been assumed since the end of the seventeenth century
that his inscription also included the second half of the sentence. The words were later
adopted as the founding motto of the State of Massachusetts. See B. Worden, *Roundhead
Reputations: The English Civil Wars and the Passions of Posterity* (London: Allen Lane,
2001), 126–27.]
† Burke's Speech at Bristol, page 13. [Burke, "Speech at Bristol Previous to the Election, 6 September 1780," in *The Writings and Speeches of Edmund Burke,* 3:630.]
‡ Id., 631.
100. Burke, *Reflections,* 144.

the present moment peculiarly auspicious to exertions in the cause of freedom.

But nothing *can* be more absurd than to assert, that all who *admire* wish to *imitate* the French Revolution. In ONE view there is room for diversity of opinion among the warmest and wisest friends of freedom, as to the *portion* of Democracy infused into the Government of France. In another, and a more important one, it is to be recollected, that the conduct of nations is to vary with the circumstances in which they are placed.—Blind admirers of Revolutions take them for implicit models. Thus Mr. Burke admires that of 1688; but we, who conceive that we pay the purest homage to the authors of that <351> Revolution, not in contending for what they *then* DID, but for what they *now* WOULD DO, can feel no inconsistency in looking on France, not to model our conduct, but to invigorate the spirit of freedom. We permit ourselves to imagine how Lord Somers, in the light and knowledge of the eighteenth century, how the patriots of France, in the tranquillity and opulence of England, would have acted. We are not bound to copy the conduct to which the last were driven by a bankrupt Exchequer and a dissolved Government, nor to maintain the establishments which were spared by the first in a prejudiced and benighted age. Exact imitation is not necessary to reverence. We venerate the principles which presided in both events, and we adapt to political admiration a maxim which has long been received in polite letters, that the only manly and liberal imitation is to speak as a great man would have spoken, had he lived in our times, and been placed in our circumstances. <352>

But let us hear the charge of Mr. Burke. "Is our Monarchy to be annihilated, with all the laws, all the tribunals, all the ancient corporations of the kingdom? Is every land-mark of the kingdom to be done away in favour of a geometrical and arithmetical Constitution? Is the House of Lords to be useless? Is Episcopacy to be abolished?"[101]—and, in a word, is France to be imitated? Yes! if our Governors imitate her policy, the State must follow her catastrophe. Man is every where MAN—imprisoned grievance will at length have vent, and the storm of popular passion will find a feeble obstacle in the solemn imbecility of human institutions. But who are the true friends

101. Ibid., 145.

to the order of Government, the prerogative of the Monarch, the splendor of the hierarchy, and the dignity of the peerage? Those most certainly who inculcate, that to with-hold reform is to stimulate convulsion; those who admonish all to whom honor, and rank, and <353> dignity, and wealth are dear, that they can only in the end preserve them by conceding, while the moment of concession remains; those who aim at draining away the fountains that feed the torrent, instead of opposing puny barriers to its course.

"The beginnings of confusion in England are at present feeble enough, but with you we have seen an infancy still more feeble growing by moments into a strength to heap mountains upon mountains, and to wage war with Heaven itself.—Whenever our neighbour's house is on fire, it cannot be amiss for the engines to play a little upon our own."[102] This language, taken in its most natural sense, is exactly what the friends of reform in England would adopt. Every gloomy tint that is added to the horrors of the French Revolution by the tragic pencil of Mr. Burke, is a new argument in support of their claims, and those only are <354> the real enemies of the Nobility and the Priesthood, and other bodies of men that suffer in such convulsions, who stimulate them to unequal and desperate conflicts.

Such are the sentiments of those who can admire without servilely copying recent changes, and can venerate the principles without superstitiously defending the corrupt reliques of old Revolutions.

"Grand swelling sentiments of liberty," says Mr. Burke, "I am sure I do not despise. Old as I am, I still read the fine raptures of Lucan and Corneille with pleasure."[103] Long may that virtuous and venerable age enjoy such pleasures. But why should he be indignant that "the glowing sentiment and the lofty speculation" should have passed from the schools and the closet to the Senate, and no longer serving "to point a moral or adorn a tale,"[104] should be brought home to the busi-<355>ness and the bosoms of men. The sublime genius whom Mr. Burke admires, and who sung the obsequies of Roman freedom, has one sentiment, which the friends of liberty in En-

---

102. Ibid., 95.
103. Ibid., 361.
104. Samuel Johnson, "Vanity of Human Wishes," in *Works,* 16 vols. (New Haven, Conn.: Yale University Press, 1958–90), 6:102 (line 221).

gland, if they are like him condemned to look abroad for a free government, must adopt—

> ———Redituraque nunquam
> LIBERTAS ultra Tigrim Rhenumque recessit
> Et *toties* nobis JUGULO quaesita negatur!—[105] <356>

---

105. "And that Freedom, banished by civil war, has retreated beyond the Tigris and the Rhine, never to return; often as we have wooed her with our life-blood, she wanders afar." (The last word should be *vagatur.*) Lucan, "The Civil War," in *Lucan,* 400–401 (VII.432–35).

Speculations on the probable Consequences of the French Revolution in Europe.

There is perhaps only *one* opinion about the French Revolution in which its friends and its enemies agree. They both conceive that its influence will not be confined to France; they both predict that it will produce important changes in the general state of Europe. This is the theme of the exultation of its admirers, this is the source of the alarms of its detractors. It were indeed difficult to suppose that a Revolution so unparalelled should take place in the most renowned of the European nations, without spreading its influence throughout the Christian Commonwealth; <357> connected as it is by the multiplied relations of politics, by the common interest of commerce, by the wide intercourse of curiosity and of literature, by similar arts and by congenial manners. The channels by which the prevailing sentiments of France may enter into the other nations of Europe, are so obvious and so numerous, that it were unnecessary and tedious to detail them, but I may remark as among the most conspicuous, a central situation, a predominating language, an authority almost *legislative* in the ceremonial of the private intercourse of life. These and many other causes must facilitate the diffusion of French politics among the neighbouring nations, but it will be justly remarked, that their effect must in a great measure depend on the *stability* of the REVOLUTION. The suppression of *an honourable revolt* would strengthen all the governments of Europe; the view of a splendid *Revolution* would be the signal of insurrection to their subjects. Any reasonings on the influ-<358>ence of the French Revolution may therefore be supposed to be premature until its permanence be ascertained.

155

Of that permanence my conviction is firm, but I am sensible that in the field of political prediction, where veteran sagacity* has so often been deceived; it becomes me to harbour with distrust, and to propose with diffidence a conviction influenced by partial enthusiasm, and perhaps produced by the inexperienced ardour of youth. The moment at which I write is peculiarly critical (August 25th 1791). The invasion of FRANCE is now spoken of as immediate by the exiles and their partizans; and the confederacy of <359> despots† is announced with new confidence; but notwithstanding these threats, I retain my doubts whether the jarring interests of the European courts will permit this alliance to have much energy or cordiality; and whether the cautious prudence of despots will send their military slaves to a school of freedom in France; but if there be doubts about the likelihood of the enterprize being undertaken, there can be few about the probability of its event. History celebrates many conquests of obscure tribes whose valour was animated by enthusiasm, but she records no example where <360> foreign force has subjugated a powerful and gallant people, governed by the most imperious passion‡ that can sway the human

---

* Witness the memorable example of HARRINGTON, who published a demonstration of the impossibility of reestablishing monarchy in England *six months* before the restoration of CHARLES II. [Probably a reference to James Harrington, *Valerius and Publicola* (London, 1659). For a recent edition see *The Political Works of James Harrington*, ed. J. G. A. Pocock (Cambridge: Cambridge University Press, 1977), 781–806.] Religious prophecies have usually the inestimable *convenience* of relating to a distant futurity.

† The malignant hostility displayed against French freedom by a perfidious Prince, who occupies and dishonours the throne of GUSTAVUS VASA, cannot excite our wonder, though it may provoke our indignation. The *Pensioner* of French despotism could not rejoice in its destruction, nor could a monarch, whose boasted talents have hitherto been confined to perjury and usurpation, fail to be wounded by the establishment of freedom; for freedom demands genius, not intrigue; wisdom, not cunning.

‡ May I be permitted to state how the ancestors of a nation now stigmatized for servility, felt this powerful sentiment. The Scottish nobles contending for their liberty under ROBERT BRUCE, thus spoke to the Pope, *"Non pugnamus propter divitias honores, aut dignitates sed propter* LIBERTATEM *tantummodo quam* nemo bonus *nisi simul cum vita amittit!"*—Nor was this sentiment confined to the *Magnates,* for the same letter declares the assent of the Commons: "TOTAQUE COMMUNITAS REGNI SCOTIAE!"— ["It is in truth not for glory, nor riches, nor honors that we are fighting, but for freedom— for that alone, which no honest man gives up but with life itself"; and "the whole community of the realm of Scotland." Declaration of Abroath, 1320.] Reflecting on the

breast. Whatever wonders fanaticism has performed, may be again effected
by a passion as ardent, though not so transitory, because it is sanctioned by
virtue and reason. To animate <361> patriotism, to silence tumult, to banish
division, would be the only effects of an invasion in the present state of
France. A people abandoned to its own inconstancy, have often courted the
yoke which they had thrown off; but to oppose foreign hostility to the enthusiasm of a *nation,* can only have the effect of adding to it ardour, and
constancy, and force. These and similar views must offer themselves to the
European cabinets, but perhaps they perceive themselves to be placed in so
peculiar a situation, that exertion and inactivity are equally perilous. If they
fail in the attempt to crush the infant liberty of France, the ineffectual effort
will recoil on their own Governments, and hasten their destruction. If they
tamely suffer a school* of <362> freedom to be founded in the *centre* of
Europe, they must foresee the hosts of disciples that are to issue from it for
the subversion of their despotism.

   They cannot be blind to a species of danger which the history of Europe

---

various fortunes of my country, I cannot exclude from my mind the comparison between
its present reputation and our ancient character— *"terrarum et libertatis extremos"* ["Here
at the world's end, on its last inch of liberty." Tacitus, *Agricola,* in *Dialogus, Agricola,
Germania,* trans. W. Peterson (London and New York: Heinemann and G. P. Putnam's
Sons, 1920), 220–21 (§30).]—nor can I forget the honourable reproach against the Scottish name in the character of BUCHANAN by THUANUS, who remarks of that illustrious
scholar *"Libertate* GENTI INNATA *in regium fastigium accibior."* ["Harsher against the
royal dignity by the sense of freedom innate in his people." Thuanus (Jacques-Auguste
de Thou), *Historiae suorum temporum* (Geneva, 1626), 3:582 (bk. 76).] This melancholy
retrospect is however relieved by the hope that a gallant and enlightened people will not
be slow in renewing the *aera* of such reproaches.

   * The most important materials for the philosophy of history are collected from remarks on the *coincidence* of the situations and sentiments of distant periods, and it may
be curious as well as instructive, to present to the Reader the topics by which the CA-
LONNES of CHARLES I. were instructed, to awaken the jealousy and solicit the aid of
the European Courts. "A dangerous combination of his Majesty's subjects have laid a
design to dissolve the Monarchy and frame of Government—becoming a dangerous
precedent to all the MONARCHIES of Christendom, if attended with success in their
design."
   King Charles I's Instructions to his Minister in Denmark,
             in LUDLOW's MEMOIRS, vol. iii. p. 257.
[Edmund Ludlow, *Memoirs of Edmund Ludlow, Esq; Lieutenant-General of the Horse,
&c.,* 3d ed., 3 vols. (Edinburgh: Sands, Murray and Cochran, 1751), 3:257.]

reveals to them in legible characters. They see, indeed, that the negocia-
tions, the wars, and the revolutions of vulgar policy, pass away without
leaving behind them any vestige of their tran-<363>sitory and ignominious
operation. But they must remark, that besides this *monotonous villainy,*
there are cases in which Europe, actuated by a *common* passion, has appeared as *one* nation. When a society of nations are so closely united as to
resemble the union of the provinces of a State, the propagation of sentiment is indeed inevitable, and the European annals already afford sufficient
evidence of its effect. The religious passion animated and guided the spirit
of chivalry—Hence arose the *Crusades.* "A nerve was touched of exquisite
feeling, and the sensation vibrated to the heart of Europe."* In the same
manner the Reformation gave rise to religious wars, the duration of which
exceeded a century and a half. Both examples prove the existence of that
sympathy, by the means of which a great passion, taking its rise in any considerable State of Europe, must circulate through the whole <364> Christian Commonwealth. Illusion is, however, transient, and truth is immortal.
The epidemical fanaticism of former times was short-lived, for it could only
flourish in the eclipse of reason. But the virtuous enthusiasm of liberty,
though it be like that fanaticism contagious, it is not like it transitory.

But besides the facility with which we have seen a common passion to
be diffused in Europe, there are other circumstances which entitle us to
expect, that the example of France will have a mighty influence on the
subjects of despotic Governments. *The Gothic Governments of Europe have
lived their time.* Man, and for ever! is the sage exclamation of Mr. HUME.[106]
Limits are no less rigorously prescribed by Nature to the age of Governments than to that of individuals. Whether it be owing to our fickleness or
our wisdom, to the inflexibility or the imperfection of our institutions, or
to the combined operation of these <365> various causes, certain it is, that
the wide survey of history discovers with as much clearness, the growth,
the decay, and the dissolution of Governments, as the narrow view of personal experience can remark the progress and the death of individual man.

* Gibbon. [Edward Gibbon, *The Decline and Fall of the Roman Empire,* ed. D. Wom-
ersley, 3 vols. (London: Allen Lane, 1994), 3:554 (vol. 5, chap. 57).]

106. Hume, "Idea of a Perfect Commonwealth," in *Essays Moral, Political, and Literary* (Indianapolis: Liberty Fund, 1985), 528.

The heroic Governments of Greece yielded to a body of legislative republics. They were in their turn swallowed up by the conquests of Rome. That great empire itself, under the same forms, passed through various modes of Government. The first usurpers concealed it under a republican disguise; their successors threw off the mask, and avowed a military despotism. The empire expired in the ostentatious feebleness of an Asiatic monarchy.* <366> It was overthrown by savages, whose rude institutions and barbarous manners have, until our days, influenced Europe with a permanence refused to wiser and milder laws. But, unless historical analogy be altogether delusive, the *decease* of the *Gothic* Governments cannot be distant. Their maturity is long past, and symptoms of their decrepitude are rapidly accumulating. Whether they are to be succeeded by more beneficial or more injurious Governments may be doubted, but that they are about to perish, we are authorized to suppose, from the usual age to which the Governments recorded in history have arrived.

There are also other presumptions furnished by historical analogy, which favour the supposition that *legislative Governments* are about to succeed the rude usurpations of Gothic Europe. The commonwealths which in the sixth and seventh centuries before the Christian aera were erected on the ruins of the *he-*<367>*roic* monarchies of Greece, are perhaps the only genuine example of Governments truly *legislative* recorded in history. A close inspection will, perhaps, discover some coincidence between the circumstances which formed these Governments and those which now influence the state of Europe. The Phenecian and Egyptian colonies were not like our colonies in America, numerous enough to subdue or extirpate the native savages of Greece. They were, however, sufficiently numerous to instruct and civilize them. From that alone could their power be derived. To that therefore were their efforts directed. Imparting the arts and the knowledge of polished nations to rude tribes, they attracted, by avowed superiority of

---

* See this progress stated by the concise philosophy of MONTESQUIEU, and illustrated by the copious eloquence of GIBBON. [Montesquieu, *Considérations sur les causes de la grandeur des Romains* (Amsterdam: Mortier, 1734) and Gibbon, *The Decline and Fall of the Roman Empire.*] The republican disguise extends from *Augustus* to *Severus*. The military despotism from *Severus to Diocletian*. The Asiatic *Sultanship* from DIOCLETIAN to the final extinction of the Roman name.

knowledge, a submission necessary to the effect of their legislation; a submission which impostors acquire from superstition, and conquerors derive from force. An age of legislation supposes a great inequality of knowledge between the legislators and those who <368> receive their institutions. The Asiatic Colonists, who first scattered the seeds of refinement, possessed this superiority over the *Pelasgic hordes,* and the legislators who in subsequent periods organized the Grecian commonwealths, acquired from their travels in the polished States of the East, that reputation of superior knowledge, which enabled them to dictate laws to their fellow-citizens. Let us then compare Egypt and Phenicia with the enlightened part of Europe, separated as widely from the general mass by the *moral* difference of instruction, as these countries are from Greece by the *physical* obstacles which impeded a rude navigation. We must discern, that when philosophers become legislators, they are colonists from an enlightened country reforming the institutions of rude tribes. The present moment indeed resembles with wonderful exactness the legislative age of Greece. The multitude have attained sufficient knowledge to value the superiority of <369> enlightened men, and they retain a sufficient consciousness of ignorance to preclude rebellion against their dictates. This is the precise state in which the human mind is equally by discernment and deference prepared for legislation. This is the present condition of Europe. Philosophers have long remained a distinct nation in the midst of an unenlightened multitude. It is only now that the conquests of the press are enlarging the dominion of reason, as the vessels of *Cadmus* and *Cecrops* spread the arts and the wisdom of the East among the Pelasgic barbarians.* <370>

These general causes, the *unity* of the European Commonwealth, the *decrepitude* on which its *fortuitous* governments are verging, and the sim-

---

* The subject of this argument merits a more ample illustration. Profound and ingenious philosophers have even questioned the existence of Grecian Legislation. No competent judge will refuse these *epithets* to PROFESSOR MILLAR. [John Millar, professor of civil law at Glasgow. Probably a reference to his *An Historical View of the English Government,* 4 vols. (1787), vol. 4, chap. 7, "The Progress of Science Relative to Law and Government."] But this important subject, and more especially the similarity between the legislative age of Greece and the present condition of Europe, I reserve for a more undisturbed leisure; for a reflection and research which may enable me to reason with more force, and entitle me to decide with more confidence.

ilarity between our age and the only recorded period when the ascendant of philosophy dictated laws, entitle us to hope that freedom and reason will be rapidly propagated from their source in France. But there are not wanting symptoms of their probable progress, which justify the speculalation. The first symptoms which indicate the approach of a contagious disease are the precautions adopted against it. The first marks of the probable progress of French principles are the alarms betrayed by despots. The *Courts* of Europe seem to look on France, and to exclaim in their despair—

> *Hinc* POPULUM late REGEM belloque superbum
> Venturum excidio Libyae—[107] <371>

The Courts of Europe have in various modes paid the homage of their fears to the French Revolution. The King of Spain already seems to tremble for his throne, though it be erected on so firm a basis of general ignorance and triumphant priestcraft. By the expulsion of foreigners, and by subjecting the entrance of travellers to such multiplied restraints, he seeks the preservation of his despotism in a vain attempt to convert his kingdom into a *Bastile,* and to banish his subjects from the European Commonwealth. The Chinese Government has indeed thus maintained its permanency, but it is insulated by *nature* more effectually than by *policy.* Let the Court of Madrid recall her Ambassadors, shut up her ports, abandon her commerce, sever every tie that unites her to Europe; the effect of such shallow policy must be that of all ineffectual rigors (and all rigors short of extirpation are here ineffectual) to awaken reflexion, to stimulate enquiry, to aggravate <372> discontent, and to provoke convulsion.—*There are no longer Pyrenees,* said Louis XIV. on the accession of his grandson to the Spanish throne. *There are no longer Pyrenees,* exclaim the alarmed statesmen of *Aranjuez,* to protect our despotism from being consumed by the Sun of Liberty.

The alarms of the Pope for the little remnant of his authority naturally increase with the probability of the diffusion of French principles. Even the mild and temperate Aristocracies of Switzerland seem to apprehend the

---

107. "That from it a people, kings of broad realms and proud in war, should come forth for Libya's downfall." Virgil, "Aeneid," in *Virgil,* trans. H. Rushton Fairclough, 2 vols. (London and Cambridge, Mass.: Heinemann and Harvard University Press, 1967), 1:242–43 (I, 21–22).

arrival of that period, when men will not be content to owe the benefits of Government to the fortuitous character of their Governors, but to the intrinsic excellence of its constitution. Even the unsuccessful struggle of *Liege,* and the *Theocratic* insurrection of *Brabant,* have left behind them traces of a patriotic party, whom a more favourable moment may call into more successful action. The despotic <373> Court of the Hague are betraying alarms that the Dutch Republic may yet revive. The *Stadtholderian* Government, supported only by the terror of foreign arms, naturally dreads the destruction of a Government odious and intolerable to an immense majority of the people.

Every where then are those alarms discernible, which are the most evident symptoms of the approaching downfall of the European despotisms. But the impression produced by the French Revolution in England, in an enlightened country, which had long boasted of its freedom, merits more particular remark. Before the publication of Mr. Burke, the public were not recovered from that astonishment into which they are plunged by unexampled events, and the general opinion could not have been collected with precision. But that performance divided the nation into marked parties. It produced a controversy, <374> which may be regarded as the trial of the French Revolution before the enlightened and independent tribunal of the English public.—What its decision* has been, I shall not presume

---

* Those who doubt the service done by Mr. BURKE to his cause may be pleased with this passage of MILTON.—"Magnam a regibus iniisse te gratiam omnes principes et terrarum Dominos demeruisse Defensione hâc regiâ te fortè putas Salmasi; cum illi si bona sua remque suam ex veritate potius quam ex adulationibus tuisvellent aestimare neminem te pejus, odisse, neminem a se longius abigere, atque arcere debeant. Dum enim regiam potestatem in immensum extollas admones eâdem operâ omnes fere populos servitutis suae nec opinatae; eoque vehementius impellis ut veternum illum *quo se esse liberos inaniter somniabant* repentè excutiant."

MILTON, *Def. Pop. Anglic. apud opera, tom. ii. p.* 266. *Ed. Lond.* 1738.

["Perhaps you think, Salmasius, that by this Royal Defence you have much ingratiated yourself with kings, and deserved well of all princes and lords of the earth; but if they would reckon their interest and advantage according to truth, not according to your flatteries, they ought to hate their presence. For in the very act of exalting the power of kings above law and beyond measure, you remind most nations that they are under a slavery they had not guessed before, and the more violently drive them to shake off upon a sudden that lethargy in which they kept vainly dreaming they were freemen." Milton,

to decide; for it does not become an advocate to announce the decision of the Judge. But this I may be permitted to remark, that the conduct of our enemies has not resembled the usual triumph of those who <375> have been victorious in the war of reason. Instead of the triumphant calmness that is ever inspired by conscious superiority, they have betrayed the bit- terness of defeat, and the ferocity of resentment, which is peculiar to the black revenge of detected imposture. Priestcraft and Toryism were sup- ported only by literary advocates of the most miserable description.* But they were abundantly supported by auxiliaries of another kind. Of the two great classes of enemies to political reform—the INTERESTED and the PREJUDICED—the activity of the first usually supplies what may be want- ing in the talents of the <376> last.† Judges forgot the dignity of their function, Priests the mildness of their religion; the Bench, which should have

---

"Pro Populo Anglicano Defensio," in *The Works of John Milton,* ed. F. A. Patterson, 18 vols. (New York: Columbia University Press, 1931–40), 7:212–13 (chap. 4).]

* *A* DOCTOR COOPER, or *a* DOCTOR TATHAM, cannot be so infatuated as to dream, that even their academical titles can procure them the perusal, not to mention the refutation of men of sense. The insolence of the latter pedant had, indeed, nearly obtained him the honor of a castigation, which would have made him for ever sick of political controversy!

† Both are admirably delineated by HELVETIUS.

"Entre ceux-ci il en est qui, naturellement portés au vrai, ne sont ennemis des verités nouvelles, que parce qu'ils sont paresseux, et qu'ils voudroient se soustraire a la fatigue d'attention necessaire pour les examiner.

"Il en est d'autres qu'animent des motifs dangereux & ceux-ci sont plus a craindre: ce sont des hommes dont l'esprit est depourvu de talents & l'ame de vertus: incapables de vues elevées et neuves ces derniers croient que leur consideration tient au respect imbecille ou feint qu'ils affichent pours toutes les opinions & les erreurs reçues: furieux contre tout homme qui veut en ebranler l'Empire, ils ARMENT *contre lui les passions & les prejugés* mêmes qu'ils MEPRISENT & ne cessent d'effaroucher les foibles esprits par le mot de *nouveauté!*" ["Among them are those who, naturally inclined to the truth, are enemies of new truths, only because they are lazy, and because they would like to escape from the fatigue of attention necessary to examine them. There are others animated by dangerous motives and there is more to fear from them: these are the men whose spirit is lacking in talent and whose soul is lacking in virtue: incapable of elevated and new views these latter believe that their [consideration holds to the imbecilic or feigned re- spect] that they attach to all received opinions and errors: furious at any man who wishes to disturb the Empire, they ARM *against him the passions and the prejudices* even those they DESPISE & do not cease to scare away the weak spirits by the word *novelty.*" C. Helvetius, *De l'ésprit* (Paris: Durand, 1758), *discours* 2, chap. 23. For a modern edition,

spoken with the serene temper of justice; the Pulpit, whence only should have issued the healing sounds of charity, were prostituted to party purposes, and polluted with invective against <377> freedom. The churches resounded with language at which *Laud* would have shuddered, and *Sacheverell* would have blushed; the most profane comparisons between the duty to the Divinity and to Kings, were unblushingly pronounced; flattery to Ministers was mixed with the solemnities of religion, by the servants, and in the temple of God. These profligate proceedings were not limited to a single spot. They were general over England. In many churches the French Revolution was *expressly named!* In a majority it was the constant theme of invective for many weeks before its intended celebration. Yet these are the peaceful pastors who so sincerely and meekly deprecate political sermons!* <378>

Nor was this sufficient. The grossness of the popular mind, on which political invective made but a faint impression, was to be roused into action by religious fanaticism, the most intractable and domineering of all destructive passions. A clamour which had for half a century lain dormant was revived. *The* CHURCH *was in danger!* The spirit of persecution against an unpopular sect was artfully excited, and the friends of freedom, whom it might be odious and dangerous professedly to attack, were to be overwhelmed as Dissenters. That the majority of the advocates for the French Revolution were not so, was, indeed, sufficiently known to their enemies. They were well known to be philosophers and friends of humanity, who were superior to the creed of any sect, and indifferent to the *dogmas* of any popular faith. But it suited the purpose of their profligate adversaries to confound them with Dissenters, and to animate against them <379> the fury of prejudices which they themselves despised.

The diffusion of these invectives produced those obvious and inevitable

---

see *De l'esprit; Or Essays on the Mind and Its Several Faculties* (New York: B. Franklin, 1970).]

The last passage must be explained by some WARWICKSHIRE COMMENTATOR!

* These are no vague accusations. A sermon was preached in a parish church in *Middlesex* on the anniversary of the restoration of CHARLES II. in which ETERNAL PUNISHMENT *was denounced* against POLITICAL DISAFFECTION! Persons for whose discernment and veracity I can be responsible, were among the indignant auditors of this infernal homily.

effects, which it may require something more than candour to suppose not foreseen and desired. A *banditti,* who had been previously stimulated, as they have since been excused and panegyrized by incendiary libellists, wreaked their vengeance on a PHILOSOPHER, illustrious by his talents and his writings, venerable for the spotless purity of his life, and amiable for the unoffending simplicity of his manners.[108] The excesses of this mob of *churchmen and loyalists* are to be poorly expiated by the few misguided victims who are sacrificed to the vengeance of the law.

We are, however, only concerned in these facts, as they are *evidence* from our enemies of <380> the probable progress of freedom. The probability of that progress they all conspire to prove. The briefs of the Pope, and the pamphlets of Mr. BURKE,* the edicts of the <381> Spanish Court, and the mandates of the Spanish inquisition, the Birmingham rioters, and the Oxford graduates, equally render to Liberty the involuntary homage of their alarms.

FINIS.

* The only thing that I recollect to have the air of argument in the *two last* pamphlets of Mr. Burke is, the reasoning against the right of a majority to change a Government. [Presumably a reference to Burke's "Letter to a Member of the National Assembly" (May 1791) and "Appeal from the New to the Old Whigs" (August 1791). For recent editions see E. Burke, *Further Reflections on the Revolution in France,* ed. D. E. Ritchie (Indianapolis: Liberty Fund, 1992), 27–72 and 73–201.] Whatever be the plausibility or dexterity of this reasoning, its *originality* will be best estimated by the following passage of a PROFANE PHILOSOPHER!

"The controversies that arise concerning the RIGHTS of the PEOPLE proceed from the equivocation of the word. The word PEOPLE has *two* significations. In one sense it signifieth a number of men distinguished only by the place of their habituation, as the people of England, or the people of France, which is no more than the multitude of those particular persons inhabiting these regions, without consideration of any covenants or contracts between them. In another sense it signifieth a person civil, either one man or one Council, in the will whereof is included and involved the will of every individual. Such as do not distinguish between these two senses do usually attribute such rights to a *dissolved* MULTITUDE as belong only to the PEOPLE virtually contained in the body of the Commonwealth or Sovereignty."

See HOBBES' *Tripos,* p. 170, et seq. edit. 12mo. Lond. 1684. [Thomas Hobbes, *Tripos, in Three Discourses,* 3d ed. (London, 1684), 170, second discourse: "De Corpore Politico," pt. 2, chap. 2, §110.]

108. Joseph Priestley.

A LETTER

TO

THE RIGHT HONOURABLE

WILLIAM PITT,

ON

HIS APOSTACY

FROM THE CAUSE OF

PARLIAMENTARY REFORM.

TO WHICH IS SUBJOINED

AN APPENDIX,

CONTAINING

IMPORTANT DOCUMENTS

ON THAT SUBJECT.

Audax venali comitatur CURIO linguâ
Vox quondam Populi libertatemque tueri
Ausus!—
LUCAN PHARSALIA, *Lib. i. l.* 269–71.[1]

LONDON:

PRINTED BY T. GILLET, (19) BARTHOLOMEW-CLOSE,

AND SOLD BY

H. D. SYMONDS, PATERNOSTER-ROW.

1792. <iii>

---

1. "With them came Curio of the reckless heart and venal tongue; yet once he had been the spokesman of the people and a bold champion of freedom." Lucan, "The Civil War," in *Lucan,* trans. J. D. Duff (London and New York: Heinemann and G. P. Putnam's Sons, 1928), 22–23 [bk. 1, lines 269–71].

Advertisement

Publications on fugitive topics, though from their nature sometimes less dubiously useful to mankind than more permanent works, are so little a source of reputation, that their Authors have commonly thought it prudent to withhold their names. If an Author be obscure, such publications will not exalt him—if he be eminent, they may be supposed to derogate from the gravity of more serious occupations, or from the dignity of a more solid fame.

These common reasons may be sufficient for anonymous publication, especially in a case like the present, which consists either of argument, which a name can neither strengthen nor impair; or of facts, which are so acknowledged as to need no testimony for their support.

The Author may be supposed by some to owe an apology for the severity of the language which he has sometimes used.—The only language, however, which he could have used, on such an occasion, was that of indignant honesty. He could neither palliate truth, nor compromise virtue; nor does he profess to emulate those Courtly Writers, the gentleness of whose censures almost mitigates guilt into innocence.

A Letter
to the
Right Honourable
William Pitt, &c. &c.

<1>

SIR,

History records too many examples of political apostacy to make any case
of that sort new or singular. Yet with all your knowledge in that branch of
history, to which congenial sentiments must have naturally pointed your
studies, I doubt whether you can produce many instances in which the
political apostate, <2> instead of the language which becomes his wretched
situation, dares to assume the tone of parade and of triumph; and with the
most eccentric originality of insolence labours to convert his own desertion
of principle into an argument against these principles themselves, instead
of feeling the principles as a *stigma* on his desertion. We do not find that
Curio was shameless enough, when he deserted the cause of his country,
to urge against it the boldness of his own apostacy with the same confidence
that Cato would have used in its support the authority of his virtue. The
annals of ancient or modern apostacy contain nothing so flagrant. It was
reserved for our days to add this variety to the various combinations of
fraud and insolence, which have in former ages duped and oppressed mankind; and it was peculiarly reserved for a Statesman, whose character rec-
onciles the most repugnant extremes of political depravity, the pliancy of
the most abject intrigue, with the vaunting of the most lofty hypocrisy. It
was re-<3>served for him, not alone silently to abandon, not alone even
publicly to abjure the doctrines of his former life; not alone to oppose, with
ardour, with vehemence, with virulence, those propositions from others,
by which he himself had earned unmerited popularity, and climbed to un-

exampled power; but by a refinement of insolent apostacy, to convert into a source of obloquy against other men, a measure which had been the basis of his own reputation and importance. It was reserved for such a man to repeat those very common-place objections to the measure, and those very common-place slanders against its movers which had been urged against himself, and which he himself had justly despised, or victoriously refuted.* It was reserved for him, unblushingly <4> to renew all the clamour against novelty, and all those affectionate alarms for the British Constitution, which patriotic borough-mongers had so successfully employed against himself. Yes, Sir, it was reserved for the son of Chatham thus to stigmatize the "dying legacy" of his father, and thus to brand his own "virgin effort."

You will have already perceived, that it is on your late conduct in the case of Parliamentary Reform, that I am about to animadvert. Though I feel a dislike not unmixed with contempt for politics purely personal, and though I should be the last man to betray and degrade the great cause of Reform, by mingling it with the petty squabbles of party, yet when I see the authority of an apostate character opposed with impudent absurdity to the cause from which he apostatized, <5> I think it at least fit that that obstacle should be removed, and that the vapouring language of such a delinquent should be counteracted by the merited brand of his crimes.

The cause of Reform demands that the nature of your present opposition to it should be understood by the people. The interest of the people demands that they should well understand the character of him who may yet be likely, in some possible combination of events, to offer himself to them as the champion of Reform, and perhaps ultimately to prove the

---

* See the debate on Mr. Pitt's motion for Parliamentary Reform on the 7th May, 1782. Compare the reply of the Chancellor of the Exchequer to the alarms and arguments of Mr. T. Pitt, *proprietor of Old Sarum,* with his speech on the notice of Mr. Grey, the 30th April, 1792, in which he expresses those alarms which he had then scouted, and retails those arguments which he had then contemned!—*Ergo referens haec nuncius ibit Pelidae genitori!* ["Then thou shalt bear this news and go as messenger to my sire, Peleus' son Virgil." "Aeneid," in *Virgil,* trans. H. Rushton Fairclough, 2 vols. (London and Cambridge, Mass.: Heinemann and Harvard University Press, 1967), 1:330–31 (bk. 2, lines 547–48). For Pitt's motion of May 7, 1782, see *Parliamentary History of England from the Norman Conquest, in 1066, to the Year 1803,* 36 vols. (London: Hansard, 1806–20), 22:1416–22. The other speeches appear in appendix 9, below.]

leader in more extensive and dangerous measures. And it is generally fit that no signal example of triumphant apostacy should pass with impunity.

These are the public reasons, Sir, which lead me to call public attention to your conduct; reasons which have influenced one who has no respect for your principles, and no exaggerated opinion of your abilities, which he has some-<6>times admired without idolatry, and often opposed without fear. That I am in no abject or devoted sense a partizan; I trust even my present sentiments will prove. I am only, therefore, your enemy so far as I believe you to be the enemy of my country; and I am not unwilling to adopt for the creed of my *personal* politics the dying prayer of a great man, *"Ut ita cuique eveniat ut quisque de Republica mereatur?"*[2]

The three general grounds then on which I shall proceed to examine your conduct are, your apostacy—your present pretexts for opposing reform—and the probability of such a future conduct in you as may render it extremely important that the people should justly appreciate your character.

Your entrance into public life was marked by circumstances more favourable than any English Statesman has ever experienced. With all the <7> vigor of your own talents, with all the reflected lustre of your Father's character, you appeared at a moment when the ungracious toil of opposition was almost past, when little remained but to profit by the effect of other men's efforts, and to urge the fall of a tottering Ministry, whose misconduct had already been fatally proved by national misfortune. The current of popularity had already set strongly against the Minister. The illusions of American conquest and American revenue were dispelled. The eyes of the people were opened to the folly of the Cabinet. You had only to declaim against it. The attention of the people was called to those defects in their Constitution, which permitted such a Cabinet so long to betray the public interest, and to brave the public opinion. You had only to put yourself at the head of the people, to declare yourself the Leader of Reform. In this character you had recourse to the same means, and you were assailed by the same objections, with every past and every future Leader of Reform.

---

2. "That each man's fortune may be according to his deserts towards the state." Cicero, "The Second Philippic of M. Tullius Cicero against M. Antonius," in M. Tullius Cicero, *Orationes: Pro Milaon, Pro Marcello, Pro Ligario . . .* trans. W. Kerr (London: Heinemann, 1957), 182–83 (speech 2, chap. 46, sect. 118).

De-<8>spairing that a corrupt body should spontaneously reform itself, you invited the interposition of the people. You knew that dispersed effort must be unavailing. You therefore encouraged them to associate. You were not deterred from appealing to the people by such miserable common places of reproach as those of advertising for grievances, diffusing discontents, and provoking sedition. You well knew that in the vocabulary of corrupt power enquiry is sedition, and tranquillity is synonimous with blind and abject obedience. You were not deterred from joining with the associations of the people by being told they were to overawe Parliament. You knew the value of a jargon that does not deserve to be dignified by so high a name as Sophistry. You felt for it that contempt which every man of sense *always* feels, and which every man of *sincerity* will always express.

As you were regardless of the clamour against the necessary *means* for the accomplishment of <9> your object—as you knew that whoever would substantially serve the people in such a cause, must appeal to the people, and associate with the people; so you must have had a just and a supreme contempt for the sophistry which was opposed to the measure of reforming the Representation itself. You were told (every Reformer has been told, and every Reformer will be told) that of innovations there is no end, that to adopt one is to invite a succession; and that though you knew the limits of your own Reforms, you could not prescribe bounds to the views which their success might awaken in the minds of others. To so battered a generality it was easy to oppose another common-place. It was easy to urge that as no Government could be secure if it were to be perpetually changed; so no abuse could be reformed if institutions are to be inflexibly maintained. If they call the courage of a Reformer temerity, he is equally entitled to represent their caution as cowardice. If they speak from conjecture of his future interest in <10> confusion, he may from knowledge speak of their actual interest in corruption.

They told you that extravagant speculations were abroad;* that it was no moment to hope for the accomplishment of a temperate Reform, when there were so many men of mischievous and visionary principles, whom your attempts would embolden; and whom your Reforms would not con-

---

* Lord Camelford's speech. [Also known as Thomas Pitt; see appendix 9, below.]

tent. You replied, that the redress of real grievances was the surest remedy against imaginary alarms; that the existence of acknowledged corruptions is the only circumstance that renders incendiaries formidable; and that to correct these corruptions is to wrest from them their most powerful weapon.

By a conduct thus natural you pursued your measure. Of that conduct indeed I should not now have reminded you, *had it not been for the* <11> *sake of contrasting it with some recent transactions.* It is almost unnecessary to add that you found it easy to practise on the generous credulity of the English people, and that for the first time in the present reign, the King's advisers thought fit to chuse *their* minister from the knowledge of his being popular, actuated by the double policy of debauching a popular leader, and of surrounding with the splendour of popularity, the apostate agent of *their* will. But with the other parts of your public life I have nothing to do, nor will I trace minutely the progress of your pretended efforts for Parliamentary Reform.

The curtain was dropped in 1785. The farce then closed. Other cares then began to occupy your mind. To dupe the enthusiasts of Reform ceased to be of any further moment, and the question itself slept, until it was revived by Mr. Flood in 1790. <12>

There was little danger of the success of his motion, maintained by himself with little pertinacity, and seconded neither by any Parliamentary connexion, nor by any decisive popular opinion. To it therefore you thought a languid opposition from you sufficient. You reserved more active opposition for more formidable dangers, and you abandoned the motion of Mr. Flood to the declamation of Mr. Grenville, the logic of Mr. Windham, and the invective of Mr. Burke.[3]

That more formidable danger at length arrived. A Reform in the Representation was brought forward by a gentleman of the most powerful abilities, of high consideration in the country, and of a character the most happily untainted by any of those dubious transactions of which political parties are rarely able, for any long period to escape at least the imputation.

3. Henry Flood, M.P., a member of the Society for Constitutional Information, had moved for parliamentary reform on March 4, 1790.

Such a character was odious to apostacy. Such an enemy was formidable to corruption. <13>

The debate on the notice of Mr. Grey illustrated the fears of corrupt men, and the malignity of apostates.[4] It was then that alarms which had slumbered so long over incendiary writings were suddenly called forth by the dreadful suggestion of a moderate, and therefore, of a practicable Reform.

Nor is the reason of this difficult to discover. These incendiary publications might render signal service to a corrupt government, by making the cause of freedom odious, and perhaps by provoking immatured and ill-concerted tumults, the suppression of which might increase the strength, and justify the violence of Government. No such happy effects were to be hoped from the proposition of Mr. Grey. Impracticable schemes are never terrible, but that fatal proposition threatened the overthrow of corruption itself. Then your exertions were indeed demanded: Then your pious zeal for the constitution was called forth. <14>

Theoretical admirers of the Constitution had indeed supposed its excellence to consist in that trial by jury which you had narrowed by excise; and its salvation to depend on that liberty of the press which you had scared by prosecution. Such might have been the idle ravings of Locke or Montesquieu. But you well knew its practical excellence to depend on very different things.

Already, in your imagination, that citadel of the Constitution *Queenborough,* that sanctuary of freedom *Midhurst,* tottered to their foundations. Already, even *Cornwall* itself, the holy land of freedom, was pierced by the impious din of Reform. Actuated by alarms so honest and so wise, for such sacred bulwarks of the Constitution, no wonder that you magnanimously sacrificed your own character. No wonder that you stooped to rake together every clumsy sophism, and every malignant slander that the most frontless corruption had ever circulated, or the most stupid credulity believed. Nor was it <15> even wonderful, when we consider it in this view, that you

4. On April 30, 1792, Charles Grey, the leader of the Association of the Friends of the People, had given notice of his intention to introduce a reform bill in the following year.

should have pronounced an elaborate, a solemn, a malignant invective, against the principles which you yourself had professed, the precise measures which you had promoted, and the very means which you had chosen for their accomplishment. There is something in such a parade of apostacy, which, in the minds of *certain persons,* may efface those vestiges of distrust and repugnance, that the recollection of a popular conduct in early life must have imprinted.

The disgraceful triumph of that night will indeed long be remembered by those who were indignant spectators of it. A Minister reprobating associations, and condemning any mode of collecting the opinion of the people for the purpose of influencing the House of Commons.—HE who commenced his career by being an Associator, and who avowedly placed all his hopes of success in the authority which general <16> opinion was to have over the House of Commons. HE who continued a Minister in defiance of the House of Commons, because he supposed himself to possess the confidence of the people. HE who gave the first example of legitimating and embodying the opinion of the people against the voice of their representatives.* HE was the Minister who adopted this language. It was not, Sir, on that night to the splendor of your words, nor the music of your periods, that you owed the plaudits of the borough-mongers of Wiltshire or of Cornwall. They take no cognizance of any dexterities of sophistry or felicities of declamation; the pompous nothingness of ABERCORN, and the sordid barbarity of ROLLE, are more on a level with their under-<17>standing and more in unison with their taste. They applauded you for virtues like their own, for impudence in asserting falsehood, for audacity in defending corruption. Their assent was condemnation—their applause was ignominy—Their disgraceful *hear hims* ought to have called to your recollection the depth of infamy into which you had at length plunged. They were the very usurpers whom you pledged yourself to your country to attack; and at the only time of your life when your conduct had the semblance of virtue, these are the men in whose enmity you would have

---

* These remarks are neither stated to justify or to condemn the conduct of Mr. Pitt in the celebrated contest of 1784. They are merely intended to contrast his then measures with his present professions, and that any example of inconsistency so gross and notorious is to be found in the black annals of apostacy, I am yet to learn.

justly gloried. At that time your claim on the confidence of the people would have been almost solely founded on the virulence of hostility, and the vehemence of clamor which such men would employ against you. And these *therefore* are the men whose applause now justly seals the sentence of your apostacy.

Nor, SIR, is this brief history of that apostacy more flagrant than the plain statement of <18> your pretexts will appear absurd. The frank and good-natured prostitution of DUNDAS, which assumes no disguise, and affects no principle, almost disarms censure, and relaxes us into a sort of contemptuous indulgence for one whom we can neither hate nor respect.[5] The unblushing steadiness of avowed Toryism, whether it frowns in Thurlow, or sneaks in Hawkesbury, we can neither blame as inconsistent, nor dread as contagious. Many men may be intimidated by their power, and many seduced by their corruption, but no man is deceived by their professions. It is not therefore to such men that the FRIEND of the PEOPLE desires to point their jealousy and their resentment. Against such men it is not necessary to guard them. But it will, indeed, be his duty to detect the *pretexts* by which the specious and successful hypocrite not only disguises his own character, but triumphantly deludes the people. <19>

It is now then fit to examine those *pretexts* by which you would evade the ignominy of having deserted your cause. Such a discussion is not only necessary to convict you, but to the defence of those whom you have attacked. For unless the fallacy of these pretexts be exposed, the Friends of Reform may be branded as the thoughtless or malignant disturbers of their country, while the apostate from Reform may be regarded as the provident and honest preserver of its quiet. It is only by the exposure of his pretexts that this apostate can be shown in his genuine character, sacrificing for the preservation of corrupt power, not only the present liberty, but the future probable peace of his country.

Let us then, SIR, consider what those pretexts are, by which you labour to ascribe to insanity or profligacy in 1792, that attempt to reform, which in 1782 was the purest exertion of the most heroic patriotism. By what sort of *chronological* morality virtue could so shortly <20> have been trans-

---

5. Henry Dundas, Pitt's home secretary.

muted into vice, may be in itself a curious enquiry. Has the generous enthusiasm of your youth been corrected by the juster views of experience? Has it been repressed by the selfish coldness of advancing years? Or has it been laid asleep by the genial indulgences, and the seductive blandishments of power? Such are the questions which a discussion of your pretexts must resolve.

You are in the first place pleased to inform us, that those grievances which once so clamorously pleaded for a Reform of Parliament, have, under your wise and virtuous Administration, ceased to exist. The reasons, if we may believe the Duke of Richmond and yourself, which then justified Reform, no longer operate. The nation is prosperous. The people are contented. The statement of facts is as incontestibly true, as the inference from it is impudently false. It is because the nation is prosperous, it is because the people are tranquil, that this is an auspicious moment <21> for averting from our country calamities which a corrupt House of Commons (by your confession) did *once* produce; and which therefore an unreformed House of Commons may again equally occasion.

The logic of apostasy is happily on a level with its morals. In 1782, when general discontent might indeed have furnished some colour for an alarm that Reform would degenerate into convulsion, then you and that noble Duke placed yourselves at the head of different bodies of Reformers. You suppose, it seems, that change is only to be attempted with safety, and bounded by moderation, when the temper of the people is inflamed, and exasperated by a succession of public calamities.

Such is the reasoning, such the politics of these honest Patriots, and accomplished Legislators! Other men might have supposed, that a state of convulsion and irritation was not the temper in <22> which moderate Reforms were likely to be adopted by the people; and that to defer all proposition of Reform until grievances should produce again such a fatal state, was to delay them to a moment when there would infallibly be no choice, but to take refuge in despotism, or to plunge into civil war. The very circumstance of the content of the people is that which gives us a perfect security, that Reforms will not be hurried away into violence. It is therefore that which most powerfully invites all men to exertion, who desire a wise and measured improvement of the Constitution.

Granting even that no *actual* or urgent evil arises from the corrupt state of the pretended Representation of the People—Granting that it has not within the last eight years cost us thirteen Colonies, a hundred thousand lives, and the accumulation of a hundred and fifty millions of debt—Making all these concessions, what argument do they furnish to you? Are the *necessary* <23> *tendencies* of an institution no reason for reforming it? Is it because these *tendencies* are suspended by some accidental circumstance, that we are to tolerate them until they are again called forth into destructive energy? Had you been a Senator under TITUS, if any man had proposed controls on the despotic authority of the Emperor, and if he had justified his proposition by reminding the Senate of the ferocity of Nero, or the brutality of Vitellius, you must, on such a principle, have opposed to his arguments the happiness derived from the existing Government, till your sophistry was confuted, and your servility rewarded by DOMITIAN.

It is thus easy to expose your pretexts, even without disputing your assumptions. But it is time to retract concessions which truth does not permit, and to prove that the absurdity of your conclusions is equalled by the falsehood of those premises on which they are established. <24>

The question, whether those grievances now exist, which in your opinion once justified a Parliamentary Reform, will be best decided by considering the nature of such grievances, and the tendency of such a Reform to redress them. The grievance is, the perpetual acquiescence of the House of Commons in the dictates of the Ministers of the Crown. The source of this grievance is the enormous influence of the Crown in the House of Commons. The remedy is, to render that House, by changing the modes of its election, and shortening the duration of its trust, dependent upon the people, instead of being dependent upon the Crown.

Such is the brief state of the subject. Can you then have the insolence to assert, that the influence has decreased in your time, or that it has produced a less abject acquiescence? That influence and that acquiescence are the grievances which are to be reformed; and as no impudence can deny that they exist in their full force, so no <25> sophistry can escape the inference, that the necessity for reforming them remains undiminished. Have majorities in your time been less devoted? Have the measures of the Court been less indiscriminately adopted? Has the voice of the people been less neglected? Has the voice of the Minister been less obeyed? Not one of these things are true; not one, therefore, of the reasons for Reform have ceased to operate.

But to argue the question in this manner is to do injustice to its strength. It is not only true that the acquiescence of Parliament has not been less indiscriminate; it is not only true that the House of Commons have betrayed no symptoms of such ungovernable independence and impracticable virtue, as might seem to render its Reform less necessary or less urgent; but it is uncontrovertibly true, that your recent experience furnishes a more fantastic example of that ignominious servitude, from which Reform can only rescue the Commons, than any other that is to be found in <26> our history. I allude to your Russian armament, which I do not bring forward that I may speak of its absurdity, because I will not stoop to wound a prostrate enemy, nor to insult a convicted criminal.[6] I allude to it only as an example of the parade with which the dependence of the House of Commons on the Minister was exhibited to an indignant country. On former occasions it had been equally corrupt; on former occasions it had been equally absurd; but on no former occasion had it displayed such ostentatious and *versatile* dependence. The Minister in one session determines on his armament. His obsequious majority register the edict; but the absurdity, the odium, and the unpopularity of the measure, shake the resolution of the Cabinet. The voice of the people, despised by their pretended representatives, is listened to by the Minister. The House of Commons are at his nod ready to plunge their country into the most ruinous and unjust war; but the body of the people declare their sentiments, and the Minister recedes. He <27> commands his majority to retrace their steps, to condemn their former proceedings, and thus to declare most emphatically, that their interest is not the interest, that their voice is not the voice of the people.

6. A reference to the Ochakov crisis, which followed Russia's capture of a fortress from the Turks. In March 1791 the government obtained parliamentary support for a naval attack on Russia to secure return of the fortress to Turkey, but Pitt, perceiving a lack of popular support for war, had retreated on the question.

The obsequious majority obey without a murmur. *"Tibi summum rerum judicium dii dedere—nobis obsequii gloria relicta est."*[7]

Nothing could more forcibly illustrate the mockery and nullity of what is strangely called the Representation of the People, than this splendid victory of public opinion. The Minister yielded to that natural authority of public opinion, which is independent of forms of Government, and which would have produced the same effect in most of the simple monarchies of civilized Europe. The Cabinet of Versailles would have been compelled to exhibit a similar deference to the general sentiment before the fall of their despotism; and the people of England experienced no more aid from their supposed Representatives, than if the House of Commons had <28> been in form and avowal, what it is in truth and substance, a chamber for registering ministerial edicts.

Thus wretched are the pretexts to which you have been driven. It is not only easy to expose the emptiness and futility of these pretexts, but to establish with all the evidence of which any topic of civil prudence is susceptible, that the *circumstances of the times,* instead of rendering it dangerous to attempt a Reform in our Constitution, make it infinitely dangerous to delay such a Reform.

On the French Revolution, it is not my intention to offer any observations. It has no natural nor direct relation to my subject, and were I disposed to treat it, it would be my aim to attempt what has not *hitherto* been attempted, and what perhaps it may *yet* be too early to execute with success, an impartial and philosophical estimate of the most unexampled event in history. But <29> on its *intrinsic* merits it is not now my province to observe. I have only to consider it as marking the present time, either as auspicious or inauspicious to attempts to reform our Constitution. These attempts to obtain Reform disclaim all alliance with the magnificent principles, or the perilous speculations, by which men, according to their various prepossessions, will suppose our neighbours to have been nobly animated or fatally deluded.

---

7. "You the gods have made the sovereign arbiter of things; to us has been left the glory of obedience." Tacitus, *Annals,* in *The Histories, The Annals,* trans. J. Jackson, 4 vols. (London and Cambridge, Mass.: Heinemann and Harvard University Press, 1961), 3:166–67 (bk. 6, chap. 8).

Whether the boldness of these principles, and the wideness of these speculations, be as reconcileable with the order of freedom as they were instrumental in the destruction of tyranny, is a question on which wise men will not be prone to anticipate the decision of experience. But the schemes of Reform which we have now in view, the only Reforms which, under the circumstances I could approve, are founded on other principles, on sentiments long naturalized among us, on notions of liberty purely English. <30>

Not engaged either in the discussion or defence of the French Revolution, we then have only to contemplate it as it is supposed to render the present moment favourable or unfavourable to mediated Reforms in England. In this view it will be easy to prove, that the probable future influence of that Revolution, *whatever be its issue,* on the general sentiments of Europe, marks the *present moment* as that in which a Reform of the English Constitution is not only safe and prudent, but urgent and indispensible. Nothing indeed can be more evident, than that a mighty change in the direction of the public sentiments of Europe is likely to arise from that Revolution, whether it be successful or unsuccessful. If it be successful, the spirit of extreme Democracy is likely to spread over all Europe, and to swallow up in a volcanic eruption every remnant of Monarchy and of Nobility in the civilized world. The probability of such effects is so strongly believed by the enemies of that Revolution, that it is the ground of their alarm, the subject of their <31> invective, and the pretext of their hostilities. It was to prevent such consequences, that Mr. Burke so benevolently counselled the Princes of Europe to undertake that *crusade* in which they are now so piously engaged.

If, on the other hand, the efforts of France be unsuccessful; if her liberties be destroyed, there can be little doubt that such a shock will most powerfully impel the current of opinion to the side of Monarchy; a direction in which it will be likely for several ages to continue. The example of the destruction of the great French republic would diffuse dismay and submission among a multitude, who only judge by events; and the bloody scenes which must attend such a destruction, would indeed be sufficient to appall the sternest and most ardent champions of Liberty. The spirit of Europe would crouch under the dark shade of Despotism, in dead repose and fearful obedience. The Royal confederacy which had effected this sub-version, would doubt-<32>less continue its concert and its efforts. The principle of maintaining the internal independence of nations, being de-stroyed by the example of France, no barrier would any longer be opposed to the arbitrary will of Kings. The internal laws of all the European States would be dictated by a Counsel of Despots, and thus the influence of moral causes on public opinion, co-operating with the combined strength and policy of Princes, "every faint vestige and loose remnant" of free govern-ment will be swept from the face of the earth.

In either alternative England cannot be exempt from the general spirit. If the phrenzy of Democracy be excited by the success of France; if the spirit of abject submission and of triumphant Despotism be produced by her failure, in the first event the peace, in the second the liberty of England is endangered. In the first event a furious Republicanism, in the second a desperate Toryism is likely to pervade the country. Against <33> the prev-alence of both extremes there only exists one remedy. It is to invigorate the democratic part of the Constitution; it is to render the House of Commons so honestly and substantially the representative of the people, that Repub-licans may no longer have topics of invective, nor Ministers the means of corruption. If the one spirit prevail, it is necessary to reform the House of Commons, that the discontents of the people may be prevented. If the other spirit prevails, the same Reform is necessary, that it may be strong enough to resist the encroachments of the Crown. In the one case, to pre-vent our Government from being changed into a pure Democracy; in the other, to prevent it from being changed into a simple Monarchy. In either event the same precaution is necessary. The same Reform will preserve the English Constitution from the sap of Royal influence, and from the storm of tumultuous Democracy. A Constitution which provided a pure repre-sentative of the people, and which included only enough of Monarchy for vigor, and only <34> enough of Aristocracy for deliberation, would bid a just defiance to the most magnificent and seductive visions of democratic enthusiasm. A people who felt that they possessed a vigorous popular con-trol on their Government, could see little obnoxious, and nothing formi-dable in the powers of the Peerage and the Crown, and would feel none of that discontent which alone could make them accessible to the arts of

Republican missionaries. The success of the French, the fascinating example of their superb Democracy will have no dangerous effects on the
minds of *contented* ENGLISHMEN. But what wisdom can avert the effects
which must arise from such a model of representation, and such a spirit as
the success of France will produce in Europe, if that spirit is to operate on
a dissatisfied people, and that model be perpetually compared with the ruins
of a free Government. In the alternative then of the success of the French
Revolution, nothing surely can be so indispensible as a speedy Reform in
the Representation of the People. <35>

That to infuse a new portion of popular vigor into the House of Commons is the only remedy that can be opposed to the triumphant Toryism
which the subversion of the French Republic must produce, is a proposition so evident, as neither to demand proof nor to admit illustration. We
have seen the influence of an odious and unpopular Court victorious during a long reign, in hostility to the prejudice, and in defiance of the jealousy
of the people. What then are we to expect from that increased and increasing influence, conducted perhaps with more dexterity in the Cabinet, seconded with equal devotion in the House of Commons, and aided by the
blind enthusiasm of a people, who are intoxicated by commercial prosperity, and infatuated by all the prejudices of the most frantic Toryism?
Under such a state of things, what can prevent the formation of an un-
controled Monarchy, and the absorption of every power by a Court, from
which Englishmen are to learn what remnant of personal security it will
vouchsafe to spare, what <36> formality of public freedom it will deign to
endure, with what image of the Constitution it will indulge and amuse an
infatuated rabble.

Such are the effects which the success or the subversion of French Democracy seem calculated to produce on the temper and sentiments of the
European nations. This therefore is the moment to repair and to strengthen
the English Constitution. The fate of France hangs in suspense. Her success
is yet too dubious, widely or dangerously to diffuse a spirit of imitation;
and the contest between her and the Despotic League is still too equal to
plunge the people of Europe into the lethargy of servility or despair. This
then is that pause of tranquillity, during which we have to prepare against
the hurricane with which we are menaced. This therefore is the moment

when what was before expedient is become necessary; when that Reform is now safe, which in future may be impracticable or dangerous. Reform was before useful to im-<37>prove; it is now necessary (and perhaps the period of its efficacy is shorter than we may imagine) to preserve the Government. Menaced by the predominance of a Democratical or a Monarchical spirit, give the people their rights, and they will not be provoked to demand more; create an independent House of Commons, and the power of the Crown will be checked; Despotism and tumult will be equally averted; the peace of the country will be preserved; the liberty of the country will be immortalized.

Such a moment must have been chosen by a Statesman, who to an enlightened love for public tranquillity united an honest zeal for political Reform. Such a moment therefore was not chosen by YOU. The opportunities which it furnished, and the public duties which it imposed, you neither felt nor regarded. But it afforded an opportunity of another kind, which you did not neglect, and of which, I must confess, you have availed yourself with no mean dexterity. <38>

The discussions produced by the French Revolution had given birth to exaggerated ideas of liberty on one hand, and had furnished a ground to some men, and a pretext to more, for exaggerated fears of anarchy on the other. No such ferment of the human mind had ever arisen without producing many extravagant opinions. Every passion and every frailty, in the ardor of dispute, seduced men into extremes. Many honest men were driven into Toryism by their fears. Many sober men were betrayed into Republicanism by their enthusiasm. Such a division of sentiment was precisely that which a good Minister would labor to heal; but which a crafty Minister would inflame into faction, that he might use it to strengthen and extend his power. You had to chuse under which of these characters you were to pass to posterity, and you have made your election. It was in your choice to mitigate extremes, to conciliate differences, to extend the impartial beneficence of Government to all parties and sects of citizens. But you chose to take the <39> most effectual means to exaggerate extremes, to inflame differences, to give the sanction and countenance of power to one party, to put the Government of the country at the head of a triumphant faction. You disseminated alarms of designs to subvert the Constitution so widely and so successfully, that you have created in this country a spirit of Toryism more indiscriminate, more abject, and more rancorous than has existed in England since the accession of the House of Hanover. Bigotry animates servility, servility mingles with the fear of confusion; the honest fear of confusion becomes the dupe of the corrupt monopolists of power; and from the fermentation of these various passions practised on by your emissaries, there has arisen a pusillanimous and merciless Toryism, which is ready to support the most corrupt Minister, and to proscribe the most temperate advocates of freedom. No spirit could be so valuable to a Minister; nothing could ensure him such cheap and indiscriminate support. You could not fail <40> to recollect the happy use which the dread of Jacobitism was of to Sir Robert Walpole, and you easily saw that the dread of Republicanism might be an equally successful engine in your hands. The reformers of abuse are in such cases called enemies to establishment—The enemies of the *Government* are to be called enemies of the Constitution. To have proposed the retrenchment of a *Tellership* of the *Exchequer* from a Walpole, was once to aim at the introduction of the Pretender; to doubt the consistency of William Pitt, or to impeach the purity of George Rose! is now to meditate the establishment of a democracy.[8]

The progress of such a valuable spirit you saw with a joy which your hirelings boasted, which your higher dependents but ill dissembled, and which was even clumsily concealed by the plausible and pompous hypocrisy of your own character. What wonder that you should see with rapture and triumph the likelihood of even honest <41> men gratuitously enrolling themselves among your Janissaries—What did it import to you, that in the mean while the phrenzy of Republicanism was likely to gain ground among a populace, provoked into wild extremes by the wild extremes of their superiors? What signified the dangers that might in time arise from the awakening understanding of SCOTLAND, from the honest indignation of IRELAND? What were these dangers to you! The Toryism of the higher classes would *last your time,* and any collision between the opposite orders in so-

---

8. George Rose, secretary to the treasury, was implicated in corruption charges during the Westminster election, but a motion to inquire into further irregularities by him was defeated on March 13, 1792; see *Parliamentary History*, 29:1014–33.

ciety, which the diffusion of extreme opinions among them might produce, was viewed without terror by him whose heart had no virtuous interest in the future fate of his country.

It had not however appeared necessary to declare by any overt act the alliance of Government with the favored faction, till an attempt was made to mediate between parties, and to avert the evils which impended over the country. <42>

An association of gentlemen was formed for these purposes. They erected the standard of the British Constitution. They were likely, by the liberality of their principles, to reclaim every thinking man who had been seduced into Republicanism, and by the moderation of their views, to attract every honest man who had for a moment been driven into Toryism. They had already almost effected an union of the friends of liberty and order, and reduced to a miserable handful the two extreme factions; the dread of one of which, and the fury of the other, were to be the instruments of your power.

Such a danger demanded an extreme remedy. No man has more studied or more experienced the *gullibility* of mankind than yourself. You knew that the popular grossness would not distinguish between what it was your policy to confound. You therefore issued a PROCLAMATION, which by directing a vague and indiscriminate odium against all political change, confounded <43> in the same storm of unpopularity the wildest projects of subversion, and the most measured plans of Reform.

A Statesman, emboldened by success, and instructed by experience in all the arts of popular delusion, easily perceived the assailable position of every MEDIATORIAL party, the various enemies they provoke, the opposite imputations they incur. In their labors to avert that fatal collision of the opposite orders of society, which the diffusion of extreme principles threatened, you saw that they would be charged by the corrupt with violence, and accused by the violent of insincerity. It was easy you knew to paint moderation as the virtue of cowards, and compromise as the policy of knaves, to the stormy and intolerant enthusiasm of faction; and the malignant alarms of the corrupt would, it is obvious, be forward to brand every moderate sentiment and every mediatorial effort as symptoms of collusion with the violent, and of treachery to the cause of public <44> order. It scarcely required the incentive and the sanction of a solemn public measure from the Government to let loose so many corrupt interests and malignant passions on the natural object of their enmity. But such a sanction and incentive might certainly add something to the activity of these interests, and to the virulence of these passions. Such a sanction and incentive you therefore gave in your Proclamation.[9] To brand mediation as treachery, and neutrality as disguised hostility; to provoke the violent into new indiscretions, and to make those indiscretions the means of aggravating the Toryism of the timid by awakening their alarms; to bury under one black and indiscriminate obloquy of licentiousness the memory of every principle of freedom; to rally round the banners of religious perfection, and of political corruption, every man in the kingdom who dreads anarchy, and who deprecates confusion; to establish on the broadest foundation oppression and servility for the present, and to heap up in store all the causes of anarchy and civil commotion for <45> future times; such is the malignant policy, such are the mischievous tendencies, such are the experienced effects of that PROCLAMATION. It is sufficient that, *for the present,* it converts the kingdom into a camp of janissaries, enlisted by their alarms to defend your power. It is indeed well adapted to produce other remoter and collateral effects, which the *far-sighted* politics of the Addressers have not discerned. It is certainly well calculated to blow into a flame that spark of Republicanism which moderation must have extinguished, but which may, in future *conceivable circumstances,* produce effects, at the suggestion of which good men will shudder, and on which wise men will rather meditate than descant. It is certain that in this view your Proclamation is as effectual in irritating some men into Republicanism, as Mr. Paine's pamphlets have been in frightening others into Toryism.[10]

Perhaps, however, the events which such a spirit might produce, are contingencies that enter <46> into the calculations of certain Statesmen. Perhaps they anticipate the moment when the Republican mob of the lower orders may be as valuable to them as the Tory vulgar of the higher are now.

9. A reference to the royal proclamation against seditious writings and meetings issued on May 21, 1792.

10. Thomas Paine, *The Rights of Man, Part the First* (London: Johnson, 1791) and Paine, *The Rights of Man, Part the Second* (London: Jordan, 1791–92).

Perhaps they may deem it a master stroke of Machiavelian policy to foment the animosity of two factions, one of whom maintains the present Dictator, and the other of whom may aggrandize the future Demagogue.

Such a policy is not altogether improbable; and if the eternal alliance of wisdom with virtue could be broken, might not be thought altogether unwise. The man who was capable of it would not be deceived by the present appearance of prosperity and content. He would easily see, how rapidly public calamity, acting upon Republican theories, might change the scene; far less would be hindered by the present appearances of furious loyalty among some of the lower classes of society. He would perceive this state of sentiment to be the forced produce of artificial causes, and he <47> could anticipate the violence with which they would rebound to an opposite extreme, more natural to their situation, more congenial to their feelings, and more gratifying to their pride.

The success of such a policy would certainly demand in the Statesman who adopted it an union of talents and dispositions which are not often combined. Cold, stern, crafty, and ambiguous, he must be, without those entanglements of friendship and those restraints of feeling, by which tender natures are held back from desperate enterprizes. No ingenuousness must betray a glimpse of his designs; no compunction must suspend the stroke of his ambition. He must never be seduced into any honest profession of *precise* public principle, which might afterwards arise against him as the record of his apostacy; he must be prepared for acting every inconsistency, by perpetually veiling his political professions in the *nomeaning* of lofty generalities. The absence of gracious and popular manners, which can find no <48> place in such a character will be well compensated by the austere and ostentatious virtues of insensibility. He must possess the parade without the restraints of morals. He must unite the most profound dissimulation with all the ardor of enterprize; he must be prepared by one part of his character for the violence of a multitude, and by another for the duplicity of a Court. If such a man arose at any critical moment in the fortune of a State; if he were unfettered by any great political connexion; if his interest were not linked to the stability of public order by any ample property; if he could carry with him to any enterprize no little authority and splendor of character; he indeed would be an object of more rational dread than a thousand Republican pamphleteers.

Against such a man it would be fit to warn the people whom he might delude, and the opulent whom he might destroy. Whether such be the character of any living Statesman, it belongs to History to determine. <49>

I shall dwell no longer on portraits that may be imaginary, and speculations which may be illusive. The dangers which have haunted my imagination may be unreal; but if ever such dangers should be realized in a moment of public calamity, and if public confidence should then be triumphantly seized by a convicted delinquent, like the present Minister of England; if the people should then forget the blackest treachery to their cause, and the meanest malignity against their friends; then indeed the parade of your confidence in popular folly will be justified; and a contempt for the understanding of the people will be proved to be the best requisite for ruling them absolutely, as well as the best proof of having estimated them correctly.

If such be the state of the People of England, no human power can save them; they must be abandoned to their misfortunes and to your delusions. In the confidence that they are more generous, and more wise, I have now arraigned <50> you before their tribunal. Events will decide whether my respect or your contempt be best founded, and the decision involves the fate of liberty and of our country.

I will not conclude this letter with expressions of respect which I do not entertain, but I will close it with confidently asserting, that every line of it contains the unbiassed sentiments of

AN HONEST MAN.

No. I
Opinion of Mr. Locke on Representation.

"Things of this world are in so constant a flux, that nothing remains long in the same state. Thus people, riches, trade, power, change their stations, flourishing mighty cities come to ruin, and prove in time neglected desolate corners, whilst other unfrequented places grow into populous countries, filled with wealth and inhabitants. But things not always changing equally, and private interest often keeping up customs and privileges, when the reasons of them are ceased, it often comes to pass, that in governments, where part of the legislative consists of representatives chosen by the people, that in tract of time this representation becomes very unequal and disproportionate to the reasons it was at first established upon. To what gross absurdities the following of custom, when reason has left it, may lead, we may be satisfied, when we see the bare name of a town, of which there remains not so much as the ruins, where scarce so much housing as a sheep-cot, or more inhabitants than a shepherd is to be found, sends *as many Representatives* to the grand Assembly of Law makers, as a whole county, numerous <2> in people, and powerful in riches. This strangers stand amazed at, and every one must confess needs a remedy. For it being the interest, as well as the intention of the people to have a fair and *equal Representative;* whoever brings it nearest to that, is an undoubted FRIEND TO, AND ESTABLISHER OF THE GOVERNMENT, and cannot miss the consent and approbation of the community. 'Tis not a change from the present state, which perhaps corruption or decay has introduced, that makes an inroad upon the Government, but the tendency of it to injure or oppress the people, and to set up one part, or party, with a distinction from, and an unequal subjection of the rest."

Locke on Civil Government, Book II.
Chap. 13. Sect. 157, 158.[1]

No. II
Opinion of Mr. Justice Blackstone.

This is the SPIRIT of our Constitution: not that I assert it is in fact quite so perfect as I have here endeavoured to describe it; for, if any alteration might be wished or suggested in the present frame of Parliaments, it should be in favour of a more COMPLEAT REPRESENTATION OF THE PEOPLE.

Blackstone's Commentaries, Vol. 1. Page 171, 172.[2]

Such is the confession extorted by the force of truth from our cautious and courtly commentator. <3>

No. III

Extracts from a letter written by the Duke of Richmond to Lieutenant Colonel Sharman, Chairman of the Committee of Correspondence at Belfast, dated August 15th, 1783.[3]

"I have no hesitation in saying, that from every consideration which I have been able to give to this great question, that for many years has occupied my mind; and from every day's experience to the present hour I am more and more convinced, that the restoring the right of voting universally to every man not incapacitated by nature for want of reason, or by law for the commission of crimes,

1. John Locke, *Two Treatises of Government,* bk. 2, chap. 13, secs. 157 and 158.
2. William Blackstone, *Commentaries on the Laws of England. A Facsimile of the First Edition of 1765–1769,* ed. S. N. Katz, 4 vols. (Chicago and London: University of Chicago Press, 1979, 2002), 1:166.
3. *A Letter from His Grace the Duke of Richmond to Lieutenant Colonel Sharman, Chairman to the Committee of Correspondence Appointed by the Delegates of Forty-Five Corps of Volunteers, Assembled at Lisburn in Ireland; With Notes, by a Member of the Society for Constitutional Information* (London: Johnson, 1792), 4–8.

together with annual elections, is the only reform that can be effectual and permanent. I am further convinced, that it is the only reform that is practicable. [. . .] The lesser reform *(alluding to Mr. Pitt's motion in the House of Commons)* has been attempted with every possible advantage in its favor; not only from the zealous support of the advocates for a more effectual one, but from the assistance of men of great weight both in and out of power. But with all those temperaments and helps it has failed; not one *proselyte* has been gained from *corruption;* nor has the least ray of hope been held out from any quarter, that the House of Commons was inclined to adopt any other mode of reform. The weight of corruption has crushed this more gentle, as it would have defeated any more efficacious plan in the same circumstances. From that quarter, therefore, I have nothing to hope. It is from the people <4> at large that I expect any good, and I am convinced that the only way to make them feel that they are really concerned in the business, is to contend for their full, clear, and indisputable rights of universal representation. But in the more liberal and great plan of universal representation a clear and distinct principle at once appears, that cannot lead us wrong. Not CONVENIENCY, but RIGHT. If it is not a maxim of our Constitution, that a British subject is to be governed only by laws to which he has consented by himself or his representative, we should instantly abandon the error; but if it is the essential of Freedom, founded on the eternal principles of justice and wisdom, and our unalienable birth-right, we should not hesitate in asserting it. Let us then but determine to act upon this broad principle of giving to every man his own, and we shall immediately get rid of all the perplexities to which the narrow notions of partiality and exclusion must ever be subject."

No. IV

Opinion of the City of London.[4]

Guildhall, Tuesday, April 11, 1782.
"At a meeting of the Livery of London, appointed to correspond with the Committees of the several counties, cities, &c. of the kingdom,"
Mr. ALDERMAN CROSBY in the Chair,
"Resolved Unanimously,
"That in the judgment of this Committee, unless a melioration of Parliament

4. Unable to find source of this extract.

can be obtained, the best official <5> regulations may soon be set aside, the wisest and most virtuous ministers may soon be displaced; by the prevalence of that corrupt influence now subsisting in the House of Commons, which its defective frame naturally generates, and which has already so nearly effected the ruin of this unhappy country."

No. V
Opinion of Associated English Counties.[5]

Extracts from the proceedings of a Meeting of Deputies appointed by the several petitioning or associated bodies hereinafter mentioned.

The counties of York, Surry, Hertford, Huntingdon, Middlesex, Essex, Kent, Devon, and Nottingham, and the city of Westminster, held on the 3rd day of March, and by different adjournments on the 10th, 17th, 19th, 24th, and 31st days of March, and 21st day of April, 1781,

"Resolved,

"That the parliamentary representation of this kingdom is extremely inadequate."

"Resolved,

"That the extensive public evils have been produced by the gross inadequacy of the representation of the people in parliaments." <6>

No. VI
Thatched House Tavern, May 16, 1782.[6]

At a numerous and respectable meeting of members of parliament friendly to a Constitutional Reformation, and of members of several committees of counties and cities,

5. Unable to find source of this extract.
6. "Proceedings of the Meeting at the Thatched House Tavern, 16 May 1782," in *A Complete Collection of State Trials and Proceedings for High Treason and Other Crimes and Misdemeanors from the Earliest Period to the Year 1783, with Notes and Other Illustrations,* ed. T. B. Howell and continued from the year 1783 to the present time by T. J. Howell (London: Hansard, 1817), 22:492–93.

PRESENT,

The Duke of RICHMOND,	The Hon. WILLIAM PITT,
Lord SURREY,	The Rev. Mr. WYVILL,
Lord MAHON,	Major CARTWRIGHT,
The LORD MAYOR,	Mr. JOHN HORNE TOOKE,
Sir WATKIN LEWES,	Alderman WILKES,
Mr. DUNCOMBE,	Doctor JEBB,
Sir C. WRAY,	Mr. CHURCHILL,
Mr. B. HOLLIS,	Mr. FROST,
Mr. WITHERS,	&c. &c. &c.

"Resolved unanimously,

"That the motion of the HON. WILLIAM PITT, on the 7th inst. for the appointment of a Committee of the House of Commons to enquire into the State of the Representation of the People of Great Britain, and to report the same to the House, and also what steps it might be necessary to take, having been defeated by a motion for the order of the day, it is become indispensibly necessary that application should be made to Parliament by petitions from the collective body of the people, in their respective districts, requesting a substantial Reformation of the Commons House of Parliament. <7>

"Resolved unanimously,

"That this meeting, considering that a general application by the collective body of the people to the House of Commons cannot be made before the close of the present session, is of opinion that THE SENSE OF THE PEOPLE SHOULD BE TAKEN AT SUCH TIMES AS MAY BE CONVENIENT DURING THIS SUMMER, IN ORDER TO LAY THEIR SEVERAL PETITIONS BEFORE PARLIAMENT EARLY IN THE NEXT SESSION, WHEN THEIR PROPOSALS FOR A PARLIAMENTARY REFORMATION (WITHOUT WHICH NEITHER THE LIBERTY OF THE NATION CAN BE PRESERVED, NOR THE PERMANENCE OF A WISE AND VIRTUOUS AD-MINISTRATION CAN BE SECURE) MAY RECEIVE THAT AMPLE AND MATURE DISCUSSION, WHICH SO MOMENTOUS A QUESTION DEMANDS."

No. VII

Until the report of the Committee of the Friends of the People on the present state of the Representation shall appear, the following may serve as a specimen of the wretched tenure by which the privileges and liberties of the People of England are now held.

"If we take the places where the majority of the electors comes below 20, it is shameful what a proportion of the 513 (members for England and Wales) is sent into the House by a handful, and that handful mostly people in low circumstances, and therefore obnoxious to bribery, or under the power of their superiors. <8>

		Sends members		Chosen by
Lestwithiel	—	2	—	13
Truro	—	2	—	14
Bodmin	—	2	—	19
Saltash	—	2	—	15
Camelford	—	2	—	10
Bossiney	—	1	—	11
St. Michael	—	2	—	14
St. Mawes	—	2	—	16
Tiverton	—	2	—	14
Malden	—	2	—	14
Harwich	—	2	—	17
Thetford	—	2	—	17
Brackley	—	2	—	17
Banbury	—	2	—	11
Bath	—	2	—	17
Newport, Wight	—	2	—	13
Newton, ditto	—	2	—	1
Andover	—	2	—	13
Gatton	—	2	—	11
Bramber	—	2	—	8
East Grinstead	—	2	—	19
Calne	—	2	—	18
Malmsbury	—	2	—	7
Old Sarum	—	2	—	1
Bewdley	—	2	—	18
New Romney	—	2	—	17
Marlborough	—	2	—	2
Buckingham	—	2	—	7
		56		364

<9> "Here we see 56 members (about a ninth-part of the whole for England) are sent into the House of Commons by 364 votes, which number ought not to send in one member. For no member ought to be elected by fewer than the majority of 800, upon the most moderate calculation, in order to give 410,000 voters their due and equally distributed share of legislative power, without which equal distribution the majority of the men of property are enslaved to the handful of beggars, who, by electing the majority of the House of Commons, have so great an overbalance of power over them, as to be able to carry every point in direct opposition to their opinion and to their interest."

Burgh's Political Disquisitions, vol. I. page 47–8.[7]

No. VIII

Sentiments delivered by Mr. Pitt on Parliamentary Reform, in his speech in the House of Commons, on Monday the 19th of April, 1785.[8]

"He said he was sensible of the difficulty which there was now, and ever must be in proposing a plan of reform. The number of gentlemen who were hostile to reform, were a phalanx which ought to give alarm to any individual upon rising to suggest such a measure. Those who, with a sort of superstitious awe, reverence the constitution so much as to be fearful of touching even its defects, had always reprobated every attempt to purify the representation. They acknowledged its inequality and corruption, but in their enthusiasm for the grand fabric, they would <10> not suffer a reformer with unhallowed hands to repair the injuries which it suffered from time. Others, who perceiving the deficiencies that had arisen from circumstances, were solicitous of their amendment, yet resisted the attempt, under the argument, that when once we had presumed to touch the Constitution in one point, the awe which had heretofore kept us back from the daring enterprize of innovation, might abate, and there was no foreseeing to what alarming lengths we might progressively go under the mask of Reformation. Others there were, but for these he confessed he had not the same respect, who considered the present state of representation as pure and adequate to all its purposes, and perfectly consistent with the first principles of represen-

7. James Burgh, *Political Disquisitions,* 3 vols. (London: E. & C. Dilly, 1774), 1:47–48.

8. *Parliamentary History of England from the Norman Conquest, in 1066, to the Year 1803,* 36 vols. (London: Hansard, 1806–20), 25:432–50.

tation. The fabric of the House of Commons was an ancient pile, on which they had been all taught to look with reverence and awe: from their cradles they had been accustomed to view it as a pattern of perfection; their ancestors had enjoyed freedom and prosperity under it; and therefore an attempt to make any alterations in it, would be deemed by some enthusiastic admirers of antiquity, as impious and sacrilegious. No one reverenced the venerable fabric more than he did; but all mankind knew, that the best institutions, like human bodies, carried in themselves the seeds of decay and corruption; and therefore he thought himself justifiable in proposing remedies against this corruption, which the frame of the constitution must necessarily experience in the lapse of years, if not prevented by wise and judicious regulations. [. . .]

"The argument of withstanding all reformation, from the fear of the ill consequences that might ensue, made <11> gentlemen come to a sort of compromise with themselves. We are sensible of certain defects; we feel certain inconveniences in the present state of representation; but fearing that we may make it worse by alteration, we will be content with it as it is." This was a sort of argument to which he could not give his countenance. If gentlemen had at all times been content with this sort of average, the nation would have lost much of that excellence of which our Constitution now had to boast. [. . .]

"If there always had been a House of Commons who were the faithful stewards of the interests of their country, the diligent checks on the administration of the finances, the constitutional advisers of the executive branch of the Legislature, the steady and uninfluenced friends of the People, he asked, IF THE BURDENS WHICH THE CONSTITUENTS OF THAT HOUSE WERE NOW DOOMED TO ENDURE, WOULD HAVE BEEN INCURRED? Would the People of England have suffered the calamities to which they had lately been made subject? [. . .]

"He needed not, he believed, to enumerate the arguments that presented themselves to his mind in favor of a reform. Every gentleman who had taken pains to investigate the subject, must see that it was most materially wanted. To conquer the corruption that existed in those decayed boroughs, he believed that gentlemen would acknowledge to be impossible. The temptation were too great for poverty to resist, and the consequence of this corruption was so visible, that some plan of reforming the boroughs had clearly become absolutely necessary. In times <12> of calamity and distress, how truly important was it to the people of this country that the House of Commons should sympathize with themselves, and that their interests should be indissoluble? It was most material that the People should have confidence in their own branch of the Legislature; the force of the Constitution, as well as its beauty, depended on that confidence, and on the union and sympathy which existed between the constituent and representative. The source of our glory and the muscles of our strength were the pure character of freedom which our Constitution bore. To lessen that character, to taint it, was to take from our vitals a part of their vigor, and to lessen not only our importance but our energy with our neighbours. [. . .]

"The purity of representation was the only true and permanent source of such confidence; for though occasionally bright characters had arisen, who, in spite of the general corruption and depravity of the day in which they lived, had manifested the superior influence of integrity and virtue, and had forced both Parliament and People to countenance their Administration; yet it would be unwise for the People of England to leave their fate to the chance of such characters often arising, when prudence must dictate that the certain way of securing their properties and freedom was to purify the sources of representation, and to establish that strict relation between themselves and the House of Commons which it was the original idea of the Constitution to create. He hoped that the plan which he had mentioned was likely to re-establish such a relation; and he recommended to gentlemen not to suffer their minds to be alarmed by unnecessary <13> fears. NOTHING WAS SO HURTFUL TO IMPROVEMENT AS THE FEAR OF BEING CARRIED FARTHER THAN THE PRINCIPLE ON WHICH A PERSON SET OUT.

"It was common for gentlemen to reason with themselves, and to say that they would have no objection to go so far, and no farther, if they were sure, that in countenancing the first step, they might not either be led themselves, or lead others farther than they intended to go. So much they were apt to say was right— so far they would go—of such a scheme they approved—but fearing that it might be carried too far, they desisted from doing even what they conceived to be proper. He deprecated this conduct, and hoped that gentlemen would come to the consideration of this business, without fearing that it would lead to consequences that would either ruin or alarm us."

Debrett's Parliamentary Register for 1785, p. 43, et seq.

No. IX

Extracts from the speech of Mr. Thomas Pitt, Proprietor of Old Sarum, on the 7th of May 1783.[9]

"That his honorable friend had truly stated that the principal objection that had been urged to what he then proposed, the going into <14> a committee to examine into the state of the representation, was that no specific remedy was then submitted to the House; and that at a time when wild and impracticable ideas of reform, and visionary speculations of imagined rights were floating on the public, such a committee would tend to alarm the minds of sober men, to inflame the madness of theorists, and to hold out expectations that neither could, nor ought, nor were intended to be satisfied. [. . .]

"That it was true that the temper of the times, was a very great additional ground to the opposition which he gave to the former motion; and that he certainly could have wished, that whatever alterations were to take place could have been brought on at a time, when men's minds were less heated by speculative opinions; that however he <15> could not but congratulate that House, and the country in general, that these dangerous doctrines were disavowed by a person of the weight of the right honorable mover of these resolutions, as well in what he had so ably stated in his opening, as in the propositions themselves; which if adopted by the House, would stand as the strongest protest against these wild speculations. That an honorable friend of his (Mr. Powys) had read such extracts from some of these incendiaries, as could not fail to make known the tendency of their tenets; that he had never thought, with all the industry that had been used, that such opinions had extended very far in the body of the people; and that he was convinced, that even by the interval of a few months <16> they had already visibly subsided amongst many of the most zealous. [. . .]

"That he could not, at the same time that he approved of such an experiment, even in the present moment deny the weight of such arguments as were founded upon the unreasonable spirit of innovation, which certainly his honorable friend could not suppose it was in his power to satisfy by such concessions as these, or indeed by any practicable reform whatever. The clamor would not be appeased by it among those who are the loudest in their calls for alterations; he wished therefore sincerely, that some such plan had already taken place in times of more calm and sober judgment." <17>

9. Ibid., 23:839–44.

Extracts from the speech of the Right Hon. William Pitt,
Chancellor of the Exchequer, on the 30th of April, 1792.[10]

"It was obvious," Mr. Pitt said, "to every rational and reflecting man, that two
objects present themselves for their consideration; the first, the probability of
carrying a Reform in Parliament at all; and the other, whether or not that Reform, if carried, would not be attended with a risk that would outweigh the
advantages that might accrue from it. To the first, he declared, he did not think
that Gentlemen would readily be persuaded to believe by what they had seen,
and by what they knew, that there existed any alteration in the minds of the
people tending to shew that a change in their Representation would be agreeable
to their wishes; there was infinitely greater reason to believe that an attempt to
carry any scheme into effect would produce consequences to which no man can
look without horror and apprehension.

"That there were out of that House men who were anxious to destroy the
Constitution he was perfectly ready to admit: that their numbers were great, or
their power vigorous he was happy enough to doubt; their force, he was persuaded, if it should come to be opposed to the sound part of the Constitution
and its defenders, would be found to be weak and trivial. He did not, Mr. Pitt
declared, deem the conduct of those Members of Parliament to be the most
meritorious, who agitated the propriety of a Reform in the shape of an Adver-
tisement in the newspaper,* rather than by discussions in that House; he would
not, however, enter on that point, as he was willing to impute the best motives
to every man. As far, Mr. Pitt said, as he had had opportunities of learning the
opinions of the people, and of observing their condition, he had reason to think
them perfectly tranquil and happy: the principles, however, that some men had
adopted, tended, he feared, to overturn that tranquillity, and destroy that happiness. In regard to that matter, however, he had a stronger reason for his conduct; he was firmly convinced that the allies to whom the Hon. Gentleman was
to look for support, were not those whose object was to repair the Constitution,
but to sap the foundation, and destroy the edifice; they were persons who had
condemned hereditary monarchy, abused aristocracy, and decried all proper and
regulated Government whatever; men, who while they for one minute talked

---

* For the decency and confidency with which the Right Hon. Gentleman makes this
remark. See the Resolutions at the Thatched House Tavern, No. VI. of this Appendix.

10. A slightly different version of this speech appears in *Parliamentary History*,
29:1310–12.

of a Parliamentary Reform, libelled the Revolution itself the other, who ridiculed the idea of rank and subordination, and endeavoured to impress upon the mind of the public, a desire to substitute for the happy constitution they at present enjoy, a plan founded on what was absurdly termed the Rights of Man; a plan which never existed in any part of the habitable globe, and which, if it should exist in the morning, must perish ere sunset; as must be the inevitable fate of the government of any kingdom which should be formed on that absurd and impracticable system. To the last hour of his life, Mr. Pitt declared, he was determined to maintain and defend the Constitution of his country, for he was convinced that it was the best that ever was formed for the happiness of men; and he was convinced that there existed no chance of success from the proceedings of the Hon. Gentleman, and from any frauds which might be practised, but that they tended to risk <18> the incurring consequences the most dreadful. Were he put to the disagreeable alternative of giving his vote for ever to forego reform, or to risk the inevitable and dreadful consequences which would arise from the attempts, if permitted, of the new reformers, he declared upon his honour, as an Englishman, and as a friend to the Constitution, that he should have no doubt of voting the former. Thus much, Mr. Pitt said, he had offered as to the *time* of bringing forward the business, which, when coupled with the *mode,* rendered it still more dangerous. The minds of men were led to no plan, nor had they any grievance stated to them. Their opinions were set afloat,* and their understandings were endeavoured to be poisoned by <19> the general assertion of the existence of grievances, and the inadequacy of the Representation in Parliament they had that held out to them as innocent and harmless, which was destructive and iniquitous."

FINIS.

---

* The Reader is again requested to study the character of Mr. Pitt in the contrast between this assertion and the Thatched House Resolution.

A Discourse on the
Law of Nature and Nations

<341>

Before I begin a course of lectures on a science of great extent and importance, I think it my duty to lay before the public the reasons which have induced me to undertake such a labour, as well as a short account of the nature and objects of the course which I propose to deliver. I have always been unwilling to waste in unprofitable inactivity that leisure which the first years of my profession usually allow, and which diligent men, even with moderate talents, might often employ in a manner neither discreditable to themselves, nor wholly useless to others. Desirous that my own leisure should not be consumed in sloth, I anxiously looked about for some way of filling it up, which might enable me, according to the measure of my humble abilities, to contribute somewhat to the stock of general usefulness. I had long been convinced that public lectures, which have been used in most <342> ages and countries to teach the elements of almost every part of learning, were the most convenient mode in which these elements could be taught;—that they were the best adapted for the important purposes of awakening the attention of the student, of abridging his labours, of guiding his inquiries, of relieving the tediousness of private study, and of impressing on his recollection the principles of a science. I saw no reason why the law of England should be less adapted to this mode of instruction, or less likely to benefit by it, than any other part of knowledge. A learned gentleman, however, had already occupied that ground,* and will, I doubt not, persevere in the useful labour which he has undertaken. On his prov-

---

* See "A Syllabus of Lectures on the Law of England, to be delivered in Lincoln's-Inn Hall by M. Nolan, Esq."

ince it was far from my wish to intrude. It appeared to me that a course of lectures on another science closely connected with all liberal professional studies, and which had long been the subject of my own reading and reflection, might not only prove a most useful introduction to the law of England, but might also become an interesting part of general study, and an important branch of the education of those who were not destined for the profession of the law. I was confirmed in my opinion by the assent and approbation of men, whose names, if it were becoming to mention them on so slight an occasion, would add authority to truth, and furnish some excuse even for error. Encouraged by their approbation, I resolved without delay to commence the undertaking, of which I shall now proceed to give some account; without interrupting the progress of my discourse by anticipating or answering the remarks of those who may, perhaps, sneer at me for a departure from the usual course of my profession, because I am desirous of employing in a rational and useful pursuit that leisure, of which the same men would have required no account, if it had been wasted on trifles, or even abused in dissipation. <343>

The science which teaches the rights and duties of men and of states, has, in modern times, been called "the law of nature and nations." Under this comprehensive title are included the rules of morality, as they prescribe the conduct of private men towards each other in all the various relations of human life; as they regulate both the obedience of citizens to the laws, and the authority of the magistrate in framing laws, and administering government; and as they modify the intercourse of independent commonwealths in peace, and prescribe limits to their hostility in war. This important science comprehends only that part of private ethics which is capable of being reduced to fixed and general rules. It considers only those general principles of jurisprudence and politics which the wisdom of the lawgiver adapts to the peculiar situation of his own country, and which the skill of the statesman applies to the more fluctuating and infinitely varying circumstances which affect its immediate welfare and safety. "For there are in nature certain fountains of justice whence all civil laws are derived, but as streams; and like as waters do take tinctures and tastes from the soils through which they run, so do civil laws vary according to the regions and governments where they are planted, though they proceed from the same fountains."*

On the great questions of morality, of politics, and of municipal law, it is the object of this science to deliver only those fundamental truths of which the particular application is as extensive as the whole private and public conduct of men;—to discover those "fountains of justice," without pursuing the "streams" through the endless variety of their course. But another part of the subject is to be treated with greater <344> fulness and minuteness of application; namely, that important branch of it which professes to regulate the relations and intercourse of states, and more especially, (both on account of their greater perfection and their more immediate reference to use), the regulations of that intercourse as they are modified by the usages of the civilized nations of Christendom. Here this science no longer rests on general principles. That province of it which we now call the "law of nations," has, in many of its parts, acquired among European ones much of the precision and certainty of positive law; and the particulars of that law are chiefly to be found in the works of those writers who have treated the science of which I now speak. It is because they have classed (in a manner which seems peculiar to modern times) the duties of individuals with those of nations, and established their obligation on similar grounds, that the whole science has been called, the "law of nature and nations."

Whether this appellation be the happiest that could have been chosen for the science, and by what steps it came to be adopted among our modern moralists and lawyers,† are inquiries, perhaps, of more curiosity <345> than

---

* Advancement of Learning, book ii. [*The Works of Francis Bacon . . . in Five Volumes* (London: A. Millar, 1765), 1:101.] I have not been deterred by some petty incongruity of metaphor from quoting this noble sentence. Mr. Hume had, perhaps, this sentence in his recollection, when he wrote a remarkable passage of his works. See his Essays, vol. ii. p. 352. [Hume, *Essays,* 2 vols. (London, 1788), 2:352, "A Dialogue."]

† The learned reader is aware that the "jus naturae" and "jus gentium" of the Roman lawyers are phrases of very different import from the modern phrases, "law of nature" and "law of nations." "Jus naturale," says Ulpian, "est quod natura omnia animalia docuit." "Quod naturalis ratio inter omnes homines constituit, id apud omnes peraeque custoditur; vocaturque jus gentium." ["Natural law is that which nature instils in all animals." "But what natural reason has established among all men is observed equally

use, and ones which, if they deserve any where to be deeply pursued, will be pursued with more propriety in a full examination of the subject than within the short limits of an introductory discourse. Names are, however, in a great measure arbitrary; but the distribution of knowledge into its parts, though it may often perhaps be varied with little disadvantage, yet certainly depends upon some fixed principles. The modern method of considering individual and national morality as the subjects of the same science, seems to me as convenient and reasonable an arrangement as can be adopted. The same rules of morality which hold together men in families, and which form families into commonwealths, also link together these commonwealths as members of the great society of mankind. Commonwealths, as well as private men, are liable to injury, and capable of benefit, from each other; it is, therefore, their interest, as well as their duty, to rev-

---

by all nations and is designated *ius gentium* or the law of nations." Justinian, *The Institutes of Justinian, Text, Translation, and Commentary,* ed. J. A. C. Thomas (Cape Town: Juta, 1975), 4 (Bk. 1, Tit.).] But they sometimes neglect this subtle distinction—"Jure naturali quod appellatur jus gentium." ["Natural Law which is known as the Law of Nations."] "Jus feciale" was the Roman term for our law of nations. "Belli quidem aequitas sanctissimè populi Rom. feciali jure perscripta est." De Officiis, lib. i. cap. ii. ["As for war, humane laws touching it are drawn up in the fetial code of the Roman People under all the guarantees of religion." Cicero, *De Officiis,* trans. W. Miller (London and Cambridge, Mass.: Heinemann and Harvard University Press, 1956), 38–39 (I.36).] Our learned civilian Zouch has accordingly entitled his work, "De Jure Feciali, sive de Jure inter Gentes." [R. Zouch, *Iuris et Iudicii Fecialis, sive, Iuris Inter Gentes, et Quaestionum de Eodem Explicatio* (An exposition of fecial law and procedure, or of law between nations), ed. T. Erskine Holland (Washington: Carnegie Institution, 1911).] The Chancellor D'Aguesseau, probably without knowing the work of Zouch, suggested that this law should be called, "Droit entre les Gens" (oeuvres, vol. ii. p. 337) [Literally "law between people." This is perhaps a reference to d'Aguesseau: "Elle sont le seul appui ordinaire de ce droit, qui merité proprement le nom de Droit des gens, c'est à dire, de celui qui a lieu de Royaume à Royaume ou d'Etat à d'Etat." *Oeuvres de Monseigneur le chancelier d'Aguesseau,* 10 vols. (Yverdun, 1772–75), 2:76. Unable to trace the edition to which Mackintosh refers, but he may simply have taken it from Bentham; see below.], in which he has been followed by a late ingenious writer, Mr. Bentham, (Introduction to the Principles of Morals and Legislation, p. 324.) [Jeremy Bentham, *An Introduction to the Principles of Morals and Legislation* (London: T. Payne & Son, 1789), 324.]. Perhaps these learned writers do employ a phrase which expresses the subject of this law with more accuracy than our common language; but I doubt whether innovations in the terms of science always repay us by their superior precision for the uncertainty and confusion which the change occasions.

erence, to practise, and to enforce those rules of justice which control and restrain injury,—which regulate and augment benefit,—which, even in their present imperfect observance, preserve civilized states in a tolerable condition of security from wrong, and which, if they could be generally obeyed, would establish, and permanently maintain, the well-being of the universal commonwealth of the human race. It is therefore with justice, that one part of this science has been called "the natural law of *individuals,*" and the other "the natural law of *states*"; and it is too obvious to require observation,* that the application of both these laws, of the former as much as of the latter, is modified and varied by customs, conventions, character, and situation. With a view to these principles, the writers on general jurisprudence have considered states as moral persons; a mode of expression which has been called a fiction of law, but which may be regarded with more propriety as a bold metaphor, used to convey the important truth, that nations, though they acknowledge no <346> common superior, and neither can, nor ought, to be subjected to human punishment, are yet under the same obligations mutually to practise honesty and humanity, which would have bound individuals,—if the latter could be conceived ever to have subsisted without the protecting restraints of government, and if they were not compelled to the discharge of their duty by the just authority of magistrates, and by the wholesome terrors of the laws. With the same views this law has been styled, and (notwithstanding the objections of some writers to the vagueness of the language) appears to have been styled with great propriety, "the law of nature." It may with sufficient correctness, or at least by an easy metaphor, be called a "law," inasmuch as it is a supreme, invariable, and uncontrollable rule of conduct to all men, the violation of which is avenged by natural punishments, necessarily flowing from the constitution of things, and as fixed and inevitable as the order of nature. It is "the law of nature," because its general precepts are essentially adapted to pro-

---

* This remark is suggested by an objection of Vattel, which is more specious than solid. See his Preliminaries, § 6 [E. de Vattel, *Le droit des gens, ou Principes de la loi naturelle appliqués á la conduite et aus affaires de nations et des souverains,* vol. 3, *The Law of Nations or the Principles of Natural Law Applied to the Conduct and to the Affairs of Nations and of Sovereigns,* trans. of 1758 ed. by C. G. Fenwick (New York: Oceana Publications, 1964), 4 (introduction §6)].

mote the happiness of man, as long as he remains a being of the same nature
with which he is at present endowed, or, in other words, as long as he continues to be man, in all the variety of times, places, and circumstances, in
which he has been known, or can be imagined to exist; because it is discoverable by natural reason, and suitable to our natural constitution; and
because its fitness and wisdom are founded on the general nature of human
beings, and not on any of those temporary and accidental situations in
which they may be placed. It is with still more propriety, and indeed with
the highest strictness, and the most perfect accuracy, considered as a law,
when, according to those just and magnificent views which philosophy and
religion open to us of the government of the world, it is received and reverenced as the sacred code, promulgated by the great Legislator of the Universe for the guidance of His creatures to happiness;—guarded and enforced, as our own experience may inform us, by <347> the penal sanctions
of shame, of remorse, of infamy, and of misery; and still farther enforced
by the reasonable expectation of yet more awful penalties in a future and
more permanent state of existence. It is the contemplation of the law of
nature under this full, mature, and perfect idea of its high origin and tran-
scendent dignity, that called forth the enthusiasm of the greatest men, and
the greatest writers of ancient and modern times, in those sublime descriptions, in which they have exhausted all the powers of language, and surpassed all the other exertions, even of their own eloquence, in the display
of its beauty and majesty. It is of this law that Cicero has spoken in so many
parts of his writings, not only with all the splendour and copiousness of
eloquence, but with the sensibility of a man of virtue, and with the gravity
and comprehension of a philosopher.* It is of this law that Hooker speaks

---

* "Est quidem vera lex recta ratio, naturae congruens, diffusa in omnes, constans,
sempiterna; quae vocet ad officium jubendo, vetando à fraude deterreat, quae tamen
neque probos frustra jubet aut vetat, neque improbos jubendo aut vetando movet. Huic
legi neque obrogari fas est, neque derogari ex hac aliquid licet, neque tota abrogari potest.
Nec verò aut per senatum aut per populum solvi hac lege possumus: neque est quaeren-
dus explanator aut interpres ejus alius. Nec erit alia lex Romae, alia Athenis, alia nunc,
alia posthac; sed et omnes gentes et omni tempore una lex et sempiterna, et immutabilis
continebit; unusque erit communis quasi magister et imperator omnium Deus, ille legis

in so sublime a strain:—"Of Law, no less can be said, than that her seat is the bosom of God, her voice the harmony of the world; all things in heaven and earth do her homage, the very least as feeling her care, the greatest as not exempted from her power; both angels and men, and creatures of what condition soever, though each in different sort and manner, yet all with uniform consent admiring her as the mother of their peace and joy."* <348>

Let not those who, to use the language of the same Hooker, "talk of truth," without "ever sounding the depth from whence it springeth,"¹ hastily take it for granted, that these great masters of eloquence and reason were led astray by the specious delusions of mysticism, from the sober consideration of the true grounds of morality in the nature, necessities, and interests of man. They studied and taught the principles of morals; but they thought it still more necessary, and more wise,—a much nobler task, and more becoming a true philosopher, to inspire men with a love and reverence

----

hujus inventor, disceptator, lator: cui qui non parebit *ipse se fugiet et naturam hominis aspernabitur,* atque hoc ipso luet maximas poenas, etiamsi caetera supplicia, quae putantur, effugerit."—De Repub. lib. iii. cap. 22. ["True law is right reason in agreement with nature; it is of universal application, unchanging and everlasting; it summons to duty by its commands, and averts from wrongdoing by its prohibitions. And it does not lay its commands or prohibitions upon good men in vain, though neither have any effect on the wicked. It is a sin to try to alter this law, nor is it allowable to attempt to repeal any part of it, and it is impossible to abolish it entirely. We cannot be freed from its obligations by senate or people, and we need not look outside ourselves for an expounder or interpreter of it. And there will not be different laws at Rome and at Athens, or different laws now and in the future, but one eternal and unchangeable law will be valid for all nations and all times, and there will be one master and ruler, that is, God, over us all, for he is the author of this law, its promulgator, and its enforcing judge. Whoever is disobedient is fleeing from himself and denying his human nature, and by reason of this very fact he will suffer the worst penalties, even if he escapes what is commonly considered punishment. . . ." Cicero, *De re publica,* in *De re publica, De legibus,* trans. C. Walker Keyes (London and Cambridge, Mass.: Heinemann and Harvard University Press, 1959), 210–11 (III, xxii, 33). The son's edition omitted an additional paragraph: "It is impossible to read such precious fragments without deploring the loss of a work which, for the benefit of all generations, *should* have been immortal."]

* Ecclesiastical Polity, book i. in the conclusion [Richard Hooker, *Of the Laws of Ecclesiastical Polity,* ed. A. S. McGrade (Cambridge: Cambridge University Press, 1989), 127 (bk. 1, chap. 16.8)].

1. Possibly based on Hooker, *Of the Laws of Ecclesiastical Polity,* 121.

for virtue.* They were not contented with elementary speculations: they examined the foundations of our duty; but they felt and cherished a most natural, a most seemly, a most rational enthusiasm, when they contemplated the majestic edifice which is reared on these solid foundations. They devoted the highest exertions of their minds to spread that beneficent enthusiasm among men. They consecrated as a homage to Virtue the most perfect fruits of their genius. If these grand sentiments of "the good and fair" have sometimes prevented them from delivering the principles of ethics with the nakedness and dryness of science, at least we must own that they have chosen the better part,—that they have preferred virtuous feeling to moral theory, and practical benefit to speculative exactness. Perhaps these wise men may have supposed that the minute dissection and anatomy of Virtue might, to the ill-judging eye, weaken the charm of her beauty.

It is not for me to attempt a theme which has perhaps been exhausted by these great writers. I am indeed much less called upon to display the worth <349> and usefulness of the law of nations, than to vindicate myself from presumption in attempting a subject which has been already handled by so many masters. For the purpose of that vindication it will be necessary to sketch a very short and slight account (for such in this place it must unavoidably be) of the progress and present state of the science, and of that succession of able writers who have gradually brought it to its present perfection.

We have no Greek or Roman treatise remaining on the law of nations. From the title of one of the lost works of Aristotle, it appears that he com-

---

* "Age verò urbibus constitutis, ut fidem colere et justitiam retinere discerent, et aliis parere suâ voluntate consuescerent, ac non modò labores excipiendos communis commodi causâ, sed etiam vitam amittendam existimarent; qui tandem fieri potuit, nisi homines ea, quae ratione invenissent, eloquentiâ persuadere potuissent?"—De Invent. Rhet. lib. i. cap. 2. ["Consider another point; after cities had been established how could it have been brought to pass that men should learn to keep faith and observe justice and become accustomed to obey others voluntarily and believe not only that they must work for the common good but even sacrifice life itself, unless men had been able by eloquence to persuade their fellows of the truth of what they had discovered by reason?" Cicero, *De inventione*, trans. H. M. Hubbell (London and Cambridge, Mass.: Heinemann and Harvard University Press, 1960), 6–7 (I.ii.3).]

posed a treatise on the laws of war,* which, if we had the good fortune to possess it, would doubtless have amply satisfied our curiosity, and would have taught us both the practice of the ancient nations and the opinions of their moralists, with that depth and precision which distinguish the other works of that great philosopher. We can now only imperfectly collect that practice and those opinions from various passages which are scattered over the writings of philosophers, historians, poets, and orators. When the time shall arrive for a more full consideration of the state of the government and manners of the ancient world, I shall be able, perhaps, to offer satis-factory reasons why these enlightened nations did not separate from the general province of ethics that part of morality which regulates the inter-course of states, and erect it into an independent science. It would require a long discussion to unfold the various causes which united the modern nations of Europe into a closer society,—which linked them together by the firmest bands of mutual dependence, and which thus, in process of time, gave to the law that regulated their intercourse, greater importance, higher improvement, and more binding force. Among these causes, we may enumerate a common extraction, a common religion, similar manners, in-stitutions, and languages; <350> in earlier ages the authority of the See of Rome, and the extravagant claims of the imperial crown; in later times the connexions of trade, the jealousy of power, the refinement of civilization, the cultivation of science, and, above all, that general mildness of character and manners which arose from the combined and progressive influence of chivalry, of commerce, of learning, and of religion. Nor must we omit the similarity of those political institutions which, in every country that had been over-run by the Gothic conquerors, bore discernible marks (which the revolutions of succeeding ages had obscured, but not obliterated) of the rude but bold and noble outline of liberty that was originally sketched by the hand of these generous barbarians. These and many other causes conspired to unite the nations of Europe in a more intimate connexion and a more constant intercourse, and, of consequence, made the regulation of

---

* ικαιώματα των πολέμων. [Though Mackintosh has translated this as "the laws of war," in fact the word used for "of war" is a corruption in one source for "of cities," the work being a catalogue of the various claims of the Greek cities against each other.]

their intercourse more necessary, and the law that was to govern it more important. In proportion as they approached to the condition of provinces of the same empire, it became almost as essential that Europe should have a precise and comprehensive code of the law of nations, as that each country should have a system of municipal law. The labours of the learned, accordingly, began to be directed to this subject in the sixteenth century, soon after the revival of learning, and after that regular distribution of power and territory which has subsisted, with little variation, until our times. The critical examination of these early writers would perhaps not be very interesting in an extensive work, and it would be unpardonable in a short discourse. It is sufficient to observe that they were all more or less shackled by the barbarous philosophy of the schools, and that they were impeded in their progress by a timorous deference for the inferior and technical parts of the Roman law, without raising their views to the comprehensive principles which will for ever inspire mankind with veneration for that grand monument of human wisdom. <351> It was only, indeed, in the sixteenth century that the Roman law was first studied and understood as a science connected with Roman history and literature, and illustrated by men whom Ulpian and Papinian would not have disdained to acknowledge as their successors.* Among the writers of that age we may perceive the ineffectual attempts, the partial advances, the occasional streaks of light which always precede great discoveries, and works that are to instruct posterity.

The reduction of the law of nations to a system was reserved for Grotius. It was by the advice of Lord Bacon[2] and Peiresc that he undertook this

* Cujacius, Brissonius, Hottomannus, &c., &c.—See Gravina Origines Juris Civilis (Lips. 1737.), pp. 132–138. [Jani Vincentii Gravinae, *Opera, seu originum Juris Civiliis, libri tres, quibus accedunt, de Romano Imperis liber Singularis; ejusque orationes et opuscula Latina. Recensuit et adnotationibus auxit G. Mascovius* (Libsiae, 1737), 132–38.] Leibnitz, a great mathematician as well as philosopher, declares that he knows nothing which approaches so near to the method and precision of Geometry as the Roman law.—Op. vol. iv. p. 254. [Leibnitz, *Opera*, 6 vols. (Geneva, 1768), vol. 4, pt. 3, p. 254.]

2. Footnote omitted in son's edition: "I have here been misled by an expression of a modern panegyrist of Grotius. He tells us that the book *'De Jure Belli'* was undertaken *'hortante* BACONE VERULAMIO' [with Lord Bacon's encouragement]. Vid. CRAS *Idea perfecti Jurisconsulti in Hugone Grotio* [*Henrici Constantini Cras Oratio, qua perfecti*

arduous task. He produced a work which we now, indeed, justly deem imperfect, but which is perhaps the most complete that the world has yet owed, at so early a stage in the progress of any science, to the genius and learning of one man. So great is the uncertainty of posthumous reputation, and so liable is the fame even of the greatest men to be obscured by those new fashions of thinking and writing which succeed each other so rapidly among polished nations, that Grotius, who filled so large a space in the eye of his contemporaries, is now perhaps known to some of my readers only by name. Yet if we fairly estimate both his endowments and his virtues, we may justly consider him as one of the most memorable men who have done honour to modern times. He combined the discharge of the most important duties of active and public life with the attainment of that exact and various learning which is generally the portion only of the recluse student. He was distinguished as an advocate and a magistrate, and he composed the most valuable works on the law of his own country; he was almost equally celebrated as an historian, a scholar, a poet, and a divine;—a disinterested <352> statesman, a philosophical lawyer, a patriot who united moderation with firmness, and a theologian who was taught candour by his learning. Unmerited exile did not damp his patriotism; the bitterness of controversy did not extinguish his charity. The sagacity of his numerous and fierce adversaries could not discover a blot on his character; and in the midst of all the hard trials and galling provocations of a turbulent political life, he never once deserted his friends when they were unfortunate, nor insulted his enemies when they were weak. In times of the most furious civil and religious faction he preserved his name unspotted, and he knew how to reconcile fidelity to his own party, with moderation towards his opponents.

---

iuris consulti forma in Hugone Grotio spectatur (Amsterdam, 1776)]. Though aware of the ambiguity of the expression, I thought that it referred more naturally to personal exhortation. I now find, however, that it alludes only to the plan sketched out in Lord Bacon's writings, in which sense Sir Isaac Newton might be said to have composed his Principia *'hortante Bacone Verulamio.'* The authentic history of the work of Grotius is to be found in his own most interesting Letters, and in Gassendi's very able and curious life of Peiresc." This carries the following note: "Gassendi, *Viri illustris N.C. Fabricii de Peiresc . . . vira (Peireskii laudatio habita in concione funebri Academicorum romanorum . . . JJ Buccardo . . . Perorante,* 2 parts (Paris, 1641)."

Such was the man who was destined to give a new form to the law of nations, or rather to create a science, of which only rude sketches and undigested materials were scattered over the writings of those who had gone before him. By tracing the laws of his country to their principles, he was led to the contemplation of the law of nature, which he justly considered as the parent of all municipal law.* Few works were more celebrated than that of Grotius in his own days, and in the age which succeeded. It has, however, been the fashion of the last half-century to depreciate his work as a shapeless compilation, in which reason lies buried under a mass of authorities and quotations. This fashion originated among French wits and declaimers, and it has been, I know not for what reason, adopted, though with far greater moderation and decency, by some respectable writers among ourselves. As to those who first used this language, the most candid supposition that we can make with respect to them is, that they never read the work; for, if they had not been deterred from the perusal of it by such a formidable display of Greek characters, they must soon have discovered that Grotius <353> never quotes on any subject till he has first appealed to some principles, and often, in my humble opinion, though not always, to the soundest and most rational principles.

But another sort of answer is due to some of those† who have criticised Grotius, and that answer might be given in the words of Grotius himself.‡ He was not of such a stupid and servile cast of mind, as to quote the opinions of poets or orators, of historians and philosophers, as those of judges, from whose decision there was no appeal. He quotes them, as he tells us himself, as witnesses whose conspiring testimony, mightily strengthened and confirmed by their discordance on almost every other subject, is a conclusive proof of the unanimity of the whole human race on the great rules of duty and the fundamental principles of morals. On such matters, poets and orators are the most unexceptionable of all witnesses; for they address

---

* "Proavia juris civilis."—De Jure Belli ac Pacis, proleg. § xvi. ["Great-grandmother of municipal law." H. Grotius, *De Jure Belli ac Pacis Libri Tres*, trans. Francis W. Kelsey, 3 vols. (repr. New York: Oceana; London: Wildy and Sons, 1964), 2:15 (prolegomena §16).]

† Dr. Paley, Principles of Moral and Political Philosophy, pref. pp. xiv. xv. [W. Paley, *Principles of Moral and Political Philosophy*, 2 vols. (Dublin, 1785).]

‡ De Jure Belli, proleg. § 40. [Grotius, *De Jure Belli*, 2:23 (prolegomena §40).]

themselves to the general feelings and sympathies of mankind; they are neither warped by system, nor perverted by sophistry; they can attain none of their objects, they can neither please nor persuade, if they dwell on moral sentiments not in unison with those of their readers. No system of moral philosophy can surely disregard the general feelings of human nature and the according judgment of all ages and nations. But where are these feelings and that judgment recorded and preserved? In those very writings which Grotius is gravely blamed for having quoted. The usages and laws of nations, the events of history, the opinions of philosophers, the sentiments of orators and poets, as well as the observation of common life, are, in truth, the materials out of which the science of morality is formed; and those who neglect them are justly chargeable with a vain attempt to philosophise <354> without regard to fact and experience,—the sole foundation of all true philosophy.

If this were merely an objection of taste, I should be willing to allow that Grotius has indeed poured forth his learning with a profusion that sometimes rather encumbers than adorns his work, and which is not always necessary to the illustration of his subject. Yet, even in making that concession, I should rather yield to the taste of others than speak from my own feelings. I own that such richness and splendour of literature have a powerful charm for me. They fill my mind with an endless variety of delightful recollections and associations. They relieve the understanding in its progress through a vast science, by calling up the memory of great men and of interesting events. By this means we see the truths of morality clothed with all the eloquence,—not that could be produced by the powers of one man,—but that could be bestowed on them by the collective genius of the world. Even Virtue and Wisdom themselves acquire new majesty in my eyes, when I thus see all the great masters of thinking and writing called together, as it were, from all times and countries, to do them homage, and to appear in their train.

But this is no place for discussions of taste, and I am very ready to own that mine may be corrupted. The work of Grotius is liable to a more serious objection, though I do not recollect that it has ever been made.[3] His method

3. Footnote omitted in son's edition: "This objection against the method of Grotius is stated by Mr. WARD, in his learned work on *The History of the Law of Nations before*

is inconvenient and unscientific: he has inverted the natural order. That natural order undoubtedly dictates, that we should first search for the original principles of the science in human nature; then apply them to the regulation of the conduct of individuals; and lastly employ them for the decision of those difficult and complicated questions that arise with respect to the intercourse of nations. But Grotius has chosen the reverse of this method. He begins with the consideration of the states of peace and war, and he examines original principles only occasionally and incidentally as they grow out of the questions <355> which he is called upon to decide. It is a necessary consequence of this disorderly method,—which exhibits the elements of the science in the form of scattered digressions, that he seldom employs sufficient discussion on these fundamental truths, and never in the place where such a discussion would be most instructive to the reader.

This defect in the plan of Grotius was perceived, and supplied, by Puffendorff, who restored natural law to that superiority which belonged to it, and, with great propriety, treated the law of nations as only one main branch of the parent stock. Without the genius of his master, and with very inferior learning, he has yet treated this subject with sound sense, with clear method, with extensive and accurate knowledge, and with a copiousness of detail sometimes indeed tedious, but always instructive and satisfactory.[4] His work will be always studied by those who spare no labour to acquire a deep knowledge of the subject; but it will, in our times, I fear, be oftener found on the shelf than on the desk of the general student. In the time of Mr. Locke it was considered as the manual of those who were intended for active life; but in the present age, I believe it will be found that men of business are too much occupied,—men of letters are too fastidious,—and men of the world too indolent, for the study or even the perusal of such

---

the Time of Grotius, though at the time of writing this Discourse I had forgotten that passage of his work." This carries the following note: "Robert Ward (later Plumer Ward), *An Enquiry into the Foundations and History of the Law of Nations in Europe, from the Time of the Greeks and Romans to the Age of Grotius,* 2 Volumes (London, 1795)."

4. Footnote omitted in son's edition: "I am not induced to retract this commendation by the great authority even of LEIBNITZ himself, who, in one of his incomparable letters, calls Puffendorff '*Vir parum jurisconsultus et minime philosophus.*'" [A man too little of a lawyer and not at all a philosopher.]

works. Far be it from me to derogate from the real and great merit of so useful a writer as Puffendorff. His treatise is a mine in which all his successors must dig. I only presume to suggest, that a book so prolix, and so utterly void of all the attractions of composition, is likely to repel many readers who are interested in its subject, and who might perhaps be disposed to acquire some knowledge of the principles of public law.

Many other circumstances might be mentioned, which conspire to prove that neither of the great works of which I have spoken, has superseded the necessity of a new attempt to lay before the public a system of the law of nations. The language of <356> Science is so completely changed since both these works were written, that whoever was now to employ their terms in his moral reasonings would be almost unintelligible to some of his hearers or readers,—and to some among them too who are neither ill qualified, nor ill disposed, to study such subjects with considerable advantage to themselves. The learned, indeed, well know how little novelty or variety is to be found in scientific disputes. The same truths and the same errors have been repeated from age to age, with little variation but in the language; and novelty of expression is often mistaken by the ignorant for substantial discovery. Perhaps, too, very nearly the same portion of genius and judgment has been exerted in most of the various forms under which science has been cultivated at different periods of history. The superiority of those writers who continue to be read, perhaps often consists chiefly in taste, in prudence, in a happy choice of subject, in a favourable moment, in an agreeable style, in the good fortune of a prevalent language, or in other advantages which are either accidental, or are the result rather of the secondary, than of the highest, faculties of the mind. But these reflections, while they moderate the pride of invention, and dispel the extravagant conceit of superior illumination, yet serve to prove the use, and indeed the necessity, of composing, from time to time, new systems of science adapted to the opinions and language of each succeeding period. Every age must be taught in its own language. If a man were now to begin a discourse on ethics with an account of the "moral entities" of Puffendorff,* he would speak an unknown tongue.

* I do not mean to impeach the soundness of any part of Puffendorff's reasoning

It is not, however, alone as a mere translation of <357> former writers into modern language that a new system of public law seems likely to be useful. The age in which we live possesses many advantages which are peculiarly favourable to such an undertaking. Since the composition of the great works of Grotius and Puffendorff, a more modest, simple, and intelligible philosophy has been introduced into the schools; which has indeed been grossly abused by sophists, but which, from the time of Locke, has been cultivated and improved by a succession of disciples worthy of their illustrious master. We are thus enabled to discuss with precision, and to explain with clearness, the principles of the science of human nature, which are in themselves on a level with the capacity of every man of good sense, and which only appeared to be abstruse from the unprofitable subtleties with which they were loaded, and the barbarous jargon in which they were expressed. The deepest doctrines of morality have since that time been treated in the perspicuous and popular style, and with some degree of the beauty and eloquence of the ancient moralists. That philosophy on which are founded the principles of our duty, if it has not become more certain (for morality admits no discoveries), is at least less "harsh and crabbed,"[5] less obscure and haughty in its language, and less forbidding and disgusting in its appearance, than in the days of our ancestors. If this progress of leaning towards popularity has engendered (as it must be owned that it has) a multitude of superficial and most mischievous sciolists,[6] the antidote must come from the same quarter with the disease: popular reason can alone correct popular sophistry.

Nor is this the only advantage which a writer of the present age would possess over the celebrated jurists of the last century. Since that time vast additions have been made to the stock of our knowledge of human nature.

---

founded on moral entities: it may be explained in a manner consistent with the most just philosophy. He used, as every writer must do, the scientific language of his own time. I only assert that, to those who are unacquainted with ancient systems, his philosophical vocabulary is obsolete and unintelligible.

5. J. Milton, *A Mask (Comus)*, in *Comus and Some Shorter Poems of Milton*, ed. E. M. W. Tillyard (London: Harrap, 1952), 90, lines 477–78.

6. Taken by Godwin to be a reference to himself.

Many dark periods of history have since been explored: many hitherto unknown regions of the globe have been visited and described by <358> travellers and navigators not less intelligent than intrepid. We may be said to
stand at the confluence of the greatest number of streams of knowledge
flowing from the most distant sources that ever met at one point. We are
not confined, as the learned of the last age generally were, to the history of
those renowned nations who are our masters in literature. We can bring
before us man in a lower and more abject condition than any in which he
was ever before seen. The records have been partly opened to us of those
mighty empires of Asia* where the beginnings of civilization are lost in the
darkness of an unfathomable antiquity. We can make human society pass
in review before our mind, from the brutal and helpless barbarism of Terra
del Fuego, and the mild⁷ and voluptuous savages of Otaheite, to the tame,
but ancient and immoveable civilization of China, which bestows its own
arts on every successive race of conquerors,—to the meek and servile na-
tives of Hindostan, who preserve their ingenuity, their skill, and their science, through a long series of ages, under the yoke of foreign tyrants,—

* I cannot prevail on myself to pass over this subject without paying my humble
tribute to the memory of Sir William Jones, who has laboured so successfully in Oriental
literature; whose fine genius, pure taste, unwearied industry, unrivalled and almost prodigious variety of acquirements,—not to speak of his amiable manners, and spotless
integrity,—must fill every one who cultivates or admires letters with reverence, tinged
with a melancholy which the recollection of his recent death is so well adapted to inspire.
In hope I shall be pardoned if I add my applause to the genius and learning of Mr.
Maurice, who treads in the steps of his illustrious friend, and who has bewailed his death
in a strain of genuine and beautiful poetry, not unworthy of happier periods of our
English literature.

7. Footnote omitted in son's edition: "The Otaheiteans will probably not be thought
to deserve either to be praised for their mildness or envied for their happiness, after the
interesting account of their character and situation, which has been lately laid before the
Public in 'The MISSIONARY VOYAGE,' an account which has the strongest marks
of accuracy and authenticity, and which, as it was derived from intimate intercourse,
must far outweigh the hasty and superficial observations of panegyrists, who allowed
themselves no sufficient time either to gain accurate information, or to let the first enthusiasm, excited by novelty, subside." [W. Wilson, *A Missionary Voyage to the Southern
Pacific Ocean, . . . in the years 1796–1798, in the ship Duff, commanded by Captain J. Wilson.
Compiled from journals of the officers and the missionaries, (chiefly by W.W.) . . . with a
preliminary discourse on the geography and civil state of Otaheite. By a committee appointed
. . . by . . . the Missionary Society* (London, 1799).]

and to the gross and incorrigible rudeness of the Ottomans, incapable of improvement, and extinguishing the remains of civilization among their unhappy subjects, once the most ingenious nations of the earth. We can examine almost every imaginable variety in the character, manners, opinions, feelings, prejudices, and institutions of mankind, into <359> which they can be thrown, either by the rudeness of barbarism, or by the capricious corruptions of refinement, or by those innumerable combinations of circumstances, which, both in these opposite conditions, and in all the intermediate stages between them, influence or direct the course of human affairs. History, if I may be allowed the expression, is now a vast museum, in which specimens of every variety of human nature may be studied. From these great accessions to knowledge, lawgivers and statesmen, but, above all, moralists and political philosophers, may reap the most important instruction. They may plainly discover in all the useful and beautiful variety of governments and institutions, and under all the fantastic multitude of usages and rites which have prevailed among men, the same fundamental, comprehensive truths, the sacred master-principles which are the guardians of human society, recognised and revered (with few and slight exceptions) by every nation upon earth, and uniformly taught (with still fewer exceptions) by a succession of wise men from the first dawn of speculation to the present moment. The exceptions, few as they are, will, on more reflection, be found rather apparent than real. If we could raise ourselves to that height from which we ought to survey so vast a subject, these exceptions would altogether vanish; the brutality of a handful of savages would disappear in the immense prospect of human nature, and the murmurs of a few licentious sophists[8] would not ascend to break the general harmony. This consent of mankind in first principles, and this endless variety in their application, which is one among many valuable truths which we may collect from our present extensive acquaintance with the history of man, is itself of vast importance. Much of the majesty and authority of virtue is derived from their consent, and almost the whole of practical wisdom is founded on their variety.

What former age could have supplied facts for such a work as that of

8. William Godwin.

Montesquieu? He indeed <360> has been, perhaps justly, charged with abusing this advantage, by the undistinguishing adoption of the narratives of travellers of very different degrees of accuracy and veracity. But if we reluctantly confess the justness of this objection; if we are compelled to own that he exaggerates the influence of climate,—that he ascribes too much to the foresight and forming skill of legislators, and far too little to time and circumstances, in the growth of political constitutions,—that the substantial character and essential differences of governments are often lost and confounded in his technical language and arrangement,—that he often bends the free and irregular outline of nature to the imposing but fallacious geometrical regularity of system,—that he has chosen a style of affected abruptness, sententiousness, and vivacity, ill suited to the gravity of his subject;—after all these concessions (for his fame is large enough to spare many concessions), *the Spirit of Laws* will still remain not only one of the most solid and durable monuments of the powers of the human mind, but a striking evidence of the inestimable advantages which political philosophy may receive from a wide survey of all the various conditions of human society.

In the present century a slow and silent, but very substantial, mitigation has taken place in the practice of war; and in proportion as that mitigated practice has received the sanction of time, it is raised from the rank of mere usage, and becomes part of the law of nations. Whoever will compare our present modes of warfare with the system of Grotius* will clearly discern the immense improvements which have taken place in that respect since the publication of his work, during a period, perhaps in every point of view the happiest to be found in the history of the world. In the same period many important points of public law have been the subject of contest both by argument <361> and by arms, of which we find either no mention, or very obscure traces, in the history of preceding times.

There are other circumstances to which I allude with hesitation and reluctance, though it must be owned that they afford to a writer of this age

---

* Especially those chapters of the third book, entitled, "Temperamentum circa Captivos," &c. [Grotius, *De Jure Belli,* bk. 3, chap. 14, "Moderation in Regard to Prisoners of War."]

some degree of unfortunate and deplorable advantage over his predecessors. Recent events have accumulated more terrible practical instruction on every subject of politics than could have been in other times acquired by the experience of ages. Men's wit sharpened by their passions has penetrated to the bottom of almost all political questions. Even the fundamental rules of morality themselves have, for the first time, unfortunately for mankind, become the subject of doubt and discussion.[9] I shall consider it as my duty to abstain from all mention of these awful events, and of these fatal controversies. But the mind of that man must indeed be incurious and indocile, who has either overlooked all these things, or reaped no instruction from the contemplation of them.

From these reflections it appears, that, since the composition of those two great works on the law of nature and nations which continue to be the classical and standard works on that subject, we have gained both more convenient instruments of reasoning and more extensive materials for science,—that the code of war has been enlarged and improved,—that new questions have been practically decided,—and that new controversies have arisen regarding the intercourse of independent states, and the first principles of morality and civil government.

Some readers may, however, think that in these observations which I offer, to excuse the presumption of my own attempt, I have omitted the mention of later writers, to whom some part of the remarks is not justly applicable. But, perhaps, further consideration will acquit me in the judgment of such readers. Writers on particular questions of public law are not within the scope of my observations. <362> They have furnished the most valuable materials; but I speak only of a system. To the large work of Wolfius, the observations which I have made on Puffendorff as a book for general use, will surely apply with tenfold force. His abridger, Vattel, deserves, indeed, considerable praise: he is a very ingenious, clear, elegant, and useful writer. But he only considers one part of this extensive subject,—namely, the law of nations, strictly so called; and I cannot help thinking, that, even in this department of the science, he has adopted some doubtful and dan-

9. William Godwin.

gerous principles,[10]—not to mention his constant deficiency in that fulness of example and illustration, which so much embellishes and strengthens reason. It is hardly necessary to take any notice of the textbook of Heineccius, the best writer of elementary books with whom I am acquainted on any subject. Burlamaqui is an author of superior merit; but he confines himself too much to the general principles of morality and politics, to require much observation from me in this place. The same reason will excuse me for passing over in silence the works of many philosophers and moralists, to whom, in the course of my proposed lectures, I shall owe and confess the greatest obligations; and it might perhaps deliver me from the necessity of speaking of the work of Dr. Paley, if I were not desirous of this public opportunity of professing my gratitude for the instruction and pleasure which I have received from that excellent writer, who possesses, in so eminent a degree, those invaluable qualities of a moralist,—good sense, caution, sobriety, and perpetual reference to convenience and practice; and who certainly is thought less original than he really is, merely because his taste and modesty have led him to disdain the ostentation of novelty, and because he generally employs more art to blend his own arguments with the body of received opinions (so as that they are scarce to be distinguished), than other men, in the pursuit of a <363> transient popularity, have exerted to disguise the most miserable common-places in the shape of paradox.[11]

No writer since the time of Grotius, of Puffendorff, and of Wolf, has combined an investigation of the principles of natural and public law, with a full application of these principles to particular cases; and in these circumstances, I trust, it will not be deemed extravagant presumption in me to hope that I shall be able to exhibit a view of this science, which shall, at least, be more intelligible and attractive to students, than the learned trea-

---

10. Footnote omitted in son's edition: "I was unwilling to have expressed more strongly or confidently my disapprobation of some parts of Vattel; though I might have justified more decisive censure by the authority of the greatest lawyers of the present age. His politics are fundamentally erroneous; his declamations are often insipid and impertinent; and he has fallen into great mistakes in important practical discussions of public law."

11. William Godwin.

tises of these celebrated men. I shall now proceed to state the general plan and subjects of the lectures in which I am to make this attempt.

I. The being whose actions the law of nature professes to regulate, is man. It is on the knowledge of his nature that the science of his duty must be founded.* It is impossible to approach the threshold of moral philosophy without a previous examination of the faculties and habits of the human mind. Let no reader be repelled from this examination by the odious and terrible name of "metaphysics"; for it is, in truth, nothing more than the employment of good sense, in observing our own thoughts, feelings, and actions; and when the facts which are thus observed are expressed, as they ought to be, in plain language, it is, perhaps, above all other sciences, most on a level with the capacity and information of the generality of thinking men. When it is thus expressed, it requires no previous qualification, but a sound judgment perfectly to comprehend it; and those who wrap it up in a technical and mysterious jargon, always give us strong reason to suspect that they are not philosophers, but impostors. Whoever thoroughly understands such a science, must be able to teach it plainly to all men of common sense. The proposed course will therefore open with a very short, <364> and, I hope, a very simple and intelligible account of the powers and operations of the human mind. By this plain statement of facts, it will not be difficult to decide many celebrated, though frivolous and merely verbal, controversies, which have long amused the leisure of the schools, and which owe both their fame and their existence to the ambiguous obscurity of scholastic language. It will, for example, only require an appeal to every man's experience, to prove that we often act purely from a regard to the happiness of others, and are therefore social beings; and it is not necessary to be a consummate judge of the deceptions of language, to despise the sophistical trifler, who tells us, that, because we experience a gratification in our benevolent actions, we are therefore exclusively and uniformly selfish. A correct examination of facts will lead us to discover that

---

* "Natura enim juris explicanda est nobis, eaque ab hominis repetenda naturâ."— De Leg. lib. i. c. 5. ["For we must explain the nature of Justice, and this must be sought for in the nature of man." Cicero, *De legibus,* in *De re publica, De legibus,* trans. C. Walker Keyes (London and Cambridge, Mass.: Heinemann and Harvard University Press, 1959), 314–17 (I.v.17).]

quality which is common to all virtuous actions, and which distinguishes them from those which are vicious and criminal. But we shall see that it is necessary for man to be governed, not by his own transient and hasty opinion upon the tendency of every particular action, but by those fixed and unalterable rules, which are the joint result of the impartial judgment, the natural feelings, and the embodied experience of mankind. The authority of these rules is, indeed, founded only on their tendency to promote private and public welfare; but the morality of actions will appear solely to consist in their correspondence with the rule. By the help of this obvious distinction we shall vindicate a just theory, which, far from being modern, is, in fact, as ancient as philosophy, both from plausible objections, and from the odious imputation[12] of supporting those absurd and monstrous systems which have been built upon it. Beneficial tendency is the foundation of rules, and the criterion by which habits and sentiments are to be tried: but it is neither the immediate standard, nor can it ever be the principal motive of action.[13] An action to be completely virtuous, must accord with moral rules, and must flow <365> from our natural feelings and affections, mod-

---

12. Footnote omitted in son's edition: "See a late ingenious tract by Mr. Green, entitled, 'An Enquiry into the leading Principle of the new System of Morals.'" [T. Green, *An examination of the leading principle of the new system of morals, as that principle is stated and applied in Mr. Godwin's Enquiry concerning political justice* (London, 1799).]

13. The following passage was omitted in the son's edition along with its footnotes: "No precept, indeed, deserves a place among the rules of morality, unless its observance will promote the happiness of mankind; and no man ought to cultivate in his own mind any disposition of which the natural fruits are not such actions as conduce to his own well-being, and to that of his fellow-men. Utility is doubtless always the ultimate test of general rules, but it can very rarely be the direct test of the morality of single actions. It is also the test of our habitual sentiments, but it can still more rarely supply their place as motives to virtue. A *rule* is moral, of which the observance tends to produce general happiness." After "the happiness of mankind" a footnote is inserted which reads: "Or, to use the language of Cicero, unless it be adapted 'AD TUENDAM MAGNAM ILLAM SOCIETATEM GENERIS HUMANI'" [to protect that great fellowship of the human race]. After "to produce general happiness" a footnote is inserted which reads: "Whoever is desirous of studying these questions thoroughly, will do well to consult 'Search's Light of Nature,' vol. ii. a work which, after much consideration, I think myself authorized to call the most original and profound that has ever appeared on moral philosophy." [Abram Tucker, *The Light of Nature Pursued by Edward Search, Esq.*, 7 vols. (London: T. Jones, 1765–74), vol. 2.]

erated, matured, and improved into steady habits of right conduct.* Without, however, dwelling longer on subjects which cannot be clearly stated, unless they are fully unfolded, I content myself with observing, that it shall be my object, in this preliminary, but most important, part of the course, to lay the foundations of morality so deeply in human nature, as to satisfy the coldest inquirer; and, at the same time, to vindicate the paramount authority of the rules of our duty, at all times, and in all places, over all opinions of interest and speculations of benefit, so extensively, so universally, and so inviolably, as may well justify the grandest and the most apparently extravagant effusions of moral enthusiasm. If, notwithstanding all my endeavours to deliver these doctrines with the utmost simplicity, any of my auditors should still reproach me for introducing such abstruse matters, I must shelter myself behind the authority of the wisest of men. "If they (the ancient moralists,) before they had come to the popular and received notions of virtue and vice, had staid a little longer upon the inquiry concerning *the roots of good and evil,* they had given, in my opinion, a great light to that which followed; and especially if they had consulted with nature, they had made their doctrines less prolix, and more profound."† What Lord Bacon desired for the mere gratification of scientific curiosity, the welfare of mankind now imperiously demands. Shallow systems of metaphysics have given birth to a brood of abominable and pestilential paradoxes, which nothing but a more profound philosophy can destroy.[14] However we may, perhaps, lament the necessity of discussions which may shake the habitual reverence of some men for those rules which it is the chief interest of all men to practise, we have now no choice left. We <366> must either dispute, or abandon the ground. Undistinguishing and unmerited invectives against philosophy will only harden sophists and their disciples in the insolent conceit, that they are in possession of an undisputed su-

---

* "Est autem virtus nihil aliud, quam in se perfecta atque ad summum perducta natura."—Ibid. lib. i. c. 8. ["Virtue, however, is nothing else than Nature perfected and developed to its highest point." Cicero, *De legibus,* in *De re publica, De legibus,* 324–25 (I.viii.25).]

† Advancement of Learning, book ii. [Bacon, "The Dignity and Advancement of Learning," in *Works,* 3:420.]

14. William Godwin.

periority of reason; and that their antagonists have no arms to employ against them, but those of popular declamation. Let us not for a moment even appear to suppose, that philosophical truth and human happiness are so irreconcilably at variance. I cannot express my opinion on this subject so well as in the words of a most valuable, though generally neglected writer: "The science of abstruse learning, when completely attained, is like Achilles's spear, that healed the wounds it had made before; so this knowledge serves to repair the damage itself had occasioned, and this perhaps is all it is good for; it casts no additional light upon the paths of life, but disperses the clouds with which it had overspread them before; it advances not the traveller one step in his journey, but conducts him back again to the spot from whence he wandered. Thus the land of philosophy consists partly of an open champaign country, passable by every common understanding, and partly of a range of woods, traversable only by the speculative, and where they too frequently delight to amuse themselves. Since then we shall be obliged to make incursions into this latter track, and shall probably find it a region of obscurity, danger, and difficulty, it behoves us to use our utmost endeavours for enlightening and smoothing the way before us."* We shall, however, remain in the forest only long enough to visit the fountains of those streams which flow from it, and which water and fertilise the cultivated region of morals, to become acquainted with the modes of warfare practised by its savage inhabitants, and to learn the means of guarding our fair and fruitful land against their desolating incursions. I shall hasten from speculations, to which I am naturally, <367> perhaps, but too prone, and proceed to the more profitable consideration of our practical duty.

The first and most simple part of ethics is that which regards the duties of private men towards each other, when they are considered apart from the sanction of positive laws. I say *apart* from that sanction, not *antecedent* to it; for though we *separate* private from political duties for the sake of greater clearness and order in reasoning, yet we are not to be so deluded by this mere arrangement of convenience as to suppose that human society ever has subsisted, or ever could subsist, without being protected by government, and bound together by laws. All these relative duties of private

* [Tucker], Light of Nature, vol. i. pref. p. xxxiii.

life have been so copiously and beautifully treated by the moralists of antiquity, that few men will now choose to follow them, who are not actuated by the wild ambition of equalling Aristotle in precision, or rivalling Cicero in eloquence. They have been also admirably treated by modern moralists, among whom it would be gross injustice not to number many of the preachers of the Christian religion, whose peculiar character is that spirit of universal charity, which is the living principle of all our social duties. For it was long ago said, with great truth, by Lord Bacon, "that there never was any philosophy, religion, or other discipline, which did so plainly and highly exalt that good which is communicative, and depress the good which is private and particular, as the Christian faith."* The appropriate praise of this religion is not so much that it has taught new duties, as that it breathes a milder and more benevolent spirit over the whole extent of morals.

On a subject which has been so exhausted, I should naturally have contented myself with the most slight and general survey, if some fundamental principles had not of late been brought into question, which, in all former times, have been deemed too evident to require the <368> support of argument, and almost too sacred to admit the liberty of discussion. I shall here endeavour to strengthen some parts of the fortifications of morality which have hitherto been neglected, because no man had ever been hardy enough to attack them. Almost all the relative duties of human life will be found more immediately, or more remotely, to arise out of the two great institutions of property and marriage. They constitute, preserve, and improve society. Upon their gradual improvement depends the progressive civilization of mankind; on them rests the whole order of civil life. We are told by Horace, that the first efforts of lawgivers to civilize men consisted in strengthening and regulating these institutions, and fencing them round with rigorous penal laws.

> Oppida coeperunt munire, et ponere leges,
> Ne quis fur esset, neu latro, neu quis adulter.†

---

* Advancement of Learning, book ii. [Bacon, "The Dignity and Advancement of Learning," in *Works*, 3:421.]

† Sermon. lib. i. Serm. iii. 105. ["To build towns, and to frame laws that none should thieve or rob or commit adultery." Horace, *Satires*, in *Satires, Epistles, and Ars poetica*,

A celebrated ancient orator, of whose poems we have but a few fragments remaining, has well described the progressive order in which human society is gradually led to its highest improvements under the guardianship of those laws which secure property and regulate marriage.

> Et leges sanctas docuit, et chara jugavit
> Corpora conjugiis; et magnas condidit urbes.[15]

These two great institutions convert the selfish as well as the social passions of our nature into the firmest bands of a peaceable and orderly intercourse; they change the sources of discord into principles of quiet; they discipline the most ungovernable, they refine the grossest, and they exalt the most sordid propensities; so that they become the perpetual fountain of all that strengthens, and preserves, and adorns society: they sustain the individual, and they perpetuate the race. Around these institutions all our social duties will be found at various distances to range themselves; <369> some more

---

trans. H. Rushton Fairclough (London and Cambridge, Mass.: Heinemann and Harvard University Press, 1978), 40–41 (I.iii.105–6).]

15. "[Ceres] instructed men in her holy laws and joined loving bodies in wedlock and founded great cities." This fragment is cited by "Deutero-Servius" (i.e., the expanded version of Servius's *Commentary* on Virgil, *Aeneid* 4.58). It is Calvus fragment 6 in modern collections of Latin poetic fragments, e.g., Edward Courtney, *The Fragmentary Latin Poets* (Oxford: Clarendon Press, 1993), 203–4.

In the third edition an extra paragraph appears at this point that is omitted in the son's edition: "Nothing can be more philosophical than the succession of ideas here presented by Calvus: for it is only when the general security is maintained by the laws, and when the order of domestic life is fixed by marriage, that nations emerge from barbarism, proceed by slow degrees to cultivate science, to found empires, to build magnificent cities, and to cover the earth with all the splendid monuments of civilized art." Later on the same page after "perpetuate the race" a further additional paragraph appears: "As they were at first the sole authors of all civilization, so they must for ever continue its sole protectors. They alone make the society of man with his fellows delightful, or secure, or even tolerable. Every argument and example, every opinion and practice which weakens their authority, tends also to dissolve the fellowship of the human race, to replunge *men* into that state of helpless ferocity, and to condemn the earth to that unproductive wildness, from which they were both originally raised, by the power of these sacred principles; which animate the activity of exertion and yet mitigate the fierceness of contest, which move every plough and feed every mouth, and regulate every household and rear every child; which are the great nourishers and guardians of the world. The enemy of these principles is the enemy of mankind."

near, obviously essential to the good order of human life; others more remote, and of which the necessity is not at first view so apparent; and some
so distant, that their importance has been sometimes doubted, though
upon more mature consideration they will be found to be outposts and
advanced guards of these fundamental principles,—that man should se-
curely enjoy the fruits of his labour, and that the society of the sexes should
be so wisely ordered, as to make it a school of the kind affections, and a fit
nursery for the commonwealth.

The subject of property is of great extent. It will be necessary to establish
the foundation of the rights of acquisition, alienation, and transmission,
not in imaginary contracts or a pretended state of nature, but in their subserviency to the subsistence and well-being of mankind. It will not only be
curious, but useful, to trace the history of property from the first loose and
transient occupancy of the savage, through all the modifications which it
has at different times received, to that comprehensive, subtle, and anxiously
minute code of property which is the last result of the most refined
civilization.

I shall observe the same order in considering the society of the sexes, as
it is regulated by the institution of marriage.* I shall endeavour to lay open
those unalterable principles of general interest on which that institution
rests;[16] and if I entertain a hope that on this subject I may be able to add
something to what our masters in morality have taught us, I trust, that the

---

* See on this subject an incomparable fragment of the first book of Cicero's Economics, which is too long for insertion here, but which, if it be closely examined, may
perhaps dispel the illusion of those gentlemen, who have so strangely taken it for granted
that Cicero was incapable of exact reasoning. [Cicero's *Economics* is in fact his translation
(cited by Columella in the preface to book 12 of his *De re rustica*) from Xenophon,
Oeconomics, 7.18–28. But, like its original, it seems to have been in only one book.]

16. In emphasizing the laws of property and marriage as fundamental to social life,
Mackintosh could also have been referring to William Godwin's speculations on a future
society in which they would not exist; see W. Godwin, *An Enquiry Concerning Political
Justice* (1793), book 8. Defending these laws as the only means of countering the effects
of excessive population growth lay at the heart of T. R. Malthus's criticisms of Godwin's
system of equality in his *Essay on the Principle of Population* (1798). Godwin linked Malthus with Samuel Parr and Mackintosh in his reply to critics in *Thoughts occasioned by
the perusal of Dr Parr's Spital Sermon . . . a reply to the attacks of Dr Parr, Mr. Mackintosh,
the author of the Essay on Population and others* (1801).

reader will bear in mind, as an excuse for my presumption, that *they* were not likely to employ much argument where they did not foresee the possibility of doubt. I shall also consider the <370> history* of marriage, and trace it through all the forms which it has assumed, to that descent and happy permanency of union, which has, perhaps above all other causes, contributed to the quiet of society, and the refinement of manners in modern times. Among many other inquiries which this subject will suggest, I shall be led more particularly to examine the natural station and duties of the female sex, their condition among different nations, its improvement in Europe, and the bounds which Nature herself has prescribed to the progress of that improvement; beyond which every pretended advance will be a real degradation.

Having established the principles of private duty, I shall proceed to consider man under the important relation of subject and sovereign, or, in other words, of citizen and magistrate. The duties which arise from this

---

* This progress is traced with great accuracy in some beautiful lines of Lucretius:—

———— Mulier, conjuncta viro, concessit in unum;
Castaque privatae Veneris connubia laeta
Cognita sunt, prolemque ex se vidêre creatam;
Tum genus humanum primum mollescere coepit.
———— puerique parentum
Blanditiis facile ingenium fregere superbum.
Tunc et amicitiam coeperunt jungere, habentes
Finitimi inter se, nec laedere, nec violare;
Et pueros commendârunt, muliebreque saeclum,
Vocibus et gestu; cum balbè significarent,
Imbecillorum esse aequum miserier omni.
                              De Rerum Nat. lib. v.

["And woman mated with man moved into one [[home, and the laws of wedlock]] became known, and they saw offspring born of them, then first the human race began to grow soft. For the fire saw to it that their shivering bodies were less able to endure cold under the canopy of heaven, and Venus sapped their strength, and children easily broke their parents' proud spirit by coaxings. Then also neighbours began to join friendship amongst themselves in their eagerness to do no hurt and suffer no violence, and asked protection for their children and womankind, signifying by voice and gesture with stammering tongue that it was right for all to pity the weak." Lucretius, *De rerum natura,* trans. W. H. D. Rouse, rev. M. F. Smith (London and Cambridge, Mass.: Heinemann and Harvard University Press, 1975), 456–59 (lines 1012–23).]

relation I shall endeavour to establish, not upon supposed compacts, which are altogether chimerical, which must be admitted to be false in fact, and which, if they are to be considered as fictions, will be found to serve no purpose of just reasoning, and to be equally the foundation of a system of universal despotism in Hobbes, and of universal anarchy in Rousseau; but on the solid basis of general convenience. Men cannot subsist without society and mutual aid; they can neither maintain social intercourse <371> nor receive aid from each other without the protection of government; and they cannot enjoy that protection without submitting to the restraints which a just government imposes. This plain argument establishes the duty of obedience on the part of the citizens, and the duty of protection on that of magistrates, on the same foundation with that of every other moral duty; and it shows, with sufficient evidence, that these duties are reciprocal;— the only rational end for which the fiction of a contract should have been invented. I shall not encumber my reasoning by any speculations on the origin of government,—a question on which so much reason has been wasted in modern times; but which the ancients* in a higher spirit of philosophy have never once mooted. If our principles be just, our origin of government must have been coeval with that of mankind; and as no tribe has ever been discovered so brutish as to be without some government, and yet so enlightened as to establish a government by common consent, it is surely unnecessary to employ any serious argument in the confutation of the doctrine that is inconsistent with reason, and unsupported by experience. But though all inquiries into the origin of government be chimerical, yet the history of its progress is curious and useful. The various stages through which it passed from savage independence, which implies every man's power of injuring his neighbour, to legal liberty, which consists in

* The introduction to the first book of Aristotle's Politics is the best demonstration of the necessity of political society to the well-being, and indeed to the very being, of man, with which I am acquainted. Having shewn the circumstances which render man necessarily a social being, he justly concludes, "καὶ ὅτι ὁ ἄνθρωπος φύσει πολιτικὸν ζῷον." ["And that man is by nature a political animal." Aristotle, Politics, trans. H. Rackham (London: Heinemann, 1932), i.1253a2–3.] The same scheme of philosophy is admirably pursued in the short, but invaluable fragment of the sixth book of Polybius, which describes the history and revolutions of government.

every man's security against wrong; the manner in which a family expands into a tribe, and tribes coalesce into a nation,—in which public justice is gradually engrafted on private revenge, <372> and temporary submission ripened into habitual obedience; form a most important and extensive subject of inquiry, which comprehends all the improvements of mankind in police, in judicature, and in legislation.

I have already given the reader to understand that the description of liberty which seems to me the most comprehensive, is that of *security against wrong*. Liberty is therefore the object of all government. Men are more free under every government, even the most imperfect, than they would be if it were possible for them to exist without any government at all: they are more secure from wrong, more undisturbed in the exercise of their natural powers, and therefore more free, even in the most obvious and grossest sense of the word, than if they were altogether unprotected against injury from each other.[17] But as general security is enjoyed in very different degrees under different governments, those which guard it most perfectly, are by the way of eminence called "free." Such governments attain most completely the end which is common to all government. A free constitution of government and a good constitution of government are therefore different expressions for the same idea.

Another material distinction, however, soon presents itself. In most civilised states the subject is tolerably protected against gross injustice from his fellows by impartial laws, which it is the manifest interest of the sovereign to enforce: but some commonwealths are so happy as to be founded on a principle of much more refined and provident wisdom. The subjects of such commonwealths are guarded not only against the injustice of each other, but (as far as human prudence can contrive) against oppression from

17. The following note was omitted in the son's edition: "I have never pretended to offer this description of liberty as a logical definition. According to my principles it would be folly to attempt logical definitions of political terms. The simple and original notion of *liberty* is, doubtless, that of the absence of restraint. Now if men are restrained in fewer actions by Government than they would be by violence in the supposed state of nature; if they are always less restrained in proportion as they are more secure; it will follow, that security and liberty must always practically coincide; that the degree of security may always be considered as a test of the degree of liberty, and that for all practical purposes one of these words may constantly be substituted for the other."

the magistrate. Such states, like all other extraordinary examples of public or private excellence and happiness, are thinly scattered over the different ages and countries of the world. In them the will of the sovereign is limited with so exact a measure, that <373> his protecting authority is not weakened. Such a combination of skill and fortune is not often to be expected, and indeed never can arise, but from the constant though gradual exertions of wisdom and virtue, to improve a long succession of most favourable circumstances. There is, indeed, scarce any society so wretched as to be destitute of some sort of weak provision against the injustice of their governors. Religious institutions, favourite prejudices, national manners, have in different countries, with unequal degrees of force, checked or mitigated the exercise of supreme power. The privileges of a powerful nobility, of opulent mercantile communities, of great judicial corporations, have in some monarchies approached more near to a control on the sovereign. Means have been devised with more or less wisdom to temper the despotism of an aristocracy over their subjects, and in democracies to protect the minority against the majority, and the whole people against the tyranny of demagogues. But in these unmixed forms of government, as the right of legislation is vested in one individual or in one order, it is obvious that the legislative power may shake off all the restraints which the laws have imposed on it. All such governments, therefore, tend towards despotism, and the securities which they admit against misgovernment are extremely feeble and precarious. The best security which human wisdom can devise, seems to be the distribution of political authority among different individuals and bodies, with separate interests, and separate characters, corresponding to the variety of classes of which civil society is composed,—each interested to guard their own order from oppression by the rest,—each also interested to prevent any of the others from seizing on exclusive, and therefore despotic power; and all having a common interest to co-operate in carrying on the ordinary and necessary administration of government. If there were not an interest to resist each other in extraordinary cases, there would not be liberty: if there were not an interest to co-operate <374> in the ordinary course of affairs, there could be no government. The object of such wise institutions, which make selfishness of governors a security against their injustice, is to protect men against wrong both from their rulers and their fellows. Such governments are, with justice, peculiarly and emphatically called "free" and in ascribing that liberty to the skilful combination of mutual dependence and mutual check, I feel my own conviction greatly strengthened by calling to mind, that in this opinion I agree with all the wise men who have ever deeply considered the principles of politics;—with Aristotle and Polybius, with Cicero and Tacitus, with Bacon and Machiavel, with Montesquieu and Hume.* It is impossible in such a cursory sketch as the present, even to allude to a very small part of those philosophical principles, political reasonings, and historical facts, which are necessary for the illustration of this momentous subject. In a full discussion of it I shall be obliged to examine the general frame of the most celebrated governments of ancient and modern times, and especially of those which have been most renowned for their freedom. The result of such an examination will be, that no institution so detestable as an absolutely <375> unbalanced government, perhaps ever existed; that the simple governments are mere creatures of the imagination of theorists, who have transformed names used for convenience of arrangement into real politics; that, as constitutions of government approach more nearly to that unmixed and uncontrolled simplicity they become despotic, and as they recede farther from that simplicity they become free.

By the constitution of a state, I mean "the body of those written and

* To the weight of these great names let me add the opinion of two illustrious men of the present age, as both their opinions are combined by one of them in the following passages: "He (Mr. Fox) always thought any of the simple unbalanced governments bad; simple monarchy, simple aristocracy, simple democracy; he held them all imperfect or vicious, all were bad by themselves; the composition alone was good. These had been always his principles, in which he agreed with his friend, Mr. Burke."—Speech on the Army Estimates, 9th Feb. 1790. In speaking of both these illustrious men, whose names I here join, as they will be joined in fame by posterity, which will forget their temporary differences in the recollection of their genius and their friendship, I do not entertain the vain imagination that I can add to their glory by any thing that I can say. But it is a gratification to me to give utterance to my feelings; to express the profound veneration with which I am filled for the memory of the one, and the warm affection which I cherish for the other, whom no one ever heard in public without admiration, or knew in private life without loving.

unwritten[18] fundamental laws which regulate the most important rights of the higher magistrates, and the most essential privileges* of the subjects." Such a body of political laws must in all countries arise out of the character and situation of a people; they must grow with its progress, be adapted to its peculiarities, change with its changes, and be incorporated with its habits. Human wisdom cannot form such a constitution by one act, for human wisdom cannot create the materials of which it is composed. The attempt, always ineffectual, to change by violence the ancient habits of men, and the established order of society, so as to fit them for an absolutely new scheme of government, flows from the most presumptuous ignorance, requires the support of the most ferocious tyranny, and leads to consequences which its authors can never foresee,—generally, indeed, to institutions the most opposite to those of which they profess to seek the establishment.† But human wisdom <376> indefatigably employed in remedying abuses, and in seizing favourable opportunities of improving that order of society

* Privilege, in Roman jurisprudence, means the *exemption* of one individual from the operation of a law. Political privileges, in the sense in which I employ the terms, mean those rights of the subjects of a free state, which are deemed so essential to the well-being of the commonwealth, that they are *excepted* from the ordinary discretion of the magistrate, and guarded by the same fundamental laws which secure his authority.

† See an admirable passage on this subject in Dr. Smith's Theory of Moral Sentiments (vol. ii. pp. 101–112), in which the true doctrine of reformation is laid down with singular ability by that eloquent and philosophical writer. [Adam Smith, *The Theory of Moral Sentiments* (Indianapolis: Liberty Fund, 1984), 230–34 (VI.ii.2.7–18). This is a reference to the famous criticism of the "man of system," and since it belongs to the additions made by Smith in 1790, it has been taken by some to be a warning about the need for caution in matters of legislation evoked by French revolutionary events. While this may be speculative, there can be no doubt about the applicability of a message of gradualism to Mackintosh's postrevolutionary predicament.] See also Mr. Burke's Speech on Economical Reform ["February 11, 1780," in *The Writings and Speeches of Edmund Burke,* ed. P. Langford, vol. 3, *Party, Parliament, and the American War 1774–1780* (Oxford: Clarendon Press, 1996), 481–551]; and Sir M. Hale on the Amendment of Laws, in the Collection of my learned and most excellent friend, Mr. Hargrave. [Sir Matthew Hale, "Considerations Touching the Amendment or Alteration of Lawes," in *A Collection of Tracts Relative to the Law of England, from Manuscripts,* ed. Francis Hargrave (Dublin, 1787), 1:249–89.]

18. The following note was omitted in the son's edition: "The reader will observe that I insert this word *'unwritten'* with a view to the ignorant and senseless cavils of those who contend that every country which has not a *written constitution* must be without a constitution." Presumed to be a reference to Paine.

which arises from causes over which we have little control, after the reforms and amendments of a series of ages, has sometimes, though very rarely, shown itself capable of building up a free constitution, which is "the growth of time and nature, rather than the work of human invention."19* Such a constitution can only be formed by the wise imitation of "the great innovator Time, which, indeed, innovateth greatly, but quietly, and by degrees scarce to be perceived."† Without descending to the puerile ostentation of panegyric, on that of which all mankind confess the excellence, I may observe, with truth and soberness, that a free government not only establishes a universal security against wrong, but that it also cherishes all the noblest powers of the human mind; that it tends to banish both the mean and the ferocious vices; that it improves the national character to which it is adapted, and out of which it grows; that its whole administration is a practical school of honesty and humanity; and that there the social affections, expanded into public spirit, gain a wider sphere, and a more active spring.

I shall conclude what I have to offer on government, by an account of

---

* Pour former un gouvernement modéré, il faut combiner les puissances, les régler, les tempérer, les faire agir; donner pour ainsi dire un lest à l'une, pour la mettre en état de résister à une autre; c'est un chef-d'oeuvre de législation que le hasard fait rarement, et que rarement on laisse faire à la prudence. Un gouvernement despotique au contraire saute, pour ainsi dire, aux yeux; il est uniforme partout: comme il ne faut que des passions pour l'établir, tout le monde est bon pour cela.—Montesquieu, De l'Esprit de Loix, liv. v. c. 14. ["In order to form a moderate government, it is necessary to combine powers, to regulate them, to temper them, to make them act, to provide, so to speak, one to resist another, this is the main aim of legislation that chance rarely achieves and prudence is rarely allowed to achieve. A despotic government, by contrast, leaps to view, so to speak, it is uniform everywhere as only passions are required to establish it, everyone can do that."]

† Bacon, Essay xxiv. (Of Innovations.) [*The Works of Francis Bacon . . . in Five Volumes* (London: A. Millar, 1765), 6:433.]

19. Bishop Shipley, *The Works of the Right Reverend Jonathan Shipley, D.D., Lord Bishop of St Asaph,* 2 vols. (London: T. Cadell, 1792), 2:112. The following statement was omitted in the son's edition: "I quote this passage from Bishop Shipley's beautiful account of the English constitution one of the finest parts of a writer, whose works I cannot help considering as the purest and most faultless model of composition that the present age can boast. Greater vigour and splendour may be found in others; but so perfect a taste, such chaste and modest elegance, it will, I think, be hard to discover in any other English writer of this reign."

the constitution of England. I shall endeavour to trace the progress of that constitution by the light of history, of laws, and of records, from the earliest times to the present age; and to show how the general principles of liberty, originally common to it with the other Gothic monarchies of <377> Europe, but in other countries lost or obscured, were in this more fortunate island preserved, matured, and adapted to the progress of civilization. I shall attempt to exhibit this most complicated machine, as our history and our laws show it in action; and not as some celebrated writers have most imperfectly represented it, who have torn out a few of its more simple springs, and putting them together, miscal them the British constitution. So prevalent, indeed, have these imperfect representations hitherto been, that I will venture to affirm, there is scarcely any subject which has been less treated as it deserved than the government of England. Philosophers of great and merited reputation* have told us that it consisted of certain portions of monarchy, aristocracy, and democracy,—names which are, in truth, very little applicable, and which, if they were, would as little give an idea of this government, as an account of the weight of bone, of flesh, and of blood in a human body, would be a picture of a living man. Nothing but a patient and minute investigation of the practice of the government in all its parts, and through its whole history, can give us just notions on this important subject. If a lawyer, without a philosophical spirit, be unequal to the examination of this great work of liberty and wisdom, still more unequal is a philosopher without practical, legal, and historical knowledge; for the first may want skill, but the second wants materials. The observations of Lord Bacon on political writers, in general, are most applicable to those who have given us systematic descriptions of the English constitution. "All those who have written of governments have written as philosophers, or as lawyers, *and none as statesmen.* As for the philosophers, they make imaginary laws for imaginary commonwealths, and their discourses are as the stars, which give little light <378> because they are so

---

* The reader will perceive that I allude to Montesquieu, whom I never name without reverence, though I shall presume, with humility, to criticise his account of a government which he only saw at a distance. [Montesquieu, *The Spirit of the Laws,* bk. 2, chap. 6.]

high."[20]—"Haec cognitio ad viros civiles propriè pertinet,"[21] as he tells us in another part of his writings; but unfortunately no experienced philosophical British statesman has yet devoted his leisure to a delineation of the constitution, which such a statesman alone can practically and perfectly know.

In the discussion of this great subject, and in all reasonings on the principles of politics, I shall labour, above all things, to avoid that which appears to me to have been the constant source of political error:—I mean the attempt to give an air of system, of simplicity, and of rigorous demonstration, to subjects which do not admit it. The only means by which this could be done, was by referring to a few simple causes, what, in truth, arose from immense and intricate combinations, and successions of causes. The consequence was very obvious. The system of the theorist, disencumbered from all regard to the real nature of things, easily assumed an air of speciousness: it required little dexterity, to make his arguments appear conclusive. But all men agreed that it was utterly inapplicable to human affairs. The theorist railed at the folly of the world, instead of confessing his own; and the man of practice unjustly blamed Philosophy, instead of condemning the sophist.[22] The causes which the politician has to consider are, above all others, multiplied, mutable, minute, subtile, and, if I may so speak, evanescent,—perpetually changing their form, and varying their combinations,—losing their nature, while they keep their name,—exhib-

20. Bacon, "The Dignity and Advancement of Learning," in *Works*, 3:475.

21. "Certe cognitio ista ad viros civiles proprie spectat." "The science of such matters certainly belongs more particularly to the province of men [who by habits of public business have been led to take a comprehensive survey of the social order]; of the interests of the community at large; of the rules of natural equity; of the manners of nations; of the different forms of government; and who are thus prepared to reason concerning the wisdom of laws, both from considerations of justice and of policy." Bacon, *De Augmentis Scientiarum*, bk. 8, chap. 3. The full passage is quoted, with a translation, in Dugald Stewart, *Account of the Life and Writings of Adam Smith*, sec. 4. *Transactions of the Royal Society of Edinburgh*, 1793. (Now in *Essays on Philosophical Subjects*, vol. 3 of The Glasgow Edition of the Works and Correspondence of Adam Smith, Liberty Fund, 1982, 311–12.)

22. The son's edition omits the following sentences: "The reason of this constant war between speculation and practice is not difficult to discover. It arises from the very nature of political science."

iting the most different consequences in the endless variety of men and nations on whom they operate,—in one degree of strength producing the most signal benefit, and, under a slight variation of circumstances, the most tremendous mischiefs. They admit indeed of being reduced to theory; but to a theory formed on the most extensive views, of the most comprehensive and flexible principles, to embrace all their varieties, and to fit all their rapid transmigrations,—a theory, of which the <379> most fundamental maxim is, distrust in itself, and deference for practical prudence. Only two writers of former times have, as far as I know, observed this general defect of political reasoners; but these two are the greatest philosophers who have ever appeared in the world. The first of them is Aristotle, who, in a passage of his Politics,[23] to which I cannot at this moment turn, plainly condemns the

23. The following note was omitted in the son's edition: "I have since discovered the passage or rather passages of Aristotle to which I alluded; I have collected several of these passages from various parts of his writings, that the reader may see the anxiety of that great philosopher to inculcate, even at the expense of repetition, the absurdity of every attempt to cultivate or teach moral philosophy with a geometrical exactness, which, in the vain pursuit of an accuracy which never can be more than *apparent,* betrays the inquirer into real, innumerable, and most mischievous fallacies.

Περὶ μὲν οὖν τῶν πολιτευομένων, πόσους τε ὑπάρχειν δεῖ καὶ ποίους τινὰς τὴν φύσιν, ἔτι δὲ τὴν χώραν πόσην τέ τινα καὶ ποίαν τινά, διώρισται σχεδόν· οὐ γὰρ τὴν αὐτὴν ἀκρίβειαν δεῖ ζητεῖν διά τε τῶν λόγων καὶ τῶν γιγνομένων διὰ τῆς αἰσθήσεως. ["We have now approximately decided what are the proper numbers and the natural qualities of those who exercise the right of citizens, and the proper extent and nature of the territory (for we must not seek to attain the same exactness by means of theoretical discussions as is obtained by means of the facts that come to us through sense-perceptions)." Aristotle, *Politics,* trans. H. Rackham (London: Heinemann, 1932), 568–69 (VII.vi.4.1328a17–21).]

τὴν δ᾽ ἀκριβολογίαν τὴν μαθηματικὴν οὐκ ἐν ἅπασιν ἀπαιτητέον, ἀλλ᾽ ἐν τοῖς μὴ ἔχουσιν ὕλην. ["Mathematical accuracy is not to be demanded in everything, but only in things which do not contain matter." Aristotle, *Metaphysics,* trans. H. Tredennick (Cambridge, Mass.: Harvard University Press, 1933), 94–95 (II.iii.3.995a14–16).]

πεπαιδευμένου γάρ ἐστιν ἐπὶ τοσοῦτον τἀκριβὲς ἐπιζητεῖν καθ᾽ ἕκαστον γένος ἐφ᾽ ὅσον ἡ τοῦ πράγματος φύσις ἐπιδέχεται· παραπλήσιον γὰρ φαίνεται μαθηματικοῦ τε πιθανολογοῦντος ἀποδέχεσθαι καὶ ῥητορικὸν ἀποδείξεις ἀπαιτεῖν. ["For it is the mark of the educated mind to expect that amount of exactness in each kind which the nature of the particular subject admits. It is equally unreasonable to accept merely probable conclusions from a mathematician, and to demand strict demonstration from an orator."

pursuit of a delusive geometrical accuracy in moral reasonings as the constant source of the grossest error. The second is Lord Bacon, who tells us, with that authority of conscious wisdom which belongs to him, and with that power of richly adorning Truth from the wardrobe of Genius which he possessed above *almost* all men, "Civil knowledge is conversant about a subject which, above all others, is most immersed in matter, and hardliest reduced to axiom."*[24]

I shall next endeavour to lay open the general principles of civil and criminal laws. On this subject I may with some confidence hope that I shall be enabled to philosophise with better materials by my acquaintance with the laws of my own country, which it is the business of my life to practise, and of which the study has by habit become my favourite pursuit.

The first principles of jurisprudence are simple maxims of Reason, of which the observance is immediately discovered by experience to be essential to the security of men's rights, and which pervade the laws of all countries. An account of the gradual application of these original principles, first to more simple, and afterwards to more complicated cases, <380>

Aristotle, *The Nicomachean Ethics,* trans. H. Rackham (London: Heinemann, 1926), 8–9 (I.iii.4.I.1094b23–27).]

"In the first of these remarkable passages he contradistinguishes morality from the physical sciences; in the second, from the abstract sciences. The distinction, though of a different nature, is equally great in both cases. Morality can neither attain the *particularity* of the sciences which are conversant with external nature, nor the *simplicity* of those, which, because they are founded on a few elementary principles, admit of rigorous demonstration; but this is a subject which would require a long dissertation. I am satisfied with laying before the reader the authority and the reasoning of Aristotle."

* This principle is expressed by a writer of a very different character from these two great philosophers,—a writer, "qu'on n'appellera plus philosophe, mais qu'on appellera le plus éloquent des sophistes," ["That one will no longer call him a philosopher, but that one will call him the most eloquent of the sophists."] with great force, and, as his manner is, with some exaggeration. "Il n'y a point de principes abstraits dans la politique. C'est une science des calculs, des combinaisons, et des exceptions, selon les lieux, les tems, et les circonstances." ["There are no longer abstract principles in politics. It is a science of calculations, or combinations, and of exceptions, according to the place, the time, and the circumstances."]—Lettre de Rousseau au Marquis de Mirabeau. [*Correspondence complète de Jean Jacques Rousseau,* ed. R. A. Leigh, 52 vols. (Genève and Oxford, 1965–98), 33:239 (July 1767).] The second proposition is true; but the first is not a just inference from it.

24. Bacon, "The Dignity and Advancement of Learning," in *Works,* 3:445.

forms both the history and the theory of law. Such an historical account of the progress of men, in reducing justice to an applicable and practical system, will enable us to trace that chain, in which so many breaks and interruptions are perceived by superficial observers, but which in truth inseparably, though with many dark and hidden windings, links together the security of life and property with the most minute and apparently frivolous formalities of legal proceeding. We shall perceive that no human foresight is sufficient to establish such a system at once, and that, if it were so established, the occurrence of unforeseen cases would shortly altogether change it; that there is but one way of forming a civil code, either consistent with common sense, or that has ever been practised in any country,—namely, that of gradually building up the law in proportion as the facts arise which it is to regulate. We shall learn to appreciate the merit of vulgar objections against the subtilty and complexity of laws. We shall estimate the good sense and the gratitude of those who reproach lawyers for employing all the powers of their mind to discover subtle distinctions for the prevention of injustice;* and we shall at once perceive that laws ought to be neither more simple nor more complex than the state of society which they are to govern, but that they ought exactly to correspond to it. Of the two faults, however, the excess of simplicity would certainly be the greatest; for laws, more complex than are necessary, would only produce embarrassment; whereas laws more simple than the affairs which they regulate would occasion a defeat of Justice. More understanding has perhaps been in this manner exerted to fix the rules of life than in any other science;† and it is <381> certainly the most honourable occupation of the understanding, because it is the most immediately subservient to general safety and comfort.

---

* "The casuistical subtilties are not perhaps greater than the subtilties of lawyers; but the latter are innocent, and even necessary."—Hume, Essays, vol. ii. p. 558. [A reference to "An Enquiry Concerning the Principles of Morals," sec. 3, "Of Justice," in *Essays*, 2 vols. (London: A. Millar, 1765).]

† "Law," said Dr. Johnson, "is the science in which the greatest powers of the understanding are applied to the greatest number of facts." [Unable to find the source of this quotation.] Nobody, who is acquainted with the variety and multiplicity of the subjects of jurisprudence, and with the prodigious powers of discrimination employed upon them, can doubt the truth of this observation.

There is not, in my opinion, in the whole compass of human affairs, so noble a spectacle as that which is displayed in the progress of jurisprudence; where we may contemplate the cautious and unwearied exertions of a succession of wise men, through a long course of ages, withdrawing every case as it arises from the dangerous power of discretion, and subjecting it to inflexible rules,—extending the dominion of justice and reason, and gradually contracting, within the narrowest possible limits, the domain of brutal force and of arbitrary will. This subject has been treated with such dignity by a writer who is admired by all mankind for his eloquence, but who is, if possible, still more admired by all competent judges for his philosophy,—a writer, of whom I may justly say, that he was "gravissimus et dicendi et intelligendi auctor et magister,"[25]—that I cannot refuse myself the gratification of quoting his words:—"The science of jurisprudence, the pride of the human intellect, which, with all its defects, redundancies, and errors, is the collected reason of ages combining the principles of original justice with the infinite variety of human concerns."*

I shall exemplify the progress of law, and illustrate those principles of Universal Justice on which it is founded, by a comparative review of the two greatest civil codes that have been hitherto formed,—those of Rome[26]

---

* Burke, [The Works of the Right Honourable Edmund Burke, Collected in Three Volumes (Dublin, 1792), 3:134. For a modern version see Reflections on the Revolution in France, vol. 2 of Select Works of Edmund Burke, 3 vols. (Indianapolis: Liberty Fund, 1999), 191–92.]

25. "That eminent master and teacher both of style and of thought." Compare Cicero, Orator, in Brutus, Orator, trans. H. M. Hubbell (London and Cambridge, Mass.: Heinemann and Harvard University Press, 1952), 312–13 (iii.10), said of Plato.

26. The following note was omitted in the son's edition: "It may perhaps not be disagreeable to the reader to find here the passage of LEIBNITZ, to which I have referred in the former editions of the Discourse. 'Caeteroquin ego Digestorum Opus vel potius auctorum unde excerpta sunt labores admiror, nec quidquam vidi sive rationum pondere sive dicendi nervos spectes quod magis accedat ad mathematicorum laudem.'—Leibnitz Op. vol. iv. p. 254." ("In other respects I admire the Digest, or rather the labours of the authors from whom the excerpts were made, and have not seen anything, whether in regard to the weight of the reasons or the tautness of the diction, that approaches more nearly to the merits of mathematics." Leibnitz, Opera, 6 vols. (Geneva, 1768), vol. 4, pt. 3, p. 254.)

and of England,*—of their agreements <382> and disagreements, both in general provisions, and in some of the most important parts of their minute practice. In this part of the course, which I mean to pursue with such detail as to give a view of both codes, that may perhaps be sufficient for the purposes of the general student,[27] I hope to convince him that the laws of civilized nations, particularly those of his own, are a subject most worthy of scientific curiosity; that principle and system run through them even to the minutest particular, as really, though not so apparently, as in other sciences, and applied to purposes more important than those of any other science. Will it be presumptuous to express a hope, that such an inquiry may not be altogether a useless introduction to that larger and more detailed study of the law of England, which is the duty of those who are to profess and practise that law?

In considering the important subject of criminal law it will be my duty to found, on a regard to the general safety, the right of the magistrate to inflict punishments, even the most severe, if that safety cannot be effectually protected by the example of inferior punishments. It will be a more agreeable part of my office to explain the temperaments which Wisdom, as well as Humanity, prescribes in the exercise of that harsh right, unfortunately so essential to the preservation of human society. I shall collate the penal codes of different nations, and gather together the most accurate statement of the result of experience with respect to the efficacy of lenient and severe punishments; and I shall endeavour to ascertain the principles on which must be founded both the proportion and the appropriation of

---

* On the intimate connection of these two codes, let us hear the words of Lord Holt, whose name never can be pronounced without veneration, as long as wisdom and integrity are revered among men:—"Inasmuch as the laws of all nations are doubtless raised out of the ruins of the civil law, as all governments are sprung out of the ruins of the Roman empire, it must be owned that the principles of our law are borrowed from the civil law, therefore grounded upon the same reason in many things." [The extract comes from Chief Justice Holt's judgment. The full legal citation is *Lane v. Sir Robert Cotton* (1701), 12. mod. 472 at 482 per Holt C.J.]

27. The following note was omitted in the son's edition: "On a closer examination, this part of my scheme has proved impracticable in the extent which I have here proposed, and within the short time to which I am necessarily confined. A general view of the principles of law, with some illustrations from the English and Roman codes, is all that I can compass."

penalties to crimes. As to the law of criminal proceeding,[28] my labour will be very easy; for on that subject an English lawyer, if he were to delineate the model of perfection, would find that, with few exceptions, he had transcribed the institutions of his own country.

The next great division of the subject is the "law of nations," strictly and properly so called. I have <383> already hinted at the general principles on which this law is founded. They, like all the principles of natural jurisprudence, have been more happily cultivated, and more generally obeyed, in some ages and countries than in others; and, like them, are susceptible of great variety in their application, from the character and usage of nations. I shall consider these principles in the gradation of those which are necessary to any tolerable intercourse between nations, of those which are essential to all well-regulated and mutually advantageous intercourse, and of those which are highly conducive to the preservation of a mild and friendly intercourse between civilized states. Of the first class, every understanding acknowledges the necessity, and some traces of a faint reverence for them are discovered even among the most barbarous tribes; of the second, every well-informed man perceives the important use, and they have generally been respected by all polished nations; of the third, the great benefit may be read in the history of modern Europe, where alone they have been carried to their full perfection. In unfolding the first and second class of principles, I shall naturally be led to give an account of that law of nations, which, in greater or less perfection, regulated the intercourse of savages, of the Asiatic empires, and of the ancient republics. The third brings me to the consideration of the law of nations, as it is now acknowledged in Christendom. From the great extent of the subject, and the par-

---

28. The following note was omitted in the son's edition: "By the *'Law of criminal proceeding,'* I mean those laws which regulate the *trial* of men accused of crimes, as distinguished from *penal law,* which fixes the *punishment* of crimes. 'tanda quae composita sunt et descripta, jura et jussa populorum; in quibus NE NOSTRI QUIDEM POPULI LATEBUNT QUAE VOCANTUR JURA CIVILIA.' Cic. de Leg. lib. i. c. 5." Mackintosh begins the passage halfway through a word—*traditanda;* the full passage reads, "then we must deal with the enactments and decrees of nations which are already formulated and put in writing; and among these the civil law, as it is called, of the Roman people will not fail to find a place." Cicero, *De legibus,* in *De re publica, De legibus,* trans. C. Walker Keyes (London: Heinemann, 1959), 314–17 (I.V.17).

ticularity to which, for reasons already given, I must here descend, it is impossible for me, within my moderate compass, to give even an outline of this part of the course. It comprehends, as every reader will perceive, the principles of national independence, the intercourse of nations in peace, the privileges of ambassadors and inferior ministers, the commerce of private subjects, the grounds of just war, the mutual duties of belligerent and neutral powers, the limits of lawful hostility, the rights of conquest, the faith to be observed in warfare, the force of an armistice,—of safe conducts and passports, <384> the nature and obligation of alliances, the means of negotiation, and the authority and interpretation of treaties of peace. All these, and many other most important and complicated subjects, with all the variety of moral reasoning, and historical examples which is necessary to illustrate them, must be fully examined in that part of the lectures, in which I shall endeavour to put together a tolerably complete practical system of the law of nations, as it has for the last two centuries been recognised in Europe.

"Le droit des gens est naturellement fondé sur ce principe, que les diverses nations doivent se faire, dans la paix le plus de bien, et dans la guerre le moins de mal, qu'il est possible, sans nuire à leurs véritables intérêts. L'objet de la guerre c'est la victoire; celui de la victoire la conquête; celui de la conquête la conservation. De ce principe et du précédent, doivent dériver toutes les loix qui forment le droit des gens. Toutes les nations ont un droit des gens; et les Iroquois même, qui mangent leurs prisonniers, en ont un. Ils envoient et reçoivent des embassades; ils connoissent les droits de la guerre et de la paix: le mal est que ce droit des gens n'est pas fondé sur les vrais principes."*

As an important supplement to the practical system of our modern law

---

* De l'Esprit des Loix, liv. i. c. 3. ["The *law of nations* is naturally founded on this principle; that the various nations should do to one another in times of peace the most good possible, and in times of war the least evil possible, without harming their own interests. The object of war is victory, that of victory conquest, that of conquest preservation. From this principle and from the preceding one, all laws which form the *law of nations* must be derived. All nations have a law of nations; even the Iroquois who eat their prisoners have one. They send and receive ambassadors; they know the laws of war and peace; the problem is that their law of nations is not founded on true principles." Montesquieu, *The Spirit of the Laws*, bk. 1, chap. 3.]

of nations, or rather as a necessary part of it, I shall conclude with a survey of the diplomatic and conventional law of Europe, and of the treaties which have materially affected the distribution of power and territory among the European states,—the circumstances which gave rise to them, the changes which they effected, and the principles which they introduced into the public code of the Christian commonwealth. In ancient times the knowledge of this conventional law was thought one of the greatest praises that could be bestowed on a name loaded with all the honours that eminence in the arts of peace and war can confer: "Equidem existimo, judices, <385> cùm in omni genere ac varietate artium, etiam illarum, quae sine summo otio non facilè discuntur, Cn. Pompeius excellat, singularem quandam laudem ejus et praestabilem esse scientiam, in foederibus, pactionibus, conditionibus, populorum, regum, exterarum nationum: in universo denique belli jure ac pacis."* Information on this subject is scattered over an immense variety of voluminous compilations, not accessible to every one, and of which the perusal can be agreeable only to a very few. Yet so much of these treaties has been embodied into the general law of Europe, that no man can be master of it who is not acquainted with them. The knowledge of them is necessary to negotiators and statesmen; it may sometimes be important to private men in various situations in which they may be placed; it is useful to all men who wish either to be acquainted with modern history, or to form a sound judgment on political measures. I shall endeavour to give such an abstract of it as may be sufficient for some, and a convenient guide for others in the farther progress of their studies. The treaties which I shall more particularly consider, will be those of Westphalia, of Oliva, of the Pyrenees, of Breda, of Nimeguen, of Ryswick, of Utrecht, of Aix-la-Chapelle, of Paris (1763), and of Versailles (1783). I shall

---

* Cic. Orat. pro L. Corn. Balbo, c. vi. ["For my part, gentlemen, I think on the contrary, that while Gnaeus Pompeius excels in every sort and variety of accomplishments, even those which it is not easy to acquire without much leisure, his quite outstanding merit is his most remarkable knowledge of treaties, of agreements, of terms imposed upon peoples, kings, and foreign races, and, in fact, of the whole code of law that deals with war and peace." Cicero, "Pro Balbo," in *Orationes,* trans. R. Gardner (London and Cambridge, Mass.: Heinemann and Harvard University Press, 1958), 640–42 (vi, 15).]

shortly explain the other treaties, of which the stipulations are either alluded to, confirmed, or abrogated in those which I consider at length. I
shall subjoin an account of the diplomatic intercourse of the European
powers with the Ottoman Porte, and with other princes and states who are
without the pale of our ordinary federal law; together with a view of the
most important treaties of commerce, their principles, and their consequences.

As an useful appendix to a practical treatise on the law of nations, some
account will be given of those tribunals which in different countries of
Europe decide controversies arising out of that law; of their <386> constitution, of the extent of their authority, and of their modes of proceeding;
more especially of those courts which are peculiarly appointed for that purpose by the laws of Great Britain.

Though the course, of which I have sketched the outline, may seem to
comprehend so great a variety of miscellaneous subjects, yet they are all in
truth closely and inseparably interwoven. The duties of men, of subjects,
of princes, of lawgivers, of magistrates, and of states, are all parts of one
consistent system of universal morality. Between the most abstract and elementary maxim of moral philosophy, and the most complicated controversies of civil or public law, there subsists a connection which it will be
the main object of these lectures to trace. The principle of justice, deeply
rooted in the nature and interest of man, pervades the whole system, and
is discoverable in every part of it, even to its minutest ramification in a legal
formality, or in the construction of an article in a treaty.

I know not whether a philosopher ought to confess, that in his inquiries
after truth he is biassed by any consideration,—even by the love of virtue.
But I, who conceive that a real philosopher ought to regard truth itself
chiefly on account of its subserviency to the happiness of mankind, am
not ashamed to confess, that I shall feel a great consolation at the conclusion
of these lectures, if, by a wide survey and an exact examination of the conditions and relations of human nature, I shall have confirmed but one individual in the conviction, that justice is the permanent interest of all men,
and of all commonwealths. To discover one new link of that eternal chain
by which the Author of the universe has bound together the happiness and
the duty of His creatures, and indissolubly fastened their interests to each

other, would fill my heart with more pleasure than all the fame with which the most ingenious paradox ever crowned the most eloquent sophist. I shall conclude this Discourse in the noble language of two great orators and <387> philosophers, who have, in a few words, stated the substance, the object, and the result of all morality, and politics, and law. "Nihil est quod adhuc de republicâ putem dictum, et quo possim longius progredi, nisi sit confirmatum, non modo falsum esse illud, sine injuriâ non posse, sed hoc verissimum, sine summâ justitiâ rempublicam geri nullo modo posse."* "Justice is itself the great standing policy of civil society, and any eminent departure from it, under any circumstances, lies under the suspicion of being no policy at all."†

---

* Cic. De Repub. lib. ii. ["We must consider all the statements we have made so far about the commonwealth as amounting to nothing, and must admit that we have no basis whatever for further progress, unless we can not merely disprove the contention that a government cannot be carried on without injustice, but are also able to prove positively that it cannot be carried on without the strictest justice." Cicero, De re publica, in De re publica, De legibus, trans. C. Walker Keyes (London and Cambridge, Mass.: Heinemann and Harvard University Press, 1959), 182–83 (II, xliv).]

† Burke, Works, vol. iii. p. 207. [For a recent version see Burke, Reflections, 260.]

Appendix to the *"Discourse"*:
Extracts from the Lectures

In laying open this plan, I am aware that men of finished judgment and experience will feel an unwillingness, not altogether unmingled with disgust, at being called back to the first rudiments of their knowledge. I know with what contempt they look down on the sophistical controversies of the schools. I own that their disgust is always natural, and their contempt often just. Something had already been said in vindication of myself on this subject in my published discourse, but perhaps not enough. I entreat such men to consider the circumstances of the times in which we live. A body of writers has arisen in all the countries of Europe, who represent all the ancient usages, all the received opinions, all the fundamental principles, all the most revered institutions of mankind, as founded in absurdity, requiring the aid both of oppression and imposture, and leading to the degradation and misery of the human race. This attack is conducted upon principles which are said to be philosophical, and such is the state of Europe, that I will venture to affirm, that, unless our ancient opinions and establishment can also be vindicated upon philosophical principles, they will not long be able to maintain that place in the affection and <112> veneration of mankind, from which they derive all their strength. In this case, I trust I shall be forgiven if I dig deeply into theory, and explore the solid foundations of practice—if I call in the aid of philosophy, not for the destruction, but for the defence, of experience. Permit me to say, the unnatural separation and, much more, the frequent hostility of speculation and practice, have been fatal to science and fatal to mankind. They are destined to move harmoniously, each in its own orbit, as members of one grand system of universal Wisdom. Guided by one common law, illuminated from one common source, reflecting light on each other, and conspiring, by their movements, to the use and beauty [of one grand] whole. Believe me, gentlemen, when we have examined this question thoroughly, we shall be persuaded that that refined and exquisite good sense, applied to the most important matters, which is called Philosophy, never differs, and never can differ in its dictates, from that other sort of good sense, which is employed in the guidance of human life. There is, indeed, a philosophy, falsely so called, which, on a hasty glance over the surface of human life, condemns all our institutions to destruction, which stigmatises all our most natural and useful feelings as prejudices; and which, in the vain effort to implant in us principles which take no root in human nature, would extirpate all those principles which sweeten and ennoble the life of man. The general character of this system is diametrically opposite to that of true philosophy:—wanting philosophical modesty, it is arrogant—philosophical caution, it is rash—philosophical calmness, it is headstrong and fanatical. Instead of that difference, and, if I may so speak, of that scepticism and cowardice, which is the first lesson of philosophy, when we are to treat of the happiness of human beings, we find a system as dog-<113>matical, boastful, heedless of every thing but its own short-sighted views, and intoxicated with the perpetual and exclusive contemplation of its own system of disorder, and demonstrations of insanity. This is not that philosophy which Cicero calls "philosophiam illam matrem omnium benefactorum beneque dictorum";[1] for its direct tendency is to wither and blast every amiable and every exalted sentiment, from which either virtue, or eloquence can flow, by holding up to the imagination an ideal picture of I know not what future perfection of human society. The doctors of this system teach their disciples to loathe that state of society in which they must live and act, to despise and abhor what they cannot be virtuous and happy without loving and revering—to consider all our present virtues either as specious vices, or at best but as the inferior and contemptible duties of a degraded condition, from which the human race must and will speedily escape. Of this supposed state of future perfection (though it be utterly irreconcilable with reason, with experience, or with analogy), the masters of this sect speak as confidently, as if it were one of the best authenticated

---

1. "Philosophy, that mother of all good deeds and eloquent sayings."

events in history. It is proposed as an object of pursuit and attainment. It is said to be useful to have such a model of a perfect society before our eyes, though we can never reach it. It is said at least to be one of the harmless speculations of benevolent visionaries. But this is not true. The tendency of such a system (I impute no evil intentions to its promulgators) is to make the whole present order of human life appear so loathsome and hideous, that there is nothing to justify either warm affection, or zealous exertion, or even serious pursuit. In seeking an unattainable perfection, it tears up by the roots every principle which leads to the substantial and practicable improvement of mankind. It thwarts its own purpose, <114> and tends to replunge men into depravity and barbarism. Such a philosophy, I acknowledge, must be at perpetual variance with practice, because it must wage eternal war with truth. From such a philosophy I can hope to receive no aid in the attempt, which is the main object of these lectures, to conclude a treaty of peace, if I may venture so to express myself, between the worlds of speculation and practice, which were designed by nature to help each other, but which have been so long arrayed against each other, by the pretended or misguided friends of either. The philosophy from which I shall seek assistance in building up [my theory of] morals, is of another character; better adapted, I trust, to serve as the foundation of that which has been called, with so much truth, and with such majestic simplicity, "amplissimam omnium artium, bene vivendi disciplinam."[2] The true philosophy of morality and politics is founded on experience. It never, therefore, can contradict that practical prudence, which is the more direct issue of experience. Guided by the spirit of that philosophy, which is

> Not harsh or crabbed, as dull fools suppose,
> But musical, as is Apollo's lute,[3]

I shall, in my inquiries into human nature, only to take to pieces the principles of our conduct, that I may the better show the necessity of putting

---

2. "This the most fruitful of all arts, which teaches the way of right living." Cicero, *Tusculan Disputations,* trans. J. E. King (London and Cambridge, Mass.: Heinemann and Harvard University Press, 1960), 332–33 (IV.iii.5).

3. John Milton, *A Mask (Comus),* in *Comus and Some Shorter Poems of Milton,* ed. E. M. W. Tillyard (London: Harrap, 1952), 90, lines 477–78.

them together—analyse them, that I may display their use and beauty, and that I may furnish new motives to cherish and cultivate them. In the examination of laws, I shall not set out with the assumption, that all the wise men of the world have been hitherto toiling to build up an elaborate system of folly, a stupendous edifice of injustice. As I think the contrary presumption more reasonable as well as more modest, I shall think it my duty to explore the codes of nations, for those treasures of reason which <115> must have been deposited there by that vast stream of wisdom, which, for so many ages, has been flowing over them.

Such a philosophy will be terrible to none of my hearers. Empirical statesmen have despised science, and visionary speculators have despised experience; but he who was both a philosopher and a statesman, has told us, "This is that which will indeed dignify and exalt knowledge, if contemplation and action may be more nearly conjoined and united than they have hitherto been."[4] These are the words of Lord Bacon;* and in his spirit I shall, throughout these lectures, labour with all my might to prove, that philosophical truth is, in reality, the foundation of civil and moral prudence. In the execution of this task, I trust I shall be able to avoid all obscurity of language. Jargon is not philosophy—though he who first as-

---

* In his copy of Lord Bacon's Works was the following note:—"Jus naturae et gentium diligentius tractaturus, omne quod in Verulamio ad jurisprudentiam universalem spectat relegit J M apud Broadstairs in agro Rutupiano Cantiae, anno salutis humanae 1798, latè tum flagrantè per Europae felices quodam populos misero fatalique bello, in quo nefarii et scelestissimi latrones infando consilio apertè et audacter, virtutem, libertatem, Dei Immortalis cultum, mores et instituta majorum, hanc denique pulcherrimè et sapientissimè constitutam rempublicam labefactare, et penitùs evertere conantur." ["When he came to deal with the Law of Nature and of Nations J[ames] M[ackintosh] reread everything in Verulam [Lord Bacon's writings] that had to do with universal jurisprudence. He did this reading in Broadstairs in the district of Richborough in Kent, in the year of Salvation 1798, a time when there was a dreadful and deadly war raging widely among the once happy peoples of Europe. In this war impious and criminal mercenaries, with unspeakably evil intent, openly and boldly tried to dislodge and completely overturn virtue, freedom, worship of the Everlasting God, ancestral customs and practices, and lastly this finely and wisely founded commonwealth."]—A plan of study, which, some time after he wrote out for a young friend, concludes thus: "And as the result of all study, and the consummation of all wisdom, Bacon's Essays to be read, studied, and converted into part of the substance of your mind."
4. Bacon, "The Dignity and Advancement of Learning," in *Works*, 3:294.

sumed the name of philosopher, is said by Lucian to have confessed that he made his doctrines wonderful to attract the admiration of the vulgar. You will, I hope, prefer the taste of a greater than Pythagoras, of whom it was said, "that it was his course to make wonders plain, not plain things wonderful."[5] <116>

As a part of general education, I have no intention to insinuate that there is any deficiency in the original plan, or in the present conduct of those noble seminaries of learning where the youth of England are trained up in all the liberal and ingenious arts: far be such petulant, irreverent insinuations from my mind. Though I am in <117> some measure a foreigner in England, though I am a stranger to their advantages, yet no British heart can be a stranger to their glory.

Non obtusa adeo gestamus pectora.[6]

I can look with no common feelings on the schools which sent forth a Bacon and a Milton, a Hooker and a Locke. I have often contemplated with mingled sensations of pleasure and awe, those magnificent monuments of the veneration of our ancestors for piety and learning. May they long flourish, and surpass, if that be possible, their ancient glory.

I am not one of those who think that, in the system of English education, too much time and labour are employed in the study of the languages of Greece and Rome; it is a popular, but, in my humble opinion, a very shallow and vulgar objection. It would be easy, I think, to prove that too much time can be scarcely employed on these languages by any nation which is desirous of preserving either that purity of taste, which is its brightest ornament, or that purity of morals, which is its strongest bulwark.

You may be sure, gentlemen, that I am not going to waste your time by expanding the common-places of panegyric on classical learning. I shall not speak of the necessity of recurring to the best models for the formation of taste. When any modern poets or orators shall have excelled Homer and Demosthenes; and when any considerable number of unlettered modern

---

5. Unable to find the source of this quotation.
6. "Not so dull are our Punic hearts." Virgil, "Aeneid," in *Virgil,* trans. H. Rushton Fairclough, 2 vols. (London and Cambridge, Mass.: Heinemann and Harvard University Press, 1967), 1:280–81 (bk. 1, line 567).

writers (for I have no concern with extraordinary exceptions) shall have attained eminence, it will be time enough to discuss the question. But I entreat you to consider the connexion between classical learning and morality, which I think as real and as close as its connexion with taste, although I do not find that it has been so often noticed. If we were to <118> devise a method for infusing morality into the tender minds of youth, we should certainly not attempt it by arguments and rules, by definition and demonstration. We should certainly endeavour to attain our object by insinuating morals in the disguise of history, of poetry, and of eloquence; by heroic examples, by pathetic incidents, by sentiments that either exalt and fortify, or soften and melt, the human heart. If philosophical ingenuity were to devise a plan of moral instruction, these, I think, would be its outlines. But such a plan already exists. Classical education is that plan; nor can modern history and literature even be substituted in its stead. Modern example can never imprint on the youthful mind the grand and authoritative sentiment, that in the most distant ages, and in states of society the most unlike, the same virtues have been the object of human veneration. Strip virtue of the awful authority which she derives from the general reverence of mankind, and you rob her of half her majesty. Modern character never could animate youth to noble exertions of duty and of genius, by the example of that durable glory which awaits them after death, and which, in the case of the illustrious ancients, they see has survived the subversion of empires, and even the extinction of nations. Modern men are too near and too familiar, to inspire that enthusiasm with which we must view those who are to be our models in virtue. When our fancy would exalt them to the level of our temporary admiration, it is perpetually checked by some trivial circumstance, by some mean association,—perhaps by some ludicrous recollection,—which damps and extinguishes our enthusiasm. They had the same manners which we see every day degraded by ordinary and vicious men; they spoke the language which we hear polluted by the use of the ignorant and the vulgar. But ancient sages and patriots are, <119> as it were, exalted by difference of language and manners, above every thing that is familiar, and low, and debasing. And if there be something in ancient examples not fit to be imitated, or even to be approved in modern times, yet, let it be recollected, that distance not only adds to their authority, but softens their fierceness. When we contemplate them at such a distance, the ferocity is lost, and the magnanimity only reaches us. These noble studies preserve, and they can only preserve the unbroken chain of learning which unites the most remote generations; the grand catholic communion of wisdom and wise men throughout all ages and nations of the world. "If," says Lord Bacon, "the intention of the ship was thought so noble, which carrieth riches and commodities from place to place, and consociateth the most remote regions in participation of their fruits, how much more are letters to be magnified, which, as ships, pass through the vast seas of time, and make ages so distant participate of the wisdom, illuminations, and inventions, the one of the other."[7] Alas! gentlemen; what can I say that will not seem flat, and tame, and insipid, after this divine wisdom and divine eloquence? But this great commerce between ages will be broken and intercepted; the human race will be reduced to the scanty stock of their own age, unless the latest generations are united to the earliest by an early and intimate knowledge of their language, and their literature. From the experience of former times, I will venture to predict, that no man will ever obtain lasting fame in learning, who is not enlightened by the knowledge, and inspired by the genius, of those who have gone before him. But if this be true in other sciences, it is ten thousand times more evident in the science of morals.

I have said in my printed Discourse, that morality admits no discoveries; and I shall now give you some <120> reasons for a position, which may perhaps have startled some, in an age when ancient opinions seem in danger of being so exploded, that when they are produced again, they may appear novelties, and even be suspected of paradox. I do not speak of the theory of morals, but of the rule of life. First examine the fact, and see whether, from the earliest times, any improvement, or even any change, has been made in the practical rules of human conduct. Look at the code of Moses. I speak of it now as a mere human composition, without considering its sacred origin. Considering it merely in that light, it is the most ancient and the most curious memorial of the early history of mankind. More than three thousand years have elapsed since the composition of the Pentateuch;

7. Bacon, "The Dignity and Advancement of Learning," in *Works,* 3:318.

and let any man, if he is able, tell me in what important respects the rule of life has varied since that distant period. Let the Institutes of Menu be explored with the same view; we shall arrive at the same conclusion. Let the books of false religion be opened; it will be found that their moral system is, in all its grand features, the same. The impostors who composed them were compelled to pay this homage to the uniform moral sentiments of the world. Examine the codes of nations, those authentic depositories of the moral judgments of men; you every where find the same rules prescribed, the same duties imposed: even the boldest of these ingenious sceptics who have attacked every other opinion, has spared the sacred and immutable simplicity of the rules of life. In our common duties, Bayle and Hume agree with Bossuet and Barrow. Such as the rule was at the first dawn of history, such it continues till the present day. Ages roll over mankind; mighty nations pass away like a shadow; virtue alone remains the same, immortal and unchangeable.

The fact is evident, that no improvements have been <121> made in practical morality. The reasons of this fact it is not difficult to discover. It will be very plain, on the least consideration, that mankind must so completely have formed their rule of life, in the most early times, that no subsequent improvements could change it. The chances of a science being improvable, seem chiefly to depend on two considerations.

When the facts which are the groundwork of a science are obvious, and when the motive which urge men to the investigation of them is very powerful, we may always expect that such a science will be so quickly perfected, in the most early times, as to leave little for after ages to add. When, on the contrary, the facts are remote and of difficult access, and when the motive which stimulates men to consider them is not urgent, we may expect that such a science will be neglected by the first generations of mankind; and that there will be, therefore, a boundless field for its improvement left open to succeeding times. This is the grand distinction between morality, and all other sciences. This is the principle which explains its peculiar history and singular fortune. It is for this reason that it has remained for thirty centuries unchanged, and that we have no ground to expect that it will be materially improved, if this globe should continue inhabited by men for twice thirty centuries more. The facts which lead to the formation of moral rules are as accessible, and must be as obvious, to the simplest barbarian, as to the most enlightened philosopher. It requires no telescope to discover that un-distinguishing and perpetual slaughter will *terminate* in the destruction of his race. The motive that leads him to consider them is the most powerful that can be imagined. It is the care of preserving his own existence. The case of the physical and speculative sciences is directly opposite. There the facts are remote, and scarcely acces-<122>sible; and the motive that induces us to explore them is comparatively weak. It is only curiosity; or, at most, only a desire to multiply the conveniences and ornaments of life. It is not, therefore, till very late in the progress of refinement, that these sciences become an object of cultivation. From the countless variety of the facts, with which they are conversant, it is impossible to prescribe any bounds to their future improvement. It is otherwise with morals. They have hitherto been stationary; and, in my opinion, they are likely for ever to continue so.

On the State of France <184> <185>
in 1815.

To appreciate the effects of the French Revolution on the people of France, is an undertaking for which no man now alive has sufficient materials, or sufficient impartiality, even if he had sufficient ability. It is a task from which Tacitus and Machiavel would have shrunk; and to which the little pamphleteers, who speak on it with dogmatism, prove themselves so unequal by their presumption, that men of sense do not wait for the additional proof which is always amply furnished by their performances. The French Revolution was a destruction of great abuses, executed with much violence, injustice, and inhumanity. The destruction of abuse is, in itself, and for so much, a good: injustice and inhumanity would cease to be vices, if they were not productive of great mischief to society. This is a most perplexing account to balance.

As applied, for instance, to the cultivators and cultivation of France, there seems no reason to doubt the unanimous testimony of all travellers and observers, that agriculture has advanced, and that the condition of the agricultural population has been sensibly improved. M. de la Place calculates agricultural produce to have increased one fifth during <186> the last twenty-five years. M. Cuvier, an unprejudiced and dispassionate man, rather friendly than adverse to much of what the Revolution destroyed, and who, in his frequent journeys through France, surveyed the country with the eyes of a naturalist and a politician, bears the most decisive testimony to the same general result. M. de Candolle, a very able and enlightened Genevese, who is Professor of Botany at Montpellier, is preparing for the press the fruit of several years devoted to the survey of French cultivation, in which we are promised the detailed proofs of its progress.[1] The apprehensions lately entertained by the landed interest of England, and countenanced by no less an authority than that of Mr. Malthus, that France, as a permanent exporter of corn, would supply our market, and drive our inferior lands out of cultivation,—though we consider them as extremely unreasonable,—must be allowed to be of some weight in this question.[2] No such dread of the rivalship of French corn-growers was ever felt or affected in this country in former times. Lastly, the evidence of Mr. Birkbeck, an independent thinker, a shrewd observer, and an experienced farmer, though his journey was rapid, and though he perhaps wished to find benefits resulting from the Revolution, must be allowed to be of high value.[3]

But whatever may have been the benefits conferred by the Revolution on the cultivators, supposing them to have been more questionable than they appear to have been, it is at all events obvious, that the division of the confiscated lands among the peasantry must have given that body an interest and a pride in the maintenance of the order or disorder which that revolution had produced. All confiscation is unjust. The French confiscation, being the most extensive, is the most abominable example of that species of legal robbery. But we speak only of its political effects on the temper of the peasantry. These effects are by no means confined to those who had become proprietors. The promotion of many inspired all with <187> pride: the whole class was raised in self-importance by the proprietary dignity acquired by numerous individuals. Nor must it be supposed that the apprehensions of such a rabble of ignorant owners, who had acquired their ownerships by means of which their own conscience would distrust the fairness, were to be proportioned to the reasonable probabilities of danger. The alarms of a multitude for objects very valuable to them, are always extravagantly beyond the degree of the risk, especially when they

---

1. Augustin Pyramus de Candolle, *Botanicon Gallicum seu Synopsis Plantarum in Flora Gallica Descriptarum,* 2d ed. (Paris, 1828).

2. T. R. Malthus, *The Grounds of an Opinion on the Policy of Restricting the Importation of Foreign Corn* (London, 1815), 12–14.

3. Morris Birkbeck, *Notes on a Journey through France from Dieppe through Paris and Lyons to the Pyrenees, and back through Toulouse, in July, August, and September 1814* (London, 1814).

are strengthened by any sense, however faint and indistinct, of injustice, which, by the immutable laws of human nature, stamps every possession which suggests it with a mark of insecurity. It is a panic fear;—one of those fears which are so rapidly spread and so violently exaggerated by sympathy, that the lively fancy of the ancients represented them as inflicted by a superior power.

Exemption from manorial rights and feudal services was not merely, nor perhaps principally, considered by the French farmers as a relief from oppression. They were connected with the exulting recollections of deliverance from a yoke,—of a triumph over superiors,—aided even by the remembrance of the licentiousness with which they had exercised their saturnalian privileges in the first moments of their short and ambiguous liberty. They recollected these distinctions as an emancipation of their caste. The interest, the pride, the resentment, and the fear, had a great tendency to make the maintenance of these changes a point of honour among the whole peasantry of France. On this subject, perhaps, they were likely to acquire that jealousy and susceptibility which the dispersed population of the country rarely exhibit, unless when their religion, or their national pride, or their ancient usages, are violently attacked. The only security for these objects would appear to them to be a government arising, like their own property and privileges, out of the Revolution.

We are far from commending these sentiments, and <188> still farther from confounding them with the spirit of liberty. If the forms of a free constitution could have been preserved under a counter-revolutionary government, perhaps these hostile dispositions of the peasants and new proprietors against such a government, might have been gradually mitigated and subdued into being one of the auxiliaries of freedom. But, in the present state of France, there are unhappily no elements of such combinations. There is no such class as landed gentry,—no great proprietors resident on their estates,—consequently no leaders of this dispersed population, to give them permanent influence on the public counsels, to animate their general sluggishness, or to restrain their occasional violence. In such a state they must, in general, be inert;—in particular matters, which touch their own prejudices and supposed interest, unreasonable and irresistible. The extreme subdivision of landed property might, under some circumstances, be favourable to a democratical government. Under a limited monarchy it is destructive of liberty, because it annihilates the strongest bulwarks against the power of the crown. Having no body of great proprietors, it delivers the monarch from all regular and constant restraint, and from every apprehension but that of an inconstant and often servile populace. And, melancholy as the conclusion is, it seems too probable that the present state of property and prejudice among the larger part of the people of France, rather disposes them towards a despotism deriving its sole title from the Revolution, and interested in maintaining the system of society which it has established, and armed with that tyrannical power which may be necessary for its maintenance.

Observations of a somewhat similar nature are applicable to other classes of the French population. Many of the tradesmen and merchants, as well as of the numerous bodies of commissaries and contractors grown rich by war, had become landed proprietors. These classes in general had participated in the early <189> movements of the Revolution. They had indeed generally shrunk from its horrors; but they had associated their pride, their quiet, almost their moral character, with its success, by extensive purchases of confiscated land. These feelings were not to be satisfied by any assurances, however solemn and repeated, or however sincere, that the sales of national property were to be inviolable. The necessity of such assurance continually reminded them of the odiousness of their acquisitions, and of the light in which the acquirers were considered by the government. Their property was to be spared as an evil, incorrigible from its magnitude. What they must have desired, was a government from whom no such assurances could have been necessary.

The middle classes in cities were precisely those who had been formerly humbled, mortified, and exasperated by the privileges of the nobility,—for whom the Revolution was a triumph over those who, in the daily intercourse of life, treated them with constant disdain,—and whom that Revolution raised to the vacant place of these desposed chiefs. The vanity of that numerous, intelligent, and active part of the community—merchants, bankers, manufacturers, tradesmen, lawyers, attorneys, physicians, surgeons, artists, actors, men of letters—had been humbled by the monarchy, and had triumphed in the Revolution: they rushed into the stations which the gentry—emigrant, beggared, or proscribed—could no longer fill: the whole government fell into their hands.

Buonaparte's nobility was an institution framed to secure the triumph of all these vanities, and to provide against the possibility of a second humiliation. It was a body composed of a Revolutionary aristocracy, with some of the ancient nobility,—either rewarded for their services to the Revolution, by its highest dignities, or compelled to lend lustre to it, by accepting in it secondary ranks, with titles inferior to their own,—and with many lawyers, men of letters, <190> merchants, physicians, &c., who often receive inferior marks of honour in England, but whom the ancient system of the French monarchy had rigorously excluded from such distinctions. The military principle predominated, not only from the nature of the government, but because military distinction was the purest that was earned during the Revolution. The Legion of Honour spread the same principle through the whole army, which probably contained six-and-thirty thousand out of the forty thousand who composed the order. The whole of these institutions was an array of new against old vanities,—of that of the former roturiers against that of the former nobility. The new knights and nobles were daily reminded by their badges, or titles, of their interest to resist the re-establishment of a system which would have perpetuated their humiliation. The real operation of these causes was visible during the short reign of Louis XVIII. Military men, indeed, had the courage to display their decorations, and to avow their titles: but most civilians were ashamed, or afraid, to use their new names of dignity; they were conveyed, if at all, in a subdued voice, almost in a whisper; they were considered as extremely unfashionable and vulgar. Talleyrand renounced his title of Prince of Beneventum; and Massena's resumption of his dignity of Prince was regarded as an act of audacity, if not of intentional defiance.

From these middle classes were chosen another body, who were necessarily attached to the Revolutionary government,—the immense body of civil officers who were placed in all the countries directly or indirectly subject to France,—in Italy, in Germany, in Poland, in Holland, in the Netherlands,—for the purposes of administration of finance, and of late to enforce the vain prohibition of commerce with England. These were all thrown back on France by the peace. They had no hope of employment:

their gratitude, their resentment, and their expectations bound them to the fortune of Napoleon. <191>

The number of persons in France interested, directly or indirectly, in the sale of confiscated property—by original purchase, by some part in the successive transfers, by mortgage, or by expectancy,—has been computed to be ten millions. This must be a great exaggeration: but one half of that number would be more than sufficient to give colour to the general sentiment. Though the lands of the Church and the Crown were never regarded in the same invidious light with those of private owners, yet the whole mass of confiscation was held together by its Revolutionary origin: the possessors of the most odious part were considered as the outposts and advanced guards of the rest. The purchasers of small lots were peasants; those of considerable estates were the better classes of the inhabitants of cities. Yet, in spite of the powerful causes which attached these last to the Revolution, it is certain, that among the class called *"La bonne bourgeoisie"* are to be found the greatest number of those who approved the restoration of the Bourbons as the means of security and quiet. They were weary of revolution, and they dreaded confusion: but they are inert and timid, and almost as little qualified to defend a throne as they are disposed to overthrow it. Unfortunately, their voice, of great weight in the administration of regular governments, is scarcely heard in convulsions. They are destined to stoop to the bold;—too often, though with vain sorrow and indignation, to crouch under the yoke of the guilty and the desperate.

The populace of great towns (a most important constituent part of a free community, when the union of liberal institutions, with a vigorous authority, provides both a vent for their sentiments, and a curb on their violence,) have, throughout the French Revolution, showed at once all the varieties and excesses of plebeian passions, and all the peculiarities of the French national character in their most exaggerated state. The love of show, or of change,—the rage for liberty or slavery, for war or for peace, soon <192> wearing itself out into disgust and weariness,—the idolatrous worship of demagogues, soon abandoned, and at last cruelly persecuted,—the envy of wealth, or the servile homage paid to it,—all these, in every age, in every place, from Athens to Paris, have characterised a populace not educated by habits of reverence for the laws, or bound by ties of character and

palpable interest to the other classes of a free commonwealth. When the
Parisian mob were restrained by a strong government, and compelled to
renounce their democratic orgies, they became proud of conquest,—proud
of the splendour of their despotism,—proud of the magnificence of its
exhibitions and its monuments. Men may be so brutalised as to be proud
of their chains. That sort of interest in public concerns, which the poor,
in their intervals of idleness, and especially when they are met together, feel
perhaps more strongly than other classes more constantly occupied with
prudential cares, overflowed into new channels. They applauded a general
or a tyrant, as they had applauded Robespierre, and worshipped Marat.
They applauded the triumphal entry of a foreign army within their walls
as a grand show; and they huzzaed the victorious sovereigns, as they would
have celebrated the triumph of a French general. The return of the Bourbons was a novelty, and a sight, which, as such, might amuse them for a
day; but the establishment of a pacific and frugal government, with an
infirm monarch and a gloomy court, without sights or donatives, and the
cessation of the gigantic works constructed to adorn Paris, were sure
enough to alienate the Parisian populace. There was neither vigour to overawe them,—nor brilliancy to intoxicate them,—nor foreign enterprise to
divert their attention.

Among the separate parties into which every people is divided, the Protestants are to be regarded as a body of no small importance in France. Their
numbers were rated at between two and three millions; but their importance was not to be estimated <193> by their numerical strength. Their
identity of interest,—their habits of concert,—their common wrongs and
resentments,—gave them far more strength than a much larger number of
a secure, lazy, and dispirited majority. It was, generally speaking, impossible
that French Protestants should wish well to the family of Louis XIV., peculiarly supported as it was by the Catholic party. The lenity with which
they had long been treated, was ascribed more to the liberality of the age
than that of the Government. Till the year 1788, even their marriages and
their inheritances had depended more upon the connivance of the tribunals, than upon the sanction of the law. The petty vexations, and ineffectual
persecution of systematic exclusion from public offices, and the consequent
degradation of their body in public opinion, long survived the detestable

but effectual persecution which had been carried on by missionary dragoons, and which had benevolently left them the choice to be hypocrites, or exiles, or galley-slaves. The Revolution first gave them a secure and effective equality with the Catholics, and a real admission into civil office. It is to be feared that they may have sometimes exulted over the sufferings of the Catholic Church, and thereby contracted some part of the depravity of their ancient persecutors. But it cannot be doubted that they were generally attached to the Revolution, and to governments founded on it.

The same observations may be applied, without repetition, to other sects of Dissidents. Of all the lessons of history, there is none more evident in itself, and more uniformly neglected by governments, than that persecutions, disabilities, exclusions,—all systematic wrong to great bodies of citizens,—are sooner or later punished; though the punishment often falls on individuals, who are not only innocent, but who may have had the merit of labouring to repair the wrong.

The voluntary associations which have led or influenced the people during the Revolution, are a very material object in a review like the present. The <194> very numerous body who, as Jacobins or Terrorists, had participated in the atrocities of 1793 and 1794, had, in the exercise of tyranny, sufficiently unlearned the crude notions of liberty with which they had set out. But they all required a government established on Revolutionary foundations. They all took refuge under Buonaparte's authority. The more base accepted clandestine pensions or insignificant places: Barrere wrote slavish paragraphs at Paris; Tallien was provided for by an obscure or a nominal consulship in Spain. Fouché, who conducted this part of the system, thought the removal of an active Jacobin to a province cheaply purchased by five hundred a year. Fouché, himself, one of the most atrocious of the Terrorists, had been gradually formed into a good administrator under a civilized despotism,—regardless indeed of forms, but paying considerable respect to the substance, and especially to the appearance of justice,—never shrinking from what was necessary to crush a formidable enemy, but carefully avoiding wanton cruelty and unnecessary evil. His administration, during the earlier and better part of Napoleon's government, had so much repaired the faults of his former life, that the appointment of Savary to the police was one of the most alarming acts of the internal policy during the violent period which followed the invasion of Spain.

At the head of this sort of persons, not indeed in guilt, but in the conspicuous nature of the act in which they had participated, were the Regicides. The execution of Louis XVI. being both unjust and illegal, was unquestionably an atrocious murder: but it would argue great bigotry and
ignorance of human nature, not to be aware, that many who took a share
in it must have viewed it in a directly opposite light. Mr. Hume himself,
with all his passion for monarchy, admits that Cromwell probably considered his share in the death of Charles I. as one of his most distinguished
merits.[4] Some of those who voted for the death of Louis XVI. have proved
that they acted only from erroneous judgment, by <195> the decisive evidence of a virtuous life. One of them perished in Guiana, the victim of an
attempt to restore the Royal Family.[5] But though among the hundreds who
voted for the death of that unfortunate Prince, there might be seen every
shade of morality from the blackest depravity to the very confines of purity—at least in sentiment, it was impossible that any of them could be
contemplated without horror by the brothers and daughter of the murdered Monarch. Nor would it be less vain to expect that the objects of this
hatred should fail to support those Revolutionary authorities, which secured them from punishment,—which covered them from contempt by
station and opulence,—and which compelled the monarchs of Europe to
receive them into their palaces as ambassadors. They might be—the far
greater part of them certainly had become—indifferent to liberty,—perhaps partial to that exercise of unlimited power to which they had been
accustomed under what they called a "free" government: but they could
not be indifferent in their dislike of a government, under which their very
best condition was that of pardoned criminals, whose criminality was the
more odious on account of the sad necessity which made it pardoned. All
the Terrorists, and almost all the Regicides, had accordingly accepted emol-

4. "The murder of the King, the most atrocious of all [Cromwell's] actions, was to
him covered under a mighty cloud of republican and fanatical illusions; and it is not
impossible, but he might believe it, as many others did, the most meritorious action,
that he could perform." David Hume, *History of England,* 6 vols. (Indianapolis: Liberty
Fund, 1983), 6:110.

5. This is probably a reference to Jean-Marie Collot d'Herbois (1749–96). Involved
in the theater under the ancien régime, Collot d'Herbois was a member of both the
National Convention and the Committee of Public Safety. He played a leading role in
Thermidor and was subsequently deported to Guiana, where he died.

uments and honours from Napoleon, and were eager to support his authority as a Revolutionary despotism, strong enough to protect them from general unpopularity, and to ensure them against the vengeance or the humiliating mercy of a Bourbon government.

Another party of Revolutionists had committed great errors in the beginning, which co-operated with the alternate obstinacy and feebleness of the Counter-revolutionists, to produce all the evils which we feel and fear, and which can only be excused by their own inexperience in legislation, and by the prevalence of erroneous opinions, at that period, throughout the most enlightened part of Europe. These were the best leaders of the Constituent Assembly, who never <196> relinquished the cause of liberty, nor disgraced it by submissions to tyranny, or participation in guilt.

The best representative of this small class, is M. de La Fayette, a man of the purest honour in private life, who has devoted himself to the defence of liberty from his earliest youth. He may have committed some mistakes in opinion; but his heart has always been worthy of the friend of Washington and of Fox. In due time the world will see how victoriously he refutes the charges against him of misconduct towards the Royal Family, when the palace of Versailles was attacked by the mob, and when the King escaped to Varennes. Having hazarded his life to preserve Louis XVI., he was imprisoned in various dungeons, by Powers, who at the same time released Regicides. His wife fell a victim to her conjugal heroism. His liberty was obtained by Buonaparte, who paid court to him during the short period of apparent liberality and moderation which opened his political career. M. de la Fayette repaid him, by faithful counsel; and when he saw his rapid strides towards arbitrary power, he terminated all correspondence with him, by a letter, which breathes the calm dignity of constant and intrepid virtue. In the choice of evils, he considered the prejudices of the Court and the Nobility as more capable of being reconciled with liberty, than the power of an army. After a long absence from courts, he appeared at the levee of Monsieur, on his entry into Paris; and was received with a slight,—not justified by his character, nor by his rank—more important than character in the estimate of palaces. He returned to his retirement, far from courts or conspiracies, with a reputation for purity and firmness, which, if it had been less rare among French leaders, would have secured the liberty of that great nation, and placed her fame on better foundations than those of mere military genius and success.

This party, whose principles are decisively favourable to a limited monarchy, and indeed to the general outlines of the institutions of Great Britain, had some <197> strength among the reasoners of the capital, but represented no interest and no opinion in the country at large. Whatever popularity they latterly appeared to possess, arose but too probably from the momentary concurrence, in opposition to the Court, of those who were really their most irreconcileable enemies,—the discontented Revolutionists and concealed Napoleonists. During the late short pause of restriction on the press, they availed themselves of the half-liberty of publication which then existed, to employ the only arms in which they were formidable,— those of argument and eloquence. The pamphlets of M. Benjamin Constant were by far the most distinguished of those which they produced; and he may be considered as the literary representative of a party, which their enemies, as well as their friends, called the "Liberal," who were hostile to Buonaparte and to military power, friendly to the general principles of the constitution established by Louis XVIII., though disapproving some of its parts, and seriously distrusting the spirit in which it was executed, and the maxims prevalent at Court. M. Constant, who had been expelled from the *Tribunat,* and in effect exiled from France, by Buonaparte, began an attack on him before the Allies had crossed the Rhine, and continued it till after his march from Lyons. He is unquestionably the first political writer of the Continent, and apparently the ablest man in France. His first Essay, that on Conquest, is a most ingenious development of the principle, that a system of war and conquest, suitable to the condition of barbarians, is so much at variance with the habits and pursuits of civilized, commercial, and luxurious nations, that it cannot be long-lived in such an age as ours.[6] If the position be limited to those rapid and extensive conquests which tend towards universal monarchy, and if the tendency in human affairs to resist them be stated only as of great force, and almost sure within no long time

6. Benjamin Constant, *De l'ésprit de conquête et de l'usurpation* (Hanover, 1814). For a recent English translation see "The Spirit of Conquest and Usurpation and Their Relation to European Civilization," in Constant, *Political Writings,* ed. B. Fontana (Cambridge: Cambridge University Press, 1988).

of checking their progress, the doctrine of M. Constant will be generally
<198> acknowledged to be true. With the comprehensive views, and the
brilliant poignancy of Montesquieu, he unites some of the defects of that
great writer. Like him, his mind is too systematical for the irregular variety
of human affairs; and he sacrifices too many of those exceptions and limitations, which political reasonings require, to the pointed sentences which
compose his nervous and brilliant style. His answer to the Abbé Montesquiou's foolish plan of restricting the press, is a model of polemical politics,
uniting English solidity and strength with French urbanity.[7] His tract on
Ministerial Responsibility, with some errors (though surprisingly few) on
English details, is an admirable discussion of one of the most important
institutions of a free government, and, though founded on English practice, would convey instruction to most of those who have best studied the
English constitution.[8] We have said thus much of these masterly produc-
tions, because we consider them as the only specimens of the Parisian press,
during its semi-emancipation, which deserve the attention of political philosophers, and of the friends of true liberty, in all countries. In times of
more calm, we should have thought a fuller account of their contents, and
a free discussion of their faults, due to the eminent abilities of the author.
At present we mention them, chiefly because they exhibit, pretty fairly, the
opinions of the liberal party in that country.

But, not to dwell longer on this little fraternity (who are too enlightened
and conscientious to be of importance in the shocks of faction, and of
whom we have spoken more from esteem for their character, than from an
opinion of their political influence), it will be already apparent to our readers, that many of the most numerous and guiding classes in the newly ar-
ranged community of France, were bound, by strong ties of interest and
pride, to a Revolutionary government, however little they might be qualified or sincerely disposed for a free constitution,—which they <199> strug-
gled to confound with the former; that these dispositions among the civil
classes formed one great source of danger to the administration of the Bour-

7. B. Constant, *Observations sur le discours de M. de Montesquiou* (Paris, 1814).
8. B. Constant, *De la responsabilité des ministres* (Paris, 1815). Translated into English
as "The Responsibility of Ministers," *The Pamphleteer* (London) 5 (1815): 299–329.

bons; and that they now constitute a material part of the strength of Napoleon. To them he appeals in his Proclamations, when he speaks of "a new dynasty founded on the same bases with the new interests and new institutions which owe their rise to the Revolution."[9] To them he appeals, though more covertly, in his professions of zeal for the dignity of the people, and of hostility to feudal nobility, and monarchy by Divine right.

It is natural to inquire how the conscription, and the prodigious expenditure of human life in the campaigns of Spain and Russia, were not of themselves sufficient to make the government of Napoleon detested by the great majority of the French people. But it is a very melancholy truth, that the body of a people may be gradually so habituated to war, that their habits and expectations are at last so adapted to its demand for men, and its waste of life, that they become almost insensible to its evils, and require long discipline to re-inspire them with a relish for the blessings of peace, and a capacity for the virtues of industry. The complaint is least when the evil is greatest:—it is as difficult to teach such a people the value of peace, as it would be to reclaim a drunkard, or to subject a robber to patient labour.

A conscription is, under pretence of equality, the most unequal of all laws; because it assumes that military service is equally easy to all classes and ranks of men. Accordingly, it always produces pecuniary commutation in the sedentary and educated classes. To them in many of the towns of France it was an oppressive and grievous tax. But to the majority of the people, always accustomed to military service, the life of a soldier became perhaps more agreeable than any other. Families even considered it as a means of provision for their children; each parent labouring to persuade himself that his children would <200> be among those who should have the fortune to survive. Long and constant wars created a regular demand for men, to which the principle of population adapted itself. An army which had conquered and plundered Europe, and in which a private soldier might reasonably enough hope to be a marshal or a prince, had more allurements, and not more repulsive qualities, than many of those odious, disgusting, unwholesome, or perilous occupations, which in the common

9. No statement to this effect can be found in any of the proclamations or decrees issued by Napoleon during the period of his advance on Paris.

course of society are always amply supplied. The habit of war unfortunately perpetuates itself: and this moral effect is a far greater evil than the mere destruction of life. Whatever may be the justness of these speculations, certain it is, that the travellers who lately visited France, neither found the conscription so unpopular, nor the decay of male population so perceptible, as plausible and confident statements had led them to expect.

It is probable that among the majority of the French (excluding the army), the restored Bourbons gained less popularity by abolishing the conscription, than they lost by the cession of all the conquests of France. This fact affords a most important warning of the tremendous dangers to which civilized nations expose their character by long war. To say that liberty cannot survive it, is saying little:—liberty is one of the luxuries which only a few nations seem destined to enjoy;—and then only for a short period. It is not only fatal to the refinements and ornaments of civilized life:—its long continuance must inevitably destroy even that degree (moderate as it is) of order and security which prevails even in the pure monarchies of Europe, and distinguishes them above all other societies ancient or modern. It is vain to inveigh against the people of France for delighting in war, for exulting in conquest, and for being exasperated and mortified by renouncing those vast acquisitions. These deplorable consequences arise from an excess of the noblest and most necessary principles in the character of a nation, acted upon by <201> habits of arms, and "cursed with every granted prayer,"[10] during years of victory and conquest. No nation could endure such a trial. Doubtless those nations who have the most liberty, the most intelligence, the most virtue,—who possess in the highest degree all the constituents of the most perfect civilization, will resist it the longest. But, let us not deceive ourselves,—long war renders all these blessings impossible: it dissolves all the civil and pacific virtues; it leaves no calm for the cultivation of reason; and by substituting attachment to leaders, instead of reverence for laws, it destroys liberty, the parent of intelligence and of virtue.

10. "Cursed with every granted prayer" is from Alexander Pope, *Moral Essays,* epistle 2, *To a Lady,* line 147, in *The Twickenham Edition of the Poems of Alexander Pope,* ed. John Butt, 6 vols. (London: Methuen; New Haven: Yale University Press, 1951–1969), 62.

The French Revolution has strongly confirmed the lesson taught by the history of all ages, that while political divisions excite the activity of genius, and teach honour in enmity, as well as fidelity in attachment, the excess of civil confusion and convulsion produces diametrically opposite effects,—subjects society to force, instead of mind,—renders its distinctions the prey of boldness and atrocity, instead of being the prize of talent,—and concentrates the thoughts and feelings of every individual upon himself,—his own sufferings and fears. Whatever beginnings of such an unhappy state may be observed in France,—whatever tendency it may have had to dispose the people to a light transfer of allegiance, and an undistinguishing profession of attachment,—it is more useful to consider them as the results of these general causes, than as vices peculiar to that great nation.

To this we must add, before we conclude our cursory survey, that frequent changes of government, however arising, promote a disposition to acquiesce in change. No people can long preserve the enthusiasm, which first impels them to take an active part in change. Its frequency at last teaches them patiently to bear it. They become indifferent to governments and sovereigns. They are spectators of revolutions, instead of actors in them. They are a prey to be fought for by the hardy and bold, and are generally disposed of <202> by an army. In this state of things, revolutions become bloodless, not from the humanity, but from the indifference of a people. Perhaps it may be true, though it will appear paradoxical to many, that such revolutions as those of England and America, conducted with such a regard for moderation and humanity, and even with such respect for established authorities and institutions, independently of their necessity for the preservation of liberty, may even have a tendency to strengthen, instead of weakening, the frame of the commonwealth. The example of reverence for justice,—of caution in touching ancient-institutions,—of not innovating, beyond the necessities of the case, even in a season of violence and anger, may impress on the minds of men those conservative principles of society, more deeply and strongly, than the most uninterrupted observation of them in the ordinary course of quiet and regular government.

Appendix to "On the State of France in 1815"

We have no time to say much at present on the remaining division of this great subject. Wise administration, in the situation of Louis XVIII, was so extremely arduous a task, that the consideration of his misfortunes is not necessary to repress all propensity to severe censure. The restoration of the French Monarchy was impossible. Its elements were destroyed. No proprietary nobility, no opulent church, no judiciary bodies, no army. Twenty-five years had destroyed and produced more than several centuries usually do. A Bourbon Prince was placed at the head of revolutionized France. It was not merely a loose stone in the edifice, it was a case of repulsion between the Government and all the Elements of the Society.

It is difficult to determine whether any prudence could have averted the catastrophe. In justice it ought to be allowed, that more civil liberty was enjoyed during these ten months, than during any period of French history. There were no arbitrary imprisonments; not above one or two feeble attempts to exile obnoxious men to their country houses. Once, or perhaps twice, during the Revolution, there had been more political liberty, more freedom of the press, more real debate in the Legislative assemblies. But, in those tumultuous times there was no tranquillity, no security of person and property.

The King and the Court could not indeed love liberty; few Courts do; and they had much more excuse than most others for hating it. It was obvious that his policy consisted in connecting himself with the purest part of the Revolutionists, in seeing only in the Revolution the abuses which it had destroyed, in keeping out of sight those claims which conveyed too obvious a condemnation of it, in conquering his most natural and justifiable repugnance to individuals, when the display of such a repugnance produced or confirmed the alienation of numerous classes and powerful interests, and, lastly, the hardest but most necessary part of the whole, in the suppression of gratitude, and the delay of justice itself, to those whose suffering and fidelity deserved his affection, but who inspired the majority of Frenchmen with angry recollections and dangerous fears. It is needless to say that so arduous a scheme of policy, which would have required a considerable time for a fair experiment, and which, in the hands of an un-military Prince, was likely enough, after all, to fail, was scarcely tried by this respectable and unfortunate Monarch. The silly attack made by his ministers on the press, rendered the Government odious, without pre-venting the publication, or limiting the perusal of one libel. It answered no purpose, but that of giving some undeserved credit for its suppression to Buonaparte, who has other means of controuling the press than those which are supplied by laws and tribunals. Macdonald, who spoke against it with most rigour and spirit in the House of Peers, was one of the last Marshals who quitted the King (if he has quitted him); and Constant, who wrote against it with such extraordinary talent and eloquence, was the last French writer of celebrity who threw himself into the breach, and defied the vengeance of the Conqueror.

The policy of some of the restored Governments in other countries of Europe, was extremely injurious to the Bourbon administration. Spain, governed by a Bourbon Prince, threw discredit, or rather disgrace, upon all ancient Governments. The conduct of Ferdinand at Valencay was noto-rious in France. It was well known that he had importuned Napoleon for a Princess of the Imperial Family, and that he wrote constant letters of congratulation to Joseph on his victories over the Spanish armies, whom Ferdinand called the rebel subjects of Joseph. It was known, that, besides all those imbecilities of superstition which disgraced his return, besides the re-establishment of the Inquisition, besides the exile, on various grounds or pretexts, of several thousand families, he had thrown into prison more than five thousand persons, for no other crime than that of administering or seconding a Government which all Europe had recognized, which had resisted all the offers of Buonaparte, and under whom resistance was made to which he owed his Crown. Many cases of oppression were familiarly known in France, which are hitherto little spoken of in this country. Among them, that of *M. Antillon* deserves to be mentioned. That gentleman, a pre-eminent Professor in an University, had distinguished himself both in the Cortes, of which he was a Member, and by his writings, especially by several excellent works against the Slave Trade, of which he was the most determined enemy. The first care of King Ferdinand was to imprison such mischievous men. Early in June, he issued a warrant for the apprehension of M. Antillon, whom the officer appointed to execute the warrant found labouring under a severe and dangerous malady at his house in Arragon. Upon the representation of the physicians, the officer hesitated to remove the prisoner, and applied for farther instructions to the Captain General of Arragon. The Captain General suspended the execution of the order till his Majesty's pleasure could be ascertained. The Ministers immediately intimated to the Viceroy the Royal dissatisfaction at the delay. They commanded M. Antillon to be instantly conducted to Madrid. The order was executed; and M. Antillon died on the road, shortly after he had begun the journey! Such is the narrative which we have received from persons who appear to us worthy of faith. If it be entirely false, it may easily be confuted. If it be exaggerated, it may with equal ease be reduced within the limits of the exact truth. Until it be confuted, we offer it as a specimen of the administration of the Spanish Monarchy.

The Pope and the King of Sardinia seemed to be ambitious of rivalling Ferdinand in puerile superstition, if their limited means forbade them to aspire to rivalship in political oppression. They exerted every effort to give a colour to the opinion, that the restored governments were the enemies of civilization and of reason, and that the great Destroyer was necessary to pave the way for wise institutions, even at the expense of tyranny for a time. Spain was represented at Paris as a mirror, in which all nations might see the destiny prepared for them by restored Princes, and the yoke which would be imposed on them if the Sovereigns were not restrained by fear of their people. These impressions were not effaced even by the policy which induced Louis XVIII to suffer the Journal of Paris to discuss the administration of his Cousin in Spain, as freely as those of London.

THE ARMY! We have not time to develop all that is suggested by this terrible word. And it is unnecessary. The word conveys more than any commentary could unfold.

Many readers will say, that this word alone might have been substituted for the whole of what we have written. Short and dogmatical explanations of great events are at once agreeable to the pride of intellect, and very suitable to the narrow capacity and indolent minds of ordinary men. To explain a revolution by a maxim, has an imposing appearance of decisive character and practical good sense. But great revolutions are always produced by the action of some causes, and by the absence of others, without the full consideration of which it is impossible to form a true judgment of their origin. In the case before us, we must consider as well what might have prevented, as what actually produced the catastrophe. The spirit of a soldiery inured to victory, and indignant at defeat—the discontent of officers whose victories were gained over the allies of the government whom they now served—the ambition of generals whose companions had obtained principalities and kingdoms—the disrespect of a conquering army for an unwarlike sovereign—the military habits spread over the whole population of France—did certainly constitute a source of danger to the restored monarch, against which no wisdom could advise, or even conceive a perfect security. But, to retard, is, in such cases, to gain a chance of preventing. Every delay had at least a tendency to unsoldier the army. Time was the Ally of Tranquillity. Two years of quiet might have given the people of France a superiority over the Soldiery, and thus might have ensured Europe against military barbarism. It is true, that the frame of society produced by the Revolution, which we have attempted to describe, contributed to render perhaps the larger, certainly the more active part of the civil population, not cordially affected to the authority of the Bourbons. Even in this very difficult case much had been accomplished to appease the alarms, and (what was harder) to soothe the wounded pride of that numerous body who derived new wealth or consequence from the Revolution. But the wisest policy of this sort required a long time, and an undisturbed operation. The moderate administration of Louis might have accomplished, in a great degree, the work of conciliation. But it was indispensable that it should have been secure against violent interruption for a reasonable period, and that it should not have been brought in to a state of continual odium and suspicion by the contemptible ambition of others in their projects of foreign policy. It was essential that the French people would not be goaded into daily rage at the treaty which confined them within their own ancient limits, by the spectacle of the great military powers bartering republics, confiscating monarchies, adding provinces and kingdoms to their vast dominions. Notwithstanding the natural sources of internal danger, if even some of these unfavourable causes had been absent, the life of Napoleon Buonaparte (supposing him to have been as vigilantly watched as it would have been just and easy to watch him) might have proved a security to the Throne of the Bourbons, by preventing any other military chief from offering himself to the army till they had subsided into a part of the people, and imbibed sentiments compatible with the peace and order of civil life.

As things stand at present, the prospects of the world are sufficiently gloomy; and the course of safety and honour by no means very plain before us. Two things, however, seem clear in the midst of the darkness; one, that a crusade in behalf of the Bourbons and the old monarchy is as palpably hopeless as it is manifestly unjust; and the other, that that course of policy is the wisest and most auspicious, which tends most to reclaim the population of France from its military habits and to withhold it from those scenes of adventure in which its military spirit has been formed.

Chronology of James Mackintosh's Life

1765: Born at Aldowrie on the banks of Loch Ness, the child of a minor landowning family, his father being a professional soldier.

1775: Begins school in Fortrose.

1780–84: Studies at King's College Aberdeen under William Ogilvie.

1784: Moves to Edinburgh University to take up medical studies with William Cullen and becomes a member of the Speculative Society and other debating clubs. Forms lifelong friendships with Benjamin Constant and the circle of students surrounding Dugald Stewart, professor of moral philosophy, who founded the *Edinburgh Review* in 1803.

1787: Graduates with a thesis on muscular motion and moves to London to begin a medical career.

1788: Publishes anonymously *Arguments Concerning the Constitutional Right of Parliament to Appoint a Regency* in support of Fox's position during the Regency crisis.

1789: Marries Catherine Stuart and visits the Low Countries, partly to improve his knowledge of French in Brussels. Writes on French subjects for the *Oracle* and joins the Society for Constitutional Information.

1790: Takes part in the Westminster election on behalf of John Horne Tooke.

1791: Visits Birmingham with Samuel Parr to view the effects of the Birmingham "church and king" riots on Joseph Priestley's house and laboratory. Attends celebrations of the storming of the Bastille. Publishes three editions of *Vindiciae Gallicae*.

1792: Appointed honorary secretary to the Association of the Friends of the People, and publishes *A Letter to the Right Honourable William Pitt*. Makes another visit to France and hears of the early scenes of violence before departure for London.

1795: Called to the Bar. Reviews Burke's *Two Letters on Peace with the Regicide Directory of France* sympathetically in the *Monthly Review*, while remaining opposed to war with France.

1796:   Sends letter to Burke recanting support for the French Revolution.
          Entertained by Burke at the end of the year.

1797:   Death of first wife.

1798:   Marries Catherine Allen.

1799:   Publishes *A Discourse on the Study of the Law of Nature and Nations;
          Introductory to a Course of Lectures on that Science,* and gives lectures at
          Lincoln's Inn. Applies, via George Canning, for the support of Pitt
          and Henry Dundas to his claims for a judicial post in India.

1800:   Repeats lectures at Lincoln's Inn.

1802:   Visits Paris during Peace of Amiens and attends a reception given by
          Napoleon.

1803:   Defends Jean Peltier, a French émigré royalist and publisher, in the
          course of which he attacks the autocracy of the Napoleonic regime.
          Joins Loyal North Britons' militia formed to repel a threatened French
          invasion. Receives knighthood.

1804:   Accepts appointment as recorder of Bombay from Addington. Founds
          Literary Society of Bombay and delivers opening address.

1812:   Returns to England. Offered, but rejects, a Tory seat in Parliament.

1813:   Elected as a Whig member of Parliament for Nairn.

1814:   Visits France during the interval between Napoleon's first abdication
          and his return from exile on Elba. Renews acquaintance with Constant
          and Mme. de Stael.

1815:   Publishes "On the State of France in 1815" in the *Edinburgh Review*
          during Napoleon's Hundred Days.

1816:   Reviews part 1 of Dugald Stewart's *Dissertation Exhibiting the Progress
          of Metaphysical, Ethical and Political Philosophy* in the *Edinburgh
          Review.*

1818:   Elected as member of Parliament for Knaresborough and is appointed
          as professor of law and general politics at Haileybury College, one of
          his colleagues being T. R. Malthus. Criticizes universal suffrage in the
          Edinburgh Review.

1819:   Speech against foreign establishments bill in Parliament.

1820:   Reluctantly turns down offer of the Edinburgh Chair of Moral Philos-
          ophy in succession to Thomas Brown in favor of retaining his political
          position in London. Outlines Whig case for variegated representation
          in the *Edinburgh Review* in opposition to the Benthamite case for uni-
          form and universal manhood suffrage.

1821:   Reviews Simonde de Sismondi's *History of France* and part 2 of Stew-
          art's *Dissertation* in the *Edinburgh Review.*

1822:   Carries motion in House of Commons on reform of criminal law.

1823:   Defeats Sir Walter Scott in election to rectorship of Glasgow
         University.

1830:   Begins publication of his three-volume *History of England from the
         Earliest Times to the Final Establishment of the Reformation* and *A Gen-
         eral View of the Progress of Ethical Philosophy During the Seventeenth
         and Eighteenth Centuries* for the *Encyclopedia Britannica,* part of which
         extends the attack on Benthamite utilitarianism.

1832:   Death of Sir James Mackintosh.

1834:   Posthumous publication of an unfinished *History of the Revolution in
         England in 1688.*

1835:   Publication of James Mill's *Fragment on Mackintosh,* a hypercritical
         response to Mackintosh's attack on the Benthamites.

1836:   Publication by his son, Robert, of *Memoirs of the Life of the Right
         Honourable Sir James Mackintosh.*

1846:   Publication by his son of *The Miscellaneous Works of Sir James
         Mackintosh.*

Selective Chronology of Events Relating to the French Revolution and Parliamentary Reform in Britain

1787

22 February:	Meeting of the Assembly of Notables. The Assembly was called to discuss Calonne's reforms for dealing with the French state's financial crisis. However, the Assembly proved hostile to Calonne's ideas.
8 April:	Following the hostile reception by the Assembly of Notables to the proposed tax reforms, Calonne was dismissed.
1 May:	Appointment of Loménie de Brienne, archbishop of Toulouse, as head of the Royal Council of Finances. Brienne went on to propose a modified version of Calonne's reforms.
25 May:	Assembly of Notables refused to ratify Brienne's reform program and consequently was dispersed.
14 August:	*Parlement* of Paris exiled to Troyes.

1788

4 May:	*Lettres de cachet* issued against Goislard de Montsabert and Duval d'Eprémesnil.
8 May:	Attempted French royal coup against the *parlements*.
8 August:	Louis XVI agrees to the summoning of the Estates General.
25 September:	Paris *parlement* reconvened.
4 November:	Celebrations of the Glorious Revolution of 1688 organized by London Revolution Society, coinciding with the illness of George III and the Regency crisis.
6 November:	Meeting of second Assembly of Notables in France.

1789

24 January:	Letters patent issued setting out electoral procedure for forthcoming Estates General.
January:	Abbé Sieyès's *Qu'est-ce que le tiers état?* published in France.
5 May:	Opening meeting of French Estates General.

May: Bill to remove the civil disabilities imposed on English dissenters by the Test and Corporation Acts narrowly defeated.

17 June: Third Estate of France adopted the title National Assembly and declared their intention to rule on behalf of the nation.

20 June: The *serment du jeu de paume* (*Tennis Court Oath*); owing to the closure of its normal meeting place, the National Assembly met in the royal tennis court where they swore not to disband until a constitution had been firmly established.

23 June: National Assembly rejected Louis XVI's order that the three estates meet separately and reiterated its earlier decrees.

9 July: National Assembly adopted the title "National Constituent Assembly."

11 July: Dismissal of Necker.

14 July: Storming of the Bastille.

4 August: National Assembly abolished many privileges of the nobility and the church.

26 August: Declaration of the rights of man and of the citizen.

10 September: National Assembly voted for a unicameral legislature in the forthcoming constitution.

11 September: National Assembly voted to give the king a suspensive veto over legislation.

5–6 October: People of Paris marched to Versailles and forced Louis XVI to return to the capital. Soon after, the National Assembly voted to move to Paris.

2 November: Nationalization of church property.

3 November: Suspension of *parlements*.

4 November: Richard Price gave his sermon on "Love of Our Country" at the annual meeting of the London Revolution Society, after which an address was sent to French National Assembly.

19 December: Assignats issued.

22 December: Decree setting out plans for primary elections to the forthcoming legislature.

1790

9 February: Burke's first public attack on the French Revolution in his speech on the army estimates (published 20 February).

4 March: Henry Flood's motion for parliamentary reform defeated in House of Commons.

15 March: National Assembly declared abolition of feudal regime in France.

22 May:	National Assembly voted to abolish king's prerogative over declarations of war and peace.
19 June:	Abolition of titles of hereditary nobility.
June:	Horne Tooke stood as candidate for Westminster on the program of reform agreed by the Society for Constitutional Information.
12 July:	Civil Constitution of the Clergy voted by National Assembly.
4 September:	Resignation of Necker.
6 September:	Abolition of the *parlements*.
October:	Publication of Calonne's *De l'état de la France*.
1 November:	Publication of Burke's *Reflections on the Revolution in France*.
29 November:	Publication of Mary Wollstonecraft's *Vindication of the Rights of Man*.
December:	Publication of Catharine Macaulay's *Observations on the Reflections of the Rt. Hon. Edmund Burke*.

1791

January:	Publication of Joseph Priestley's *Letters to the Rt. Hon. Edmund Burke*.
12 March:	Publication of Thomas Paine's *Rights of Man. Part the First*.
7 May:	Publication of Mackintosh's *Vindiciae Gallicae*.
May:	Open rift between Burke and Fox in the House of Commons.
20 June:	Louis XVI's flight to Varennes.
2 July:	Publication of second edition of *Vindiciae Gallicae*.
15–17 July:	Birmingham "church and king" riots; destruction of Priestley's house and laboratory.
17 July:	Massacre on the Champ de Mars.
28 August:	Publication of third edition of *Vindiciae Gallicae*.
3 September:	Adoption of a constitution declaring France to be a constitutional monarchy (Constitution of 1791).
1 October:	The National Constituent Assembly replaced by the National Legislative Assembly.

1792

9 February:	Property of French *émigrés* forfeited to the nation.
16 February:	Publication of Thomas Paine's *Rights of Man. Part the Second*.
16 March:	Abolition of *lettres de cachet*.
11 April:	Formation of Society of Friends of the People.
20 April:	France declared war on Austria; Prussia joined war against France.

30 April:	Charles Grey pledges to introduce a motion for parliamentary reform on behalf of the Friends of the People in the following year.
21 May:	Royal proclamation against seditious writings (strengthened in December). Publication of Mackintosh's *Letter to the Right Honourable William Pitt*.
10 August:	A popular uprising involving the killing of Swiss troops at the Tuileries, which brought down the French monarchy.
12 August:	French royal family imprisoned.
2–6 September:	The September massacres: the killing, by a mob, of counter-revolutionary prisoners in Paris jails.
21 September:	The National Legislative Assembly replaced by the National Convention, the task of which was to draw up a new Constitution.
22 September:	First French republic officially declared.
19 November:	Decree of Convention offering fraternal aid to promote revolutions abroad.
18 December:	Paine tried in London *in absentia*.

1793

21 January:	Execution of Louis XVI.
25 January:	Inaugural meeting of London Corresponding Society affiliated to the Society for Constitutional Information and partly inspired by Paine's *Rights of Man*.
1 February:	France declared war on Britain and the Dutch Republic and the first coalition against France (Britain, Prussia, Holland, Spain, and Austria) was formed.
March:	Start of the rising in the Vendée against the French Revolution.
6 April:	Committee of Public Safety took power.
7 May:	Grey's promised motion on parliamentary reform heavily defeated in House of Commons.
5 September:	Terror declared the "order of the day."
16 October:	Execution of Marie Antoinette.
November:	Height of dechristianization campaign.

1794

May:	Suspension of habeas corpus in Britain in response to radical agitation.
21 June:	Burke resigned from Parliament.

July: Split within Whig Party widened when conservative Whigs under Portland lent support to Pitt's policies.

28 July
(10 Thermidor): Execution of Robespierre; end of the Terror.

1795
17 February: Armistice in the Vendée.
2 November: Establishment of the French Directory.
29 October: George III's carriage stoned at opening of Parliament.
10 November: Bills to curb seditious meetings and "treasonable practices" introduced in Parliament.

1796
20 October: Publication of Burke's *Two Letters on the Proposals for Peace with the Regicide Directory of France.*

1797
9 July: Death of Edmund Burke.

1799
9 November
(18 Brumaire): Napoleon Bonaparte's coup d'état established a military dictatorship in France.

1802
27 March: Peace of Amiens.
2 August: Napoleon becomes first consul for life.

1803
May: War resumed.

1804
2 December: Napoleon crowned as hereditary emperor of the French.

1814
30 March: Allies entered Paris.
6 April: Napoleon abdicated and was sent to Elba.
3 May: Louis XVIII entered Paris.
4 June: Louis XVIII issued a constitutional charter.
1 November: Congress of Vienna opened.

1815
1 March: Napoleon landed in France.
19 March: Louis XVIII fled.

20 March:	Napoleon entered Paris to begin Hundred Days (until June 29).
2 June:	Napoleon issued liberal constitution, *Le Champ de Mai.*
18 June:	Napoleon defeated by Wellington and Blucher at Waterloo.
22 June:	Napoleon abdicated for a second time.
7 July:	Allies entered Paris.
8 July:	Louis XVIII returned.
2 August:	Napoleon departed for exile to St. Helena.

Dramatis Personae

Abercorn: James Hamilton, eighth Earl Abercorn, 1712–89. Politician.

Aguesseau: Henri François d'Aguesseau, 1668–1751. French jurist, three times chancellor of France under Louis XV.

Princess Anne: 1665–1714. Second daughter of James II, later queen of Great Britain and Ireland (1702–14).

Anne of Austria (Antonietta of Austria): 1601–66. Queen of France, wife of Louis XIII.

Antillon: Don Isidore d'Antillon, 1778–1814. Professor and member of the Cortes who became a victim of the Spanish restoration.

Artois: Charles Philippe de Bourbon, comte d'Artois, 1757–1836. Brother of Louis XVI, émigré leader during the French Revolution. King of France as Charles X 1824–30.

Bacon: Sir Francis Bacon, 1561–1626. Baron Verulam of Verulam and Viscount St. Albans. English philosopher and statesman.

Bailly (Bailli): Jean-Sylvain Bailly, 1736–93. Member of the Estates General and mayor of Paris from 1789.

Barrere (Barère): Bertrand Barère (de Vieuzac), 1755–1841. French revolutionary—originally a monarchist but was later a member of the Committee of Public Safety. Attacked Robespierre at Thermidor.

Bayard: Pierre du Terrail, Chevalier de Bayard, 1473–1524. French soldier.

Beccaria: Cesare, Marchese de Beccaria, 1738–94. Italian jurist and philosopher, author of *Dei delitti e delle pene* (on crimes and punishments).

Bentham: Jeremy Bentham, 1748–1832. English philosopher and social reformer, pioneer of utilitarianism.

Birkbeck: Morris Birkbeck, 1764–1825. Author of *Notes on a Journey through France from Dieppe through Paris and Lyons to the Pyrenees, and back through Toulouse, in July, August, and September 1814* (1814).

Blackstone: Sir William Blackstone, 1723–80. English judge and jurist, author of *Commentaries on the Laws of England* (1765–69).

Blackwood: Adam Blackwood, 1539–1613. Scottish author and critic of George Buchanan.

Boileau: Nicolas Boileau, known as Boileau Despréaux, 1636–1711. French poet and critic.

Bolingbroke: Henry St. John, first Viscount Bolingbroke, 1678–1751. English statesman and author.

Bossuet: Jacques Bénigne Bossuet, 1627–1704. French cleric and orator.

Breteuil: Louis Auguste Le Tennelier, baron de Breteuil, 1730–1807. Diplomat and statesman.

Brienne: Etienne Charles, Loménie de Brienne, 1727–94. French statesman and cleric who replaced Calonne as Louis XVI's principal minister and tried to introduce reforms.

Brion de la Tour: Louis Brion de la Tour, 1756–1823. Cartographer.

Brissonius: Barnabas Brissonius, 1531–91. Jurist.

Buchanan: George Buchanan, 1506–82. Scottish scholar and humanist.

Buonaparte: Napoleon Bonaparte, Napoleon I, 1769–1821. Corsican general who became emperor of France in 1804.

Burgh: James Burgh, 1714–75. Scottish dissenter, teacher, and moral and political reformer.

Burke: Edmund Burke, 1729–97. Anglo-Irish statesman and philosopher. Author of *Reflections on the Revolution in France* (1790).

Burlamaqui: Jean Jacques Burlamaqui, 1694–1748. Swiss jurist. Author of *Principe du droit naturel* (1747) and *Principes du droit politique* (1751).

Burnet: Dr. Gilbert Burnet, 1643–1715. Bishop of Salisbury, historian and supporter of William and Mary's accession to the English throne.

Cadmus: The legendary founder of Thebes. Son of the Phoenician king Agenor and brother of Europa. Famed for having introduced the Greek alphabet from Phoenicia.

Calonne: Charles Alexandre de Calonne, 1734–1802. Controller general of French finances 1783–87. Author of *De l'état de la France* (1790).

Lord Camelford: See Thomas Pitt.

Camus: Armand Gaston Camus, 1740–1804. French revolutionary politician.

Candolle: Augustin Pyramus de Candolle, 1778–1841. Genevan botanist.

Caraman: Victor Louis Charles Riquet, duc de Caraman, 1762–1839. French soldier and diplomat.

Cartwright: Major John Cartwright, 1740–1824. English political reformer.

Chabroud: Jean Baptiste Charles Chabroud, 1750–1816. Representative of the Third Estate in Estates General, author of a report on the actions of Châtelet following the events of 5–6 October 1789.

Charles I: 1600–1649. King of Great Britain and Ireland. Executed following the English Civil War.

Charles II: 1630–85. King of Great Britain and Ireland. Came to the throne at the Restoration in 1660.

Chatham: William Pitt, first Earl of Chatham, Pitt the Elder, 1708–78. Prime minister. Father of William Pitt the Younger.

Churchill: John Churchill, first Duke of Marlborough, 1650–1722.

Clarendon: Edward Hyde, first Earl of Clarendon, 1609–74. English statesman and historian of the English Civil War.

Clermont Tonnerre: Stanislas, comte de Clermont Tonnerre, 1757–92. Moderate French revolutionary politician, associated with the *Monarchiens*.

Coke: Sir Edward Coke, 1552–1634. English judge and jurist.

Collins: Anthony Collins, 1676–1729. Deist and author of *Dissertation on Liberty and Necessity* (1729).

Constant: Henri Benjamin Constant de Rebecque, 1767–1830. Swiss politician and author.

Cooper: Dr. Thomas Cooper, 1759–1839. English reformer.

Corneille: Pierre Corneille, 1606–84. French dramatist.

Cromwell: Oliver Cromwell, 1599–1658. English soldier and statesman. Lord Protector of England 1653–58.

Crosby: Brass Crosby, 1725–93. English radical. Alderman of Bread Street ward from 1765. Lord Mayor of London from 1770.

Cujacius: Jacobus Cujacius, ca. 1522–90. French jurist.

Curran: John Philpot Curran, 1750–1817. Irish judge.

Cuvier: Jean Léopold Nicolas Frédéric (Georges) Cuvier, 1769–1832. French anatomist, zoologist, and naturalist.

De Lolme: Jean Louis De Lolme, 1741–1806. Genevan writer. Author of *Constitution de l'Angleterre, ou etat du gouvernement anglais, comparé avec la forme républicaine & avec les autres monarchies de l'Europe.*

Duncombe: Henry Duncombe, 1728–1818. MP for Yorkshire 1780–96.

Dundas: Henry Dundas, 1742–1811. First Viscount Melville and Baron Dunira. Scottish jurist and politician. Home secretary to William Pitt the Younger.

Eden (Lord Auckland): William Eden, first Baron Auckland, 1744–1814. Statesman and diplomat.

D'Epresmenil (Eprémesnil): Jean Jacques Duval d'Eprémesnil, 1745–94. Member of the *Parlement* of Paris. Critic of Calonne and Brienne. Arrested, together with Goislard de Montsabert, in May 1788.

Erskine: Thomas Erskine, first Baron Erskine, 1750–1823. Scottish jurist and member of the Society of the Friends of the People.

Fénelon: François de Salignac de la Mothe-Fénelon, 1651–1715. French cleric and writer, archbishop of Cambray and author of *Telemachus* (1699).

Ferdinand VII: 1784–1833. King of Spain. Forced into exile by the French invasion of 1808, but restored to the throne by a treaty with Napoleon in 1813.

Filmer: Sir Robert Filmer, 1588–1653. Author of *Patriarcha* (1689).

Fletcher: Andrew Fletcher of Saltoun, 1653–1716. Scottish patriot and author.

Fleury: André-Hercule de Fleury, 1653–1743. French prelate and politician. Effectively controlled the government of Louis XV until 1743.

Flood: Henry Flood, 1732–91. Irish politician and reformer.

Fouché: Joseph Fouché, 1763–1829. French revolutionary politician who supported the attacks on Christianity and was one of the people behind the Thermidor coup.

Fox: Charles James Fox, 1749–1806. Leading Whig politician. Rival of William Pitt.

Franklin: Benjamin Franklin, 1706–90. U.S. statesman, diplomat, printer, publisher, inventor, and scientist.

Frost: John Frost, 1750–1842. Reformer and supporter of the French Revolution, secretary of the London Corresponding Society.

Gassendi: Pierre Gassendi, 1592–1655. French philosopher and scientist. An advocate of the experimental approach to science and an early critic of Descartes.

Gibbon: Edward Gibbon, 1737–94. English historian, author of *The Decline and Fall of the Roman Empire* (1776–88).

Godwin: William Godwin, 1756–1836. Novelist, historian, and author of *An Enquiry Concerning Political Justice* (1793), the work attacked by Mackintosh in his lectures on law of nature and nations.

Goestard/Goislard: Goislard de Montsabert, 1763–1835. Leading member of the Paris *Parlement,* arrested alongside d'Eprémesnil in May 1788.

Green: Thomas Green, 1769–1825. Author of *An examination of the leading principle of the new system of morals, as that principle is stated and applied in Mr. Godwin's Enquiry Concerning Political Justice* (1799).

Grenville: William Wyndham Grenville, first Baron Grenville, 1759–1834. English politician and prime minister. Son of George Grenville.

Grey: Charles Grey, second Earl Grey, 1764–1845. English statesman, prime minister, and opponent of William Pitt the Younger.

Grotius: Hugo Grotius, 1583–1645. Dutch jurist, politician, and diplomat. One of the founders of international law, his great work on the subject being *De Jure Belli et Pacis* (1625).

Hale: Sir Matthew Hale, 1609–76. English judge and writer.

Hargrave: Francis Hargrave, ca. 1741–1821. Lawyer and legal historian.

Harrington: James Harrington, 1611–77. Author of *The Commonwealth of Oceana* (1656).

Hawkesbury: Charles Jenkinson, first Earl of Liverpool and first Baron Hawkesbury, 1729–1808. English aristocrat.

Heineccius: Johann Gottlieb Heineccius, 1681–1741. German jurist.

Helvetius: Claude-Adrien Helvetius, 1715–71. French philosopher, one of the *Encyclopédistes.*

Henrietta of Orleans: Henrietta Anne, duchesse d'Orléans, 1644–70. Youngest daughter of Charles I, wife of Philippe, duc d'Orléans.

Henry III: 1551–89. King of France (1574–89).

Henry the Great: Henry V, 1387–1422. King of England (1413–22).

Hobbes: Thomas Hobbes, 1588–1679. English political philosopher, author of *Leviathan* (1651).

Hollis: Thomas Brand Hollis (originally Thomas Brand), ca. 1719–1804. Gentleman.

Holt: Lord John Holt, 1642–1710. English judge.

Hooker: Richard Hooker, 1554–1600. English theologian, author of *Of the Laws of Ecclesiastical Polity* (1594).

Hottomannus: François Hotman, 1524–90. French publicist and jurist.

Howard: Sir Robert Howard, 1626–98. Politician.

Hume: David Hume, 1711–76. Scottish philosopher and historian.

Hurd: Dr. Richard Hurd, 1720–1808. Cleric and author.

James I: 1566–1625. King of Scotland as James VI from 1567. Became king of England in 1603.

James II: 1633–1701. King of Scotland as James VII, and then king of England and Ireland as James II. Second son of Charles I, brother of Charles II. On the invasion of William of Orange, James fled to France.

Jebb: Dr. John Jebb, 1736–86. English reformer.

Jeffries (Jeffreys or Jefferies): Jeffreys (of Wem), George Jeffreys, first Baron Jeffreys, 1645–89. English judge who condemned Algernon Sidney and William Russell to death for their alleged involvement in the Rye House Plot.

Jones: Sir William Jones, 1746–94. English jurist and orientalist.

Kirk: Percy Kirke, ca. 1649–91. Lieutenant-general, colonel of Kirke's Lambs. Had a reputation for brutality; escorted Judge Jeffreys during the bloody assizes.

La Fayette: Marie Joseph Paul Yves Roch Gilbert du Motier, Marquis de Lafayette, 1757–1834. French soldier and revolutionary. Fought against the British in the American War of Independence before returning to France to take part in the Revolution there.

Lally Tollendal (Tolendal): Trophime-Gérard, marquis de Lally-Tollendal, 1751–1830. Moderate French revolutionary politician, associated with the *Monarchiens.*

La Rochfoucault: François, sixth duc de la Rochefoucauld, 1613–80. French writer and opponent of Richelieu.

La Rochfoucault-Liancourt: François Alexandre Frédéric, duc de Rochefoucauld-Liancourt, 1747–1827. French revolutionary politician, philanthropist, and social reformer.

Laud: William Laud, 1573–1645. English prelate. Archbishop of Canterbury under Charles I.

Le Chapelier: Isaac René Gui Le Chapelier, 1754–94. French lawyer and revolutionary politician. Author of the Loi Le Chapelier (1791), which outlawed workers' associations. Executed during the Terror.

Leibnitz: Gottfried Wilhelm Leibnitz, 1646–1716. Prussian philosopher and mathematician.

Leopold II: 1747–92. Holy Roman Emperor, brother of Marie Antoinette.

Lewes: Sir Watkin Lewes, ca. 1740–1821. London alderman, sheriff, Lord Mayor, and MP. Radical and reformer.

Locke: John Locke, 1632–1704. English philosopher.

Louis XIII: 1601–43. King of France from 1610.

Louis XIV: 1638–1715. King of France from 1643. Son of Louis XIII and Anne of Austria. Known as Le Roi Soleil.

Louis XV: 1710–74. King of France from 1715.

Louis XVI: 1754–93. King of France from 1774. Grandson of Louis XV. Executed during the French Revolution.

Louis XVIII: Louis Stanislas Xavier, comte de Provence, 1755–1824. King of France, younger brother of Louis XVI. Declared himself king in 1795 but actually took up the throne in 1815.

Macdonald: Jacques Joseph Alexandre Macdonald, 1765–1840. Of Scottish Jacobite descent, became a general in Napoleon's armies in 1794 and governor of Rome in 1798.

Mackenzie: Sir George Mackenzie, 1636–91. Scottish jurist and author. Wrote against Buchanan and Milton.

Lord Mahon: See Earl Stanhope.

Maitland: James Maitland, Earl of Lauderdale, 1759–1839. Scottish lawyer, politician, and author.

Malthus: Thomas Robert Malthus, 1766–1834. English political economist and clergyman. Author of the *Essay on the Principle of Population* (1798).

Marat: Jean Paul Marat, 1743–93. French revolutionary, journalist, physician, and scientist. Famous for his popular newspaper *L'ami du peuple.*

Marie Antoinette (Maria Antoinetta): Josèphe Jeanne, 1755–93. Queen of France, wife of Louis XVI.

Princess Mary: 1662–94. Daughter of James II. Wife of William of Orange. Later queen of Great Britain and Ireland (1689–94).

Mary (A Queen of France): Mary Queen of Scots, 1542–87. Queen of Scotland and mother of James IV and I. Though born in Scotland, Mary was sent to France at an early age. She returned to Scotland as an adult. Executed in England on the orders of Elizabeth I in 1587.

Mary of Medicis: 1573–1642. Wife of Henry IV, mother of Louis XIII.

Masséna: André Masséna, 1758–1817. French general. Became Marshal of the Empire in 1804. In the campaign of 1809 earned the title prince of Essling.

Maurice: Thomas Maurice, 1754–1824. Oriental scholar and historian.

Maury: Jean Siffrein, Abbé Maury, 1746–1817. French prelate and counterrevolutionary orator and writer.

Maynard: Sir John Maynard, Serjeant Maynard, 1604–90. English judge.

Millar: John Millar, 1735–1801. Professor of civil law at Glasgow University, author of *The Origin of the Distinction of Ranks* (1771) and *An Historical View of the English Government* (1787).

Milton: John Milton, 1608–74. English poet who also wrote political prose works.

Mirabeau: Honoré Gabriel Riqueti, comte de Mirabeau, 1749–91. French revolutionary politician and orator.

Molyneux: William Molyneux, 1656–98. Irish philosopher and writer, author of *The Case of Ireland* (1698).

Montesquieu: Charles Louis de Secondat, baron de la Brède, 1689–1755. French jurist and author of the *Spirit of the Laws* (1748).

Montesquiou: Abbé François Xavier Marc Antoine Montesquiou-Fezensac, 1758–1832. French cleric.

Montmorencie(y): Anne, first duc de Montmorency, 1493–1567. French soldier.

Montrose: James Graham, Marquis of Montrose, 1612–50. Scottish general.

Mounier: Jean Joseph Mounier, 1758–1806. French lawyer and moderate revolutionary politician, associated with the *Monarchiens*.

Necker: Jacques Necker, 1732–1804. Genevan-born French politician and financier. In 1777 Necker was made director-general of French finances. Dismissed in 1781. Recalled in 1788 but dismissed again in 1789.

Noailles: Louis Marie, vicomte de Noialles, 1756–1804. French soldier and revolutionary politician.

Nolan: Michael Nolan, died 1827. Irish legal historian.

Nottingham: Daniel Finch, second Earl of Nottingham, 1647–1730. Tory politician.

Orleans: Louis Philippe Joseph, duc d'Orléans, also known as Philippe Égalité, 1747–93. French Bourbon prince, cousin of Louis XVI. During the French Revolution supported the Third Estate against the privileged orders, but later arrested as a Bourbon and guillotined.

Ormond(e): James Butler, second Duke of Ormonde, 1665–1745. Irish nobleman. Impeached for high treason (for Jacobitism) in 1715, went into exile in France.

Paine: Thomas Paine, 1737–1809. English radical political writer and revolutionary. Wrote *The Rights of Man* in reply to Edmund Burke's *Reflections on the Revolution in France*.

Paley: Dr. William Paley, 1743–1805. English theologian. His *Principles of Moral and Political Philosophy* expounded a form of theological utilitarianism.

Papinian: Aemilius Papinianus, ca. 140–212. Roman jurist.

Peiresc: Nicolas Claude Fabri Peiresc, 1580–1637. French scientist.

Peters: Hugh Peters, 1598–1660. Independent cleric.

Pétion: Jérôme Pétion de Villeneuve, 1756–93. French revolutionary, mayor of Paris from 1791.

Philip II: 1527–98. King of Spain and of Portugal, also ruler of the Spanish Netherlands.

Thomas Pitt: Thomas Pitt, first Baron Camelford, 1737–93. Politician and art connoisseur. Nephew of William Pitt the Elder. Spoke against parliamentary reform in 1782.

William Pitt: Known as Pitt the Younger, 1759–1806. English statesman and prime minister, 1783–1801. Son of William Pitt the Elder, first Earl of Chatham.

De la Place/De Laplace: Pierre-Simon, marquis de Laplace, 1749–1827. French astronomer and mathematician.

Powys: Sir Thomas Powys, 1649–1719. Judge.

Price: Dr. Richard Price, 1723–91. Welsh moral philosopher and Unitarian minister. Price's *A Discourse on the Love of Our Country* (1789) prompted Edmund Burke to write his *Reflections on the Revolution in France.*

Puffendorff (Pufendorf): Samuel Pufendorf, 1632–94. German writer on jurisprudence. Author of *De Jure Naturae et Gentium Libri* (of the law and nature of nations).

Richlieu/Richelieu: Armand Jean Duplessis, duc de Richelieu, Cardinal Richelieu, 1585–1642. French prelate and statesman, minister of state to Louis XIII.

Richmond: Charles Lennox, third Duke of Richmond and Lennox, 1735–1806. Peer, diplomat, and government minister.

Robespierre: Maximilien Marie Isidore de Robespierre, 1758–94. French revolutionary politician. Sat on the Committee of Public Safety 1793–94. Executed, together with other members of that committee, on 10 Thermidor (28 July 1794).

Rolle: John Rolle, baron Rolle of Stevenstone, 1750–1842. Politician, supporter of Pitt.

Rose: George Rose, 1744–1818. Secretary to the treasury under Pitt.

Rousseau: Jean-Jacques Rousseau, 1712–78. Genevan-born French political philosopher and author of *The Social Contract* (1762).

Russel/Russell: Lord William Russell, 1639–83. English politician. Arrested alongside Algernon Sidney for involvement in the Rye House Plot. Found guilty of high treason and executed.

Sacheverell: William Sacheverell, 1638–91. English politician. Sometimes called the First Whig.

Savary: Anne Jean Savary, 1774–1833. French general.

Sharman: Lieutenant Colonel Sharman, d. 1803. Recipient of *A Letter from . . . the Duke of Richmond. . . .* See *A Letter to William Pitt,* appendix 1, no. 3.

Shipley: Bishop Jonathan Shipley, 1713–88. English prelate.

Algernon Sidney (Sydney): 1623–83. English politician and writer. Grandnephew of Sir Philip Sidney. Arrested for alleged involvement in the Rye House Plot, alongside William Russell, and executed.

Sir Philip Sidney: 1554–86. English poet and patron.

Smith: Adam Smith, 1723–90. Scottish moral philosopher and political economist, author of *Theory of Moral Sentiments* (1759) and *Wealth of Nations* (1776).

Somers: John Somers, first Baron Somers (of Evesham), 1651–1716. English Whig statesman.

Sophia of Hanover: 1630–1714. Electress of Hanover, mother of George I.

Southampton: Charles Fitzroy, first Duke of Southampton and Cleveland, 1662–1730. Son of Charles II by Barbara Villiers.

Stanhope: Charles Stanhope, third Earl Stanhope, later Lord Mahon, 1753–1816. English scientist and politician. Son-in-law of William Pitt the Elder, but later fell out with Pitt the Younger over the French Revolution.

Stewart: Dugald Stewart, 1753–1828. Professor of moral philosophy at Edinburgh University, author of *A General View of the Progress of Metaphysical, Ethical, and Political Philosophy* (1816, 1820).

Sully: Maximilien de Béthune, duc de Sully, also known as baron de Rosny, 1560–1641. French financier.

Sunderland: Probably Robert Spencer, second Earl of Sunderland, 1640–1702.

Surrey: Charles Howard, Earl of Surrey, 1746–1815. MP for Carlisle 1780–86 and supporter of parliamentary reform.

Swift: Jonathan Swift, 1667–1745. Anglo-Irish clergyman and satirist.

Talleyrand: Charles Maurice de Talleyrand-Périgord, prince of Benevento, 1754–1838. French cleric and politician.

Tallien: Jean Lambert Tallien, 1767–1820. French revolutionary. One of those behind the Thermidor coup.

Target: Gui Jean Baptiste Target, 1733–1806. French lawyer and revolutionary politician.

Tatham: Dr. Edward Tatham, 1749–1834. Cleric and author.

Temple: Sir Richard Temple, 1634–97. Politician.

Thouret: Jacques Guillaume Thouret, 1746–94. French lawyer and revolutionary politician. Guillotined during the Terror.

Thuanus: Jacques-Auguste de Thou (Thuanus), 1553–1617. French statesman and historian.

Thurlow: Edward Thurlow, first Baron Thurlow, 1731–1806. Lord Chancellor.

Tooke: John Horne Tooke, originally John Horne, 1736–1812. English radical politician and philologist.

Tucker: Abraham (Abram) Tucker, 1705–74. English cleric and author of *The Light of Nature Pursued* (1765–74). Wrote under the pseudonym Edward Search.

Turgot: Anne Robert Jacques Turgot, 1727–81. French political economist and politician. Comptroller-general of finance under Louis XVI.

Ulpian: Domitius Ulpianus, ca. 170–228. Roman jurist.

Vattel: Emmerich de Vattel, 1714–67. Swiss jurist and author of *Droits des gens.*

Vergennes: Charles Gravier, comte de Vergennes, 1717–87. French diplomat, foreign minister 1774–87.

Victor Amadeus: Victor Amadeus II, 1666–1732. Duke of Savoy (1675–1713), king of Sicily (1713–20), king of Sardinia (1720–30).

Virieu: François Henri, comte de Virieu, 1754–93. Initially a supporter of the Revolution but later became a royalist.

Voltaire: Pseudonym of François Marie Arouet, 1694–1778. French Enlightenment author.

Walpole: Sir Robert Walpole, first Earl of Orford, 1676–1745. English Whig politician, seen as the first prime minister of Great Britain.

Warburton: William Warburton, 1698–1779. Cleric and author.

Ward: Robert Plumer Ward, 1765–1846. Barrister and MP. Author of *An Enquiry into the Foundations of History of the Law of Nations in Europe, from the Time of the Greeks and Romans to the Age of Grotius* (1795).

Wilkes: John Wilkes, 1725–97. English politician.

William of Orange: William III, 1650–1702. Stadtholder of the United Provinces of the Netherlands and king of Great Britain and Ireland. Replaced James II in the Glorious Revolution of 1688.

Windham: William Windham, 1750–1810. Statesman.

Wolf (Wolffius): Christian Wolff, 1679–1754. German philosopher.

Wray: Sir Cecil Wray, 1734–1805. Politician.

Wyvill: Rev. Christopher Wyvill, 1738–1822. Anglican clergyman and reformer.

Zouch: Richard Zouch, 1590–1661. English jurist.

INDEX

Abercorn, Earl of. *See* Hamilton, James, Earl of Abercorn

Addison, Joseph, 17n10

Aeneid (Virgil), 161n107, 229n15, 254n6

Agricola (Tacitus), 20, 126–27n66

agriculture, 259–60

Aguesseau, Henri François d', 206, 289

Allen, Catherine, 280

American Revolution, 75–77, 98, 144

ancient democracies, 98–99

ancient societies: benefits of studying, 254–56; conventional law in, 247; Greeks, on law of nations, 210–11

Annals (Tacitus), 180n7

Anne, queen of Great Britain and Ireland, 130, 289

Anne of Austria, 289

Antillon, Don Isadore d', 275–76, 289

apostasy, political, ix, 169–70, 173–76

Appeal from the New to the Old Whigs (Burke), 165

Archimedes, 55

Areopagitica (Milton), 101

aristocracy: Bonaparte's nobility and, 263; downfall of, 12; in English government, 238; legislative power in, 234; wealth and, 32–33. *See also* nobility

Aristotle, 210–11; on man as political animal, 232; on political reasoners, 240–41; principle of politics according to, 235

army, the: organization of, 124–26; postrevolutionary, 264, 271–72, 276–78; role of in revolution, 27–29; salary increase for, 28–29; tyranny of, 126–27

Artois, Charles Philippe de Bourbon comte d', 23–24, 289

Asia, increased knowledge of, 219–20

Asiatic monarchy, 159, 160

assignats, 66–67, 68–69

Association of the Friends of the People, ix–x, 174n4, 279

atheism, 62, 65

Auckland, Lord. *See* Eden, William, baron Auckland

De Augmentis Scientiarum (Bacon), 239n21

Augustan age, the, 88

Austria, 28, 285

Bacon, Francis, 212–13, 289; on the Christian faith, 228; on connection between knowledge and action, 253; on constitutions, 237; on learning, 238–39n20, 256; on political reasoners, 241; principles of politics according to, 235; on religious establishments, 64; on roots of morality, 226

Bailly, Jean-Sylvain, 25, 289

barbarism, in National Assembly, 88–89

This book is set in Adobe Garamond, a modern adaptation by Robert Slimbach of the typeface originally cut around 1540 by the French typographer and printer Claude Garamond. The Garamond face, with its small lowercase height and restrained contrast between thick and thin strokes, is a classic "old-style" face and has long been one of the most influential and widely used typefaces.

Printed on paper that is acid-free and meets the requirements of the American National Standard for Permanence of Paper for Printed Library Materials, z39.48-1992. ♾

Book design by Louise OFarrell
Gainesville, Florida
Typography by Apex Publishing, LLC
Madison, Wisconsin
Printed and bound by Worzalla Publishing Company
Stevens Point, Wisconsin